D0914557

JOHN LACKLAND

JOHN LACKLAND

BY

KATE NORGATE

WITH MAPS

AMS PRESS
NEW YORK

Reprinted from the edition of 1902, New York
First AMS EDITION published 1970
Manufactured in the United States of America

Library of Congress Catalog Card Number: 71-110740
SBN: 404-00614-0

AMS PRESS, INC.
NEW YORK, N. Y. 10003

CONTENTS

NOTE I

NOTE II

LIST OF MAPS

ERRATA

P. 57, note 1, *for* "the writer, John d'Erlée," *read* "John of Earley
(*d'Erlée*), on whose relation to the *Histoire* in its present form see
M. Meyer's introduction, vol. iii. pp. ii.-xiv."

P. 62, note 6, *for* "John d'Erlée, the Marshal's biographer, asserts
(*Hist. de G. le Mar.*, vv. 11909-16) that he himself," *read* "The writer
of the *Hist. de G. le Mar.* asserts, vv. 11909-16, that John of Earley."

P. 70, note 6, *for* "John d'Erlée, *Hist. de G. le Mar.*," *read* "The
writer of the *Hist. de G. le Mar.*"

P. 77, ll. 7 and 8 from foot, *for* "on or about August 26" *read* "on
August 24"; and same page, note 6, *for* "*Itin.* a. 2, and *Rot. Chart.*
p. 75," *read* "*Memorials of S. Edmund's*, vol. ii. p. 8."

P. 89, note 5, ll. 11 and 13, and p. 106, note 3, *for* "D'Erlée" *read*
"the Marshal's biographer."

" THE closer study of John's history clears away the charges of sloth and incapacity with which men tried to explain the greatness of his fall. The awful lesson of his life rests on the fact that the king who lost Normandy, became the vassal of the Pope, and perished in a struggle of despair against English freedom was no weak and indolent voluptuary but the ablest and most ruthless of the Angevins."

JOHN RICHARD GREEN.

CHAPTER I

JOHN LACKLAND

1167–1189

. . . . Johan sanz Terre,
Por qui il [1] ot tant noise e guere.
Estoire de la Guerre Sainte, vv. 101, 102.

THE fifth son, the eighth and last child, of Henry II. of
England and Eleanor of Aquitaine was born at Oxford, in
the "King's manor"—that is, the palace of Beaumont—
on Christmas Eve 1167.[2] Of their six other surviving
children, the three younger were daughters; the last of
these, Joanna, was then two years old. The eldest living
son, Henry, was nearly thirteen; Richard was ten, and
Geoffrey nine. The boy Henry had, when an infant, been
acknowledged by the barons of England as heir to the
crown,[3] and in 1160 had done homage to Louis of France
for the duchy of Normandy.[4] In 1162 preparations had
been made for his crowning in England, and he had again
received the homage of the barons,[5] to which that of the
Welsh princes and the Scot king was added in 1163.[6]
Eleanor's duchy of Aquitaine had been destined for her
second surviving son, Richard, as early as 1159,[7] when he

---

[1] *I.e.* Henry II.
[2] The place comes from the prose addition to Robert of Gloucester, ed.
Hearne, vol. ii. p. 484; on the date see Stubbs, pref. to W. Coventry, vol. ii.
p. xvii.
[3] R. Torigni, a. 1155; Gerv. of Canterbury, vol. i. p. 162.
[4] R. Torigni, a. 1160.
[5] R. Diceto, vol. i. p. 306. [6] *Ib.* p. 311.
[7] R. Torigni, a. 1159.

B

1167   was not yet two years old. In the summer of 1166 the king had secured Britanny for Geoffrey by betrothing him to its heiress.[1] The whole Angevin dominions, with one exception, were thus, in design at least, partitioned among John's brothers before John himself was born. The exception was, indeed, an important one; in the contemporary accounts of Henry's plans during this period for the distribution of his territories, there is no mention of Anjou and its dependency Touraine. The reason, however, is obvious. Anjou was the cradle of his race, the very heart and centre of his dominion, the one portion of it which he had inherited from his forefathers in unbroken male descent, by a right which had been always undisputed and indisputable. The destiny of Anjou was therefore as yet unspecified, not because Henry was reserving it for a possible younger son, but because its devolution to his eldest son, as head of the Angevin house after him, was in his mind a matter of course. It was in fact Henry himself who gave to his new-born child the name which has clung to him ever since—" Johans Sanz Terre," John Lackland.[2]

1169   Two years later the scheme of partition was fully developed, and now Anjou was explicitly included in it. At Epiphany 1169 Louis of France granted to the younger Henry the investiture of Anjou and Maine, on the understanding that the boy was to hold these fiefs, as well as Normandy, in his own person, directly of the French crown. Richard was invested, on the same terms, with the county of Poitou and the duchy of Aquitaine. Britanny was granted to young Henry, to be holden by his brother Geoffrey of him as mesne lord, under the king of France as

---

[1] R. Torigni, a. 1166.

[2] "Quartum natu minimum Johannem Sine Terra agnominans," W. Newburgh, l. ii. c. 18. Cf. W. Armor. *Philippis*, l. vi. vv. 591, 592, who says, addressing John—

> "Antea quam fato fieres ludente monarcha,
> Patris ab ore tui Sine-Terra nomen habebas."

The name seems to have been commonly used as if it were a part of John's proper designation: "Johannes . . . quem vocant Sine Terra, quamvis multas et latas habet possessiones et multos comitatus," says R. Torigni, a. 1185. So the writer of the *Estoire de la Guerre Sainte*: "Johan sanz Terre ot nom li mendres," v. 179 ; "Johan sanz Terre, Por qui il ot tant noise e guere," vv. 101, 102.

overlord.[1] The one fragment of the continental dominions   1169
of the Angevin house which the king of England formally
reserved to himself was Touraine; his homage for it was
due to a prince of inferior rank, the count of Blois, and his
paternal pride chose rather to perform that homage himself
than to suffer it to be performed by any of his sons.[2]

All these arrangements were as yet merely prospective.
Henry had no intention of abdicating, nor of depriving
Eleanor of her rights as duchess of Aquitaine and countess
of Poitou, nor even of dispossessing the reigning duke of
Britanny. His purpose was simply to insure that, were he
himself unexpectedly to become disabled or die, there should
be no fair pretext for fighting over his inheritance or
defrauding any of his sons of their shares, but that they
should be bound to each other, and their overlord Louis
bound to each and all of them, by such legal ties as none of
the parties could lightly venture to set at defiance. In June   1170
1170 the scheme was completed by the coronation of the
younger Henry at Westminster. Two months later the elder
king fell sick at La Motte-de-Ger, near Domfront. Believing
his end to be at hand, he confirmed the partition of January
1169, and solemnly bequeathed the one son who had no
share in it—John—to the guardianship of his eldest brother,
"the young king," "that he might advance him and maintain him."[3] One contemporary historian adds: "And he
(the king) gave to his youngest son John the county of
Mortain."[4] The meaning of this probably is that Henry

---

[1] Cf. R. Torigni, a. 1169; Gerv. Cant. vol. i. p. 208, and Robertson's
Materials for Hist. of Becket, vol. vi. pp. 506, 507. According to the writer of
this last account, young Henry's homage to Louis was only for Anjou and Maine,
and he adds : "In hac autem honorum distributione Franci regno suo arbitrantur
plurimum esse prospectum; eo quidem magis quod cum acerbiori dolore meminerant
Henricum filium regis Angliæ regi Francorum pro omnibus hominium fecisse,
quando inter ipsum et filiam regis Francorum sponsalia contracta sunt." But
R. Torigni's account of young Henry's homage to Louis in 1160, when compared with his account of the settlement in 1169, seems distinctly to imply that
the former was for Normandy alone.

[2] Robertson, *Materials*, vol. vi. p. 507.

[3] "Tradidit ei [*i.e.* Henrico] Johannem fratrem suum minimum ad promo-
vendum et manutenendum," *Gesta Hen.* vol. i. p. 7. The charge cannot have
been given personally, for though John may have been with his father, the young
king was in England.

[4] R. Howden, vol. ii. p. 6.

1170   expressed a wish, or made a suggestion, that his successor
should provide for John by investing him with Mortain.[1]
From the days of the Conqueror downwards, this Norman
county had always been held by some junior member of the
Norman ducal house. Henry I. had granted it to his
favourite nephew, Stephen ; it had passed to Stephen's son
William, and afterwards to his daughter Mary ; in 1168,
Mary's husband, Count Matthew of Boulogne, had ceded it
to Henry II., on condition that a heavy sum charged upon
its revenues should be paid annually to his two daughters.[2]
Its actual value, therefore, was now very small ; and Henry
on his recovery seems to have abandoned, for the time at
least, his project of bestowing it on John. A year later his
diplomacy had wrought out a scheme for providing John
with a far more splendid, as well as more valuable, endow-
ment than Mortain, by betrothing him to the presumptive
heiress of Maurienne.

1171   A proposal for this marriage was made by Count
Humbert of Maurienne and accepted by Henry in 1171.[3]
Humbert was then a widower for the third time, and had
only two daughters. The marriage contract, which was
1172   signed at the close of 1172,[4] provided that if he should yet
have a son, that son should inherit scarcely anything but the
little county of Maurienne itself, which was only a small and
comparatively unimportant part of Humbert's dominions,
stretching as they did along both sides of the Alps and
including all the passes between Gaul, Germany and Italy.
Except Maurienne, and a very trifling portion of land
reserved as a dowry for his younger daughter, all Humbert's
territories—Rossillon-en-Bugey, the county of Belley, the
valley of Novalesia, Chambéry and its dependencies, Aix,
Aspremont, Rochetta, Mont-Major, and La Chambre on the
western side of the Alps ; and on their eastern side, Turin,
Cavaur, Colegno, with the homage and service of the count
of Canavesia, and that which the viscount of Aosta owed for

---

[1] See Bishop Stubbs's notes to R. Howden, vol. ii. p. 6, and vol. iii. p. xxiv,
note 1.
[2] R. Torigni, a. 1168 ; Stapleton, *Mag. Rot. Scacc. Norm.* vol. i. introd.
pp. lxiii, cxxiii.
[3] R. Torigni, a. 1171.   [4] *Gesta Hen.* vol. i. p. 35.

Châtillon, and also Humbert's claims on the county of   1172
Grenoble—were devised absolutely and unconditionally to
John and his bride, and were, if Henry so willed, to be
secured to them immediately by the homage of all Humbert's
subjects in those regions to the little bridegroom ; while if
Humbert should die without a son, Maurienne itself was to
be added to John's inheritance. The price stipulated for all
this was five thousand marks, of which one thousand were
paid over at once by Henry to Humbert.[1] It was not till
the infant bride had been actually delivered over to her
intended father-in-law, who was to bring her up in company
with her betrothed till both were old enough to be married,
that Humbert asked what was to be John's share in the
heritage of the Angevin house. Henry, seemingly on the
spur of the moment, proposed to give the boy three castles
with the lands appertaining to them—Chinon, Loudun, and
Mirebeau.[2] Chinon was in Touraine ; but Loudun and
Mirebeau were in Anjou. The project was defeated by
young Henry's refusal to allow any part of his county to be
settled upon his little brother, and it thus gave the immediate
occasion, though it was certainly not the real cause, for his
revolt.[3]   1173

When that revolt was subdued, the political relations   1174
between King Henry and his elder sons were settled upon   Oct.
a new footing. The terms of this new settlement, while
confirming the arrangements made at Montmirail for the
devolution of Henry's territories after his death, left no room
for any doubt of his intention to keep them all, for the
present at least, in his own hands. He covenanted to give
to his eldest son, so long as he remained dutiful, two castles
in Normandy and a yearly revenue of fifteen thousand
pounds Angevin ; to Richard, two castles in Poitou, and half
the revenues of that county ; to Geoffrey, half the dowry of
Constance till they should be married, and the whole of it
after that event. Richard and Geoffrey had to do homage to
their father " for what he granted and gave them," but young
Henry was excused from doing the like in consideration

---

[1] *Gesta Hen.* vol. i. pp. 35-39.   [2] *Ib.* p. 41.
[3] Cf. *ib.* p. 41, and Gerv. Cant. vol. i. p. 242.

1174 of his regal dignity. For John there was now made a
carefully detailed provision ; he was to receive an income of
a thousand pounds from the royal demesnes in England,
any escheats which the king might choose to give him, the
castle and county of Nottingham, the castle and lordship of
Marlborough ; two castles and a revenue of one thousand
pounds Angevin in Normandy, and from the Angevin lands
the same amount in money, with one castle in Anjou, one in
Touraine, and one in Maine ; and this settlement young
Henry was made to promise that he would keep " firmly and
inviolate." [1]

The scheme looks almost as if planned purposely to give
John a foothold in every part of his eldest brother's future
dominions—a strip, so to say, in every one of young Henry's
fields. There was indeed no thought as yet of putting the
boy into possession, of investing him with the county of
Nottingham, or making him do homage either to his brother
or to his father. The clause about escheats, however, soon
furnished an opportunity for adding to John's portion. In
1175 1175 the great estates of Earl Reginald of Cornwall reverted
to the Crown at his death, and Henry set them aside for
John.[2] Henry's plans for his little " Lackland " were in fact
completely changed. The project of setting him up as
" marquis in Italy " was abandoned ; Alice of Maurienne
was dead,[3] her father had married again, and neither he nor
Henry seems ever to have thought of insisting upon the
fulfilment of the clause in her marriage-contract which
provided that in case of her premature death her sister
should take her place as John's bride. The settlement of
October 1174 seems to indicate that Henry now saw his
best hope of providing for John in his insular dominions,
1176 rather than anywhere on the continent. In 1176 there was
added to John's prospect of the earldoms of Nottingham and
Cornwall that of a third English earldom and a yet wider
lordship in the west. Earl William of Gloucester, the son

---

[1] Cf. *Gesta Hen.* vol. i. pp. 77-79 ; R. Howden, vol. ii. pp. 67-69, and
Foedera, vol. i. pt. i. p. 30.

[2] R. Torigni, a. 1175.

[3] *Art de Vérifier les Dates*, vol. xvii. p. 165.

and successor of Earl Robert and Mabel of Glamorgan, had   1176
been implicated in the recent rebellion. His three surviving
children were all daughters, two of them already married.
He bought his peace with the king by making John heir to
all his lands, Henry in return promising that John should
marry William's youngest daughter, or, if the needful dispensation could not be obtained,[1] he would bestow her on
another husband "with the utmost honour "; while a yearly
sum of one hundred pounds was to be paid by the Crown to
each of her sisters, as compensation for the loss of their shares
of the family heritage. If William should yet have another
son, that son and John were to divide the lands of the
earldom of Gloucester between them.[2]

Where John himself had been from his birth until near
the completion of his fifth year, there is nothing to show.
He seems to have been with his father at the time of the
marriage-treaty with Maurienne, and throughout the subsequent revolt ; " John alone, who was a little boy, remained
with his father," says Gervase of Canterbury, when speaking
of the defection of Henry's elder sons in 1173.[3] He was
apparently in England when the arrangement with Earl
William of Gloucester was made, September 28, 1176 ;
and he was certainly with the king at Nottingham at
Christmas in that year,[4] and also at Oxford in May 1177,   1177
when Henry bestowed on him the titular sovereignty of the
English dominions in Ireland, and made the Norman-Welsh
barons to whom he had granted fiefs in that country do
homage for those fiefs to John as well as to himself.[5] A
slight indication of the boy's increasing importance may
be found in two entries on this year's Pipe Roll ; the ex-
penditure accounted for by the fermor of Peterborough abbey
includes a corrody for " the king's son John," and fifty-two
pounds spent in buying two palfreys " for the use of the

---

[1] John and Isabel of Gloucester were cousins in the fourth degree according
to the canon law ; *i.e.* they were what is now commonly called second cousins,
being both great-grandchildren of Henry I.

[2] *Gesta Hen.* vol. i. pp. 124, 125 ; R. Diceto, vol. i. p. 415, giving the date,
September 28, 1176.

[3] Gerv. Cant. vol. i. p. 243.

[4] *Gesta Hen.* vol. i. p. 131.   [5] *Ib.* pp. 161-5.

1177   same John."[1]   In August the king returned to Normandy ;
       John followed him, travelling under the care of his half-
       brother Geoffrey, the bishop-elect of Lincoln ;[2] at Mid-Lent,
1178   March 19, 1178, he was present with his father and eldest
       brother at the consecration of the abbey church of Bec ;[3]
       and at Christmas 1178 Henry and John were together at
       Winchester.[4]   During the next four years no mention occurs
       of John, save that at some time between Michaelmas 1178
       and Michaelmas 1179 twenty shillings were spent on horses
       for him "in England and Normandy" by one William
       Franceis, who seems to have been a groom appointed by the
       king to attend him.[5]

1182   John's earliest known appearance as witness to a charter
       of his father's seems to date from the early part of the year
       1182 ; his style is simply "John, the king's son."[6]   This
       charter was given at Arundel.   When Henry went over sea,
       in March, he left John in England under the guardianship
       of the justiciar, Ranulf Glanville.[7]   Fifteen months later, the
       king's arrangements for the disposal of the Angevin succession
1183   were all upset by the death of his eldest son, June 11, 1183.
       Almost heart-broken as the father was, one consolation
       immediately suggested itself ; now at last he might secure to
       his favourite child some provision at once loftier and more
       independent than any number of Norman counties or English
       earldoms, and more substantial than his titular sovereignty
       in Ireland.   In September Henry "sent to England for his
       youngest son, John, and his master Ranulf de Glanville" ;
       when they had joined him in Normandy he sent for Richard,
       and bade him cede the duchy of Aquitaine to John and
       receive the boy's homage for it.[8]   This command shows
       clearly what Henry's present intentions were.   Richard was
       to take the place proper to the eldest son, as heir to the
       whole Angevin dominions ; when he should enter upon

---

[1] Eyton, *Itin. of Henry II.* p. 210, from Pipe Roll 1177.
[2] *Ib.* p. 222, from Pipe Roll 1178.
[3] R. Torigni, a. 1178.   [4] *Gesta Hen.* vol. i. p. 221.
[5] Eyton, *Itin. Hen. II.* p. 226, from Pipe Roll 1179.
[6] *Foedera*, vol. i. pt. i. p. 40.   For date see Eyton, p. 246.
[7] *Gesta Hen.* vol. i. pp. 304, 305.
[8] *Ib.* pp. 304, 305, 307, 308.

his inheritance, his brothers were to hold the two great underfiefs, Britanny and Aquitaine, under him, just as he and
Geoffrey had been destined to hold them under the younger
Henry; and this arrangement for the future was to be made
binding by the immediate homage of his brothers to him,
although for the present all three sons were to remain in
subjection to their father. The scheme was reasonable and
just; but in Richard's eyes it had a fatal defect. For the
last eight years he had been actual ruler of Aquitaine, as
Geoffrey had been actual ruler of Britanny. From 1175
Henry had given his second and third sons a free hand and
left them to govern their respective duchies for themselves.
Geoffrey's hold upon Britanny had been secured in 1181 by
his marriage with Constance; Richard had secured his own
hold upon Aquitaine by eight years of hard fighting with its
rebellious barons, and was now, in truth, duke by the right
of the sword. But young Henry, the crowned king, had
throughout these years been in England little more than a
cipher, held in check by the authority of his father when
present, and by that of the justiciars in his father's absence;
while in Normandy and the Angevin lands he had had no
practical authority at all. Richard had no mind to give up
substance for shadow. To be _de facto_ duke of Aquitaine was
far better than to be merely titular duke of Normandy and
count of Anjou; for the title of king, he knew, Henry would
never again grant to any one during his own lifetime.
Richard's answer therefore was that, so long as he lived, he
and he alone would rule Aquitaine.[1] In June 1184 the
king went back to England,[2] leaving John in Normandy.
John was now in his seventeenth year, and Henry is said to
have given him permission to "lead an army into Richard's
territories and win them for himself by force."[3] Whether
he also furnished him with an "army" for that purpose, or
how John was expected to find one for himself, is not stated;
possibly the permission was nothing more than a hastily
uttered word which the speaker never meant to be taken
seriously. In any case, however, Henry's departure over sea

---

[1] _Gesta Hen._ vol. i. p. 308.   [2] R. Diceto, vol. ii. p. 21.
[3] _Gesta Hen._ vol. i. p. 311.

1184   left John to his own devices, and to the influence of his next brother, Geoffrey of Britanny.

Two or three years later, Gerald of Wales sketched the portraits of Geoffrey and John both at once, in a manner highly suggestive of the close relations which the two brothers formed at this time, and of the points of likeness which drew them together. From that picture we can see what was the character of the influence under which John now fell, and what response it was likely to find in the character of John himself. Geoffrey was now a man of twenty-six years, a knight of approved valour, reputed scarcely inferior in this respect to either of his elder brothers, while he surpassed them both in eloquence of speech and subtlety of brain. " He was not easy to deceive, and would indeed have been one of the wisest of men, had he not been so ready to deceive others. He was a compound of two different natures, Ulysses and Achilles in one. In his inmost soul there was more of bitterness than of sweetness ; but outwardly he was always ready with an abundance of words smoother than oil ; with his bland and persuasive eloquence he could unbind the closest ties of confederation ; with his tongue he had power to mar the peace of two kingdoms. He was a hypocrite, never to be trusted, and with a marvellous talent for feigning or counterfeiting all things." [1]

There was nine years' difference in age between Geoffrey and John ; but already a clear-sighted onlooker could see that the two brothers were cast in the same mould, morally as well as physically. Both were short in stature—shorter than their father, and far below the height of young Henry or of Richard ; they were well built, but on a small scale. The likeness between them went deeper than that of outward form. As Gerald expresses it, "while one was corn in the blade, the other was corn in the ear " ; but the blade developed fast. Before John was twenty, Gerald, though evidently striving hard to make the best of him, was driven to confess that, " caught in the toils and snared by the temptations of unstable and dissolute youth, he was as wax to receive impressions of evil, but hardened against those who would have warned him of

[1] Gir. Cambr. vol. v. p. 200.

its danger ; compliant to the fancy of the moment ; making   1184
no resistance to the impulses of nature ; more given to
luxurious ease than to warlike exercises, to enjoyment than
to endurance, to vanity than to virtue." [1]   As soon as the
king was out of Normandy, Geoffrey and John joined hands ;
they collected "a great host," with which they marched,
burning and plundering, into Poitou.   Richard retaliated by
harrying Britanny, till Henry, on learning what was going
on, summoned all three brothers to England.   They obeyed
the summons, [2] and in December a "final concord" between
them was drawn up and sealed at Westminster. [3]   Whatever
were its terms, they evidently did not include any cession of
territory by either of the elder brothers to the youngest.
Geoffrey was at once sent back to Normandy "to take care
of it with its other guardians" ; [4] and immediately after
Christmas Richard obtained leave to return to Poitou. [5]   The   1185
king's project of transferring Aquitaine to John had been
merely a passing fancy.   Of the scheme for establishing him
in Ireland Henry had never lost sight ; and this scheme he
now determined to carry into effect.

Before he could do so, however, a yet loftier destiny
was proposed to him for his favourite son.   At the end of
January 1185 Heraclius, the patriarch of Jerusalem, came
to England to implore Henry's aid for the perishing realm
of Palestine.   King Baldwin IV. was dying ; after him
there was but one male heir left of the blood of King Fulk
of Anjou and Queen Melisenda, and that one was a little
child.   From the story as told by Gerald it seems plain
that Heraclius aimed at something more than merely per-
suading Henry to take the command of a crusade ; his
project was nothing less than a transfer of the succession
from the younger to the elder Angevin line—from the
infant son of Fulk's grand-daughter to a son of Fulk's
grandson, Henry.   When the king of England, after taking
counsel with his "faithful men," declared that he could not
in person undertake the deliverance of the Holy Land from

---

[1] Gir. Cambr. vol. v. pp. 199, 200.   [2] *Gesta Hen.* vol. i. p. 319.
[3] R. Howden. vol. ii. p. 288.   [4] *Gesta Hen.* vol. i. pp. 320, 321.
[5] *Ib.* p. 334.

1185   its enemies, Heraclius still persisted in his other request; he
implored Henry to send at least one of his sons—if even it
were only John—"that from this scion of the Angevin
house the seed royal might be raised up and spring into
new life." The king, however, would not listen. John, it
is said, was inclined to embrace the patriarch's suggestion, and threw himself at his father's feet to beg his
consent, but in vain.[1] At Mid-Lent Henry knighted
him at Windsor, and publicly gave out that he was to
proceed at once to Ireland, where he was destined to be
king.[2]

1175   The dominions of the English Crown in Ireland were
defined by the treaty made between the Irish Ard-Righ,
Roderic of Connaught, and Henry II. in October 1175 as
consisting of the ancient Irish kingdoms of Meath and
Leinster, the cities of Dublin and Waterford, and a tract
of land extending from Waterford as far as, and including,
Dungarvan.[3] Meath had been granted by Henry in 1171
to Hugh de Lacy to hold in chief of the Crown by the
service of fifty knights;[4] Leinster had been granted a few
weeks before to Richard de Clare, earl of Striguil.[5] The
cities of Dublin and Wexford and the territory appertaining
to each of them, which had been held by the Ostmen, were
not included in these grants, but were reserved by Henry
to himself, and placed under the charge of custodians
appointed by him. His authority over the whole area
occupied by his subjects in Ireland was represented by a
governor whose headquarters were at Dublin, and who at
the time of the treaty was Earl Richard, the lord of
Leinster.[6]

On the side of the invaders and their king, the treaty
was made only to be broken. Henry on his visit to

[1] Gir. Cambr. vol. v. pp. 362, 363.
[2] *Gesta Hen.* vol. i. p. 336; R. Diceto, vol. ii. p. 34.
[3] Treaty in *Gesta Hen.* vol. i. pp. 102, 103.
[4] Charter in Lyttelton, *Henry II.* (ed. 1767), vol. iv. p. 295; *Song of Dermot* (ed. Orpen), vv. 2725-32; cf. *Rot. Chart.* p. 178. The statement in *Gesta Hen.* vol. i. p. 163 (copied by R. Howden, vol. ii. p. 134) that the service was that of a hundred knights is clearly a mistake.
[5] *Song of Dermot*, vv. 2617-22.
[6] Gir. Cambr. vol. v. p. 298.

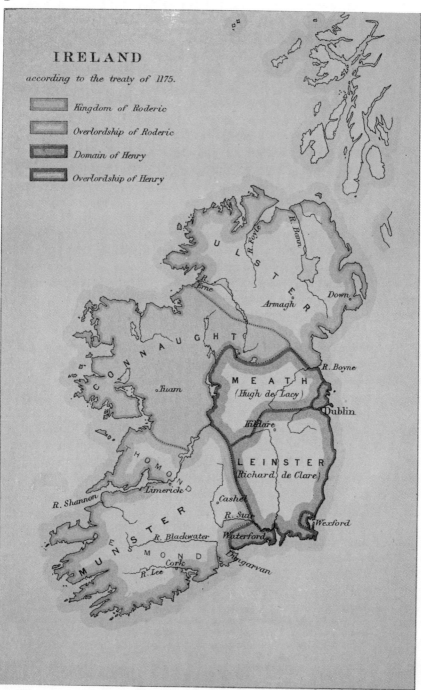

IRELAND

according to the treaty of 1175.

Kingdom of Roderic
Overlordship of Roderic
Domain of Henry
Overlordship of Henry

London: Macmillan & Co., Ltd.

Stanford's Geog.l Estab.t London

Ireland in 1171-72 had established constables of his own   1171-77
in two other towns, Limerick and Cork.[1] Cork, though not
named in the treaty, and therefore implicitly included in
that portion of the island over which he renounced all
claims to ownership, seems nevertheless to have been
continuously occupied by his officers; it was certainly in
their hands in November 1177.[2] Limerick had been
recovered by the Irish, probably when all Henry's garrisons
were recalled from Ireland to swell his forces in Normandy
in 1173. It was, however, stormed and captured early in
October 1175 — only a few days before the treaty with
Roderic was signed—by Earl Richard's brother-in-law and
constable, Raymond the Fat, and his cousin Meiler Fitz-
Henry.[3] They evacuated it, indeed, six months later, when
Raymond was recalled by Henry to England on the death
of Earl Richard in May 1176;[4] but Raymond's infraction
of the treaty was not the reason for his recall;[5] and the
withdrawal of his troops from Limerick was due not to
any order from the king, but to his own sense of the
difficulty of holding a place so remote from the other
Norman-Welsh settlements in Ireland. Henry, when he
heard of the affair, merely remarked: "Great was the
daring shown in seizing the place, but the only wisdom
was in leaving it."[6] In 1171-72 he had made, it is said,
a grant of Ulster to John de Courcy "if he could conquer
it by force."[7] At the opening of 1177 De Courcy set
forth to try whether he could make this grant effectual,
and by February 2 he had taken the city of Down.[8]
Shortly afterwards, Miles Cogan, who was constable of
Dublin under the new governor-general, William Fitz-
Audeline, made a raid into Connaught as far as Tuam.[9]
A few weeks later, Henry himself openly flung his treaty

---

[1] Gir. Cambr. vol. v. p. 277.   [2] *Ib.* p. 348.
[3] *Ib.* pp. 321-3. Cf. *Song of Dermot*, vv. 3370 to end.
[4] Gir. Cambr. vol. v. pp. 332, 333.
[5] *Ib.* pp. 327, 328.   [6] *Ib.* pp. 333, 334.
[7] *Song of Dermot*, vv. 2733-5.
[8] Gir. Cambr. vol. v. p. 339; *Gesta Hen.* vol. i. pp. 137, 138. Cf. Four
Masters and *Ann. Loch Cé*, a. 1177.
[9] Gir. Cambr. vol. v. p. 346. Cf. Four Masters and *Ann. Loch Cé*, a. 1177.

1177   with Roderic to the winds. According to one account, he
bade Earl Hugh of Chester "go into Ireland and subdue
it for him and his son John, to whom he had granted it;
for he had obtained leave from Pope Alexander to crown
and make king in Ireland whichever of his sons he might
choose; and he bade the said earl conquer the kings and
princes of Ireland who would not submit to him." The
commission was probably given not to Hugh of Chester,
but to Hugh de Lacy, who was certainly appointed governor
in Ireland shortly afterwards.[1] However this may have
been, in May 1177 Henry, in a great council at Oxford,
arrogated to himself the right of disposing at his pleasure
not only of the territories in Ireland which were already
conquered, but also of the whole of Munster. Leinster
was at this time in his own hands; for Earl Richard's heir
was a girl, and therefore a ward of the king. He confirmed
Hugh de Lacy's tenure of Meath, and gave him the custody
of Dublin, which carried with it the office of governor-
general; he appointed William Fitz-Audeline—whom Hugh
was thus to supersede as governor—custodian of Wexford,
and Robert le Poer custodian of Waterford; and he defined
the territory dependent upon the latter city as extending
not merely as far as Dungarvan (the limit specified in the
treaty of 1175), but as far as "the river which is beyond
Lismore," that is, the Blackwater. Moreover, he granted
to Robert Fitz-Stephen and Miles de Cogan in fee, for the
service of sixty knights, "the kingdom of Cork," South
Munster, or Desmond;[2] and to Herbert and William Fitz-
Herbert and their nephew Jocelyn de la Pommeraye, on
the same terms, "the kingdom of Limerick," North Munster,
or Thomond. From each of these grants the capital city,
with the Ostmen's cantred attached to it, was excluded,
being expressly reserved by Henry for "himself and his
heirs." The recipients of all these grants did liege homage
and swore fealty to John as well as to Henry.[3]

---

[1] Cf. *Gesta Hen.* vol. i. p. 161 with Gir. Cambr. vol. v. p. 347.
[2] Defined as extending "towards the Cape of S. Brendan [Knock Brandon]
on the sea-coast, and towards Limerick and other parts, and as far as the water
near Lismore." Ware's *Antiquities of Ireland*, ed. Harris, p. 194.
[3] *Gesta Hen.* vol. i. pp. 162-5.

II.

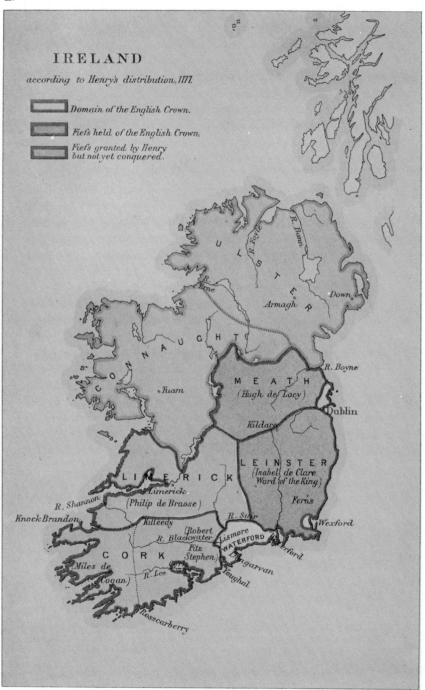

IRELAND

according to Henry's distribution, 1171.

Domain of the English Crown.

Fiefs held of the English Crown.

Fiefs granted by Henry
but not yet conquered.

U L S T E R

R. Foyle

R. Bann

R. Erne

Armagh

Down

C O N N A U G H T

Tuam

M E A T H
(Hugh de Lacy)

R. Boyne

Dublin

Kildare

L I M E R I C K

Limerick
(Philip de Braose)

R. Shannon

Knock Brandon

Killeedy

L E I N S T E R
(Isabel de Clare
Ward of the King)

Ferns

Wexford

R. Slaney

R. Blackwater

(Robert
Fitz
Stephen)

Lismore
WATERFORD

C O R K

Miles de
(Cogan)

R. Lee

Dungarvan

Youghal

Waterford

Rosscarberry

London: Macmillan & Co. Ltd.

Stanford's Geog.¹ Estab.ᵗ London.

The grant of Thomond to the two Fitz-Herberts and their nephew was shortly afterwards annulled at their own request, on the ground that this realm " was not yet won or subdued to the king's authority"; evidently they did not feel equal to the task of winning it. Henry then offered its investiture to Philip de Braose, who accepted it ; and this time the city of Limerick, with its cantred, was either included in the enfeoffment, or, more probably, Philip was appointed to hold it, when won, as custodian for the king.[1] The "kingdom of Cork" was also as yet unconquered ; but here the grantees had the advantage of being supported by an English constable, Richard of London, in Cork itself. They seem to have compelled or persuaded the king of Desmond, Dermot MacCarthy, to some agreement, in virtue of which they are said to have obtained peaceable possession of "the seven cantreds nearest to the city," and divided these between themselves, Fitz-Stephen taking the three eastern, Cogan the four western ; and they seem also to have been appointed by Henry joint custodians of the city of Cork, in succession to Richard of London.[2] As for the other twenty-four cantreds which made up the rest of their promised territory, they agreed to divide the tribute equally between them, " when it should come." [3]

Philip de Braose had helped Cogan and Fitz-Stephen to effect their settlement in Desmond ; they now went to help him to gain possession of Limerick. As the three adventurers and their little band of Welsh followers reached the bank of the Shannon, the citizens noticed their approach and fired the town before their eyes. De Braose lost heart, and "chose rather to return safe to his home than to try the risks of fortune in a land so hostile and so remote" ;[4] and it does not appear that he ever obtained any footing in the country. Cogan and Fitz-Stephen held their seven

---

[1] Cf. *Gesta Hen.* vol. i. pp. 172, 173 ; Gir. Cambr. vol. v. p. 347, with Mr. Dimock's note 6 ; and *Rot. Chart.* p. 84 b.

[2] Gir. Cambr. vol. v. p. 348. The removal of William Fitz-Audeline from the office of viceroy seems to have involved the displacement of the subordinate officers appointed by him, of whom Richard of London was one.

[3] Gir. Cambr. vol. v. p. 348. Cf. Ware, *Antiq.* pp. 194, 195.

[4] Gir. Cambr. vol. v. p. 349.

1182-83 cantreds in Desmond and the city of Cork for five years ; then, in 1182, Cogan was slain by an Irish chieftain,[1] and the natives rose at once throughout the district. They besieged Fitz-Stephen in Cork ; his nephew, Raymond the Fat, went to his rescue by sea, and managed to throw himself and some troops into the city ; while King Henry, as soon as the news reached him, despatched Miles Cogan's brother Richard, with some soldiers, from England to take Miles's place.[2] In 1183, or very soon after, Fitz-Stephen died ;[3] Henry then appointed Raymond sole constable of Cork, and Raymond contrived to restore at least some degree of "English"—more properly to be called Norman-Welsh—ascendency throughout the cantreds occupied in 1177, of which the western ones were apparently now held by Richard de Cogan as heir to Miles, while Raymond was recognized by Henry as tenant-in-chief of the eastern ones in succession to Fitz-Stephen, who had no heirs.[4] The temporary loss of ground in the south in 1182 was more than counterbalanced by the successes of John de Courcy in the same year at the opposite extremity of the island, where he seems to have effected a permanent settlement in Dalriada, though probably only along the coast.[5]

The internal condition of the so-called "English" dominion in Ireland, meanwhile, was not altogether satisfactory to the king. It was of course necessary that he should have a viceroy there to represent him and to hold the feudataries in check ; but for that very reason the viceroy was always, simply as viceroy, an object of jealousy to the other barons ; and the viceroy who had been appointed in 1177, Hugh de Lacy, presently incurred the distrust of the king himself. Hugh's rivals accused him of currying favour with the Irish in the hope of making himself an independent sovereign ; and on his marriage with a daughter of the king of Connaught, a marriage contracted "according to the

---

[1] Gir. Cambr. vol. v. p. 350. Cf. note (e) to Four Masters, a. 1182, and *Ann. Loch Cé*, a. 1182.

[2] Gir. Cambr. vol. v. pp. 350, 351.

[3] *Dic. Nat. Biog.* s.v. "Fitz-Stephen, Robert."

[4] Gir. Cambr. vol. v. p. 350.

[5] Ware, *Antiq.* pp. 196, 197.

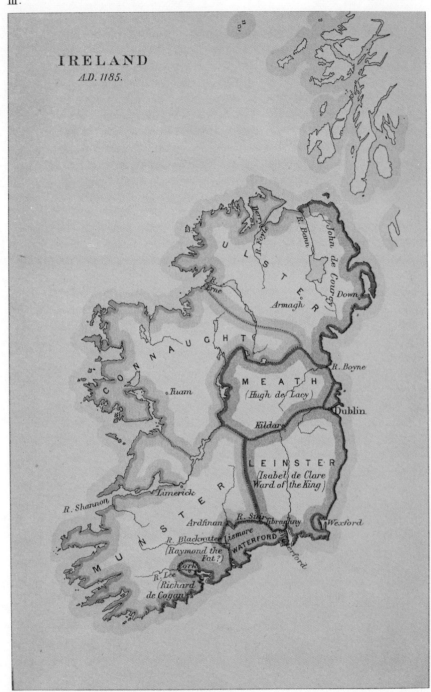

III.

IRELAND
A.D. 1185.

ULSTER

John de Courcy

Down

R. Derg

R. Bann

R. Erne

Armagh

CONNAUGHT

Tuam

R. Boyne

MEATH
(Hugh de Lacy)

Dublin

Kildare

LEINSTER
(Isabel de Clare
Ward of the King)

MUNSTER

Limerick

R. Shannon

Ardfinan

R. Suir

Jibraghny

Wexford

R. Blackwater
(Raymond the
Fat?)

Lismore

WATERFORD

R. Lee
(Richard
de Cogan)

Cork

London: Macmillan & Co., Ltd.

Stanford's Geog¹ Estab¹ London

manner of that country" and without King Henry's leave, 1181-84
Henry in May 1181 removed him from his office and summoned him to England, sending the constable of Chester
and Richard de Pec to Ireland as joint governors in his
stead. Hugh's disgrace, however, lasted only six months ;
he returned to Dublin as governor at the end of the year.[1]
Meanwhile Henry was providing himself with a new instrument for working out his purposes in Ireland. The saintly
and patriotic archbishop of Dublin, S. Laurence O'Toole,
had died in November 1180 ;[2] Henry kept the see vacant
ten months, and then, in September 1181, gave it to an
English clerk and confidant of his own, John Cumin. The
new archbishop was consecrated by the Pope on March 21,
1182 ;[3] but more than two years elapsed before he set foot
in his diocese. At last, in August 1184, he was sent over
by Henry to prepare the way for the coming of John.[4] It
was doubtless for the same purpose that Hugh de Lacy was
again superseded as governor ; at the beginning of September
he was replaced by Philip of Worcester, whose first work
was to recover for the Crown certain lands which Hugh had
alienated, and whose next undertaking was a plundering 1185
raid upon the clergy and churches of Armagh, achieved with
great success in March 1185.[5]

On April 24 John sailed from Milford [6] with a fleet of
sixty ships,[7] which carried some three hundred knights, a large
body of archers, and a train of other followers. Next day
they all landed at Waterford.[8] There the neighbouring Irish
chieftains came to salute the son of the English king. The
knights of John's suite, young and reckless like himself,
jeered at the dress and manners of these Irishmen, and
even pulled some of them by their beards, which they wore
long and flowing according to their national custom. The

---

[1] Cf. Gir. Cambr. vol. v. pp. 353-6, and *Gesta Hen.* vol. i. p. 270.
[2] Gir. Cambr. vol. v. pp. 357, 358. Cf. *Gesta Hen. l.c.*, where the date is
wrong.
[3] Cf. *Gesta Hen.* vol. i. pp. 280, 287, and Gir. Cambr. vol. v. p. 358.
[4] Gir. Cambr. vol. v. p. 359.
[5] *Ib.* pp. 359, 360 ; Four Masters, a. 1185.
[6] Gir. Cambr. vol. v. p. 380.
[7] Four Masters, a. 1185.
[8] Gir. Cambr. vol. v. p. 381.

1185   insulted chieftains reported to their brethren in more remote
districts the indignity with which they had been treated ; and
in consequence, the kings and princes of Munster and Connaught not only refused to attend John's court, but agreed
among themselves to oppose him by force.[1] Archbishop
Cumin, who had been sent over on purpose that he might
set an example of clerical submission and lend John the
support of his countenance as spiritual head of the province
over which John was to be the secular ruler, of course
welcomed the lad as his sovereign and gave him his homage
and fealty, and so did the lay barons who owed their possessions in Ireland to King Henry ; but among the survivors
and representatives of the original Norman-Welsh conquerors
the king's son—like the king himself fourteen years before
—evidently received but a half-hearted welcome ;[2] and John
did nothing to gain their confidence or their respect. He
ordered castles to be built at Lismore and at two places on
the Suir, Ardfinnan and Tibraghny ;[3] beyond this he seems
to have taken no measures to oppose the threatened coalition
of the Irish princes and people ; and while they were openly
joining hands against him, he was spending in riotous living
the money which had been destined for the pay of the
soldiers who had come with him from England. When
these soldiers demanded their wages, he met them with a
refusal.[4] Some of them, whom he had left to garrison the
new castles at Ardfinnan and Tibraghny, provided for themselves by making plundering raids into Munster, till they
were defeated with great slaughter by the king of Thomond,
Donell O'Brien ;[5] most of the others refused to serve John
any longer, and went over to the Irish.[6] Such was the
characteristic beginning of John's public life. Equally characteristic was the facility with which he escaped from the
consequences of his criminal folly. In September, finding
himself on the verge of ruin, he hurried back to his father's
court and laid the blame of his ill-success upon Hugh de

---

[1] Gir. Cambr. vol. v. p. 389.
[2] *Gesta Hen.* vol. i. p. 339.
[3] Gir. Cambr. vol. v. p. 386 ; Four Masters, a. 1185.
[4] *Gesta Hen.* vol. i. p. 339.
[5] Four Masters, a. 1185.   [6] *Gesta Hen. l.c.*

Lacy, whom he accused of plotting with the Irish against   1185
him.[1] The task of repairing the mischief wrought by his
five months' stay in Ireland was entrusted by Henry to John
de Courcy as governor-general.[2]

Within a few months, however, the king again took up
his cherished scheme with renewed eagerness and hope.
" Lord of Ireland " was the title which John had assumed
during his visit to that country,[3] as it was the title by which
Henry had claimed authority over the Irish princes ; but
ever since 1177 Henry had been planning to secure for his
son a more definite basis of power, by having him crowned
and anointed as king. For this the Pope's permission was
necessary ; Alexander III. was said to have granted it,[4] but
his grant seems never to have been embodied in a bull, and
Lucius III., who succeeded him in 1181, absolutely refused
to sanction Henry's project. When Lucius died, in November
1185, Henry at once despatched an embassy to his successor,
Urban III., " and from him he obtained many things which
Pope Lucius had strongly resisted ; of which things this was
one, that whichever of his sons he might choose should be
crowned and anointed king of Ireland." [5] This grant Urban
is said to have confirmed by a bull, and by sending to Henry
a crown of peacock's feathers set in gold.[6] Bull and crown
were probably brought by two legates who are expressly
described as commissioned by Urban as legates for Ireland,
" to crown John king of that country." But these envoys
did not reach England till Christmas Eve 1186 ;[7] and   1186
meanwhile, in August, news had come that " a certain Irishman had cut off the head of Hugh de Lacy," whereupon
Henry bade John proceed at once to Ireland and seize Hugh's

---

[1] Four Masters, *l.c.* ; *Ann. Loch Cé*, a. 1185.

[2] Gir. Cambr. vol. v. p. 392.

[3] In several of John's Irish charters granted during his father's lifetime he
styles himself simply " Johannes filius Regis " ; when he does use a title, it is
"Dominus Hiberniae," or, apparently, in one case (*Hist. MSS. Comm.* 3rd Report,
p. 231), " Dux Hiberniae."

[4] *Gesta Hen.* vol. i. p. 161.   [5] *Ib.* p. 339.

[6] R. Howden, vol. ii. pp. 306, 307. No such bull is now known, but there
seems no reason to doubt the story.

[7] Gerv. Cant. vol. i. p. 346 ; *Gesta Hen.* vol. ii. pp. 3, 4 ; R. Diceto, vol.
ii. p. 47.

1186   vast estates there.[1] John, however, was still in England
when the legates arrived ; possibly his father detained him
on learning that they were actually on their way.   But they
had no sooner landed than they offended Archbishop Baldwin of Canterbury by wearing their mitres and having their
crosses carried before them in his cathedral church ; and
they repeated the insult in the king's court, to the great
indignation of Baldwin and his suffragans.[2]   Under these
circumstances it would obviously have been impossible to let
them crown John in Baldwin's province ; and if Henry
entertained any idea of sending them and John to Ireland
together, that the rite might be performed there, he speedily
abandoned it.   Baldwin, in fact, to rid himself of the legates,
advised the king to employ them in France, as mediators in
the disputes which were arising between Henry and Philip
Augustus out of the death of Geoffrey of Britanny, the
minority of Geoffrey's daughter, and the critical condition of
his widow.   Henry accepted the suggestion, sent John to
Normandy instead of to Ireland,[3] and himself followed with
1187   the legates on February 17 (1187).[4]

No pacification between the kings was arrived at, and at
Whitsuntide both openly prepared for war.   This was the
first real war in which John took part ; for his attacks upon
Aquitaine in 1184 had been mere raids, probably directed
by Geoffrey, and it was not under his personal leadership
that his mercenaries had fought their losing fight with the
Irish in Munster.   Now he was appointed to command one
of the four bodies into which King Henry divided his host ;
the other three being entrusted to Richard, Earl William de
Mandeville, and Geoffrey the chancellor.[5]   The position of
these different bodies of troops at the opening of the campaign is obscure.   One English authority states that when
Philip began the war by laying siege to Châteauroux, Richard
and John were both within its walls.[6]   A contemporary

---

[1] Cf. *Gesta Hen.* vol. i. pp. 350, 361 ; Four Masters, a. 1186 ; Gir. Cambr.
vol. v. p. 387, and R. Diceto, vol. ii. p. 34, who gives the day of Hugh's
death—July 25—but under a wrong year.
[2] Gerv. Cant. vol. i. p. 346 ; *Gesta Hen.* vol. ii. p. 4.
[3] *Gesta Hen.* vol. ii. p. 4.   [4] *Ib.* Cf. R. Diceto, vol. ii. p. 47.
[5] *Gesta Hen.* vol. ii. p. 6.   [6] *Ib.*

French historian, however, who was probably better informed, says that when Philip besieged Châteauroux Henry and Richard proceeded together to its relief;[1] and it appears that John accompanied his father and brother, for we are told that " John who is called Lackland, being sent by his father, chanced to be present " when one of Richard's mercenaries broke off an arm of a statue in the church of Our Lady, whereupon the figure bled as if it were alive ; and John picked up the severed arm and carried it off as a holy relic.[2] One contemporary asserts that Richard's subsequent desertion of his father was owing to Philip's communicating to him a letter in which Henry proposed that Philip's sister Adela, Richard's betrothed, should marry John instead of Richard, and that John should succeed to the whole of his dominions except England and Normandy.[3] Whether this letter was genuine or forged, there is nothing to show ; if such a proposition was really made by Henry, it was probably only as a temporary expedient for putting off Philip's importunity on the awkward question of Adela's marriage. In the autumn Henry and Richard were again reconciled,[4] and a little later both were for a moment reconciled to Philip by a common vow of crusade.

On January 30, 1188, Henry returned to England, and it seems that John went with him ; for when Philip attacked Berry again in the summer, Henry " sent into Normandy his son John, who crossed from Shoreham to Dieppe." [5] The king rejoined his son in July, and they probably remained together during the greater part of the next eleven months, though there is no mention of John's presence at any of the numerous conferences between Henry and Philip. At one of these conferences—that at La Ferté Bernard, on Trinity Sunday, June 4, 1189 [6] — Philip and Richard demanded that John should be made to accompany his father and brother on the crusade ; Richard even declared that he would not go himself unless John

---

[1] Rigord, c. 52 (ed. Delaborde, p. 180).
[2] *Ib.*   Cf. Gerv. Cant. vol. i. p. 369.
[3] Gir. Cambr. vol. viii. pp. 232, 233.
[4] *Gesta Hen.* vol. ii. p. 9.   [5] *Ib.* p. 40.
[6] R. Howden, vol. ii. p. 362.

1189   went too.[1]   Henry, on the other hand, now openly proposed
to Philip that Adela should marry John instead of Richard ;
but Philip, now that Richard was at his side, would not listen
to this suggestion.[2]

Our last glimpse of John during his father's lifetime is
at Le Mans on June 12, when Philip and Richard captured the city, and Henry was compelled to flee.   A
contemporary tells us that before setting out on his flight
" the king caused his son John, whom he loved and in whom
he greatly trusted, to be disarmed." [3]   This precaution may
have been due to anxiety—groundless, as the issue proved
—lest John should thrust himself into danger in his father's
behalf; that it was not suggested by any doubts of John's
loyalty is plain, not only from the words of the writer who
records it, but also from Henry's action on the next morning, when, before setting out on his solitary ride from La
Frênaye back into Anjou, he despatched his remaining
followers to Normandy, after making the seneschal of the
duchy and Earl William de Mandeville swear that in case
of his own death the Norman castles should be given up to
John.[4]   John, however, had then already left him—under
what circumstances, or at what precise moment, we know
not ; but it seems clear that at some time between the
French attack upon Le Mans on the Monday morning and
Henry's arrival at La Frênaye on the same night, John had
either been sent away by his father for safety, or had found
some pretext for quitting his company, and that, in either
case, he used the opportunity to go his own way with such
characteristic ingenuity that for three whole weeks his father
never guessed whither that way really tended.[5]

[1] *Gesta Hen.* vol. ii. p. 66.
[2] R. Howden, vol. ii. p. 363.
[3] *Hist. de G. le Mar.* vv. 8542-4.
[4] Gir. Cambr. vol. iv. p. 369.
[5] Gerald indeed (*l.c.*) says : "In crastino vero . . . versus Audegaviam
rege properante, fidei tamen sacramentique vinculis senescallo Normanniae Guillelmo Radulphi filio et comite Guillelmo de Mandeville ante constrictis, de
munitionibus Normanniae cunctis, siquid de ipso sinistrum fore contigerit, filio suo
juniori Johanni reddendis, quanquam tamen et ipse ab eodem, proh dolor! paulo
post discesserit." But it looks very much as if " post " here were a mistake for
" ante," for the whole story indicates that John was not at La Frênaye on the
night of June 12. Cf. W. Newb. l. iii. c. 25 : "Tunc" (after the flight from

Henry and Richard had been set at strife by an illusion of their own imaginations. Richard had been spurred to rebellion by the idea that his father aimed at disinheriting him in favour of John, and might succeed in that aim, unless prevented by force. Henry's schemes for John were probably in reality much less definite and less outrageous than Richard imagined ; but there can be little doubt that the otherwise unaccountable inconsistencies and self-contra-dictions, the seemingly wanton changes of front, by which the king in his latter years had so bewildered and exas-perated his elder son, were the outcome of an insatiable desire to place John, somehow or other, in a more lofty and independent position than a younger son was fairly entitled to expect. The strange thing is that Henry never per-ceived how hopeless were his efforts, nor Richard how groundless were his fears ; neither of them, apparently, realizing that the substitution of John for Richard as heir of the Angevin house was an idea which could not possibly be carried into effect. The utter selfishness of John, however, rendered him, mere lad of one-and-twenty as he was, proof against illusions where his own interest was concerned ; and it was he who pricked the bubble. On July 4 Henry, sick unto death, made his submission to Philip and Richard, and received a list of the traitors who had transferred their homage to the latter. That night, at Chinon, he bade his vice-chancellor read him the names. The vice-chancellor hesitated ; the king insisted ; at last the truth which was to give him his death-blow came out : "Sire, the first that is written down here is Lord John, your son." [1]

Le Mans) "Johannes filiorum ejus minimus, quem tenerrime diligebat, recessit ab eo " ; and *Gesta Hen.* vol. ii. p. 72 : "Johannes filius ejus, qui mortis suae occasio, immo causa praecipua fuerat, eo quod illum tempore guerrae, cum capta esset civitas Cenomannis, reliquerat." These two writers, indeed, taken by themselves, would seem to imply that John's desertion was open ; but Henry's charge to the two Norman barons, and his subsequent horror at the final dis-covery of John's treason, indicate that it was managed with a refinement of duplicity which is really more in accord with John's character.

[1] *Hist. de G. le Mar.* vv. 9077-8.

CHAPTER II

JOHN COUNT OF MORTAIN

1189–1199

> Then ther com most wykke tydyng
> To Quer de Lyoun Richard our kyng,
> How off Yngelonde hys brother Ihon,
> That was accursyd off flesch and bon,
>
> . . . .
> . . . wolde with maystry off hand
> Be crownyd kyng in Yngeland.
> *Richard Coer de Lion*, ll. 6267-70, 6273-4.

1189 ON July 6 Henry died; on the 8th he was buried at
Fontevraud.   Richard attended the burial; John did not,
but immediately afterwards, either at Fontevraud or on the
way northward, he sought the presence of his brother.
Richard received him graciously, and on reaching Normandy
"granted him all the lands which his father had given him,
to wit, four thousand pounds' worth of lands in England, and the county of Mortain with its appurtenances."[1]
These words, and similar expressions used by two other
writers of the time,[2] would seem to imply that John had
been count of Mortain before Henry's death, and that
Richard merely confirmed to him a possession and a dignity
which he already enjoyed.   John, however, is never styled

---

[1] *Gesta Ric.* vol. ii. pp. 72, 73.

[2] "Paternae in Hibernia acquisitionis plenitudinem et comitatum in Nor-
mannia Moritanensem, de quibus scilicet paternam donationem ratam habuit"
[Ricardus], W. Newb. l. iv. c. 3.   "Comitatum de Moritonio, quem dono
patris pridem perceperat" [Johannes], Ric. Devizes (Howlett, *Chronn. of
Stephen*, etc., vol. iii.), p. 385.   Cf. above, p. 6.

"count" during Henry's lifetime ;[1] and the real meaning of the historians seems to be that Henry had in his latter days reverted to his early project of making John count of Mortain, but had never carried it into effect, probably because he could not do so without Richard's assent. Richard's grant was thus an entirely new one, though made in fulfilment of his father's desire. It set John in the foremost rank among the barons of Normandy, though the income which it brought him was not very large. The grant of lands in England, said to have been made to him at the same time, can only have been a promise ; Richard was not yet crowned, and therefore not yet legally capable of granting anything in England at all. On his arrival there in August, one of his first acts was to secure the Gloucester heritage for John by causing him to be married to Isabel. The wedding took place at Marlborough on August 29.[2] Five days later the king was crowned ; John figured at the coronation as " Earl of Mortain and Gloucester," and walked before his brother in the procession, carrying one of the three swords of state, between Earl David of Huntingdon and Earl Robert of Leicester, who bore the other two swords.[3]

At the end of the month, or early in October, Richard despatched John at the head of an armed force, to secure for the new king the homage of the Welsh princes. They all, save one, came to meet John at Worcester, and " made a treaty of peace " with him as his brother's representative. The exception was Rees of South Wales, who was in active hostility to the English Crown,[4] being at that very time engaged in besieging Caermarthen castle. John led " the host of all England " to Caermarthen, the siege was raised,[5] and Rees accompanied John back to England for a meeting with Richard at Oxford ; Richard, however, declined the interview.[6] His refusal may have been due to some suspicion

---

[1] The biographer of William the Marshal, indeed, does on two occasions before Henry's death speak of "le conte Johan," "li quens Johan" (vv. 8543, 9078). But although in one sense contemporary, he did not write till after 1219 ; his use of the title therefore proves nothing.

[2] *Gesta Ric.* p. 78. [3] *Ib.* pp. 80, 81. [4] *Ib.* pp. 87, 88.
[5] *Ann. Cambr.* p. 57. [6] *Gesta Ric.* p. 97.

1189   of a private agreement between Rees and John which is
asserted in the Welsh annals ;[1] but his suspicions, if he had
any, did not prevent him from continuing, almost to the eve
of his own departure from England, to develope an elaborate
scheme of provision for John. The very first step in this
scheme had already led to trouble, though the trouble was
easily overcome. John and Isabel had been married without a dispensation and in defiance of Archbishop Baldwin of
Canterbury, who had forbidden, as contrary to canon law,
a union between cousins under such circumstances. After
the marriage had taken place he declared it invalid, and
laid an interdict upon the lands of the guilty couple.
John, however, appealed to Rome, and got the better of the
primate ; in November the interdict was raised by a papal
legate.[2]

The Pipe Roll drawn up a month after John's marriage
shows him as holding, besides his wife's honour of Gloucester,
the honours of Peverel, Lancaster and Tickhill, two manors
in Suffolk, three in Worcestershire, and some lands in Northamptonshire, together with the profits of the Forest of Sherwood in Nottinghamshire and of that of Andover in Wiltshire. All these grants were construed as liberally as possible
in John's favour ; he was allowed the profits of the two
forests for a whole year past, and the revenues of the other
lands for a quarter of a year, while the third penny of
Gloucestershire was reckoned as due to him for half a year
—that is, from a date five months before his investiture with
the earldom.[3] The grants of Peverel's honour and Lancaster
included the castles [4] ; in the cases of Tickhill and Gloucester
the castles were reserved by the king, and so too, apparently,
was a castle on one of John's Suffolk manors, Orford.[5]

---

[1] *Ann. Cambr.* p. 57.   [2] R. Diceto, vol. ii. pp. 72, 73.
[3] Gloucester (honour), Pipe Roll 1 Ric. I. p. 7 ; Lancaster, p. 18 ; Orford
(Suffolk), p. 40 ; Staverton (*ib.*), p. 54 ; Hanley, Edersfield and Bisley
(Worcestershire), p. 250 ; Hecham (Northamptonshire), p. 97 ; " other lands " in
Northamptonshire, p. 104 ; Sherwood, p. 172 ; Andover, *ib.* ; Goucestershire,
third penny, p. 163.
[4] *Gesta Ric.* p. 78. The Peverel castles were those of Bolsover and the
Peak.
[5] Tickhill castle appears as garrisoned by the Crown in Pipe Roll 2 Ric. I.
(1190) m. 7 ; so does Orford in 1191-92, P.R. 5 Ric. I. (1193) m. 2 (among

IV.

ENGLAND, A.D. 1190.

John's lands

Royal castles
within John's lands,   *Tickhill*

IRELAND

Berwick

NORTHUMBERLAND

CUMBERLAND

WESTMORLAND

DURHAM

YORKSHIRE

Lancaster

York

LANCASTER

Tickhill

Peak

Bolsover

Lincoln

CHESTER

DERBY

NOTTINGHAM

LINCOLN

Nottingham

WALES

STAFFORD

LEICESTER

NORFOLK

SALOP

RUTLAND

CAMBRIDGE

Norwich

Radnor

LEICESTER

Northampton

HUNTS

SUFFOLK

Eye

Leominster

WARWICK

NORTHAMPTON

Orford

HEREFORD

Hereford

BEDFORD

Brecon

Gloucester

Bedford

GOWER

Strigul

GLOUCESTER

OXFORD

BUCKS

HERTS

ESSEX

GLAMORGAN

Cardiff

Wallingford

BERKS

MIDDLESEX

London

Bristol

Marlboro'

Windsor

Reading

Luggershall

Andover F.

SURREY

KENT

SOMERSET

WILTS

HANTS

Dover

Winchester

SUSSEX

DEVON

DORSET

Launceston

Exeter

CORNWALL

London: Macmillan & Co., Ltd.

Stanford's Geog.l Estab.t London.

Four other honours appear to have been given to John
at this time — Marlborough and Luggershall, including
their castles; Eye and Wallingford, seemingly without
their castles.[1]   The aggregate value of all these lands
would be about £1170; but a much greater gift soon
followed.   Before the end of the year six whole counties
— Nottinghamshire, Derbyshire, Dorset, Somerset, Devon
and Cornwall—were added to the portion of the count of
Mortain.   The words in which this grant is recorded by
the chroniclers convey a very inadequate idea of its real
importance; taken by themselves, they might be understood
to mean merely that Richard gave his brother the title and
the third penny of the revenue from each of the counties
named.[2]   That what he actually did give was something very
different we learn from the Pipe Rolls, or rather from the
significant omission which is conspicuous in them for the
next five years.   From Michaelmas 1189 to Michaelmas
1194 these six counties made no appearance at all in the
royal accounts.   They sent no returns of any kind to the

accounts "de veteri firma" of Suffolk); Gloucester castle was repaired by the
sheriff of the county in 1191, P.R. 3 Ric. I. m. 12; Bristol, the other great
castle of the Gloucester earldom, was held by the Crown in 1192, P.R. 4 Ric.
I. m. 20.

    [1] For Marlborough, Wallingford and Luggershall, see *Gesta Ric.* p. 78;
Eye is added by R. Howden, vol. iii. p. 6.   There is no mention of any of
these in the Pipe Rolls of 1188-93, except that the men of the soke of Eye
pay tallage to the Crown in 1190 (P.R. 2 Ric. I. m. 9 d), and that in 1192 the
sheriff of Suffolk charges for livery of a garrison in Eye castle for a year (*i.e.*
Michaelmas 1191 to Michaelmas 1192; P.R. 5 Ric. I. m. 2, among accounts
"de veteri firma" of Suffolk).

    [2] "Eodem mense [Decembri] Ricardus Rex Angliae dedit Johanni fratri suo
in augmentum comitatum Cornubiae, et comitatum Devoniae, et comitatum de
Dorset, et comitatum de Sumerseta," *Gesta Ric.* p. 99.   According to this
writer, Richard had granted to John "villam de Notingham cum honore illo
. . . et Derebisiram" at the same time as Gloucester, Lancaster, etc. (*ib.* p.
78).   But the sheriffs of all six shires account for them to the Crown up to
Michaelmas in Pipe Roll I Ric. I.; so they must all have been granted after
that date.   "Villam de Notingham cum honore illo" stands for the town and
the shire; there was no "honour" of that name.   W. Newburgh, though his
list of John's counties is very incomplete (l. iv. c. 3), rightly mentions "Notinge-
hamesciram" as one of them; it disappears from the Pipe Rolls like the other
five after Michaelmas 1189.   Sherwood Forest disappears likewise, being included in the shire.   On the other hand, later events show that Nottingham
castle was retained by the Crown.   At this period Nottinghamshire and Derbyshire, Dorset and Somerset, Cornwall and Devonshire, were always administered
and accounted for in pairs.

1189   royal treasury; they were visited by no justices appointed by the king. In a word, just as Chester and Durham were palatinates in the hands of earl and bishop respectively, so John's two counties in mid-England and four in the south-west formed a great palatinate in his hands. He received and retained their ferms and the profits of justice and administration within their borders, and ruled them absolutely at his own will, the Crown claiming from him no account for them whatever.

The total revenue which the Crown had derived from these six counties in the year immediately preceding their transfer to John was a little over £4000.[1] But their money value was a consideration of trifling importance compared with the territorial and political power which accompanied it. Such an accumulation of palatine jurisdictions in the hands of one man was practically equivalent to the setting up of an under-kingdom, with a king uncrowned indeed, but absolutely independent of every secular authority except the supreme king himself; and that exception, as every one knew, was only for the moment; Richard was on the eve of his departure for the Holy Land, and as soon as he was out of reach John would have, within his little realm, practically no superior at all. Moreover, his "lordship of Ireland" had changed its character at his father's death. Until then it had been, save during his five months' visit to that country in 1185, merely titular. Most of the few known charters and grants issued in his name during his father's lifetime are dateless, and it seems possible that, with one exception, all of them may have been issued during that visit.[2] On Henry's death, however, John's lordship of the English March in Ireland became something more than a name. In virtue of it he already possessed a staff of household officers whose titles and functions reproduced those of

---

[1] Stubbs, pref. to R. Howden, vol. iii. p. xxv. note 4.

[2] Gilbert, *Hist. Doc. of Ireland*, p. 49 ; *Rot. Canc. Hib. Cal.* vol. i. pt. i. pp. 1, 3 ; Carte, *Life of Ormonde* (ed. 1851), vol. i. introd. pp. xlv, xlvi ; *Hist. MSS. Commission*, 3rd Report, p. 231 ; Harris's Ware, *Antiq. Hibern.* p. 197. The exception referred to is a grant of land in Ireland, without date of day or year, but issued by "Johannes filius Regis Angliae, Dominus Hiberniae," "apud Ceneman'," *i.e.* Le Mans, and witnessed by John the Marshal, "dapifer Johannis," *Rot. Canc. Hib. Cal.* vol. i. pt. i. p. 3.

the royal household itself.   Henry had had his seneschal,   1189
his butler, his constable for Ireland as well as for England ;
and this Irish household establishment had apparently been
transferred to John, at any rate since 1185.   No doubt the
men of whom it consisted were appointed by Henry, or
at least with his sanction, and were in fact his ministers
rather than the ministers of his son ; but to the new king
they owed no obedience save the general obedience due
from all English or Norman subjects ; from the hour of
Henry's death their service belonged to the "Lord of
Ireland" alone, and John thus found himself at the head
of a little court of his own, a ready-made ministry through
which he might govern both his Irish dominion and the
ample possessions which Richard bestowed upon him in
England, as freely as the rest of the English realm was
governed by Richard himself through the ministers of the
Crown.[1]

Of the way in which John was likely to use his new
independence he had already given a significant indication.
Shortly after Richard's accession the wardship of the heiress
of Leinster, Isabel de Clare, was terminated by her marriage
with William the Marshal.[2]   Her great Irish fief, as well as
her English and Welsh lands, thus passed into the hands of
a man who was already one of the most trusted friends and
counsellors of Richard, as he had been of Henry, and whose
brother had once been seneschal to John himself.[3]   No
sooner had William entered upon the heritage of his wife
than John disseised him of a portion of Leinster and par-
celled it out among friends of his own.   The Marshal
appealed to Richard ; Richard insisted upon John's making
restitution, and John, after some demur, was compelled to
yield, but not entirely ; he managed to secure the ratification
of a grant which he had made to his butler, Theobald

---

[1] We hear of John's chancellor, Stephen Ridel, in 1191, *Gesta Ric.* p. 224 ;
of his seneschal, William de Kahanger, and his butler, Theobald Walter, in
1192, *Foedera*, vol. i. pt. i. p. 55.   We have seen already that at some date
between 1185 and 1189 he had as "dapifer" no less a personage than John the
Marshal ; and in 1191 Roger de Planes appears as "in tota terra comitis Johannis
justiciarius," R. Diceto, vol. ii. p. 99.

[2] *Gesta Ric.* p. 73.   [3] See above, p. 28, note 2.

1189　Walter, out of the Marshal's lands, although, by way of compromise, it was settled that Theobald should hold the estate in question as an under-tenant of William, not as a tenant-in-chief of John.[1]　On the other hand, John did not at once displace the governor whom his father had set over the Irish march four years before, John de Courcy.　He had no thought of undertaking the personal government of his dominions in Ireland.　To do so he must have turned his back upon the opportunities which Richard's misplaced generosity was opening to him in England—opportunities of which it was not difficult to foresee the effect upon such a mind as his.　As William of Newburgh says, " The enjoyment of a tetrarchy made him covet a monarchy." [2]

1190　That Richard presently awoke to some consciousness of the danger which he had created for himself and his realm may be inferred from the fact that in February 1190 he summoned John to Normandy, and there made him swear not to set foot in England for the next three years.　The queen-mother, however, afterwards persuaded her elder son to release the younger one from this oath ; [3] or, according to another account, to leave the decision of the matter to the justiciar and chancellor, William of Longchamp, bishop of Ely.　John was to visit the chancellor in England, and either remain there or go into exile, as William might choose.[4]　It is clear, however, that William had no real choice.　He was legate in England, and therefore absolution from him was necessary to protect John against the ecclesiastical consequences of a violated oath ; but as the violation was sanctioned by the king to whom the oath had been sworn, no ground was left to William for refusing the absolution.

In the course of the year 1190, therefore, or very early in 1191, John returned to England.[5]　In February 1191 the sole remaining check upon both John and William of Longchamp was removed : Queen Eleanor went to join her

---

[1] *Hist. de G. le Mar.* vv. 9581-618.　See charters in Carte's *Life of Ormonde* (1851), vol. i. introd. p. xlvi.

[2] W. Newb. l. iv. c. 3.　　　　　　　　[3] *Gesta Ric.* p. 106.

[4] R. Devizes, p. 392.

[5] Stubbs, pref. to R. Howden, vol. iii. p. 41.

elder son at Messina.[1]   As soon as she was gone, the results
of the concession which he had made to her wishes in John's
behalf began to show themselves.   On Mid-Lent Sunday,
March 24, the count of Mortain and the chancellor had
an interview at Winchester "concerning the keepers of
certain castles, and the money granted to the count by his
brother out of the exchequer."[2]   What passed between them
we are not told ; but it is clear that they disagreed.   Three
months elapsed without any overt act of aggression on either
side.   Then, all at once, about midsummer, it became
apparent that a party which for more than a year had been
seeking an opportunity to undermine the chancellor's power
had found a rallying-point and a leader in the king's brother.
The sheriff of Lincolnshire and constable of Lincoln Castle,
Gerard de Camville, being summoned to answer before the
justiciars for having made his great fortress into a hold of
robbers and bandits, defied their authority on the plea that
he had become John's liegeman, and was therefore answerable to no one except John.[3]   The chancellor deprived
Gerard of his sheriffdom and gave it to another man, and
laid siege to Lincoln Castle.[4]   While he was thus occupied,
the castles of Nottingham and Tickhill were given up by
their custodians to John.[5]   Thereupon John sent to the
chancellor a message of insolent defiance.   If William did
not at once withdraw from Lincoln and leave Gerard in
unmolested possession, the count of Mortain threatened to
"come and visit him with a rod of iron, and with such a
host as he would not be able to withstand."[6]   With a
cutting allusion at once to the chancellor's humble origin
and to the readiness with which the commandants of
Nottingham and Tickhill had betrayed the fortresses committed to their charge, he added that "no good came of
depriving lawful freeborn Englishmen of the offices of trust

---

[1] *Gesta Ric.* p. 157.   [2] R. Devizes, p. 402.
[3] R. Howden, vol. iii. pp. 242, 243.   Cf. W. Newb. l. iv. c. 16, and R.
Devizes, p. 406.
[4] *Gesta Ric.* p. 207 ; R. Howden, vol. iii. p. 134.   Cf. W. Newb. *l.c.*
Gerard was constable of Lincoln in right of his wife, Nicola de Haye.
[5] R. Devizes, p. 407 ; *Gesta Ric.* p. 207.   Cf. W. Newb. l. iv. c. 16.
[6] *Gesta Ric. l.c.*

to which they were entitled, and giving them to unknown strangers ; the folly of such a proceeding had just been proved in the case of the royal castles which William had entrusted to men who left them exposed to every passer-by ; any chance comer would have found their gates open to him as easily as they had opened to John himself.   Such a state of affairs in his brother's realm he was resolved to tolerate no longer."   The chancellor's retort was a peremptory summons to John to give up the two castles, and " answer before the king's court for the breach of his oath." [1]   William probably hoped to get John expelled from England, on the plea that Richard had never really consented to his return and that his absolution was therefore invalid, as having been extorted on a false pretence.   The summons appears to have been carried by Archbishop Walter of Rouen, who had come from Messina charged with a special commission from Richard to deal with the crisis in England.[2]   John, on receiving the chancellor's message, burst into one of the paroxysms of fury characteristic of his race.   " He was more than angry," says a contemporary ; " his whole body was so contorted with rage as to be scarcely recognizable ; a scowl of wrath furrowed his brow ; his eyes flashed fire, his colour changed to a livid white, and I know what would have become of the chancellor if in that hour of fury he had come within reach of John's hands ! "   In the end, however, the archbishop persuaded both John and William to hold another conference at Winchester on July 28.[3]

John secured the services of four thousand armed Welshmen, whom he apparently brought up secretly, in small parties, from the border, and hid in various places round about the city.   No disturbance, however, took place ; some of the bishops, under the direction of Walter of Rouen, drew up a scheme of agreement which, for the moment, both John and William found it advisable to accept.   The castles of Nottingham and Tickhill were surrendered by John to the

[1] R. Devizes, pp. 407, 408.
[2] Walter left Messina April 2 (cf. R. Howden, vol. iii. p. 100 ; *Itin. Ric. Cant.* Reg. p. 176, and R. Devizes, p. 404), and landed either about midsummer (Gerv. Cant. vol. i. p. 497), or, more probably, April 27 (see Bishop Stubbs's note to R. Diceto, vol. ii. p. 90).   [3] R. Devizes, p. 408.

king in the person of his special representative the archbishop of Rouen, who was to give them in charge, one to
William of Venneval—a liegeman of the king, but a friend
and follower of John—the other to William the Marshal;
these two custodians were to hold them for the king till his
return, and then "act according to his will concerning them";
but if he should die, or if meanwhile the chancellor should
break the peace with John, they were to restore them to
John. New custodians were appointed, on the like terms,
to six royal castles which stood within John's territories,[1]
and also to two castles which Richard had expressly granted
to him,—Bolsover and the Peak. Any new castles built since
the king's departure were to be razed, and no more were to
be built till his return, save, if necessary, on the royal demesnes,
or elsewhere in pursuance of special orders, written or verbal,
from himself. No man was to be disseised either by the
king's ministers or by the count of Mortain, save in execution of a legal sentence delivered after trial before the king's
court; and each party was pledged to amend, on complaint
from the other, its own infringements of this rule, which was
at once applied to the case of Gerard de Camville. Gerard,
having been disseised without trial, was reinstated in his
sheriffdom; but his reinstatement was ordered to be immediately followed by a trial before the Curia Regis on the
charges brought against him, and the decision of the Curia
was to be final; if it went against him, John was not to
support him in resistance to it; and John was further bound
not to harbour any known outlaws or enemies of the king,
nor any person accused of treason, except on condition of
such person pledging himself to stand his trial in the king's
court. The archbishop of Rouen received a promise from
John and from the chancellor, each supported by seven
sureties, that they would keep this agreement. After it was
drawn up, a postscript appears to have been added: "If any
thing should be taken or intercepted by either party during

---

[1] Wallingford, Eye, Bristol, Exeter, Launceston and "Hereford"; R.
Howden, vol. iii. p. 136. Hereford is quite out of place among "castra de
honoribus a domino rege sibi" [*i.e.* Johanni] "datis." The name may be a
mistake for Oxford; see above, p. 26.

D

1191 the truce, it shall be lawfully restored and amends made for it. And these things are done, saving always the authority and commands of our lord the king; yet so that if the king before his return should not will this agreement to be kept, the aforesaid castles of Nottingham and Tickhill shall be given up to Lord John, whatever the king may order concerning them." The last clause is obscure; but its meaning seems to be that if the arrangement just made should prove to be, in the judgment of the king's ministers, untenable, it was to be treated as void, and matters were to be restored to the position in which they had been before it was made.[1]

The contingency which seems to have been contemplated in this postscript very soon occurred. Some mercenaries whom the chancellor had summoned from over sea landed in England, and he at once repudiated the agreement, declaring there should be no peace till either he or John was driven out of the realm.[2] Hereupon it seems that Venneval and the Marshal, in accordance with the clause above quoted, restored the castles of Tickhill and Nottingham to John. On the other hand, an outrage on John's part, which is recorded only as having occurred some time in this year (1191), certainly took place before October, and most likely before the middle of September. Roger de Lacy, the constable of Chester, who was responsible to Longchamp for the safe keeping of these two castles, made a vigorous effort

---

[1] R. Howden, vol. iii. pp. 135-7. One other clause in the agreement may be noticed. After the provisions about the castles already mentioned, it is added: "Sed et tria castella ad coronam domini regis pertinentia, scilicet castellum de Windeshoveres comiti de Arundel; castellum de Wintonia Gilleberto de Lasci; castellum de Northampton Simoni de Pateshille, tradita sunt custodienda; qui fidelitatem domini Regis de ipsis ad opus ipsius fideliter custodiendis juraverunt," *ib.* p. 136. The earl of Arundel figures, at the end of the document, as one of the chancellor's sureties, and the Lacys were in close alliance with the Longchamps; taken by itself, therefore, this clause would seem to indicate a change of custodians made at the chancellor's desire, and dictated by a discovery or suspicion that the actual commandants of these three castles were in treasonable alliance with John. But the Pipe Rolls show that the appointment of Simon de Pateshill implied no change at all, for he had custody of Northampton castle without interruption from Michaelmas 1189 to Michaelmas 1191 (P.R. 2 Ric. I. m. 4; 3 Ric. I. m. 1); while the other appointments were speedily annulled, owing to the breakdown of the whole agreement.

[2] W. Newb. l. iv. c. 16.

to bring to justice the subordinate castellans to whom he had
entrusted them, and who had betrayed them to John. Of
these there had been two in each castle. Two managed to
keep out of Lacy's reach; the other two he caught and
hanged, although one of them offered to swear with com-
purgators that he had never consented to the treason of his
colleague, and even brought a letter from John requesting
that the compurgation might be allowed—the chancellor, to
whom the question had been referred, having remitted it to
the decision of Lacy. While this man's body was hanging
in cÎains, his squire drove the birds away from it; whereupon Roger de Lacy hanged the squire. Then John took
upon himself to avenge them both, not only by disseising
Roger of all the lands which he held of him, but also by
ravaging the lands which Roger possessed elsewhere.[1]

Some time in August or September another assembly
was called to endeavour after a pacification between John
and the chancellor. Three bishops and twenty-two laymen were appointed arbitrators—the laymen chosen by the
bishops, eleven from the party which had hitherto adhered
to William, eleven from the followers of John. The terms
which these twenty-five laid down amounted to a decision
wholly in John's favour. They did, indeed, again require
him to restore the two royal castles of Nottingham and
Tickhill; but they made the restoration an empty form.
They decreed that the chancellor should put these castles
under the control of two men whom they named, William
of Venneval and another friend of John's, Reginald de
Vasseville. These two were to hold the castles for the king
and give William hostages for their fidelity; but if Richard
should die before reaching home, they were at once to
surrender the castles to John, and William was to restore
their hostages. The arbitrators further confirmed Gerard
de Camville in the constableship of Lincoln castle; they
ordered the chancellor to remove the constables of royal
castles situated within the lands of the count of Mortain,
and appoint others in their stead, "if the count showed reason
for changing them"; and they added that "if the king

[1] *Gesta Ric.* pp. 232, 234.

1191   should die, the chancellor was not to disinherit the count,
but to do his utmost to promote him to the kindgom." [1]
This last clause was pointed at a negotiation which William
had been carrying on with the Scot king, for the purpose
of obtaining his recognition of Arthur of Britanny as heir-
presumptive to the English Crown.   The negotiation was
secret ; but John had discovered it,[2] and the discovery was
a useful weapon in his hands.   William's dealings with
Scotland were most probably sanctioned by Richard ; their
object was certainly in accord with Richard's own plans for
the succession at this time ; but Richard's choice of Arthur as
his heir was probably unknown as yet to the majority of his
subjects, and if it was known to them, it could not commend
itself to their ideas either of policy or of constitutional
practice.   In their eyes the king's next-of-kin and natural
successor was not his boy-nephew, but his brother.   It was
therefore easy for John to win their sympathies by
representing the scheme as part of a plot contrived against
himself by the chancellor.

The new agreement lasted no longer than its predecessor.
Scarcely was it drawn up when there occurred an excellent
opportunity for John to secure for himself a new and valuable
ally in the person of his half-brother Geoffrey, the eldest son
of Henry II. and the predecessor of Longchamp in the office
of chancellor of England.   Geoffrey, like John, had in the
spring of 1190 been sworn to keep out of England for three
years ; but, like John too, he had obtained from Richard a
release from his oath.[3]   His election to the see of York had
been confirmed by the Pope on May 11, 1191,[4] and it was
known that he intended to return to England immediately
after his consecration.[5]   Richard had given him a written
release from his vow of absence,[6] but had neglected to

---

[1] R. Devizes, pp. 409, 410.   The date which he has appended to the agreement is impossible, not only for this particular document, but for any personal
meeting of John and the chancellor this year at Winchester, where he places
it.   See Round, *Commune of London*, p. 214, and *Cal. Doc. France*, vol. i. p.
17.   As to the agreement itself, cf. W. Newb. l. iv. c. 16.

[2] W. Newb. l. iv. c. 14.

[3] Gir. Cambr. vol. iv. p. 382.

[4] *Monast. Angl.* vol. vi. pt. iii. p. 1188.

[5] Gir. Cambr. vol. iv. p. 389.   [6] *Ib.* p. 382.

apprise the chancellor of the fact; William therefore no
sooner heard of Geoffrey's purpose to return than he issued,
on July 30, a writ ordering that the archbishop should be
arrested on landing.[1]   Geoffrey had written to John, begging
for his help; John in reply promised to stand by him.[2]   On
August 18 Geoffrey was consecrated at Tours,[3] and John
then urged him to come over at once.[4]   On September 14
Geoffrey reached Dover; he escaped from an attempt to
arrest him as he landed, but four days later he was forcibly
dragged from sanctuary in S. Martin's priory and flung into
prison in the castle.[5]

John immediately wrote to the chancellor, demanding
whether these things had been done by his authority.
According to one account, William answered that they had.[6]
A letter from William himself to the chapter of Canterbury,
however, declares that he had merely ordered his officers to
administer to Geoffrey the oath of fealty to the king (which
it was usual for a bishop to take before entering upon his
see), and if he refused it, to send him back to the Continent.[7]
However this might be, it is clear that, outwardly at least,
the chancellor had put himself in the wrong.   He was
already the most unpopular man in England; now, all
parties in Church and State joined hands against him at
once; and it was inevitable that they should rally under the
command of John.   John sent another letter or message to
William, bidding him release the archbishop, and swearing
that if this were not done immediately, he, the count of
Mortain, would go in person "with a mighty hand and a
stretched-out arm" to set his brother at liberty.[8]   On
September 21 or 26 Geoffrey was released.[9]   Meanwhile
John, with his confidant Hugh of Nonant, the bishop of
Coventry, hurried down from Lancaster to Marlborough,

---

[1] Gir. Cambr. vol. iv. p. 389.   [2] R. Devizes, p. 410.
[3] R. Diceto, vol. ii. p. 96.   [4] *Gesta Ric.* p. 210.
[5] R. Diceto, vol. ii. p. 97; Gir. Cambr. vol. iv. pp. 388-93; R. Devizes,
pp. 411, 412.
[6] *Gesta Ric.* p. 211.
[7] *Epp. Cantuar.* pp. 344, 345; Gerv. Cant. vol. i. p. 506.   Cf. R. Devizes,
p. 413.
[8] *Gesta Ric.* p. 211.
[9] September 21, R. Devizes, p. 412; September 26, R. Diceto, vol. ii. p. 97.

1191 and invited all whom he thought likely to take his side to join him there. Three of the co-justiciars—William the Marshal among them—answered his call; three bishops, one of whom was the venerated Hugh of Lincoln, did likewise; and so did Archbishop Walter of Rouen. From Marlborough the party moved on to Reading; thence John despatched a personal invitation, or summons, to Geoffrey,[1] and at the same time issued, in conjunction with the three justiciars, letters calling the rest of the bishops and barons to a council to be holden on October 5 at the bridge over the Lodden between Reading and Windsor, and a summons to the chancellor to appear there and answer for his conduct.[2] William retorted by issuing counter writs, summoning all those who had joined the count of Mortain to withdraw from him, " forasmuch as he was endeavouring to usurp the kingdom to himself." [3]

John and all his party came to the Lodden bridge on the day which they had appointed; the chancellor, who was at Windsor, sent the bishop of London and three earls to excuse his absence on the plea of illness. The outcome of the day's discussion was that the assembly, by the voice of Walter of Rouen, pledged itself to depose William from the office of chief justiciar. Their warrant was a letter from the king which Walter had brought from Messina, and in which the subordinate justiciars were bidden to obey Walter's guidance in all things. The party then returned to Reading; there, next day (Sunday, October 6), the bishops among them excommunicated Longchamp and his adherents; at night a message was sent to him, bidding him appear at the bridge next morning without fail; and this he promised to do.[4] John and his friends were resolved to make sure of their game this time. On the Monday morning they took care to be first at the bridge; but instead of waiting for the chancellor, the heads of the party rode forward along the Windsor road as if to meet him, and

---

[1] Gir. Cambr. vol. iv. pp. 394-7.
[2] *Ib.* p. 397; R. Devizes, p. 413. Cf. *Gesta Ric.* p. 212. One of the summons is given in R. Diceto, vol. ii. p. 98.
[3] Gir. Cambr. *l.c.*
[4] *Ib.* vol. iv. pp. 398-402. For date see R. Diceto, vol. ii. p. 98.

sent their men-at-arms and servants towards London by way
of Staines.   Tidings of these movements reached William
just after he had set out from Windsor.   He at once turned
back and rode towards London with all speed, and reached
the junction of the two roads at the same time as the men-
at-arms of John's party.   A skirmish took place in which
John's justiciar, Roger de Planes, was mortally wounded.[1]
While the chancellor made his way into the Tower, John
and the barons were following him to London.   Next
morning (Tuesday, October 8) they assembled at S. Paul's,
renewed their resolution to depose the chancellor, and, in
the king's name, granted to the Londoners their coveted
"commune";[2] whereupon the citizens joined unreservedly
with them in voting the deposition of Longchamp and the
appointment of Walter of Rouen as chief justiciar in his
stead.[3]   According to one account, the assembly went still
further, and proposed to make John "chief governor of the
whole kingdom," with control of all the royal castles except
three which were to be left to the chancellor.[4]   As a token
that all this was done "for the safety of the realm," every
man present, John first of all, renewed his oath of fealty to
the king ; and this ceremony was followed by a second oath
of fidelity taken by all the rest to John himself, "saving their
fealty" [to the king], together with a promise that they
would acknowledge him as king if Richard should die
without issue.[5]

The barons, the bishops, the justiciars, all London, all
England, save a handful of Longchamp's own relatives,
personal friends and followers, was on John's side ; Longchamp himself, besieged in the Tower by overwhelming
forces, could not possibly hold it for more than a day or
two, and there was no hope of relief.   There was, however,
still one chance of escape from all his difficulties,—John

[1] Cf. Gir. Cambr. vol. iv. pp. 402-5 ; R. Devizes, pp. 413, 414 ; R. Diceto,
vol. ii. p. 99 ; *Gesta Ric.* p. 212, and W. Newb. l. iv. c. 17.

[2] Gir. Cambr. vol. iv. p. 405 ; *Gesta Ric.* pp. 213, 214 ; R. Diceto, *l.c.* ; R.
Devizes, pp. 416, 417.

[3] *Gesta Ric.* pp. 213, 214.

[4] R. Devizes, p. 415.

[5] *Gesta Ric.* p. 214. Cf. R. Diceto, vol. ii. p. 97.

1191 might be bribed. The project seemed a desperate one, for William had already tried it without success, two days before;[1] yet he tried it again on the Wednesday, and this time he all but succeeded. "By promising him much and giving him not a little, the chancellor so nearly turned the count of Mortain from his purpose that he was ready to withdraw from the city, leaving the business unfinished, had not the bishops of Coventry and York recalled him by their entreaties and arguments."[2] Next day the chancellor submitted. On the Oct. 11 Friday he gave up the keys of the Tower and of Windsor; within another fortnight he was reduced to surrender all the other royal castles except the three which had been nominally reserved to him, Dover, Cambridge, and Hereford.[3] Hereupon John ordered him to be released, and allowed him to sail on October 29 for France.[4]

The truth of Longchamp's assertion that John was "endeavouring to usurp the kingdom for himself" was soon made evident. Just before Christmas Philip Augustus of France came home from Acre. After a vain attempt to entrap the seneschal of Normandy into surrendering some of the border fortresses of the duchy to him, he opened negotiations for Richard's damage in a more likely quarter; he invited John to come over and speak with him immediately, proposing to put him in possession of "all the lands of England and Normandy on this (*i.e.* the French) side of the sea," on one condition, that he should marry the bride whom Richard had refused, Philip's sister Adela.[5] To this condition John's existing marriage was a bar, but not an insuperable one; it would be easy for him to divorce Isabel on the plea of consanguinity if he were so minded. He responded

---

[1] Gir. Cambr. vol. iv. p. 402.   [2] *Ib.* p. 406.

[3] *Ib.* pp. 106, 107 ; R. Devizes, pp. 417, 418 ; R. Diceto, vol. ii. p. 100. The reservation was merely nominal ; R. Diceto says the constables appointed by William to these castles were allowed to remain, but made to give hostages for their loyalty ; while Gerald says the constables were to be appointed by the new ministry. Probably the ministry decided to retain or reappoint the actual constables, on the condition mentioned by Ralph.

[4] *Gesta Ric.* p. 220 ; R. Diceto, vol. ii. pp. 100, 101.

[5] *Gesta Ric.* p. 236.

eagerly to Philip's invitation, and was on the point of sailing
from Southampton for France, when his plans were upset by
his mother's landing at Portsmouth on February 11.[1]   The
French king's treachery had come to Eleanor's knowledge,
and she had hastened back to England to do what lay in
her power for the protection of her elder son's interests.   The
justiciars, who seem to have already had their suspicions of
John's loyalty, rallied round her at once.   She was in fact the
only person whose right to represent the absent king was
treated by all parties as indisputable, although she had never
held any formal commission as regent.   She and the justiciars
conjointly forbade John to leave the country, threatening
that if he did so they would seize all his lands for the Crown.[2]
For a while John hesitated, or affected to hesitate ; he had
indeed at least two other secret negotiations on hand beside
that with France, and he was probably waiting to see which
of the three most required his personal superintendence, or
was likely to prove most profitable.   Another proposition
besides Philip's had come to him from over sea : Longchamp had offered to give him five hundred pounds if he
would get him reinstated as chief justiciar of England.[3]
John cared very little who bore the title of justiciar, if he
could secure the power for himself ; his main object in
England was to gain possession of the royal castles ; with
these in his hands, he could set any justiciar at defiance.   The
arrangement made in the previous July had been terminated
by the chancellor's fall, and the castles of Nottingham and
Tickhill had therefore, in accordance with the last clause of
the July agreement, been restored in October to John.   The
very rash project of placing all the royal castles under John's
control, said to have been mooted in London at the same
time, had evidently not been carried into effect ;[4] but John

---

[1] R. Devizes, pp. 430, 432 ; *Gesta Ric.* p. 236.

[2] *Gesta Ric.* p. 237.

[3] R. Howden, vol. iii. p. 188 ; in *Gesta Ric.* p. 239, the sum is given as
five hundred thousand marks, "which," as Bishop Stubbs says (note to R.
Howden, *l.c.*), " is of course impossible."

[4] Richard of Devizes, indeed, says (p. 418) that on the chancellor's
departure over sea " Comes omnia munita terrae quibus voluit et plus credidit sibi
reddita liberavit " : but his own story about Windsor and Wallingford shows this
to be incorrect.

1192 himself had never lost sight of it, and, as a chronicler says, "he did what he could" towards its realization. He began with two of the most important fortresses near the capital, Windsor and Wallingford. He dealt secretly with their commanding officers, so that they were delivered into his hands and filled with liegemen of his own.[1] This would be easy to manage in the case of Wallingford, which stood within an "honour" belonging to John himself. The custody of Windsor castle seems to have been, after the chancellor's fall, entrusted for a time to the bishop of Durham, Hugh of Puiset,[2] a near kinsman of the royal house. In spite of the fact that Hugh was under sentence of excommunication from his metropolitan, Geoffrey of York, John had chosen to spend the Christmas of 1191 with him at Howden; thereby of course rendering himself, in Geoffrey's estimation at least, *ipso facto* excommunicate likewise, till he made satisfaction for his offence.[3] Hugh of Durham had once hoped himself to supersede Longchamp as chief justiciar, and it is perhaps not too much to suspect that John may have so wrought upon the old bishop's jealousy of Walter of Rouen as to induce him to connive at a proceeding on the part of his representatives at Windsor which would more than compensate his wily young cousin for the temporary ecclesiastical disgrace brought upon him by that otherwise unaccountable Christmas visit.

The actual transfer of these two castles to John probably did not take place till after a council held at Windsor by the queen-mother and the justiciars, towards the end of February or beginning of March. This council was followed by another at Oxford. After Mid-Lent (March 12) a third council was called, to meet this time in London, and for the express purpose of "speaking with Count John about his seizure of the castles."[4] John, however, had taken care that another matter should come up for discussion first. He had answered Longchamp's proposal by bidding him come

---

[1] R. Devizes, p. 433.

[2] "Episcopo Dunelmensi £34 : 15s. in Pickering pro escambio custodiae castelli de Windsor quamdiu regi placuerit," Pipe Roll 4 Ric. I. (1192) m. 7.

[3] *Gesta Ric.* pp. 235, 236.

[4] R. Devizes, p. 433.

over and try his luck.   Thus the first piece of business with
which the council had to deal was a demand from the
chancellor, who had just landed at Dover, for a trial in the
Curia Regis of the charges on which he had been deposed.
Eleanor inclined to grant the demand.   One contemporary
says that Longchamp had bribed her.   In any case she
probably knew, or suspected, that Longchamp now had John
at his back ; she certainly knew in what regard he was held
by Richard ; and she urged, with considerable reason, that
his deprivation must be displeasing to the king, if it were
not justified by process of law.   The justiciars and the
barons, however, represented the chancellor's misdoings in
such glaring colours that she was reduced to silence.[1] But
she was evidently not willing to join the justiciars in driving
William out of the country ; and in the face of her reluct-
ance the justiciars dared not act without John.   He was at
Wallingford, "laughing at their conventicles."   Messenger
after messenger was sent to him with respectful entreaties
that he would come to the council and lend it his aid in
dealing with the chancellor.   He took the matter very com-
posedly, letting them all go on begging and praying till they
had humbled themselves enough to satisfy him and he had
got his final answer ready for every contingency ; then he
went to London.   The council, originally summoned to
remonstrate with him for his misconduct, now practically
surrendered itself wholly to his guidance.   Of the castles not
a word was said ; the one subject of discussion was the
chancellor.   All were agreed in desiring his expulsion, if
only the count would declare himself of the same mind.
The count told them his mind with unexpected plainness.
" This chancellor will neither fear the threats nor beg the
favour of any one of you, nor of all of you put together, if
he can but get me for his friend.   Within the next seven
days he is going to give me seven hundred pounds, if I
meddle not between him and you.   You see that I want
money ; I have said enough for wise men to understand "—
and·therewith he left them.[2]   The justiciars saw that unless
they could outbid the chancellor, their own fate was sealed.

[1] *Gesta Ric.* p. 239.   [2] R. Devizes, pp. 433, 434.

1192   As a last resource, " it was agreed that they should give him
          or lend him some money, but not of their own ; all fell upon
          the treasury of the absent king."   John's greed was satisfied
          by a gift, or a loan, out of the exchequer ; when this was
          safe in his hands, he gave the justiciars his written sanction
          to their intended proceedings against the chancellor ; [1] they
          ordered William to quit the country, and he had no choice
          but to obey.   They had, however, purchased his expulsion at
          a ruinous cost to themselves ; its real price was of course not
          the few hundreds of which they had robbed the exchequer for
          John's benefit, but their own independence.   John had out-
          witted them completely, and they had practically confessed
          themselves to be at his mercy.   Before the council broke up,
          every member of it, including the queen-mother, took another
          oath of fealty " against all men " to the king " and to his
          heir "—in other words, to John himself.[2]

          John's obvious policy now was to keep still and let
          things remain as they were till there should come some
          definite tidings of Richard.   For nine months all parties
          were quiescent.   Then, on December 28, the Emperor
          wrote to Philip of France the news of Richard's capture.
          If the messenger who brought the letter was " welcome
          above gold and topaze " [3] to Philip, no less welcome to John
          was the messenger whom Philip immediately despatched to
          carry the news to England.   John hurried over to Nor-
          mandy, where the seneschal and barons of the duchy met
          him with a request that he would join them in a council at
          Alençon to deliberate " touching the king's affairs, and his
          release."   John's answer was at least frank : " If ye will
          acknowledge me as your lord and swear me fealty, I will
          come with you and will be your defender against the king
          of France ; but if not, I will not come." [4]   The Normans

          ---

          [1] "Dare placet vel commodare pecuniam, sed non de proprio, tandemque
          totum cadit in absentis aerarium.   Creduntur comiti de fisco per fiscarios quin-
          gentae librae sterlingorum, et recipiuntur ad placitum literae in cancellarium,"
          R. Devizes, p. 343.   "Johannes . . . acceptis a Rothomagensi archiepiscopo
          et a caeteris justitiariis Angliae duobus millibus marcis argenti de thesauro regis
          fratris sui, consilio eorum adquievit," *Gesta Ric.* p. 239.   Possibly the smaller
          sum was handed over to John at once, and the remainder only promised.
          [2] *Gesta Ric.* pp. 239, 237.
          [3] W. Newb. l. iv. c. 32.   [4] R. Howden, vol. iii. p. 204.

refused thus to betray their captive sovereign; whereupon John proceeded to the court of France. There an agreement was drawn up, to which the count swore in person and the French king by proxy, and which curiously illustrates their mutual distrust and their common dread of Richard. It provided that in the event of John's succession, he should cede the Vexin to France, and should hold the rest of the Norman and Angevin dominions as his forefathers had held them, with the exception of the city of Tours and certain small underfiefs, concerning which special provisions were made, evidently with a view to securing the co-operation of their holders against Richard. On the other hand, John promised to accept no offer of peace from Richard without Philip's consent, and Philip promised to make no peace with Richard unless the latter would accept certain conditions laid down in behalf of John. These conditions were that John should not be disseised of any lands which he held at the time of the treaty; that if summoned to trial by Richard, he should always be allowed to appear by proxy; and that he should not be held liable to personal service in Richard's host. After sealing this document in Paris, in January 1193,[1] John hurried back to England and set to work secretly to stir up the Welsh and the Scots, hoping with their support to effect a junction with a body of Flemings who were to come over in a fleet prepared by Philip at Wissant.

The Scot king rejected John's overtures; but a troop of Welsh were, as usual, ready to join in any rising against the king of England.[2] With these Welshmen, and "many foreigners" whom he had brought with him from France, John secured himself at Wallingford and Windsor. Then he proceeded to London, told the justiciars that Richard was dead, and bade them deliver up the kingdom and make its people swear fealty to himself. They refused; he withdrew in a rage, and both parties prepared for war.[3] The

[1] *Foedera*, vol. i. pt. i. p. 57. The document (of which no original is known) may be slightly corrupt, but it is obviously more trustworthy than the version of John's and Philip's agreement given by Roger of Howden, vol. iii. p. 204.

[2] Gerv. Cant. vol. i. pp. 514, 515.

[3] R. Howden, vol. iii. pp. 204, 205.

justiciars organized their forces so quickly and so well that when the French fleet arrived, just before Easter, it found the coast so strongly guarded that no landing was possible. John meanwhile had openly fortified his castles, and his Welshmen were ravaging the country between Kingston and Windsor when the justiciars laid siege to the latter fortress.[1] This siege, and that of Tickhill, which was undertaken by Archbishop Geoffrey of York and Bishop Hugh of Durham, were in progress when on April 20 Hubert Walter, the bishop of Salisbury, landed in England.[2] Hubert had come direct from the captive king, and it was now useless for John to pretend any longer that Richard was dead. On the other hand, Hubert knew the prospect of Richard's release to be still so remote and so uncertain that he deemed it highly imprudent to push matters to extremity with John. He therefore, although both Windsor and Tickhill were on the verge of surrender, persuaded the justiciars to make a truce whose terms were on the whole favourable to the count of Mortain. The castles of Tickhill and Nottingham were left in John's hands; those of Windsor, Wallingford and the Peak were surrendered by him, to be given over to the custody of Queen Eleanor and other persons named, on the express understanding that unless Richard should reach home in the meanwhile, they were to be restored to John at the expiration of the truce, which was fixed for Michaelmas, or, according to another account, All Saints' Day.[3]

The immediate object of the justiciars and the queen-mother in making this truce was to gain John's co-operation in their measures for raising the king's ransom. Considering how large a portion of the kingdom was held by John in what may almost be called absolute property, it is obvious that a refusal on his part to bear his share of the burden would make a serious difference in the result of their efforts. It appears that John undertook to raise from his own territories a certain sum for his brother's ransom, that he confirmed this undertaking by an oath, and that he put it on

---

[1] Gerv. Cant. vol. i. p. 515; R. Howden, vol. iii. p. 205.
[2] Gerv. Cant. vol. i. p. 516.   [3] *Ib.*; R. Howden, vol. iii. p. 207.

record in writing.[1]   He had, however, taken no steps   1193
towards its execution when at the beginning of July a
warning reached him from Philip Augustus—" Take care of
yourself, for the devil is loosed ! "—which meant that the
terms of Richard's release had been finally agreed upon
between Richard and the Emperor on June 29.   John
immediately hurried over to France, to shelter himself under
Philip's wing against the coming storm, as was thought in
England ;[2] more probably to keep a watch upon Philip
and take care that he should not break his promises as to
the conditions of peace with Richard.   The two allies could
have no confidence in each other, and they seem to have
been both almost ridiculously afraid of the captive Lion-
heart.   He, however, was at the moment equally afraid of
them, and not without good reason.   Three months before
he had complained bitterly to the first messengers from
England who reached him in his prison of the treachery
and ingratitude of John.   " Yet," he added, " my brother is
not a man to win lands for himself by force, if there be
any one who will oppose him with another force, however
slight."[3]   The words were true ; and no less true was the
implication underlying the words.   Of John as an open
enemy Richard could afford to be contemptuous ; of John's
capacity for underhand mischief, especially in conjunction
with Philip, he was in such fear that no sooner was his
treaty with the Emperor signed than he despatched his
chancellor and three other envoys to France with orders to
make with the French king " a peace of some sort."[4]   The
envoys executed their commission literally, by accepting in
Richard's name the terms which were dictated to them by
Philip with John at his side.   These included the cession
by Richard to Philip of the places taken by the French
king during his late campaign in Normandy ; the ratification of the arrangements made by Philip and John for

[1] R. Howden, vol. iii. p. 217.
[2] *Ib.* pp. 216, 217.
[3] " 'Johannes frater meus non est homo qui sibi *vi* terram subjiciat, si fuerit
qui vim ejus vi saltem tenui repellat,' " R. Howden, vol. iii. p. 198.   I
think there can be no doubt as to the significance of the first " *vi.*"
[4] " Ad pacem cum illo faciendum qualemcumque," *ib.* p. 217.

1193 certain of their partisans ; and the payment to Philip of twenty thousand marks, for which four castles were given to him in pledge. "Touching Count John," the treaty ran, "thus shall it be : If the men of the king of England can prove in the court of the king of France that the same John has sworn, and given a written promise, to furnish money for the English king's ransom, he, John, shall be held bound to pay it ; and he shall hold all his lands, on both sides of the sea, as freely as he held them before his brother the king of England set out on his journey over sea ; only he shall be free from the oath which he then swore of not setting foot in England ; and of this the English king shall give him security by himself, and by the barons and prelates of his realm, and by the king of France. If, however, Count John shall choose to deny that those letters are his, or that he swore to do that thing, the English king's men shall prove sufficiently, by fitting witnesses, in the French king's court, that he did swear to procure money for the English king's ransom. And if it shall be proved, as hath been said, that he did swear to do this, or if he shall fail to meet the charge, the king of France shall not concern himself with Count John, if he should choose to accept peace for his lands aforesaid." [1]

This treaty was drawn up at Nantes on July 9.[2] John at once returned to Normandy and there took an oath of liege homage to his brother ; whereupon Richard ordered all the castles of John's honours to be restored to him, on

---

[1] " De comite autem Johanne sic erit : quod si homines regis Angliae poterunt sufficienter monstrare in curia domini regis Franciae quod idem Johannes juraverit ad perquirendam pecuniam ad liberationem regis Angliae, et de hoc dederit litteras suas, ipse Johannes tenebitur ad solvendum, et totam terram quam ipse tenebat quando rex Angliae frater ejus iter arripuit ultra mare, tenebit, citra mare et ultra, ita libere sicut prius tenebat ; excepto eo quod liber erit a sacramento quod fecerat de non intranda terra Angliae ; et de hoc dictus rex Angliae faciet dominum Johannem securum per se, et per barones et archiepiscopos et episcopos terrae suae, et insuper per regem Franciae. Si autem comes Johannes vellet negare quod litterae illae non essent suae, aut quod illud non jurasset, homines regis Angliae sufficienter in curia regis Franciae monstrabunt, per idoneos testes, quod juraverit ad querendam pecuniam ad liberationem regis Angliae. Si autem monstratum fuerit, sicut dictum est, quod comes juraverit ad quaerendam pecuniam ad liberationem regis, vel si defecerit de recipienda monstratione, rex Franciae non intromittat se de comite Johanne, si pacem de terra sua praedicta recipere voluerit," R. Howden, vol. iii. pp. 217, 218.   [2] *Ib.* p. 220.

both sides of the sea. "But the keepers thereof would not give up any castle to him" on the strength of this order.[1] John in a rage went back to France, and Philip immediately gave him the custody of two Norman castles, Driencourt and Arques, which by the recent treaty had been intrusted to the archbishop of Reims in pledge for the twenty thousand marks promised to Philip by Richard.[2] At Christmas the two allies made a last desperate effort to prevent the "devil" from being "loosed." They offered the Emperor three alternatives: either Philip would give him fifty thousand marks, and John would give him thirty thousand, if he would keep Richard prisoner until the following Michaelmas (1194); or the two between them would pay him a thousand pounds a month so long as he kept Richard in captivity; or Philip would give him a hundred thousand marks and John fifty thousand, if he would either detain Richard for another twelvemonth, or deliver him up into their hands. "Behold how they loved him!" says a contemporary writer.[3] A hundred and fifty thousand marks was the ransom which had been agreed upon between Henry VI. and Richard, and the one question which troubled Henry was whether he had a better chance of actually getting that sum from Richard or from his enemies. He unblushingly stated this fact to Richard himself, and on February 2, 1194, showed him the letters of Philip and John. Richard appealed to the German princes who had witnessed his treaty with Henry, and by promises of liberal revenues to be granted to them from England induced them to take his part and insist upon Henry's fulfilling his agreement. On February 4 the English king was set at liberty, and a joint letter from the Emperor and the nobles of his realm was despatched to Philip and John, bidding them restore to Richard all that they had taken from him during his

1193

1194

---

[1] "Sed custodes illorum noluerunt tradere illi aliquod castellum per breve," R. Howden, vol. iii. pp. 227, 228. Did they suspect John of having forged the king's writ? Or should the words be "*nisi* per breve," and do they mean that the individual castellans refused to act upon what seems to have been a merely general order, and require a special writ for each castle?

[2] *Ib.* p. 228.

[3] *Ib.* p. 229. Cf. W. Newb. i. iv. c. 40.

1194   captivity, and threatening that if they failed to do so, the writers would do their utmost to compel them.[1]

Before this letter could have reached its destination, John sent to England a confidential clerk, Adam of S. Edmund's, with secret letters, ordering that all the castles which he held there should be made ready for defence against the king. This man, having reached London without hindrance, foolishly presented himself on February 9 at the house of the new archbishop of Canterbury, Hubert Walter. The archbishop invited him to dinner, an unexpected honour by which Adam's head was so completely turned that he boasted openly at table of his master's hopes of political advancement. Hubert listened without remark, and thinking that to arrest the babbler on the spot would be a breach of hospitality, suffered him to depart after dinner; but the mayor of London—warned no doubt by the archbishop himself or by one of the other guests—seized Adam on his way back to his lodging, took possession of his papers, and sent them to Hubert, who on the following day laid them before a council of bishops and barons. The council unanimously decreed that John should be disseised of all his lands in England, and that his castles should be reduced by force; the bishops excommunicated him and all his adherents. Then the old bishop of Durham set off to renew the siege of Tickhill; the earls of Chester, Huntingdon and Ferrars laid siege to the castle of Nottingham; Archbishop Hubert himself undertook that of Marlborough, which he won in a few days; and Lancaster was given up to him by his brother Theobald. On March 13 Richard arrived in England. His arrival was speedily followed by the surrender of Tickhill. On the 25th he appeared before Nottingham; on the 28th he was once again master of its castle, and of all England.[2]

At Nottingham Richard held a council, on the second day of which (March 31) he "prayed that justice should be done him"[3] on John and on John's chief abettor, Bishop Hugh of Chester. The council cited both delinquents to

---

[1] R. Howden, vol. iii. pp. 232, 234.   [2] *Ib.* 236-40.
[3] "Petiit sibi fieri judicium de comite Johanne," etc., *ib.* p. 241.

appear for trial within forty days, and decreed that if they
failed to do so, or to "stand to right," Hugh should be
liable to a double sentence—from the bishops as a bishop,
and from the laity as a sheriff,[1]—and John should be
accounted to have "forfeited all claims to the kingdom,"[2]
or, as a later annalist explains, should be "deprived and
disinherited not only of all the lands which he held in the
realm, but also of all honours which he hoped or expected
to have from the Crown of England."[3]   Neither in person
nor·by proxy did John answer the citation.   At the end of
the forty days three earls set out for the court of France
"to convict him of treason there"; but of their proceedings,
too, he took no notice.   The forty days had expired on
May 10; on the 12th Richard sailed for Normandy.[4]
Landing at Barfleur, he went to Caen and thence turned
southward to relieve Verneuil, which Philip was besieging.
On the way he halted at Lisieux, where he took up his
quarters with the archdeacon, John of Alençon, who had
been his vice-chancellor.[5]   He soon noticed that his host
was uneasy and agitated, and at once guessed the cause.
"Why do you look so troubled?   You have seen my
brother John; deny it not!   Let him fear nought, but
come to me straightway.   He is my brother, and should
have no fears of me; if he has played the fool, I will never
reproach him with his folly.   Those who contrived this
mischief shall reap their due reward; but of that no more
at present."   Joyfully John of Alençon carried the tidings
to his namesake of Mortain: "Come forward boldly!   You
are in luck's way.   The king is simple and pitiful, and kinder
to you than you would have been to him.   Your masters
have advised you ill; it is meet they should be punished
according to their deserts.   Come! the king awaits you."
In spite of these assurances, it was "with much fear" that
Count John approached his brother and threw himself at his

---

[1] Hugh was sheriff of Warwickshire and Leicestershire.
[2] "Demeruisse regnum," R. Howden, vol. iii. p. 242.
[3] *Ann. Margan.* a. 1199.
[4] R. Howden, vol. iii. p. 251.
[5] For John of Alençon see Round, *Calendar of Doc. in France*, vol. i. pp.
14, 15, 90, 91, 210, 454, 528.

1194 feet. Richard raised him with a brotherly kiss, saying:
"Think no more of it, John! You are but a child, and were
left to ill guardians. Evil were their thoughts who counselled
you amiss. Rise, go and eat. John," he added, turning to
their host, "what can he have for dinner?" At that
moment a salmon was brought in, as a present for the king.
As the chronicler remarks, "it did not come amiss";
Richard immediately ordered it to be cooked for his
brother.[1]

For any other man of six-and-twenty, to be thus forgiven
—even though it were by a brother who was ten years older,
and a king—expressly on the ground that he was a child,
not responsible for his actions, would surely have been a
humiliation almost more bitter than any punishment. Nor
did John escape altogether unpunished. Richard's forgiveness was strictly personal; the decree of the council of
Nottingham was carried into effect with regard to all John's
English and Norman lands;[2] and for the next eighteen
months he was, save for his lordship of Ireland, once more

---

[1] *Hist. de G. le Mar.* vv. 10365-419. R. Diceto, vol. ii. p. 114, places
the meeting of the brothers at Brueis; and Roger of Howden, vol. iii. p. 252,
says their reconciliation took place "mediante Alienor regina matre eorum."
This may mean either that she had interceded with Richard before he left
England, or that it was she who had counselled John to throw himself on the
king's clemency.

[2] R. Howden, vol. iii. p. 252. Some of John's English lands had been
seized before the council of Nottingham; no doubt, by virtue of the decree
passed at the council in London on February 10. In the Pipe Roll of
Michaelmas 1194 the king's officers accounted to the king's treasury for the
ferms of Nottinghamshire, Derbyshire, Dorset and Somerset, the third penny of
Gloucestershire, and the ferm of Eye, for half a year (P.R. 6 Ric. I. m. 6, 13,
16, 4 d); but the sheriff of Devon and Cornwall rendered his account for three-
quarters of a year (*ib.* m. 12); while the forfeiture of John's private estates in
Dorset and Somerset seems to have been dated from Ash-Wednesday, February
23 (*ib.* m. 13 d); a part at least of the honour of Gloucester, viz. Bristol,
had been seized at Mid-Lent, four days after Richard's landing in England, and
the whole not later than Easter (*ib.* m. 16 d); and for the honours of Peverel
and Tickhill a whole year's ferm was reckoned as due to the treasury at Michaelmas (*ib.* m. 6). The king's escheators rendered a separate account of a number
of escheats in the honour of Lancaster and in the counties which John had held
(*ib.* m. 2, 2 d); and the sheriff of Dorset and Somerset gathered in for the king
a quantity of "arrears of debts which were owed to Count John for pleas and
amercements of the men and townships" of those two counties (*ib.* m. 13). The
commission issued to the itinerant justices in the same month of September contained an express order that they should inquire into and report upon all John's
property, real and personal, and all the moneys owed to him, to the intent that
the whole might be secured for the king, R. Howden, vol. iii. pp. 263, 264.

in fact as well as in name " John Lackland." He was thus
wholly dependent on Richard's goodwill, and it was obviously
politic for him to throw himself into Richard's service with
the utmost energy and zeal. Philip withdrew from Verneuil
at the tidings of Richard's approach, May 28.[1] After
securing the place the English king divided his forces ; with
part of them he himself went to besiege Beaumont-le-Roger ;
the other part he entrusted to John for the recovery of
Evreux,[2] which had been taken by Philip in February.[3]
Of the manner in which John accomplished this mission
there are at least two versions. One writer states that
John " laid siege to Evreux, and it was taken next day." [4]
Another says that its garrison were surprised and slain by
a body of Normans ; [5] while a third explains the surprise as
having been effected by means which are perhaps only too
characteristic of John. The city of Evreux, says William
the Breton, had been made over to John by Philip. John
contrived that his reconciliation with his brother should
remain unknown to the French troops who had been left
there. He now returned to the city and invited these
Frenchmen to a banquet, at which he suddenly brought in
a troop of " armed Englishmen " who massacred the un-
suspecting guests. His success, however, was only partial
and shortlived ; for he was still unable to gain possession of
the castle ; [6] and he had no sooner quitted the place than
Philip returned, drove out the Norman troops, and destroyed
the town.[7] Shortly afterwards Richard set off on a campaign
in the south, leaving John in Normandy. About the middle
of June Philip again threatened Rouen, taking and razing
Fontaines, a castle only four miles from the city. On this
John, the earl of Leicester, and " many other barons " held
a meeting at Rouen to consider what should be done ; " but
because they had no one to whom they could adhere as to

---

[1] R. Howden, vol. iii. p. 252.

[2] *Hist. de. G. le Mar.* vv. 10491-517.

[3] W. Newb. l. iv. c. 40 ; Rigord, c. 94.

[4] *Hist. de. G. le Mar.* vv. 10516-20.   [5] Rigord, c. 96.

[6] W. Armor. *Gesta Phil. Aug.* c. 72 ; *Philipp.* l. iv. vv. 445-62. The last
detail seems to imply that the victims of the surprise—whatever its character—
were, after all, not the whole garrison, but probably only the officers.

[7] Rigord, c. 96,

1194 the king himself," and their forces were no match for Philip's, they decided upon a policy of inaction.[1] This decision was probably dictated by their experience of Philip's ways. He, in fact, made no further attempt upon the Norman capital, but soon afterwards proceeded southward against Richard, only to meet with an ignominious defeat at Fréteval. On hearing of this, John and the earl of Arundel laid siege to Vaudreuil ; Philip, however, marched up from Bourges and relieved it.[2] John's next military undertaking, the siege of Brezolles, met with no better success.[3] Still he had done the best he could for his brother's interest, and thereby also for his own. Accordingly, next year Richard "laid aside all his anger and ill-will towards his brother John," and restored to him a portion of his forfeited possessions. It was indeed only a small portion, consisting of the county of Mortain and the honours of Gloucester and Eye "in their entirety, but without their castles." To this was added, as some compensation for the other lands which he had lost, a yearly pension of £8000 Angevin.[4]

This arrangement seems to have taken effect from Michaelmas 1195.[5] It gave John once more an honourable and independent maintenance, but left him without territorial power. His only chance of regaining this in Richard's lifetime was to earn it by loyalty to Richard. For the next three years, therefore, he kept quiet ; nothing is heard of him save an occasional notice of his presence in Normandy, either in his brother's company or acting for his brother's interest. When Philip seized Nonancourt in 1196 John retaliated by seizing Gamaches.[6] On May 19 in the same year he and Mercadier, the leader of Richard's foreign mercenaries, made a plundering expedition into the French king's territories as far as Beauvais, where they captured the bishop, who had long been one of

1196

---

[1] R. Howden, vol. iii. p. 253.

[2] Rigord, c. 100 ; W. Armor. *Gesta P. A.* c. 74 ; *Philipp.* l. iv. vv. 530-69.

[3] W. Armor. *Philipp.* l. v. vv. 30-32.

[4] R. Howden, vol. iii. p. 286.

[5] I can find no mention either of the honour of Eye or of that of Gloucester in Pipe Roll 7 Ric. I. (1196).

[6] R. Howden, vol. iv. p. 5.

Richard's most determined enemies; they then went on   1197
to the bishop's castle of Milli, took it by assault, razed it,
and returned to Normandy in triumph to present their
captive to Richard.[1]   On October 16, 1197, when the
king and the archbishop of Rouen made their agreement
for the building of a castle at Andely—the famous Château-
Gaillard—it was ratified in a separate charter by John; an
unusual proceeding, which has been thought to imply that
he was now again acknowledged as his brother's destined
heir.[2]   In 1198 Philip made another attack upon Nor-   1198
mandy and burned Evreux and seven other towns.   John
fired a ninth, Neubourg; Philip, seeing the flames and
supposing them to have been kindled by his own men, sent
a body of troops to bid them go no farther, on which John
fell upon the troops and captured eighteen knights and a
crowd of men-at-arms.[3]

The alliance of Richard and John had now lasted too   1199
long for Philip's satisfaction, and early in 1199 he set himself to break it.   He began by making a truce with Richard.
Then, when the Lion-heart, thinking himself safe for the
moment in Normandy, was on his way to Poitou, "that
sower of discord, the king of France, sent him word that
his brother John, the count of Mortain, had given himself
to him (Philip); and he offered to show him John's own
letter proving the fact.   O marvel!   The king of England
believed the king of France, and took to hating his brother
John, insomuch that he caused him to be disseised of his
lands on both sides of the sea.   And when John asked the
reason of this wrath and hatred, he was told what the king
of France had sent word to his brother about him.   Thereupon the count of Mortain sent two knights to represent
him at the French king's court, and they offered to prove
him innocent of this charge, or to defend him as the court
should direct.   But there was found no one in that court,
neither the king nor any other man, who would receive the
offered proof or defence.   And thenceforth the king of

---

[1] R. Howden, vol. iv. p. 16. Cf. W. Newb. l. v. c. 31.
[2] Deville, *Hist. du Château-Gaillard*, pp. 21, 22, 119-23.
[3] R. Howden, vol. iv. p. 60.

England was on more familiar terms with his brother John, and less ready to believe what was told him by the king of France." [1] This story does not necessarily show either that Philip's accusation of John was false, or that it was true. Philip may have invented it with the hope of driving John to throw himself again into his arms; but it is perhaps more likely that the two were in collusion, and that the scene in the French Curia Regis was a piece of acting on both sides. However this might be, by about the middle of March John had again left his brother "because he kept him so short of money, and on account of some disputes which had arisen between them." [2] Suddenly, at the end of the month, the question of the Angevin succession was brought to a crisis by a cross-bowman who, at the siege of Châlus, on March 26, gave Richard his death-wound. That question had haunted Richard throughout his reign; his wishes respecting its solution had wavered more than once; now that it had to be faced, however, he faced it in what was, after all, the wisest as well as the most generous way. In the presence of as many of his subjects as could be gathered hastily round him, he devised all his realms to John, gave orders that on his own death John should be put in possession of all the royal castles and three-fourths of the royal treasure, and made the assembly swear fealty to John as his successor. [3]

Richard died on April 6. [4] On the 3rd there had been delivered at Rouen a letter from him appointing William the Marshal commandant of the castle and keeper of the treasure which it contained. On the 10th—the eve of Palm Sunday—the news of the king's death came, late at night, just as the Marshal was going to bed. He dressed again in haste and went to the palace of the archbishop, who marvelled what could have brought him at such an hour, and when told, was, like William himself, overwhelmed with grief and consternation. What troubled them both

[1] R. Howden, vol. iv. p. 81.

[2] R. Coggeshall, p. 99.

[3] R. Howden, vol. iv. p. 83. The fourth part of the royal treasure was to be given to Richard's servants and to the poor.

[4] *Ib.* p. 84.

was the thought of the future. William went straight to
the point. " My lord, we must hasten to choose some one
whom we may make king." " I think and believe," answered Archbishop Walter, " that according to right, we
ought to make Arthur king." " To my thinking," said the
Marshal, " that would be bad. Arthur is counselled by
traitors ; he is haughty and proud ; and if we set him over
us he will seek evil against us, for he loves not the people
of this land. He shall not come here yet, by my advice.
Look rather at Count John ; my conscience and my knowledge point him out to me as the nearest heir to the land
which was his father's and his brother's." " Marshal, is this
really your desire ? " " Yea, my lord ; for it is reason.
Unquestionably, a son has a nearer claim to his father's
land than a grandson ; it is right that he should have it."
" So be it, then," said the archbishop ; " but mark my
words, Marshal ; of nothing that ever you did in your life
have you so much cause to repent as you will have of what
you are now doing." " I thank you," answered William ;
" nevertheless, I deem that thus it should be." [1]

In the conversation thus reported by the Marshal's
confidential squire there are several noticeable points. The
divergent views enunciated by the two speakers as to the
respective legal claims of Arthur and of John illustrate the
still uncertain condition of the rules of hereditary succession.
It is, however, plain that the legal aspect of the case was
but a minor matter in the eyes of both primate and Marshal.
For them the important question was not which of Richard's
two possible heirs had the best legal right to his heritage,
but which of the two was likely to make the least unsatis-
factory sovereign. The outlook was in any case a gloomy

[1] *Hist. de G. le Mar.* vv. 11877-908. These lines may be an almost
literal report of the interview as described by the Marshal himself to the writer,
John d'Erlée. John was the Marshal's favourite squire, and was immediately
despatched by him on an important mission to England ; see vv. 11909-16.
It has been suggested (*Dic. Nat. Biog.* " Marshal, William ") that " li arceves-
ques "—as John calls him, without either Christian name or title of see—may
have been not Walter of Rouen, but Hubert of Canterbury. Hubert was in
Normandy at the time ; but the advocacy of Arthur's claims, intelligible enough
in the mouth of a Norman prelate, is so contrary to the English political traditions
of those days that I cannot, without further evidence, ascribe it to such a
thoroughly English statesman as Archbishop Hubert Walter.

one ; the only choice was a choice of evils. Of the two evils, it was natural that Walter should regard John as the worst, if he thought of personal character alone.   Every one knew by this time what John was ; the most impartial of contemporary historians had already summed up his character in two words—" Nature's enemy," a monster.[1]   What Arthur might become was as yet uncertain ; the duke of Britanny was but twelve years old.   Yet even at that age, the " haughtiness and pride " ascribed to him by the Marshal are by no means unlikely to have shown themselves in a child whose father, Geoffrey, had been the evil genius of John's early life, and whose mother had for years set her second husband Earl Ralf of Chester, her brother-in-law King Richard, and her supreme overlord King Philip, all alike at defiance.   Not so much in Arthur's character, however, as in his circumstances, lay the main ground of the Marshal's objection to him as a sovereign.   From his cradle Arthur had been trained in hostility to the political system at the head of which the Norman primate now proposed to place him.   His very name had been given him by his mother and her people in defiance of his grandfather King Henry, as a badge of Breton independence and insubordination to the rule of the Angevin and Norman house.   From the hour of Henry's death in 1189, if not even from that of her son's birth in 1187, Constance of Britanny had governed her duchy and trained its infant heir as seemed good to herself and her people, till in 1196 she was at last entrapped and imprisoned in Normandy ; and then the result of her capture was that her boy fell into the keeping of another guardian not a whit less " traitorous," from the Norman or Angevin point of view, than the patriotic Bretons who had surrounded him hitherto—the king of the French, at whose court he was kept for some time, sharing the education of Philip's own son.   To confer the sovereignty of the Angevin dominions upon the boy Arthur would thus have been practically to lay it at the feet of Philip Augustus.   The only chance of preserving the integrity of the Angevin empire was to put a man at its head, and a man to whom

[1] " Hostis naturae Johannes," W. Newb. l. iv. c. 40.

the maintenance of that integrity would be a matter of personal interest as well as of family pride.   It was the consciousness of this that had made Richard abandon his momentary scheme of designating Arthur as his heir, and revert finally to John ; and it was the same consciousness which made William the Marshal, with his eyes fully open to John's character, hold fast, in the teeth of the primate's warning, to his conviction that " thus it should be."

John, after his last parting from his brother, had made a characteristic political venture ; he had sought to make friends with his boy-rival.   It was in Britanny, at Arthur's court, that he received the news of Richard's death.   He set off at once for Chinon ; money was his first need, and the Angevin treasury was there.   When he reached the place, on the Wednesday before Easter,[1] April 14 –three days after Richard's burial at Fontevraud—the castle and the treasure which it contained were at once given up to him by the commandant, Robert of Turnham, the seneschal of Anjou.[2]   The officers of the late king's household had hurried to meet his chosen heir, and now came to John demanding of him a solemn oath that he would carry into effect Richard's last wishes, and maintain the customs of the Angevin lands.   He took the oath, and they then acknowledged him as their lord in Richard's stead.[3]

The most venerated of English bishops then living, Hugh of Lincoln, had officiated at Richard's funeral and was still at Fontevraud.   John sent an urgent request for his presence at Chinon, welcomed him there with a great show of attachment, and proposed that they should travel to England together.   This Hugh declined, but he consented to accompany John for a few days on his journey northward.   They set out at once for Saumur, and stopped at Fontevraud to visit the tombs of Henry and Richard.   When John knocked at the choir-door for admittance, however, he was told that the abbess was away, and no visitor might enter without her leave.   He then asked Hugh to communi-

1 *Magna Vita S. Hugonis,* p. 287.
2 R. Howden, vol. iv. p. 86 ; R. Coggeshall, p. 99.
3 *Mag. Vita S. Hug. l.c.*

1199   cate to the sisters, in his name, a promise of benefactions to
their house, and a request for their prayers. "You know,"
said Hugh, "that I detest all falsehood; I will utter no
promises in your name unless I am assured that they will
be fulfilled." John swore that he would more than fulfil
them; and the bishop did what he had been asked to do.
As they left the church, John drew forth an amulet which
hung round his neck and showed it to his companion,
saying it had been given to one of his forefathers with a
promise from Heaven that whosoever of his race had it in
his possession should never lose the fulness of his ancestral
dominion.   Hugh bade him trust "not in that stone but in
the Chief Corner Stone"; and turning round as they came
out of the porch, over which was sculptured a representation
of the Last Judgement, he led him towards the group on the
left of the Judge, and besought him to take heed of the
perils attending the responsibility of a ruler during his brief
time upon earth.   John dragged his monitor across to the
other group, saying, "You should rather show me these,
whose good example I purpose to follow!"   During the
three days of his journey in Hugh's company, indeed, his
affectation of piety and humility was so exaggerated that it
seems to have rather quickened than allayed Hugh's distrust
of his good intentions.[1]   On Easter Day the mask was
suddenly dropped.   Bishop and count spent the festival
(April 18) at Beaufort,[2] probably as the guests of Richard's
widow, Berengaria.   John was said to have never communicated since he had been of an age to please himself in such
matters; and now all Hugh's persuasions failed to bring
him to the Holy Table.   He did, however, attend the high
mass on Easter Day, and at the offertory came up to Hugh
——who was officiating——with some money in his hand; but
instead of presenting the coins he stood looking at them
and playing with them till Hugh asked him, "Why do you
stand staring thus?"   "I am staring at these gold pieces,
and thinking that a few days ago, if I had had them, I
should have put them not into your hands, but rather into
my own purse; however, take them now."   The indignant

---

[1] *Mag. Vita S. Hug.* pp. 287-91.   [2] R. Howden, vol. iv. p. 87.

bishop, "blushing vehemently in John's stead," drew back
and bade him "throw into the bason what he held, and
begone." John obeyed.   Hugh then followed up his rebuke
with a sermon on the characters of a good and of a bad prince,
and the future reward of each.   John, liking neither the
matter of the sermon nor its length, thrice attempted to cut
it short by a message that he wanted his dinner ; Hugh only
preached the longer and the more pointedly, and took his
leave of John on the following day.[1]

On that day John discovered that he was in a situation
of imminent peril.   While he had been travelling from the
Breton border to Chinon and thence back to Beaufort, Philip
had mastered the whole county of Evreux and overrun
Maine as far as Le Mans ; and a Breton force, with Constance
and Arthur at its head, had marched straight upon Angers [2]
and won it without striking a blow.   City and castle were
surrendered at once by Thomas of Furnes, a nephew of the
seneschal Robert of Turnham ; [3] and on Easter Day a great
assembly of barons of Anjou, Touraine and Maine, as well
as of Britanny, gave in their adhesion to Arthur as their
liege lord and Richard's lawful heir.[4]   The forces thus
gathered in the Angevin capital, from which Beaufort was
only fifteen miles distant, must have been more than
sufficient to overwhelm John, whose suite was evidently a
very small one.   His only chance was to make for Normandy with all possible speed.   Hurrying away from
Beaufort on Easter Monday, he reached Le Mans the same
night ; its citizens received him coldly, its garrison refused
to support him, and it was only by slipping away before
daybreak on Tuesday that he escaped being caught between
two fires.   On that very morning the Bretons and their new
allies entered Le Mans in triumph,[5] and they were soon met
there by the French king, to whom Arthur did homage for
the counties of Anjou, Touraine and Maine.[6]

[1] *Mag. Vita S. Hug.* pp. 291-5.
[2] Rigord, c. 127.
[3] R. Coggeshall, p. 99 ; R. Howden, vol. iv. pp. 85, 86.
[4] R. Howden, pp. 86, 87 ; date from *Chron. S. Albini Andeg.* a. 1199.
[5] *Mag. Vita S. Hugon.* p. 296.
[6] Rigord, c. 127 ; W. Armor. *Gesta P. A.* c. 101.

1199   Meanwhile, however, John had made his way to Rouen,
and there he was safe. Richard on his death-bed had
declared that the people of Rouen were the most loyal of all
his subjects ; they proved their loyalty to his memory by
rallying round the successor whom he had chosen for
himself, and all Normandy followed their example. " By
the election of the nobles and the acclamation of the
citizens," [1] John was proclaimed duke of the Normans, and
invested with the symbols of his dukedom in the metropolitan church on Low Sunday, April 25.[2] The ducal
crown—a circlet of gold, with gold roses round the top—
was placed on his head by Archbishop Walter, and the new-
made duke swore before the clergy and people, on the holy
Gospels and the relics of saints, that he would maintain inviolate the rights of the Church, do justice, establish good
laws, and put down evil customs.[3] The archbishop then
girded him with the sword of justice, and presented him
with the lance which held among the insignia of a Norman
duke the place that belongs to the sceptre among those of a
king. A group of John's familiar friends stood close behind
him, audibly mocking at the solemn rites. He chose the
moment when the lance was put into his hands to turn
round and join in their mockery ; and, as he turned, the
lance slipped from his careless grasp and fell to the ground.[4]

          In after years it was only natural that this incident
should be recalled as an omen.[5] The indecent levity which
had caused the mishap was in itself ominous enough. Still,
however, the Marshal and the Norman and English primates
—for Hubert of Canterbury, too, was at Rouen, and fully
in accord with the policy of William and Walter—clave to
their forlorn hope and persevered in their thankless task.
In obedience to John's orders, Hubert and William now
returned to England to assist the justiciar, Geoffrey Fitz-
Peter, in securing the realm for him.[6] John himself turned

---

[1] R. Coggeshall, p. 99.
[2] *Ib.* ; R. Howden, vol. iv. p. 87 ; R. Diceto, vol. ii. p. 166 ; *Mag. Vita
S. Hugon.* p. 293 ; Gerv. Cant. vol. ii. p. 92.
[3] R. Howden, vol. iv. pp. 87-88.
[4] *Mag. Vita S. Hugon.* p. 293.   [5] *Ib.* pp. 293, 294.
[6] R. Howden, vol. iv. p. 86. John d'Erlée, the Marshal's biographer,

southward again to try whether it were possible, now that
he had the strength of Normandy at his back, to win the
Angevin lands before he went over sea.   No sooner had
the French and the Bretons withdrawn from Anjou than
it was overrun with fire and sword by Richard's mercenaries, acting under the orders of their captain Mercadier and of Queen Eleanor, who had enlisted them in
John's interests as soon as they had had time to march
up from Châlus to the Angevin border.   John despatched a
body of troops to join them, while he proceeded in person
to Le Mans.   There he wreaked his vengeance to the full.
City and castle fell into his hands ; he razed the castle,
pulled down the city walls, destroyed the houses capable of
defence, and flung the chief citizens into captivity.[1]   But the
danger in his rear was still too great to allow of his advance
farther south.   To throw the whole forces of Normandy
upon the Angevin lands would have been to leave Normandy
itself open to attack from two sides at once, and expose
himself to have his own retreat cut off by a new junction
between Philip and the Bretons.   He could only venture
to open negotiations with the barons of Anjou and of
Aquitaine, endeavour to win them over by fair words and
promises,[2] and then leave his interests in the south to the
care of his mother.   Accompanied only by a few personal
friends,[3] he went back through Normandy to the sea ; on
May 25 he landed at Shoreham ;[4] on the 26th he reached
London, and on the 27th—Ascension Day—he was crowned
at Westminster.[5]

asserts (*Hist. de G. le Mar.* vv. 11909-16) that he himself had been sent to
England by the Marshal three weeks earlier, to "take seisin" of the land,
castles, towns and royal demesnes for the count of Mortain.   Probably he was
really sent to bid the Marshal's own men in England secure for John the castles,
etc., which they held ; and also to act as a medium of communication between
the Marshal and the justiciar.

[1] R. Howden, vol. iv. pp. 87, 88, where, however, the order of events is
wrong. Cf. R. Coggeshall, p. 99.

[2] *Hist. de G. le Mar.* vv. 11925-40.

[3] "Cum privatis suis," R. Coggeshall, p. 99.

[4] R. Howden, vol. iv. p. 89 ; Gerv. Cant., vol. ii. p. 92, says Seaford.

[5] R. Howden and R. Coggeshall, *ll.cc.* ; R. Diceto, vol. ii. p. 166.

CHAPTER III

JOHN "SOFTSWORD"

1199-1206

Contempserunt etenim in eo malivoli quique juvenilem aetatem et corporis parvitatem, et quia prudentia magis quam pugna pacem optinebat ubique, "Johannem Mollegladium" eum malivoli detractores et invidi derisores vocabant. Sed processu temporis . . .

Gerv. Cant. vol. ii. pp. 92, 93 (a. 1200).

1199 IN Richard's island realm there was never a moment's question as to who should succeed him on its throne. In English eyes one successor alone was possible, no matter how undesirable he might be. The circumstances of the case, however—the unexpectedness of the vacancy, the heir's absence from England, his past relations with the government and the people there, and the existence of a rival claimant — presented an opportunity for endeavouring to make a bargain with him such as it was not often possible to make with a new sovereign. Accordingly the English barons as a body, on hearing of Richard's death, assumed an attitude of independence. All of them set to work to fortify and revictual their castles ; some of them even began to attack and plunder their neighbours, as if they deemed that there was to be again " no king in the land " ; and all the efforts of the justiciar, Geoffrey Fitz-Peter, failed to restore order, till he was joined at the end of April by Archbishop Hubert and William the Marshal. The archbishop excommunicated the evildoers,[1] and he and the Marshal conjointly tendered to all the men of the kingdom, " citizens and

1 Cf. R. Coggeshall, p. 98, and R. Howden, vol. iv. p. 88.

burghers, earls, barons, and free tenants," an oath of liege homage and fealty to John.   The lesser freemen apparently took it without hesitation, but many of the barons held back.   These reluctant ones—chief among whom were the earls of Clare, Huntingdon, Chester, Ferrars and Warwick, Roger de Lacy and William de Mowbray—were summoned by the primate, the Marshal and the justiciar to a meeting at Northampton.   There they took the oath, but only in return for a promise given by the three ministers that if they did so, John "should render to each of them his rights."[1] None of these "rights" are specified; but the expression used by the historian who records the claim distinctly implies that it was in each case the claim of an individual to some particular thing to which he considered himself personally entitled, something, it would seem, which he had been unable to obtain from the late king, and which he was therefore anxious to secure beforehand from the new one.   In several cases the grievance seems to have been that of an heir who had not yet received investiture of a dignity to which he had become entitled by inheritance some time before.[2]   With this grievance the Marshal and the justiciar could not fail to sympathize; for although they had for some years past enjoyed the estates attached to the earldoms of Striguil (or Pembroke) and Essex respectively, neither of them had yet been invested as earl.   Justly, therefore, was the promise which they had made in John's name redeemed first of all to them when he girded them with the earl's sword and belt on his coronation day.[3]

The chroniclers of the time speak of that day's ceremony in a matter-of-course way which implies that there was nothing remarkable about it.   "John," says one, "was peaceably received by the great men of all England, and was immediately crowned by Archbishop Hubert of Canterbury at Westminster on Ascension Day, amid a great array of the citizens."[4]   Sixteen prelates besides Hubert, ten earls and

[1] " Quod praedictus dux redderet unicuique illorum jus suum," R. Howden, vol. iv. p. 88.

[2] Stubbs, pref. to W. Coventry, vol. ii. pp. xxvi., xxvii.

[3] R. Howden, vol. iv. p. 90.

[4] R. Coggeshall, pp. 99, 100.

1199　"many barons" were present.[1]　The coronation oath was administered to John in almost the same words as it had been to Richard, and with the same adjuration not to take it without a full purpose of keeping it, to which John made the proper reply.[2]　Of the other details of the ceremony there is no description ; only one incident at its outset and one omission at its close are noted by contemporary writers.[3] The first was merely a formal protest made by Bishop Philip of Durham that the coronation ought not to take place in the absence of his metropolitan, the archbishop of York.[4] The second was an intentional and significant omission on the part of the newly crowned king himself.　It was customary for every Christian sovereign, after the crown had been placed on his head, to seal the vows which he had just made by receiving the Holy Communion.　John, however, did not communicate.[5]

Next day the new king received in person the homage of the barons.[6]　On this side of the sea, only Wales and Scotland remained to be secured.　Of Wales we hear nothing at the moment.　Scotland had taken the initiative immediately after Richard's death ; King William the Lion had at once despatched a message to John, offering him his liege homage and fealty, on condition that Northumberland and Cumberland should be given back to the Scottish Crown. The English primate, Marshal and justiciar, knowing the difficulties with which John was beset on the other side of

---

[1] R. Howden, vol. iv. pp. 89, 90.

[2] R. Wendover (ed. Coxe), vol. iii. pp. 139, 140.　Cf. *Gesta Ric.* pp. 81, 82.

[3] That the famous speech put into the mouth of Archbishop Hubert by Matthew Paris (*Chron. Maj.* vol. ii. pp. 454, 455) is *not* noted by contemporary writers does not indeed prove that it was never delivered, but does indicate that, if delivered, it had for contemporary ears no such significance as has been given to it by some modern writers, or as Matthew himself appears to have attached to it.　Some such address may have been made to the assembly by the archbishop before the coronation ; but if so, it was evidently regarded at the time as a part of the formalities usual on the occasion, not remarkable enough to be worth recording.　In Matthew's own MS. the passage is a marginal addition ; and in the form in which he gives it, I can only regard it as the first of the many unauthenticated interpolations into the plain text of Roger of Wendover with which Matthew has confused for later students the history of the reign of John.

[4] R. Howden, vol. iv. p. 90 ; R. Wendover, vol. iii. p. 139.

[5] *Mag. Vita S. Hugon.* p. 293.

[6] R. Wendover, vol. iii. p. 140.

the Channel, probably feared that he might be tempted to
purchase William's support at William's own price; they
intercepted the messenger, and sent word to the Scot king,
by his brother Earl David of Huntingdon, that he must
" wait patiently " till John should reach England.   John
himself—to whom they apparently reported what they had
done—sent word to William that he would "satisfy him
concerning all his demands " on his arrival, if the Scot king
would keep the peace till then.[1]   Immediately after his
coronation John despatched two envoys to summon William
to his court and conduct him safely thither.   After they had
started, there came to the English king three envoys from
Scotland with a repetition of William's former message; but
this time a threat was added; if William's terms were not
accepted " he would regain all that he was entitled to, if he
could."   John answered quietly: " When your lord, my
very dear cousin, shall come to me, I will do to him whatsoever is right concerning these things and other requests of
his "; and he bade the bishop of Durham go to meet the
Scot king, " hoping the latter would come according to his
summons." [2]   He had himself left London on the morrow of
his crowning to go on pilgrimage to S. Albans; [3] he afterwards visited Canterbury and S. Edmunds,[4] and thence went
to Northampton, to keep Whitsuntide (June 6) and wait
for William.[5]   He waited in vain; William only sent back
the English envoys, reiterated his demand for the two
counties and his threat of winning them by force, and added
a further demand for an answer within forty days.   John
meanwhile had lost patience with him, had given the two
counties in charge to a new sheriff, and started for the south
on his way back to Normandy.   The Scot king's messengers
followed him to the sea; [6] whether they overtook him is not
clear; at any rate nothing came of their mission, and on

[1] R. Howden, vol. iv. pp. 88, 89.   [2] *Ib.* p. 91.
[3] R. Wendover, vol. iii. p. 140.
[4] R. Diceto, vol. ii. p. 166.
[5] R. Howden, vol. iv. p. 91, says " Nottingham," but R. Diceto, vol. ii. p.
166, says "Northampton," and Hardy's *Itinerary of K. John,* a. 1, shows the
king at Northampton on Whit Monday, June 7.
[6] R. Howden, *l.c.*

1199 Sunday, June 20, John sailed from Shoreham for Dieppe,[1]
" taking with him a very great host from England." [2]

Within three days John and Philip met in conference at
Gaillon. They came to no agreement, and John "made up
his mind to resist the French king like a man, and to fight
manfully for the peace of his country." It is clear that his
preparations were well in train before the meeting took
place. Philip indeed made the first hostile movement by
laying siege to the castle of Gaillon ; not only, however,
was he driven away by the troops who had come over with
John,[3] but horse and foot came flocking to the muster at
Rouen, though it was fixed for June 24, only four days
after John's landing. On that day he made a truce with
Philip to last till August 16,[4] thus gaining nearly two
months in which to mature his plans and increase his forces.
He spent the greater part of this time in a progress through
eastern Normandy, and, as the sequel showed, in negotiations
with the counts of Flanders and Boulogne. On August
10 he was again at Rouen.[5] On the 13th Baldwin of
Flanders came to him there "and became his man." [6] On
the 16th, when the truce expired, representatives of the two
kings met in conference between Gouleton and Boutavant ;
on the 18th Philip and John met in person. Philip was
asked "why he so hated the king of England, who had
never done him any harm?" He answered that John had
occupied Normandy and other lands without his leave,
whereas he ought first to have applied to his overlord for
confirmation of his rights as heir, and done homage to him.
Now, Philip demanded of John the surrender of the whole
Vexin to the Crown of France, and that of Poitou, Anjou,
Touraine, and Maine to himself as overlord, that he might
transfer them to Arthur.[7]

---

[1] R. Howden, vol. iv. p. 91. R. Diceto, vol. ii. p. 166, gives the date as
June 19, but the *Itin.* a. 1 shows John at Shoreham on the 20th, which is R.
Howden's date for the crossing.   [2] R. Coggeshall, p. 100.

[3] Gerv. Cant. vol. ii. p. 92. The place called by Gervase "Ballum" and
"Wallum" can only be Gaillon, which Roger of Howden calls "Gwallum" in
vol. iv. p. 106.   [4] R. Howden, vol. iv. pp. 92, 93.   [5] *Itin.* a. 1.

[6] R. Howden, vol. iv. p. 93. See the treaty with Flanders—dateless, but
probably executed on this occasion—in *Rot. Chart.* p. 31.

[7] R. Howden, vol. iv. p. 95.

The Vexin had been a bone of contention between France and Normandy for nearly forty years, and its cession had been distinctly promised by Richard to Philip in 1195. As for the Angevin heritage, John in taking possession of it without waiting for investiture had only followed the example of his predecessor. Richard had made pecuniary amends to Philip for this irregular proceeding, which in feudal law was punishable—theoretically—by forfeiture. In his demand that John should resign the three Angevin counties, therefore, and in his previous grant of their investiture to Arthur, Philip did not exceed his legal rights. With regard to Poitou the case was more complicated. On the one hand, it is certain that at some time between Richard's death and the middle of May 1200 Eleanor and John made an agreement in legal form, whereby John granted his mother to have and to hold all the days of her life, or during her pleasure, the whole of Poitou with all its appurtenances, she having first ceded and surrendered it to him " as her right heir," received his homage for it, and made over to him the rights of government throughout the county and the fealty and services of its vassals.[1] On the other hand, at the end of June 1199 Eleanor had met Philip at Tours, and he had allowed her to do him homage for Poitou,[2] thus formally recognizing her as its lawful countess. Whatever be the precise date of the first-mentioned transaction, therefore, it seems that Eleanor, and Eleanor alone, was the person legally answerable for Poitou to the king of France at this moment.

The English historian of the conference adds that Philip further made of John " other demands which the king of England would in no wise grant, nor was it right that he should grant them." What these were he does not state ; but it seems that some of the French nobles were of his opinion as to their character, for when the meeting broke up, " such of the counts and barons of the realm of France as had been in alliance with King Richard " came to John,

---

[1] *Rot. Chart.* pp. 30, 31 (a. r. 1). "Et," adds John, "non tantum de praedictis terris nostris volumus quod sit domina, sed etiam de nobis et omnibus terris et rebus nostris."   [2] Rigord, c. 129.

1199   offered him their homage, and made offensive and defensive
alliance with him against their own sovereign.[1]   In the case
of the count of Boulogne this alliance was embodied in a
written treaty, drawn up on the same day (August 18) at
" the castle on the Rock of Andely." [2]

In September Philip recommenced hostilities with the
seizure of Conches.[3] John, who had continued hovering
about eastern Normandy until then, at once struck southward ; from September 12 to 17 he was at Bourg-le-Roi
in Maine.[4] This movement of John's apparently drew
Philip southward after him ; the next place which the French
king attacked was the Cenomannian fortress of Ballon, held
for John by one of his father's most devoted adherents,
Geoffrey of Brullon.   The castle was taken, and Philip proceeded to raze it.   William des Roches, the constable of
Britanny, protested against this as contrary to the agreement between Arthur and the king.   Philip retorted that he
should deal with his own conquests as he pleased, without
regard to Arthur.[5] On that very night—it must have been
September 17—William des Roches went to Bourg-le-
Roi,[6] begged for a private interview with John, and undertook to make Arthur, Constance, and all Anjou, Maine and
Poitou submit to him " so that all should be good friends
together," in return for an oath on John's part that he would
" do with them according to his (William's) counsel." [7]   A
written record of John's promise to abide by the terms which
William and other " lawful knights " of Normandy and
Britanny—whom William was to choose—should arrange
for peace between himself and his " very dear nephew Arthur,"
" for the honour and advantage of us both," was drawn up
before witnesses on September 18 at Anvers-le-Hamon.[8]

It may have been to facilitate negotiations with the
Bretons and Angevins that John had proceeded so far as

---

[1] R. Howden, vol. iv. p. 95.   [2] *Rot. Chart.* p. 30.
[3] R. Howden, vol. iv. p. 96.   [4] *Itin.* a. 1.
[5] R. Howden, *l.c.*
[6] John d'Erlée, *Hist. de G. le Mar.* v. 12472, calls it " Borc la *Reïne*,"
but seemingly for no other reason than that he had ended his previous line with
the word "*fine*" and wanted a rime to it.
[7] *Hist. de G. le Mar.* vv. 12471-86.   [8] *Rot. Chart. l.c.*

Anvers, which lies in the south of Maine, close to the border   1199
of Anjou.   We next find him overtaking Philip at the siege
of Lavardin.   Philip hereupon withdrew to Le Mans ; but
he had cut the ground from under his own feet ; the garrison
of Le Mans was under the orders of William des Roches,
who had been appointed commandant there by Philip himself.   John, too, was following close behind ; and when he
appeared before the city, Philip again beat a hasty retreat,
while William des Roches brought Arthur and Constance
in person to make their peace with John, and then opened
the gates of Le Mans to the new allies.   John, in anticipation of his triumph, had already summoned Almeric,
the viscount of Thouars, who was acting as seneschal of
Anjou and commandant of Chinon for Arthur, to come
and submit to him at Le Mans.   On the very day of
John's entry into the city, September 22, Almeric obeyed.
Next day John proceeded to Chinon, where he installed
Roger de Lacy as castellan in Almeric's stead.   With less
than his usual caution, he let Arthur, Constance and their
friends, including Almeric, stay behind at Le Mans.   Some
one had already suggested to Arthur a suspicion that his
uncle intended to make him a prisoner ; as soon, therefore,
as John was out of the way at Chinon, the majority of the
Bretons, with their young duke, his mother, and the viscount
of Thouars, returned on September 24 to their old headquarters at Angers.[1]   It was probably tidings of this which
made John hasten back from Chinon to Le Mans, where
he was again September 27 to 30 ; after that nothing is
known of his movements till October 6, when he was at
Saumur.[2]   His appearance there is suggestive, for Saumur
was the key of the Angevin border towards Poitou on the
south and Touraine on the east.   With Le Mans, Chinon
and Saumur all in his hands, he had only to secure a firm
foothold in Aquitaine, and then he might attack Anjou from
three sides at once.   But to attack it without such a foot-

[1] R. Howden, vol. iv. pp. 96, 97.   Cf. R. Diceto, vol. ii. p. 167, *Rot.
Chart.* p. 31, and for dates *Itin.* a. 1, which show that Roger's "mense
Octobris" cannot be right.   That Constance had come with her son is nowhere
stated, but appears from the sequel.

[2] *Itin.* a. 1.

1199   hold, and with only the small force which he had brought with him from Normandy,[1] would have been worse than useless. On October 8, therefore, John was once more at Le Mans, and thence he fell back upon Normandy.[2]

There was indeed another reason for his return. Cardinal Peter of Capua, who had at the beginning of the year negotiated a truce between Philip and Richard, was still at the French court. The truce had been made for three years; Richard's death had of course put an abrupt end to it; but Peter was urgent that it should be renewed for its original term between Philip and John. Such a proposal implied that John was recognized at Rome as Richard's lawful heir; it was therefore obviously politic for John to cherish such a valuable alliance by falling in with the cardinal's endeavours after a pacification. Through Peter's mediation a truce was made at the end of October. Its term was fixed for the ensuing S. Hilary's Day;[3] but there was evidently a tacit understanding that it was to be the forerunner of a more lasting agreement.

This truce set John free for a visit to Aquitaine. On November 8 he was at Niort, and in the beginning of December at Poitiers; by the middle of December he had returned to Normandy.[4] Meanwhile a question which had been pending for several years, as to the legality of Philip's repudiation of his queen Ingebiorg and his subsequent union with Agnes of Merania, had been, in a council at Dijon on December 6, decided by Cardinal Peter against the king, and Peter had laid the royal domain of France under an

1200   interdict which was to take effect from January 15, 1200,[5] the second day after the expiration of the truce. With this prospect before his eyes, Philip dared not insult John as he had insulted him at their last meeting. It was with a very different proposal that he met him at the old trysting-place between Gaillon and Les Andelys. A project which had been mooted just twelve months before, for a family alliance to cement peace between the houses of France and Anjou,

---

[1] *Hist. de G. le Mar.* vv. 12473-4.   [2] *Itin.* a. 1.
[3] R. Howden, vol. iv. p. 97. Rigord, c. 129, says S. John's Day.
[4] *Itin.* a. 1.   [5] Rigord, c. 131.

was now revived ; it was proposed that Philip's son Louis
should marry John's niece Blanche of Castille, and that
John should furnish the bride with a dowry in Norman lands
and English money.[1]   The two kings "rushed into each
other's arms," and renewed their truce till midsummer.[2]

While Eleanor went to Spain to fetch her grand-
daughter,[3] John seized his opportunity for a visit to England.[4]
His first business there was to concert measures with the
justiciar for raising the required sum of money.   They
decided that the taxes for the year should consist of a
scutage of two marks on the knight's fee and a payment of
three shillings for "every working plough."[5]   John then
went to York, where he had summoned the Scot king to
meet him at the end of March.   William, however, failed to
appear.[6]   During John's stay at York a claim of exemption
from the plough tax was laid before him by the heads of
some of the great Cistercian houses in Yorkshire in behalf
of their whole order ; this led to a violent quarrel between
them and the king, which was still unsettled when he returned
to Normandy at the end of April.[7]   Thither Blanche was
brought to meet him, and on Ascension Day (May 18)[8]
he and Philip, at a personal meeting on the border, made a
definite treaty of peace.   By that treaty Philip in so many
words acknowledged John as "his brother Richard's right
heir," and granted him, as such, the investiture of the whole
Angevin dominions, with the exception of certain territories
which John ceded to the crown of France.   These were the
Vexin, Auvergne, the greater part of the county of Evreux,
and the lordships of Issoudun, Graçay, and Bourges.   To
the cession of the Vexin and of the chief border castles of
the county of Evreux, as well as to the resignation of the

---

[1] R. Howden, vol. iv. pp. 106, 107 ; R. Coggeshall, pp. 100, 101.
[2] Gerv. Cant. vol. ii. p. 92.
[3] R. Howden, vol. iv. p. 107.
[4] He landed at Portsmouth on February 24, *Ann. Winton.* a. 1200.
[5] R. Coggeshall, p. 101. Cf. R. Howden, vol. iv. p. 107.
[6] R. Howden, *l.c.* John was at York March 25 to 28, *Itin.* a. 1.
[7] R. Coggeshall, pp. 102, 103. John was at Porchester on April 28, and at
Valognes on May 2, *Itin.* a. 1.
[8] Rigord, c. 132. Cf. R. Howden, vol. iv. p. 115, whose chronology is
less sound.

1200 Angevin claim upon Auvergne, Richard had been pledged by his treaty with Philip in 1195 ; Issoudun and Graçay had been restored to the English king by the same treaty, having been ceded by Richard to France in 1189.[1] Twenty thousand marks and the formal cession of all these territories —most, if not all, of which were already in Philip's hands— was not too heavy a price to pay for the personal triumph and the political gain involved in Philip's recognition of John as the lawful heir to Normandy, Maine, Anjou, Touraine and Aquitaine, and also to the overlordship of Britanny ; for not only was this last right distinctly conceded to him by Philip, but Arthur was then and there made to do homage to his uncle for his duchy[2] as soon as John himself had done homage to Philip for the whole continental heritage of the house of Anjou.[3] The marriage of Louis and Blanche took place four days later.[4]

John now set out upon a sort of triumphal progress southward, to take seisin of all his dominions. On June 18 he reached Angers, where he stayed four days and took a hundred and fifty hostages as security for the loyalty of the citizens.[5] At the end of June he was at Tours, and early in July at Poitiers, whence he proceeded into Gascony ; on the 14th he was welcomed at Bordeaux by the archbishop and the barons of the land.[6] He immediately secured the help of the Gascon primate in a scheme which he had been cherishing for some months past for getting rid of the wife to whom he had been married for eleven years, Isabel of Gloucester. The papal legate who in 1189 had revoked the sentence passed by Archbishop Baldwin upon John and Isabel had done so on the ground that, since John had appealed to Rome, his marriage must be recognized as lawful, pending the result of the appeal. A decision of the Pope on that appeal would of course have either annulled the marriage

---

[1] Cf. the treaty of 1200 in R. Howden, vol. iv. pp. 148-51, and *Foedera*, vol. i. pt. i. pp. 79, 80, with that of 1195 in *Foedera*, *ib.* p. 66.

[2] R. Howden, vol. iv. p. 150.

[3] R. Coggeshall, p. 101.

[4] Rigord, c. 132. Cf. R. Howden, vol. iv. p. 115.

[5] R. Howden, vol. iv. p. 125. Dates from *Itin.* a. 2.

[6] *Itin.* a. 2. For the reception at Bordeaux see *Hist. de G. le Mar.* vv. 11956-8.

or made it indissoluble ; but it seems that no such decision had ever been given, because the appeal had never been prosecuted. The marriage was therefore still voidable. At the close of 1199 John called upon the Norman bishops to declare it void, and they obeyed him.[1] He now, it seems, laid the case before the archbishop of Bordeaux and the bishop of Poitiers and Saintes ; and their decision was in accord with that of their Norman brethren.[2] On the bare question—which was doubtless all that John put before them—whether a marriage between cousins in the fourth degree was lawful without a dispensation, indeed, no other decision was possible according to the letter of the canon law. The Pope, however, when the matter came to his knowledge, seems to have felt that in this particular case adhesion to the letter of the law involved a violation of its spirit, and to have been extremely angry with John's episcopal tools as well as with John himself.[3] He had, however, no ground for interfering in the matter except on an appeal from Isabel ; and Isabel did not appeal.[4] There is every reason to think—and certainly no reason to wonder—that the removal of the matrimonial yoke was as welcome to her as to John, and that their divorce was in fact, like that of Louis VII. and Eleanor, a separation by mutual consent.

John had already chosen another heiress to take Isabel's place. One of the most important, and also most troublesome, feudataries of the duchy of Aquitaine was Ademar, count of Angoulême. It was in a quarrel with him and his half-brother, the viscount of Limoges, that Richard Cœur-de-Lion had met his death, which Richard's son had avenged by slaying the viscount.[5] The feud between the houses of Angoulême and Limoges thus threatened to be a considerable hindrance to Richard's successor in his efforts to secure a hold upon his southern

---

[1] R. Diceto, vol. ii. p. 167.   [2] R. Howden, vol. iv. p. 119.
[3] R. Diceto, vol. ii. p. 167. R. Coggeshall, p. 103, has another version, but it seems to be incorrect. On the whole question of this divorce see Prof. Maitland's remarks in *Eng. Hist. Rev.* Oct. 1895, vol. x. pp. 758, 759.
[4] Innoc. III. *Epp.* l. v. No. 50.
[5] R. Howden, vol. iv. p. 97.

duchy. How formidable Ademar and his nephew, the new viscount of Limoges, had already made themselves is shown by the insertion in the treaty between John and Philip of a special provision that John should " receive their homage and grant them their rights." [1]   It is said to have been Philip who counselled John to secure the fidelity of Ademar of Angoulême in another way, by taking to wife Ademar's only child.[2]   Philip's motives for giving the advice, and John's motives for following it, are alike obscure.   Nineteen years before, Richard, as duke of Aquitaine, had vainly striven to wrest Angoulême from Ademar in behalf of Matilda, the only child of Ademar's late brother, Count Vulgrin III.   Matilda was now the wife of Hugh "the Brown" of Lusignan, who in 1179 or 1180 had, in spite of King Henry, made himself master of the county of La Marche, and whose personal importance in southern Gaul was increased by the rank and fame which his brothers Geoffrey, Guy and Almeric had won in the kingdoms of Jerusalem and Cyprus.   The dispute between Matilda and her uncle had been settled by the betrothal of her son— another Hugh the Brown — to Ademar's daughter and heiress, Isabel.[3]   A marriage between John and this little Isabel of Angoulême, therefore, would be certain to provoke the bitter resentment of the whole Lusignan family.   On the other hand, it would provoke their resentment against Isabel's father as well as against her husband, and thus destroy the chance of a coalition of Angoulême and La Marche against their common overlord.   It is not impossible that for John, who gambled in politics as habitually as he did at the game of " tables," the very wantonness of the scheme and the hazards attendant upon it may have only added to its attractions.   But his subsequent conduct towards the Lusignans suggests the idea that he may have had a deeper

---

[1] R. Howden, vol. iv. p. 150.   This was in fulfilment of an agreement made between Philip on the one part, and the count of Angoulême and the viscount of Limoges on the other, just after Richard's death.   Round, *Cal. Doc. France*, vol. i. p. 471.

[2] R. Howden, vol. iv. p. 119; R. Coggeshall, p. 103.

[3] R. Howden, vol. iv. p. 119; R. Coggeshall, pp. 128, 129; R. Wendover, vol. iii. p. 168.   All these writers confuse Isabel's betrothed with his father.

motive, a deliberate purpose of goading them into some outrageous course of action which might enable him to recover La Marche and ruin them completely, or even drive them altogether out of the land.

On his way to Poitou John issued from Chinon, on June 25, a summons to Ademar of Angoulême and Guy of Limoges to come and perform their homage on July 5 at Lusignan,[1] the ancestral home of Hugh the Brown. There Hugh and Matilda were bringing up their intended daughter-in-law in company with her boy bridegroom, and there John was no doubt, at the moment, sure of a welcome, for Hugh and his brother Ralf had become his liegemen at Caen on January 28.[2]   Thus, in all likelihood, it was under Hugh's very roof, and as sharers in his hospitality, that the king of England and the count of Angoulême laid their plot for robbing Hugh's son of his plighted bride and his promised heritage.   John indeed, as soon as his divorce was ratified by the southern bishops, despatched, or gave out that he had despatched, an embassy to Portugal with instructions to ask for the hand of a daughter of the Portuguese king;[3] but their mission was a mere blind to divert suspicion till Ademar should have succeeded in getting his child back into his own hands.   The poor little betrothed—she was only about twelve years old[4]—was literally stolen by her father,[5] and carried off by him to his capital city.   There her royal suitor met them, and on or about August 26 the marriage ceremony was performed by the archbishop of Bordeaux.[6]   The newly married couple immediately afterwards set out for the north; at the beginning of October they went to England, and on the 8th they were crowned together at Westminster.[7]

Six weeks later the king of Scots made his submission.   Summoned to meet his overlord at Lincoln on

[1] *Rot. Chart.* p. 97.   [2] *Ib.* pp. 58, 59.
[3] R. Diceto, vol. ii. p. 170.   [4] R. Coggeshall, p. 103.
[5] *Hist. de G. le Mar.* vv. 11984-6. Cf. R. Howden, vol. iv. p. 119.
[6] R. Howden, vol. iv. p. 120. For date see *Itin.* a. 2, and *Rot. Chart.* p. 75.
[7] R. Howden, vol. iv. p. 139; R. Diceto, vol. ii. p. 170; R. Coggeshall, p. 103 (with a wrong date).

1200   November 21, William the Lion this time did not venture to disobey the summons ; both kings reached Lincoln on the appointed day.   Next morning John, in defiance of an old tradition which forbade a king to appear in regal state within the walls of Lincoln, went to the minster and offered a golden chalice at the altar of S. John the Baptist.   Thence he proceeded to his colloquy with William "on the top of the steep hill" outside the city.   There, amid a group of prelates and barons, and "in the sight of all the people," William performed his homage, and swore on Archbishop Hubert's cross that he would be faithful to John against all men, "saving his own right."   Then, and not till then, did he venture again to demand, "as his right and heritage," the disputed counties.   A long discussion ended in an adjournment of the question till the next Whitsuntide ; which of course meant that it was to be put off indefinitely. On the morrow (November 23) the king of Scots set out on his homeward journey, while the king of England helped with his own hands to carry to its last resting-place in Lincoln minster the body of the only man among his father's old friends for whom he seems to have felt a real liking, though he turned a deaf ear to his counsels—S. Hugh, who had died in London a week before.[1]   Soon after

1201   Christmas John was at Lincoln again, quarrelling with the canons about the election of Hugh's successor.[2]   He and his young queen afterwards made a progress through the north, almost up to the Scottish border,[3] and back through Cumberland to York, which they reached at Mid-Lent (March 1, 1201).   At Easter (March 25) they "wore their crowns" at Canterbury.[4]

Meanwhile, open hostilities had begun between John and the Lusignans ; and so far as can be made out from the scanty evidence available, it seems to have been John who began them.   A French historian of the time asserts that the castle of Driencourt in Normandy, which belonged to Ralf of Lusignan as count of Eu in right of his wife, was seized by John's orders while Ralf was in John's

[1] R. Howden, vol. iv. pp. 140-3.   [2] *Ib.* p. 156.
[3] *Itin.* a. 2.   [4] R. Howden, vol. iv. p. 160.

service in England.[1] It is certain that John, on March 6,
1201, issued letters patent to Hugh of Bailleul and Thomas
of St. Valery authorizing them to attack Ralf's territories at
the close of Easter and "do him all the harm they could,"
and promising that they should never be compelled to make
good any damage which they might inflict upon him ;
while on the same day one William "de Kaev" was
despatched on a mission to the inhabitants of Driencourt
and of the whole county of Eu to make arrangements for
mutual security between them and the king, without reference to their count.[2] Two days later John summoned all
his faithful barons, knights, clerks, burghers, and other
tenants of the county of La Marche "to come to his service,
and do to him what they had been wont to do to his
predecessors." [3] In other words, he claimed the direct
ownership of the county, to which his father had indeed
been entitled by purchase from the late Count Adelbert and
by the homage of its tenants, but of which Henry had
never been able and Richard had never even tried to take
possession, and which Hugh of Lusignan had now held for
more than twenty years. If their oath of liege homage to
John had hitherto restrained Hugh and Ralf from giving
vent to their anger at John's marriage, it restrained them
no longer now. They at once laid a complaint against
John, for unjust aggression and spoliation, before the king
of France as lord paramount of Aquitaine.[4] Ralf formally
renounced his allegiance to John,[5] and Hugh, with all the
forces that he could muster, invaded Poitou, where, as
usual, he found plenty of allies ready to join him.[6] The
most important of the Poitevin barons, indeed, Almeric of
Thouars, was won over to John's side by the diplomacy of

---

[1] Will. Armor. *Gesta P. A.* c. 110.   Cf. R. Howden, vol. iv. pp. 160, 161.
[2] *Rot. Chart.* p. 102.   [3] *Ib.*
[4] Innoc. III. *Epp.* l. vi. No. 167.   R. Coggeshall, p. 135, dates this
appeal a year too late. The Pope, on the authority of Philip himself, speaks of
it as having been made "more than a year before" Philip issued his citation to
John, a citation of which the date is by other evidence fixed at the end of
March or early in April 1202.
[5] *Rot. Pat.* vol. i. p. 2, dateless, but as the document is on the roll of
John's second year, its date must be before May 3, 1201. From its position on
the roll, it would seem to belong to October 1200.
[6] R. Howden, vol. iv. p. 160 ; R. Coggeshall, pp. 128,129.

1201   Eleanor; but the danger appeared so great that both
Eleanor and Almeric besought John to come over and deal
with it in person as soon as he possibly could; and at the
end of April the count of Angoulême and John's other
friends in the south proposed sending Almeric to confer
with John in England.[1]

John meanwhile was summoning the earls and barons
of England to meet him at Portsmouth at Whitsuntide
(May 13), ready with horses and arms to accompany him
over sea. The earls held a meeting at Leicester, and
thence unanimously sent him word that they would not go
with him " unless he gave them back their rights. For the
king, following ill counsel, was demanding their castles of
them; and beginning with William of Aubigny, he demanded of him the castle of Belvoir. William satisfied
him by giving him his son as a hostage, and thus kept his
castle." [2] Notwithstanding their protest, the barons brought
their forces to Portsmouth on the appointed day, equipped
for a campaign, and each man provided with the money
needful to cover his expenses during the usual term of
service in a feudal host. This, and nothing more, was precisely what John wanted them to do: " He took from some
of them the money which they would have spent in his
service, and let them return home." [3] The ready money
which he thus obtained was a more useful and safer weapon
for his purpose than the host itself would have been, and no
pretext was left for the discussion of inconvenient questions.
The king immediately despatched William the Marshal and
Roger de Lacy, each at the head of a hundred mercenaries,
" to check the assaults of his enemies on the borders of
Normandy." At the same time he appointed his chamberlain, Hubert de Burgh, warden of the Welsh marches, with
another hundred soldiers under his command, and sent the
bishop of Chester to William the Lion with a request that
the term fixed for answering his demands might be extended to Michaelmas.[4] Having taken these precautions to

---

[1] *Rot. Chart.* p. 102.
[2] R. Howden, vol. iv. pp. 160, 161.   [3] *Ib.* p. 163.
[4] *Ib.* pp. 163, 164.

secure England from attack, John again crossed the sea ;   1201
on June 2 he was at Bonneville.[1]

At the announcement of John's intention to return,
Philip had either compelled or persuaded the Lusignans to
suspend hostilities in Poitou.[2]   A period of negotiation
followed ; Philip remonstrating with John about his conduct
towards the Lusignans, and urging him to make them
restitution ; John, in his turn, remonstrating with Philip for
his constant aggressions and his interference with the
internal affairs of John's duchies.   Several personal inter-
views seem to have taken place between the kings ;[3] before
the end of June the treaty of Ascension-tide 1200 was
confirmed ; and on the last day of that month John, by
Philip's invitation, went to Paris, and was there lodged and
entertained for several days in the royal palace, which
Philip vacated for his convenience.[4]

This temporary pacification was effected by a promise
on John's part that the quarrel between him and the
Lusignans should be tried and settled fairly in his court as
duke of Aquitaine.[5]   Towards the end of July he went to
Chinon ; there he spent the greater part of the next six
weeks,[6] and it was probably there that he summoned the
Lusignans to the promised trial.   But meanwhile the
Lusignans had discovered that the trial which he designed
was something wholly different from that which Philip had
demanded on their behalf.   John, before he left England,
had determined to appeal " the barons of Poitou "—that is,
no doubt, the Lusignans and their friends—on a general
charge of treason against his late brother and himself, and
challenge them to ordeal of battle with a number of
champions specially chosen for the purpose.   This project
was perfectly legal ; the ordeal of battle, though it was
beginning to be discountenanced by public opinion under
the influence of the Church, was still recognized as a lawful

---

[1] *Itin.* a. 3.   [2] R. Howden, vol. iv. p. 161.
[3] Innoc. III. *Epp.* l. vi. Nos. 163, 167.
[4] Cf. R. Howden, vol. iv. p. 164 ; Rigord, c. 135 ; Gerv. Cant. vol. ii. p.
93 ; and for dates, *Itin.* a. 3.   Rigord's " pridie Kalendas Junii " is doubtless
a mistake for " Julii."
[5] Innoc. III. *Epp.* l. vi. No. 167.   [6] *Itin.* a. 3.

method of deciding upon a charge of treason. But a simultaneous challenge to so large a number of men, and men, too, of such high rank and personal distinction as the Lusignans and their allies, was a startling innovation upon feudal tradition and practice, and unwarranted by historical precedent. Moreover, there was in the scheme another feature which would make it doubly offensive to the barons concerned. The champions against whom they were called upon to prove their loyalty are described as " picked men, practised in the art of duelling, whom the king had hired and brought with him from his dominions on both sides of the sea." [1]   That is, they were professional champions— men who made a business of hiring themselves out to fight the battles of any one who either could not or would not fight in his own person, but who could afford to pay for an efficient substitute. Such hired champions, of course, in every case represented the person who hired them ; in the present case they would have represented the king ; yet nobles like the Lusignans, two of whose brothers had been, no less than John himself, crowned and anointed sovereigns, could not but feel it an intolerable insult to be challenged, even in a king's name, by creatures such as these. The accused barons all alike refused to come to John's court, " saying that they would answer to no one save to their peers." [2]   It seems that on a fresh remonstrance from Philip, John again consented, or pretended to consent, to a trial such as they demanded ; but he was very unwilling to fix a day ; and when he did fix one, he refused to give the defendants a safe conduct, without which, of course, they would not stir from their homes.[3]

Again Philip intervened, and again John promised redress. This time apparently Philip deemed it advisable to require security for the fulfilment of the promise. The security which he asked for, however, was more than John could reasonably be expected to give ; it seems to have been nothing less than three of the most important castles in Normandy—those of Falaise, Arques, and " Andely,"

---

[1] R. Howden, vol. iv. p. 176.   [2] *Ib.*
[3] W. Brito, *Philipp.* l. vi. vv. 106-43.

that is, Château-Gaillard. In December John summoned
Archbishop Hubert over from England, and sent him to
"make his excuses" to the French king ;[1] and Hubert so
far succeeded that after Christmas John was able to venture
into Aquitaine. Early in February 1202 he met the king
of Navarre at Angoulême, and made with him a treaty of
close offensive and defensive alliance.[2]

It was arranged that John and Philip should hold a
conference—seemingly on March 25—at Boutavant. John,
it appears, kept, or at least was ready to keep, the appointment ; but Philip either was or pretended to be afraid of
venturing into Norman territory, and would not advance
beyond Gouleton. Thither John came across the river to
meet him.[3] No agreement was arrived at. Finally, Philip
cited John to appear in Paris fifteen days after Easter,[4] at
the court of his overlord the king of France, to stand to its
judgement, to answer to his lord for his misdoings, and
undergo the sentence of his peers. The citation was addressed to John as count of Anjou and Poitou and duke of
Aquitaine ;[5] the Norman duchy was not mentioned in it.
This omission was clearly intentional ; when John answered
the citation by reminding Philip that he was duke of Normandy, and as such, in virtue of ancient agreement between
the kings and the dukes, not bound to go to any meeting
with the king of France save on the borders of their respective territories, Philip retorted that he had summoned not
the duke of Normandy but the duke of Aquitaine, and that
his rights over the latter were not to be annulled by the
accidental union of the two dignities in one person.[6] John
then promised that he would appear before the court in
Paris on the appointed day, and give up to Philip two

[1] Gerv. Cant. vol. ii. p. 93. Hubert crossed on December 14, R. Diceto,
vol. ii. p. 173.   [2] *Rot. Pat.* vol. i. pp. 5, 6.
[3] Cf. Gerv. Cant. vol. ii. p. 93 ; R. Diceto, vol. ii. p. 174 ; Rigord, c.
137 ; and R. Wendover, vol. iii. p. 167. John was at Orival on March 23 ;
then there is a blank for three days, and on March 27 he appears at Les Andelys,
Itin. a. 3.
[4] *I.e.* on April 28. The date is from Rigord, c. 138.
[5] R. Coggeshall, pp. 135, 136. Cf. Rigord, c. 138 ; W. Armor. *Gesta P. A.*
c. 110 ; Gerv. Cant. vol. ii. p. 93 ; and Innoc. III. *Epp.* l. vi. No. 167.
[6] R. Coggeshall, p. 136.

1202 small castles, Thillier and Boutavant, as security for his
submitting to its decision. April 28 passed, and both
these promises remained unfulfilled.[1] One English writer
asserts that thereupon " the assembled court of the king of
France adjudged the king of England to be deprived of all
his land which he and his forefathers had hitherto held of
the king of France " ;[2] but there is reason to think that this
statement is erroneous, and derived from a false report put
forth by Philip Augustus for political purposes two or three
years later.[3]   It is certain that after the date of this alleged
sentence, negotiations still went on ; " great and excellent
mediators" endeavoured to arrange a pacification ;[4] and
Philip himself, according to his own account, had another
interview with John, at which he used all his powers of
persuasion to bring him to submission, but in vain.   Then
the French king, by the advice of his barons, formally
" defied" his rebellious vassal ;[5] in a sudden burst of wrath
he ordered the archbishop of Canterbury—evidently one of
the mediators just referred to—out of his territories, and
dashing after him with such forces as he had at hand, began
hostilities by a raid upon Boutavant, which he captured and
burned.[6] Even after this, if we may trust his own report,
he sent four knights to John to make a final attempt at
reconciliation ; but John would not see them.[7]

The war which followed was characteristic of both kings
alike. Philip's attack took the form not of a regular invasion, but of a series of raids upon eastern Normandy,
whereby in the course of the next three months [8] he made
himself master of Thillier, Lions, Longchamp, La Ferté-
en-Braye, Orgueil, Gournay, Mortemer, Aumale and the

[1] Rigord, c. 138 ; W. Armor. *Gesta P. A.* c. 110. Cf. Gerv. Cant. vol.
ii. p. 93, and Innoc. III. *Epp.* l. vi. No. 167.
[2] R. Coggeshall, p. 136.
[3] See " The Alleged Condemnation of King John by the Court of France in
1202," in *Transactions of the Royal Historical Society*, new series, vol. xiv. (1900),
pp. 53-68.
[4] Gerv. Cant. vol. ii. p. 93.
[5] Innoc. III. *Epp. l.c.*
[6] Cf. Gerv. Cant. vol. ii. p. 94 ; Rigord, c. 138 ; W. Armor. *Gesta P. A.*
c. 112 ; and R. Wendover, vol. iii. p. 167.
[7] Innoc. III. *Epp. l.c.*
[8] The war had begun before May 11, *Rot. Pat.* vol. i. p. 10.

town and county of Eu.[1]   John was throughout the same
period flitting ceaselessly about within a short distance
of all these places;[2] but Philip never came up with him,
and he never but once came up with Philip.   On July 7
the French king laid siege to Radepont, some ten miles to
the south-east of Rouen.   John, who was at Bonport, let
him alone for a week, and then suddenly appeared before
the place, whereupon Philip immediately withdrew.[3]   John,
however, made no attempt at pursuit.   According to his
wont, he let matters take their course till he saw a favourable
opportunity for retaliation.   At the end of the month the
opportunity came.

At the conclusion of the treaty of Gouleton in May
1200 Arthur, after doing homage to his uncle for Britanny,
had been by him restored to the guardianship of the French
king.[4]   The death of the boy's mother in September 1201[5]
left him more than ever exposed to Philip's influence; and
it was no doubt as a measure of precaution, in view of the
approaching strife between the kings, that John on March
27, 1202—two days after his meeting with Philip at
Gouleton—summoned his "beloved nephew Arthur" to
come and "do right" to him at Argentan at the octave of
Easter.[6]   The summons probably met with no more obedience than did Philip's summons to John; and before the
end of April Philip had bound Arthur securely to his side
by promising him the hand of his infant daughter Mary.[7]
This promise was ratified by a formal betrothal at Gournay,
after the capture of that place by the French; at the same
time Philip made Arthur a knight, and gave him the investiture of all the Angevin dominions except Normandy.[8]
Towards the end of July Philip despatched Arthur, with a

---

[1] Cf. Rigord, c. 138; W. Armor. *Philipp.* l. vi. vv. 204-20, and R.
Wendover, vol. iii. p. 167.   [2] See *Itin.* a. 3, 4.

[3] R. Wendover, vol. iii. p. 167; for dates cf. *Itin.* a. 4.   Gerv. Cant. vol. ii.
p. 94, places this siege too late.   [4] R. Howden, vol. iv. p. 115.

[5] *Chron. Britann.* a. 1201, in Morice, *Hist. de Bretagne, preuves*, vol. i.
cols. 6, 106.   [6] *Rot. Pat.* vol. i. p. 7.

[7] Delisle, *Catalogue des Actes de Phil.-Aug.*, No. 726.

[8] Rigord, c. 138; W. Armor. *Gesta P. A.* c. 113.   Arthur's charter giving
full details of his homage to Philip is in Round, *Cal. Doc. France*, vol. i. p. 475.
Date, Gournay, July 1202.

1202   force of two hundred French knights, to join the Lusignans in an attack on Poitou. The barons of Britanny and of Berry had been summoned to meet him at Tours ; but the only allies who did meet him there were three of the Lusignans and Savaric de Mauléon, with some three hundred knights. Overruling the caution of the boy duke, who wished to wait for reinforcements from his own duchy, the impetuous southerners urged an immediate attack upon Mirebeau, their object being to capture Queen Eleanor, who was known to be there,[1] and whom they rightly regarded as the mainstay of John's power in Aquitaine. Eleanor, however, became aware of their project in time to despatch a letter to her son, begging him to come to her rescue. He was already moving southward when her courier met him on July 30 as he was approaching Le Mans. By marching day and night he and his troops covered the whole distance between Le Mans and Mirebeau—eighty miles at the least —in forty-eight hours, and appeared on August 1 before the besieged castle.[2] The enemies had already taken the outer ward and thrown down all the gates save one, deeming their own valour a sufficient safeguard against John's expected attack.[3] So great was their self-confidence that they even marched out to meet him. Like most of those who at one time or another fought against John, they underrated the latent capacities of their adversary. They were driven back into the castle, hotly pursued by his troops, who under the guidance of William des Roches forced their way in after the fugitives, and were in a short time masters of the place. The whole of the French and Poitevin forces were either slain or captured ; and among the prisoners were the three Lusignans, and Arthur.[4]

[1] Cf. Rigord, c. 138 ; W. Armor. *Gesta P. A.* c. 113, and *Philipp.* l. vi. vv. 262-389 ; R. Coggeshall, p. 137 ; Gerv. Cant. vol. ii. p. 94, and R. Wendover, vol. iii. p. 168.

[2] Dates from John's own letter, in R. Coggeshall, pp. 137, 138. Cf. R. Wendover, vol. iii. p. 169.

[3] R. Coggeshall, p. 137.

[4] R. Coggeshall, p. 138 ; R. Wendover, vol. iii. p. 169 ; Rigord, c. 138 ; W. Armor. *Gesta P. A.* c. 113. This last has another version in his later and less trustworthy work, the *Philippis*, l. vi. vv. 390-450. See also *Hist. des Ducs de Normandie* (ed. Michel, *Soc. de l'Hist. de France*), pp. 93-95.

Philip was at that moment busy with the siege of
Arques ; on the receipt of these tidings he left it and turned
southward,[1] but he failed, or perhaps did not attempt, to
intercept John, who, bringing his prisoners with him, made
his way leisurely back to Falaise.[2] There he imprisoned
Arthur in the castle,[3] and despatched his victorious troops
against Arthur's duchy ; they captured Dol a˙d Fougères,
and harried the country as far as Rennes.[4] Philip, after
ravaging Touraine, fired the city of Tours and took the
citadel ; immediately afterwards he withdrew to his own
territories, as by that time John was again at Chinon. As
soon as Philip was gone, John in his turn entered Tours
and wrested the citadel from the French garrison left there
by his rival ; but his success was won at the cost of another
conflagration which, an English chronicler declares, was
never forgiven him by the citizens and the barons of
Touraine.[5]

For the moment, however, he was in luck. In Aquitaine
he seemed in a fair way to carry all before him without
striking a blow. Angoulême had passed into his hands by
the death of his father-in-law on June 17.[6] Guy of
Limoges had risen in revolt again, but at the end of August
or early in September he was captured.[7] The Lusignans,
from their prison at Caen, made overtures for peace, and
by dint of protestations and promises succeeded ere long in
regaining their liberty, of course on the usual conditions of
surrendering their castles and giving hostages for their
loyalty.[8] It was almost equally a matter of course that as

---

[1] Rigord, c. 138 ; R. Wendover, vol. iii. p. 169.

[2] He reached Falaise on August 10, *Itin.* a. 4.

[3] R. Wendover, vol. iii. p. 170 ; W. Armor. *Philipp.* l. vi. vv. 455, 456.

[4] W. Armor. *Gesta P. A.* c. 120. In *Philipp.* l. vi. vv. 343-6, he dates
this expedition earlier. In both works he speaks as if John had headed it in
person, but the *Itin.* a. 3, 4, shows that this was not the case.

[5] W. Armor. *Gesta P. A.* c. 114 ; R. Coggeshall, p. 138. John was at
Chinon August 20-21, at Tours August 22-23, at Chinon again August 24-29,
and at Tours again August 30-September 1, *Itin.* a. 4.

[6] *Rer. Gall. Scriptt.* vol. xviii. p. 799.

[7] Rigord, c. 138. Cf. *Rot. Pat.* vol. i. p. 18.

[8] R. Coggeshall, p. 138 ; *Hist. de G. le Mar.* vv. 12531-35. Ralf of Eu
was set free before November 7, 1202, Hugh and Geoffrey before January 17,
1203 ; *Rot. Pat.* vol. i. pp. 20, 23.

1202 soon as they were free they began intriguing against John.[1] But the chronic intrigues of the south were in reality, as John himself seems to have discovered, a far less serious danger than the disaffection in his northern dominions. This last evil was undoubtedly, so far as Normandy was concerned, owing in great measure to John's own fault. He had entrusted the defence of the Norman duchy to his mercenaries under the command of a Provençal captain whose real name is unknown, who seems to have adopted for himself the nickname of "Lou Pescaire," "The Fisherman"—which the Normans apparently corrupted into "Louvrekaire"—and who habitually treated his employer's peaceable subjects in a fashion in which other commanders would have shrunk from treating avowed enemies.[2] Side by side with the discontent thus caused among the people there was a rapid growth of treason among the Norman barons ;—treason fraught with far greater peril than the treason of the nobles of Aquitaine, because it was more persistent and more definite in its aim ; because it was at once less visible and tangible and more deeply rooted ; because it spread in silence and wrought in darkness ; and because, while no southern rebel ever really fought for anything but his own hand, the northern traitors were in close concert with Philip Augustus. John knew not whom to trust ; he could, in fact, trust no one ; and herein lay the explanation of his restless movements, his unaccountable wanderings, his habit of journeying through bye-ways, his constant changes of plan.[3] Moreover, besides the Aquitanian rebels, the Norman traitors, and the French enemy, there were the Breton partizans of Arthur to be reckoned with. These had now found a leader in William des Roches, who, when he saw that he could not prevail upon John to set Arthur at liberty, openly withdrew from the king's service, and organized a league of the Breton nobles against him.

These Bretons, reinforced by some barons from Anjou

---

[1] *Hist. de G. le Mar.* vv. 12536-50.
[2] *Ib.* vv. 12595-606. On the name see M. Delaborde's note, *Œuvres de Rigord et de Guillaume le Breton*, vol. ii. p. 282.
[3] *Hist. de G. le Mar.* vv. 12569-84 ; Gerv. Cant. vol. ii. p. 95.

and Maine, succeeded on October 29 in gaining possession
of Angers.[1]   It may have been to watch for an opportunity
of dislodging them that John, who was then at Le Mans,
went to spend a fortnight at Saumur and another at Chinon.
Early in December, however, he fell back upon Normandy,[2]
and while the intruders were harrying his ancestral counties
with fire and sword,[3] he kept Christmas with his queen at
Caen, "faring sumptuously every day, and prolonging his
morning slumbers till dinner-time."[4]   It seems that shortly
afterwards the queen returned to Chinon, and that in the
middle of January 1203 the enemies at Angers were discovered to be planning an attempt to capture her there.
John hurried to Le Mans, only stopping at Alençon to dine
with Count Robert and endeavour to secure his suspected
loyalty by confirming him in all his possessions.   No sooner
had they parted, however, than Robert rode off to the French
court, did homage to Philip, and admitted a French garrison
into Alençon.   While John, thus placed between two fires,
was hesitating whether to go on or to go back, Peter des
Préaux succeeded in getting the queen out of Chinon and
bringing her to her husband at Le Mans ; thence they
managed to make their way back in safety to Falaise.[5]

---

[1] R. Coggeshall, p. 139.   Date from *Chron. S. Albini*, a. 1202.
[2] *Itin.* a. 4.   [3] R. Coggeshall, *l.c.*   [4] R. Wendover, vol. iii. p. 171.
[5] *Hist. de G. le Mar.* vv. 12585-662.   The writer appears to date this
affair in autumn 1202 ; and the *Itinerary*, a. 4, shows that John did in fact go
from Alençon to Le Mans on October 29, 1202.   But the rest of the story is irre-
concileable with John's subsequent movements.   The only documentary evidence
which I have found as to the date of Count Robert's treason is unluckily not
decisive ; it is a charter of John, given "apud Beccum, xx die Aprilis anno regni
nostri quarto, quo comes Robertus Sagiensis fecit nobis proditionem apud
Alenconem" (Round, *Cal. Doc. France*, vol. i. p. 131).   John in the fourth
year of his reign made three visits to Alençon besides the one already mentioned ;
viz. one on December 7, 1202, and two in January 1203.   The first of these
two January visits is probably the one recorded by D'Erlée.   John was at
Alençon January 15-19, at Le Mans January 21-23, and at Alençon again
January 25 (*Itin.* a. 4).   D'Erlée indeed asserts that the king on his return
from Le Mans

> " Ne s'en vint pas par Alençon ;
> N'i passast unques sanz tençon
> Anceis qu'il venist en sa terre ;
> Aileors ala passage quere ;
> Par Mamerz et par Belesmeis
> S'en vint en sa terre li reis " (vv. 12657-62).

It seems, however, possible to reconcile this with the dates as given in the

This incident may have suggested to John that it was
time to take some decisive step towards getting rid of
Arthur's claims.   According to one English chronicler, some
of the king's counsellors had already been urging this matter
upon him for some time past.   They pointed out that so
long as Arthur lived, and was neither physically nor legally
incapacitated for ruling, the Bretons would never be quiet,
and no lasting peace with France would be possible; and
they therefore suggested to the king a horrible scheme for
rendering Arthur incapable of being any longer a source of
danger.   The increasing boldness of the Bretons at last
provoked John into consenting to this project, and he
despatched three of his servants to Falaise to put out the
eyes of the captive.   Two of these men chose to leave the
king's service rather than obey him; the third went to
Falaise as he was bidden, but found it impossible to fulfil
his errand; Arthur's struggles were backed by the very
soldiers who guarded him, and the fear of a mutiny drove
their commander, Hubert de Burgh, to prevent the execution
of an order which he felt that the king would soon have
cause to regret.   He gave out, however, that the order had
been fulfilled, and that Arthur had died in consequence.
The effect of this announcement proved at once the wisdom
of Hubert and the folly of those to whose counsel John had
yielded.   The fury of the Bretons became boundless; they
vowed never to leave a moment's peace to the tyrant who
had committed such a ghastly crime upon their duke, his
own nephew; and Hubert soon found it necessary, for
John's own sake, to confess his fraud and demonstrate to
friends and foes alike that Arthur was still alive and un-
injured.[1]   John himself now attempted to deal with Arthur
in another way.   Being at Falaise at the end of January
1203,[2] he caused his nephew to be brought before him, and
" addressed him with fair words, promising him great honours
if he would forsake the king of France and cleave faithfully

Itinerary by supposing that, as he had an escort of "granz gens e rotiers," he
may have ventured close up to Alençon, perhaps with an idea of surprising it,
but turned away again immediately.   The *Itinerary* shows him at Séez on January
25-28, at Argentan on 28-30, and at Falaise 30-31.

[1] R. Coggeshall, pp. 139-41.   [2] *Itin.* a. 4.

to his uncle and rightful lord." Arthur, however, rejected these overtures with scorn, vowing that there should be no peace unless the whole Angevin dominions, including England, were surrendered to him as Richard's lawful heir. John retorted by transferring his prisoner from Falaise to Rouen and confining him, more strictly than ever, in the citadel.[1]

Thenceforth Arthur disappears from history. What was his end no one knows. The chronicle of the abbey of Margan in South Wales, a chronicle of which the only known manuscript ends with the year 1232, and of which the portion dealing with the early years of John's reign was not compiled in its present form till after 1221 at earliest, asserts that on Maunday Thursday (April 3) 1203, John, "after dinner, being drunk and possessed by the devil," slew his nephew with his own hand and tied a great stone to the body, which he flung into the Seine ; that a fisher-man's net brought it up again, and that, being recognized, it was buried secretly, "for fear of the tyrant," in the church of Notre-Dame-des-Prés, near Rouen.[2] William the Breton, in his poem on Philip Augustus, completed about 1216, relates in detail, but without date, how John took Arthur out alone with him by night in a boat on the Seine, plunged a sword into his body, rowed along for three miles with the corpse, and then threw it overboard.[3] Neither of these writers gives any authority for his story. The earliest authority of precisely ascertained date to which we can trace the assertion that Arthur was murdered is a document put forth by a personage whose word, on any subject whatever, is as worthless as the word of John himself—King Philip Augustus of France. In 1216—about the time when his Breton historiographer's poem was completed — Philip affected to regard it as a notorious fact that John had, either in person or by another's hand, murdered his nephew. But Philip at the same time went on to assert that John had

---

[1] R. Wendover, vol. iii. p. 170. Cf. R. Coggeshall, p. 143.

[2] *Ann. Margan.* a. 1204 ; the annalist, however, clearly meant to date the event 1203. On the value of his authority see Bémont, *Revue historique*, vol. xxxii. (1886), p. 59.

[3] W. Armor. *Philipp.* l. vi. vv. 552-66.

1203   been summoned to trial before the supreme court of France, and by it condemned to forfeiture of all his dominions, on that same charge of murder ; and this latter assertion is almost certainly false.[1]   Seven months after the date assigned by the Margan annalist to Arthur's death—in October 1203—Philip owned himself ignorant whether the duke of Britanny were alive or not.[2]   Clearly, therefore, it was not as the avenger of Arthur's murder that Philip took the field at the end of April.   On the other hand, Philip had never made the slightest attempt to obtain Arthur's release ; early in 1203, if not before, he was almost openly laying his plans in anticipation of Arthur's permanent effacement from politics.[3]   The interests of the French king were in fact no less concerned in Arthur's imprisonment, and more concerned in his death, than were the interests of John himself.   John's one remaining chance of holding Philip and the Bretons in check was to keep them in uncertainty whether Arthur were alive or dead, in order to prevent the Bretons from adopting any decided policy, and hamper the French king in his dealings with them and with the Angevin and Poitevin rebels by compelling him to base his alliance with them on conditions avowedly liable to be annulled at any moment by Arthur's reappearance on the political scene.   If, therefore, Arthur—as is most probable—was now really dead, whether he had indeed perished a victim of one of those fits of ungovernable fury in which (and in which alone) the Angevin counts sometimes added blunder to crime,

[1] See *Revue historique*, vol. xxxii. pp. 33-72 and 291-311.   M. Bémont's conclusion on this point, though disputed by M. P. Guilhiermoz in *Bibliothèque de l'École des Chartes*, vol. lx. (1899), pp. 45-85, still holds the field.   Cf. *Revue hist.* vol. lxxi. (1899), pp. 33-41, and *Bibl. de l'École des Chartes*, vol. lx. pp. 363-72.

[2] Delisle, *Catal. des Actes de Phil.-Aug.* No. 783.   According to R. Coggeshall, pp. 144, 145, Philip virtually declared himself still ignorant on the point six months later still.

[3] Thus in March he received the liege homage of Maurice of Craon "for the time of Arthur's imprisonment" ; should Arthur be released and adhere to his engagements with Philip, Maurice was to be Arthur's liegeman as he had been of old ; should Arthur break faith with Philip, then Maurice was to adhere to the latter ; should Arthur die, then Maurice was to remain a liegeman of Philip. In like manner the castles of Brissac and Chemillé were in the following October granted by Philip to Guy of Thouars, "saving the rights of Arthur if he be still alive," Delisle, *Catal. des Actes de Phil.-Aug.* Nos. 752, 783.

or whether he had died a natural death from sickness in   **1203** prison, or by a fall in attempting to escape,[1] it would be equally politic on John's part to let rumour do its worst rather than suffer any gleam of light to penetrate the mystery which shrouded the captive's fate.

John's chance, however, was a desperate one. A fortnight   **April 20** after Easter the French king attacked and took Saumur.[2] Moving southward, he was joined by some Poitevins and Bretons, with whose help he captured sundry castles in Aquitaine. Thence he went back to the Norman border, to be welcomed at Alençon by its count, and to lay siege to Conches.[3] John, who was then at Falaise, sent William the Marshal to Conches, to beg that Philip would "have pity on him and make peace." Philip refused; John hurried back to Rouen, to find both city and castle in flames [4]—whether kindled by accident or by treachery there is nothing to show. Conches was taken; Vaudreuil was betrayed; the few other castles in the county of Evreux which had not already passed, either by cession, conquest, or treason, into Philip's hands shared the like fate,[5] while John flitted restlessly up and down between Rouen and various places in the neighbourhood,[6] but made no direct effort to check the progress of the invader. Messenger after messenger came to him with the same story: "The king of France is in your land as an enemy; he is taking your castles; he is binding your seneschals to their horses' tails and dragging them shamefully to prison; he is dealing with your goods at his own pleasure." John heard them all with an unmoved countenance, and dismissed them all with one unvarying reply: "Let him alone! Some day I shall win back all that he is winning from me now." [7]

It was by diplomacy that John hoped to parry the attack which he knew he could not repel by force. Early

---

[1] These were the alternative versions proposed by John's friends, according to M. Paris, *Hist. Angl.* vol. ii. p. 95.

[2] *Chron. S. Albini Andeg.* a. 1203.

[3] Rigord, c. 140; wrongly dated.

[4] *Hist. de G. le Mar.* vv. 12675-720.

[5] Cf. Rigord, c. 140; R. Coggeshall, p. 143; and R. Wendover, vol. iii. p. 172.   [6] *Itin.* a. 5.

[7] R. Wendover, vol. iii. pp. 171, 172.

3 in the year he had complained to the Pope of the long course of insult and aggression pursued towards him by Philip, and begged Innocent to interfere in his behalf.[1] Thereupon Philip, in his turn, sent messengers and letters to the Pope, giving his own version of his relations with John, and endeavouring to justify his own conduct.[2] On May 26 Innocent announced to both kings that he was about to despatch the abbots of Casamario, Trois-Fontaines and Dun as commissioners to arbitrate upon the matters in dispute between them.[3] These envoys seem to have been delayed on their journey ; and when they reached France they, for some time, found it impossible to ascertain whether Philip would or would not accept their arbitration. When at last he met them in council at Mantes on August 26, he told them bluntly that he " was not bound to take his orders from the Apostolic See as to his rights over a fief and a vassal of his own, and that the matter in dispute between the two kings was no business of the Pope's." [4] John meanwhile had, on August 11, suddenly quitted his passive attitude and laid siege to Alençon ; but he retired on Philip's approach four days later. An attempt which he made to regain Brezolles was equally ineffectual.[5] Philip, on the other hand, was now resolved to bring the war to a crisis. It was probably straight from the council at Mantes that he marched to the siege of Château-Gaillard.[6]

Château-Gaillard was a fortress of far other importance than any of the castles which both parties had been so lightly winning, losing and winning again, during the last ten years. It was the key of the Seine above Rouen, the bulwark raised by Richard Cœur de Lion to protect his favourite city against attack from France. Not till the fortifications which commanded the river at Les Andelys were either destroyed or in his own hands could Philip hope

---

[1] Innoc. III. *Epp.* l. vi. No. 163 ; dated Anagni, Oct. 29, 1203.

[2] *Ib.* No. 167 (same date).

[3] *Ib.* Nos. 68, 69. [4] *Ib.* No. 163.

[5] W. Armor. *Gesta P. A.* cc. 117, 118. The dates of the siege of Alençon come from *Itin.* a. 5.

[6] The siege of Château-Gaillard was begun before the end of August. See below, p. 96.

to win the Norman capital. And those fortifications were 1203 of no common order. Their builder was the greatest, as he was the last, of the "great builders" of Anjou; and his "fair castle on the Rock of Andelys" was at once the supreme outcome of their architectural genius, and the earliest and most perfect example in Europe of the new developement which the Crusaders' study of the mighty works of Byzantine or even earlier conquerors, quickened and illuminated as it was by the exigencies of their own struggle with the Infidels, had given to the science of military architecture in the East. During the past year John had added to his brother's castle a chapel with an undercroft, placed at the south-eastern corner of the second ward.[1] The fortress which nature and art had combined to make impregnable was well stocked with supplies of every kind; moreover, it was one of the few places in Normandy which Philip had no hope of winning, and John no fear of losing, through treason on the part of its commandant. Roger de Lacy, to whom John had given it in charge, was an English baron who had no stake in Normandy, and whose personal interest was therefore bound up with that of the English king; he was also a man of high character and dauntless courage.[2] Nothing short of a siege of the most determined kind would avail against the "Saucy Castle"; and on that siege Philip now concentrated all his forces and all his skill. As the right bank of the Seine at that point was entirely commanded by the castle and its neighbour fortification, the walled town—also built by Richard—known as the New or Lesser Andely, while the river itself was doubly barred by a stockade across its bed, close under the foot of the Rock, and by a strong tower on an island in mid-stream just below the town, he was obliged to encamp in the meadows on the opposite shore. The stockade, however, was soon broken down by the daring of a few young Frenchmen; and the waterway being thus cleared for the transport of materials, he was enabled to construct below the island a pontoon, by means of which he could throw a portion of his troops across the river to form the

---

[1] Will. Armor. *Gesta P. A.* c. 129; *Philipp.* l. vii. vv. 739-47.
[2] R. Wendover, vol. iii. p. 180.

siege of the New Andely, place the island garrison between two fires, and at once keep open his own communications and cut off those of the besieged with both sides of the river alike.[1]

These things seem to have been done towards the end of August. On the 27th and 28th of that month John was at Montfort, a castle some five and twenty miles from Rouen, held by one of his few faithful barons, Hugh of Gournay. On the 30th, if not the 29th, he and all his available forces were back at Rouen, ready to attempt on that very night the relief of Les Andelys.[2] The king's plan was a masterpiece of ingenuity; and the fact that the elaborate preparations needed for its execution were made so rapidly and so secretly as to escape detection by an enemy so close at hand goes far to show how mistaken are the charges of sloth and incapacity which, even in his own day, men brought against " John Softsword."[3] He had arranged that a force of three hundred knights, three thousand mounted men-at-arms, and four thousand foot, under the command of William the Marshal, with a band of mercenaries under Lou Pescaire, should march by night from Rouen along the left bank of the Seine and fall, under cover of darkness, upon the portion of the French army which still lay on that side of the river. Meanwhile, seventy transport vessels which had been built by Richard to serve either for sea or river traffic, and as many more boats as could be collected, were to be laden with provisions for the distressed garrison of the island fort, and convoyed up the stream by a flotilla of small war-ships manned by " pirates " under a chief named Alan and carrying, besides their own daring and reckless crews, a force of three thousand Flemings. Two hundred strokes of the oar, John reckoned, would bring these ships to the French pontoon; they must break it if they could; if not, they

---

[1] Rigord, c. 141 ; W. Armor. *Gesta P. A.* c. 122 ; *Philipp.* l. vii. vv. 29-140.   [2] *Itin.* a. 5.

[3] " Johannem Mollegladium," Gerv. Cant. vol. ii. p. 93. This nickname is no doubt a translation of one which must have been applied to John in French, though unluckily its vernacular form is lost. A friend has suggested that " if the phrase had any English equivalent, it would probably be something embracing a more direct metaphor than ' Soft-sword ' — something like ' Tin-sword,' or, better still, if the thirteenth century knew of putty, ' John Putty-sword.' "

could at least co-operate with the Marshal and Lou Pescaire
in cutting off the northern division of the French host from
its comrades and supplies on the left bank, and throw into
the island fort provisions which would enable it to hold out
till John himself should come to its rescue.

One error brought the scheme to ruin—an error neither
of strategy nor of conduct, but of scientific knowledge. John
had miscalculated the time at which, on that night, the Seine
would be navigable up-stream; and his counsellors evidently
shared his mistake till it was brought home to them by
experience. The land forces achieved their march without
hindrance, and at the appointed hour, shortly before daybreak, fell upon the French camp with such a sudden and
furious onslaught that the whole of its occupants fled across
the pontoon, which broke under their weight. But the
fleet, which had been intended to arrive at the same time,
was unable to make way against the tide, and before it could
reach its destination the French had rallied on the northern
bank, repaired the pontoon, recrossed it in full force, and
routed John's troops. The ships, when they at last came up,
thus found themselves unsupported in their turn, and though
they made a gallant fight they were beaten back with heavy
loss. In the flush of victory one young Frenchman contrived to set fire to the island fort ; it surrendered, and the
whole population of the New Andely fled in a panic to
Château-Gaillard, leaving their town to be occupied by
Philip.[1] The Saucy Castle itself still remained to be won.
Knowing, however, that for this nothing was likely to avail
but a blockade, which was now practically formed on two
sides by his occupation of the island fort and the Lesser
Andely, Philip on the very next day[2] set off to make
another attempt on Radepont, whence he had been driven
away by John a year before. This time John made no
effort to dislodge him. It was not worth while ; the one
thing that mattered now was Château-Gaillard. Thither

---

[1] W. Armor. *Philipp.* l. vii. vv. 140-393. Cf. *Gesta P. A.* c. 123.
[2] Rigord, c. 141, says Philip laid siege to Radepont on August 31. John's
attempt to relieve Les Andelys, being made from Rouen, cannot have been
earlier than August 29, more probably 30, *Itin.* a. 5.

1203 Philip, after receiving the surrender of Radepont, returned towards the end of September to complete the blockade.[1]

No second attempt to relieve it was possible. It may have been for the purpose of endeavouring to collect fresh troops from the western districts, which were as yet untouched by the war, that John about this time visited his old county of Mortain, and even went as far as Dol,[2] which his soldiers had taken in the previous year. But his military resources in Normandy were exhausted. The Marshal bluntly advised him to give up the struggle. "Sire," said William, "you have not enough friends; if you provoke your enemies to fight, you will diminish your own force; and when a man provokes his enemies, it is but just if they make him rue it." "Whoso is afraid, let him flee!" answered John. "I myself will not flee for a year; and if indeed it came to fleeing, I should not think of saving myself otherwise than you would, wheresoever you might be." "I know that well, sire," replied William; "but you, who are wise and mighty and of high lineage, and whose work it is to govern us all, have not been careful to avoid irritating people. If you had, it would have been better for us all. Methinks I speak not without reason."[3] The king, "as if a sword had struck him to the heart," spoke not a word, but rushed to his chamber; next morning he was nowhere to be found; he had gone away in a boat, almost alone, and it was only at Bonneville that his followers rejoined him. This was apparently at the beginning of October.[4] For two months more he lingered in the duchy, where his position was growing more hopeless day by day. At the end of October, or early in November, he took the decisive step of dismantling Pont-de-l'Arche, Moulineaux, and Montfort,[5] three castles which, next to Château-Gaillard, would be of the greatest value to the French for

[1] Rigord, c. 141; W. Armor. *Gesta P. A.* c. 121; *Philipp.* l. vii. vv. 400-2.
[2] *Itin.* a. 5. He was at Dol September 19-22.
[3] *Hist. de G. le Mar.* vv. 12721-42.
[4] *Ib.* vv. 12743-67. John was at Rouen from October 4 to 7, when he went to Bonneville; *Itin.* a. 5. The poet goes on with an account of the king's wanderings till "s'en vint a Rouen arere," but his itinerary does not agree with the authentic one at any period of this year.
[5] W. Armor. *Philipp.* l. vii. vv. 827-9.

an advance upon Rouen. To Rouen itself he returned once more on November 9, and stayed there four days.[1] On the 12th he set out for Bonneville, accompanied by the queen, and telling his friends that he intended to go to England to seek counsel and aid from his barons and people there, and would soon return. In reality his departure from the capital was caused by a rumour which had reached him of a conspiracy among the Norman barons to deliver him up to Philip Augustus. At Bonneville, therefore, he lodged not in the town but in the castle, and only for a few hours; the Marshal and one or two others alone were warned of his intention to set forth again before daybreak, and the little party had got a start of seven leagues on the road to Caen before their absence was discovered by the rest of the suite, of whom "some went after them, and the more part went back." [2] Still John was reluctant to leave Normandy; he went south to Domfront and west to Vire before he again returned to the coast at Barfleur on November 28; and even then he spent five days at Gonneville and one at Cherbourg before he finally took ship at Barfleur on December 5, to land at Portsmouth next day.[3]

It was probably before he left Rouen that he addressed a letter to the commandant of Château-Gaillard in these terms: "We thank you for your good and faithful service, and desire that, as much as in you lies, you will persevere in the fidelity and homage which you owe to us; that you may receive a worthy meed of praise from God and from ourself, and from all who know your faithfulness. If however—which God forbid!—you should find yourself in such straits that you can hold out no longer, then do whatsoever our trusty and well-beloved Peter of Préaux, William of Mortimer, and Hugh of Howels our clerk, shall bid you in our name." [4] An English chronicler says that John "being unwilling"—or "unable"—"to succour the besieged, through fear of the treason of his men, went to England,

---

[1] *Itin.* a. 5.
[2] *Hist. de G. le Mar.* vv. 12783-818.
[3] Cf. *Itin.* a. 5 and R. Wendover, vol. iii. p. 173.
[4] Duchesne, *Hist. Norm. Scriptt.* p. 1059.

1203   leaving all the Normans in a great perturbation of fear."[1]
It is hard to see what they feared, unless it were John's
possible vengeance, at some future time, for their universal
readiness to welcome his rival.   Not one town manned its
walls, not one baron mustered his tenants and garrisoned his
castles, to withstand the invader.   Some, as soon as John
was out of the country, openly made a truce with Philip for
a year, on the understanding that if not succoured by John
within that time, they would receive the French king as their
lord ;[2] the rest stood passively looking on at the one real
struggle of the war, the struggle for Château-Gaillard.

1204   At length, on March 6, 1204, the Saucy Castle fell.[3]
Its fall opened the way for a French advance upon Rouen ;
but before taking this further step Philip deemed it politic
to let the Pope's envoy, the abbot of Casamario, complete
his mission by going to speak with John.   The abbot was
received at a great council in London at the end of March ;[4]
the result was his return to France early in April, in
company with the archbishop of Canterbury, the bishops of
Norwich and Ely, and the earls of Pembroke and Leicester,
all charged with a commission " to sound the French king,
and treat with him about terms of peace."   On the French
king's side the negotiation was a mere form ; to whatever
conditions the envoys proposed, he always found some
objection ; and his own demands were such as John's
representatives dared not attempt to lay before their
sovereign—Arthur's restoration, or, if he were dead, the
surrender of his sister Eleanor, and the cession to Philip,
as her suzerain and guardian, of the whole continental
dominions of the Angevin house.[5]   Finally, Philip dropped

---

    [1] " Rege vero Johanne nullum praesidium ferre obsessis volente, eo quod
suorum proditionem semper timeret, infra hyemem, mense Decembri, in Angliam
trans fretavit, omnes Normannos in magna timoris perturbatione relinquens," R.
Coggeshall, p. 144. It seems probable that "volente" may be a clerical error
for "valente."

    [2] R. Wendover, vol. iii. pp. 173, 174.   [3] Rigord, c. 141.

    [4] Gerv. Cant. (vol. ii. p. 95) says the council was held "in London"; R.
Coggeshall (p. 144) describes its result, the embassy to France, as taking place
"after Mid-Lent," *i.e.* after April 1.   The only date about this time when
John was in London was March 22-29 ; *Itin.* a. 5.

    [5] Cf. R. Coggeshall, pp. 144, 145 ; Gerv. Cant. vol. ii. pp. 95, 96, and *Hist.
de G. le Mar.* vv. 12854-68.

the mask altogether, and made a direct offer, not to John, but to John's Norman subjects, including the two lay ambassadors. All those, he said, who within a year and a day would come to him and do him homage for their lands should receive confirmation of their tenure from him. Hereupon the two English earls, after consulting together, gave him five hundred marks each, on the express understanding that he was to leave them unmolested in the enjoyment of their Norman lands for a twelvemonth and a day, and that at the expiration of that time they would come and do homage for those lands to him, if John had not meanwhile regained possession of the duchy.[1] Neither William the Marshal nor his colleague had any thought of betraying or deserting John; as the Marshal's biographer says, they "did not wish to be false"; and when they reached England they seem to have frankly told John what they had done, and to have received no blame for it.[2]

The return of the English embassy was followed by a letter from the commandant of Rouen—John's "trusty and well-beloved" Peter of Préaux—informing the English king that "all the castles and towns from Bayeux to Anet" had promised Philip that they would surrender to him as soon as he was master of Rouen, an event which, Peter plainly hinted, was not likely to be long delayed.[3] This information about the western towns was probably incorrect, for it was on western Normandy that Philip made his next attack. John meanwhile had in January imposed a scutage of two marks and a half per shield throughout England, and, in addition, a tax of a seventh of moveables, which, though it fell upon all classes alike, the clergy included, he is said to have demanded expressly on the ground of the barons' desertion of him in Normandy.[4] The hire of a mercenary force was of course the object to which the proceeds of both these taxes were destined; but they took time to collect, and John soon fell back upon a readier, though less trustworthy,

---

[1] *Hist. de G. le Mar.* vv. 12869-98. Cf. the Marshal's charter to Philip (dated May 1204) in *Cal. Doc. France,* vol. i. p. 475.

[2] *Hist. de G. le Mar.* vv. 12934-66.   [3] *Ib.* vv. 12905-20.

[4] R. Wendover, vol. iii. pp. 173, 175.

1204   resource, and summoned the feudal host of England to meet
him at Portsmouth, seemingly in the first week of May.   It
gathered, however, so slowly that he was obliged to give
up the expedition.[1]   Philip was about this time besieging
Falaise ;[2] he won it, and went on in triumph to receive the
surrender of Domfront, Séez, Lisieux, Caen, Bayeux, Cou-
tances, Barfleur, and Cherbourg.[3]   He was then joined by
John's late ally, the count of Boulogne, as well as by Guy of
Thouars, the widower of Constance of Britanny ; and these
two, their forces swelled by a troop of mercenaries who had
transferred their services from John to Philip after the
surrender of Falaise, completed the conquest of south-western
Normandy,[4] while the French king at last set his face towards
Rouen.   He was not called upon to besiege it, nor even to
threaten it with a siege.   On June 1 Peter de Préaux made
in his own name, and in the names of the commandants of
Arques and Verneuil, a truce with Philip, promising that these
two fortresses and Rouen should surrender if not succoured
within thirty days.[5]   The three castellans sent notice of this
arrangement to John, who, powerless and penniless as he was,
scornfully bade them "look for no help from him, but do
whatsoever seemed to them best."[6]   It seemed to them best
not even to wait for the expiration of the truce ; Rouen
surrendered on June 24,[7] and in a few days Arques and
Verneuil followed its example.[8]

Thus did Normandy forsake—as Anjou and Maine
had already forsaken—the heir of its ancient rulers for the
king of the French.   Philip's next undertaking, the conquest

---

[1] *Hist. de G. le Mar.* vv. 12921-6.   John was at Portsmouth on May 5,
and at Porchester on May 5-7, 1204.   The story may, however, be a mere
confusion with what happened in June 1205.

[2] R. Coggeshall, p. 145, dates Philip's siege of Falaise Easter (April 25) ;
but Rigord, a better authority on the point, places it in the May campaign
(c. 142).

[3] Cf. R. Coggeshall, p. 145 ; Rigord, c. 142 ; W. Armor. *Gesta P. A.* c. 131,
and *Philipp.* l. viii. vv. 9-39.

[4] W. Armor. *Gesta P. A.* c. 131.

[5] Duchesne, *Hist. Norm. Scriptt.* pp. 1057-9.

[6] R. Wendover, vol. iii. p. 181.   That John was penniless may be inferred
from the desertion of his mercenaries.

[7] Rigord, c. 142.   Cf. R. Coggeshall, p. 146, and *Hist. des Ducs de
Normandie*, p. 98.

[8] R. Coggeshall, p. 146.

of Aquitaine, was likely to be considerably facilitated
by the fact that there was no longer a third person
who could claim to stand between him and his rival
as lawful lady of the land ; for Eleanor had died on
April 1.[1]   In the middle of August Philip marched upon
Poitou.   Robert of Turnham, John's seneschal there, did
what he could for its defence ; but he was powerless against
the indifference of the people and the active hostility of the
Lusignans and William des Roches ;[2] and in a few weeks
the whole county, except La Rochelle, Niort, and Thouars,
had submitted to the French king.[3]   There, however,
Philip's progress ended.   He could not touch the county of
Angoulême, for it belonged not to John, but to John's wife ;
while his very successes turned Gascony against him, for the
Gascons were quick to perceive how much greater would be
their chances of practical independence under a king who
would henceforth be parted from them by the whole width
of the Bay of Biscay, than under one whose territories now
stretched without a break from the Channel to their own
border.   Nor had John failed to recognize that in this
quarter lay his best hope—at the moment indeed his only
hope—of checking Philip's advance.   He at once devoted
twenty-eight thousand marks of the treasure which he was
gathering in England to the hire of thirty thousand soldiers,
who were to be enrolled for his service in Gascony by one
Moreve, a brother of the archbishop of Bordeaux, in readiness
to join the forces of the king himself whenever he should
land on their coast.[4]   From Poitiers, therefore, Philip returned
to his own dominions, and no further military movement on
either side was made throughout the winter.

    In the middle of January 1205 John called the bishops
and barons of England to a council in London.[5]   His
nominal reason for so doing was that he feared Philip might
attempt an invasion of England, and desired to concert
measures for its defence ; but it is clear that what he really

---

[1] *Ann. Waverley*, a. 1204.   [2] R. Coggeshall, p. 146.
[3] *Ib.* ; R. Wendover, vol. iii. p. 181.
[4] R. Coggeshall, p. 147.
[5] John was in London January 16-21, 1205 (*Itin.* a. 6).   This is evidently
the date of the council.

1205 dreaded and sought to guard against was not invasion, but
treason. The precautions which he induced the council to
support him in taking against the imaginary danger were, if
insufficient to save him from the real one, at least as good a
safeguard as could be contrived against it at the moment.
The oath of fealty to the king was taken anew by all present,
and afterwards re-administered throughout the country. " It
was also decreed that, for the general defence of the realm
and for the preservation of peace, a *commune* should be made
throughout the kingdom, and that all men, from the greatest
to the least, who were over twelve years of age, should swear
to keep it firmly." The ordinance to which they swore
established constables in every shire ; and in every hundred,
city, and group of lesser townships, subordinate constables
who were to lead the men of their respective " communes "
to the muster whenever they were summoned by the chief
constables, whose orders these local levies were to obey " for
the defence of the realm and the preservation of peace
against foreigners or against any other disturbers of the
same " ; and whosoever should neglect the summons was to
be held guilty of high treason.[1]   At the beginning of February
John issued letters patent to the bailiffs of the east and south
coast, giving orders that no ship or boat should be allowed to
issue from or pass by the harbours under their jurisdiction,
unless by special licence from him.[2]   Besides the obvious
purpose of hindering treasonable communications with his
enemies on the continent, this order had probably another
object ; the vessels thus detained were most likely appropriated
to the king's service and made to form part of a fleet which
he was gathering from various quarters [3] throughout the next
two months.   The want of confidence between king and
barons was openly revealed in a council at Oxford, March
27 to 29 ; the barons made oath to John " that they
would render him due obedience," but John was first " compelled to swear that he would by their counsel maintain the
rights of the kingdom inviolate, to the utmost of his power." [4]

[1] Gerv. Cant. vol. ii. pp. 96, 97.
[2] *Rot. Pat.* vol. i. p. 50.   [3] *Ib.* pp. 51, 52.
[4] Gerv. Cant. vol. ii. pp. 97, 98. For date see *Itin.* a. 6.

On Palm Sunday, April 3, John issued letters patent from   1205
Winchester, ordering that in all the shires of England every
nine knights should "find" a tenth, and that the knights
thus provided should come to meet him in London three
weeks after Easter (that is, on May 1), " ready to go in his
service where he should bid them, and to be in his service
in defence of the realm as much as might be needful." [1] The
muster seems, however, to have been postponed, possibly to
await the result of an attempt which the king had been
making in the field of diplomacy, under somewhat peculiar
circumstances.

Of all John's ministers, the one whom he most disliked
and mistrusted was the one whose constitutional position
made him absolutely irremoveable from the royal counsels—
the archbishop of Canterbury, Hubert Walter.   That John's
suspicions of Hubert's loyalty were unjust there can be no
doubt ; but there are not wanting indications that Hubert,
whose temper was extremely masterful, and who for the six
years preceding John's accession to the throne had governed
England for Richard practically at his own sole discretion,
was inclined to press his views of policy upon Richard's
younger brother in a fashion more dictatorial than deferential,
and to magnify his own office as chief adviser of the Crown,
and his personal capabilities as a statesman and a diplo-
matist, with more emphasis than tact.   Hubert had on
several occasions tried to act as mediator between John and
Philip, and his mediation had failed.   In Lent 1205 John,
while pushing on his military preparations in England,
resolved to set on foot a new diplomatic negotiation with
France which seems to have had a twofold object—first, to
keep Philip occupied so as to hinder him, at least for a short
time, from proceeding against the few fortresses north of the
Dordogne which still held out for their Angevin lord ; [2] and
secondly, to make game of the archbishop of Canterbury.
This latter object was to be attained by keeping the project
a secret from Hubert, and carrying on the negotiations not
only without his assistance or advice, but even without his

---

[1] *Rot. Pat.* vol. i. p. 55.
[2] Chinon, Loches, Thouars, Niort and La Rochelle.

1205   knowledge.   The envoys whom John selected for this mission
were his vice-chancellor, Hugh of Wells, and Earl William
the Marshal.   Apparently it was given out that their journey
to France was on business of their own ; an assertion which
in the Marshal's case was true, though not the whole truth.
When John had communicated to them his private instructions, William spoke : " Now, sire, listen to me.   I am not
sure of obtaining peace ; and you see that my term of
truce for my Norman land is nearly expired.   Unless I do
homage for it to the French king, I shall lose it ; for I see
no hope of recovering it otherwise.   What am I to do ? "
" Save it for my service by doing the homage," answered
John.   " I know you are too loyal to withdraw your heart's
homage from me, come what may, and that the more you
possess to serve me with, the better will be your service." [1]
He seems to have given—though scarcely with equal willingness—a like permission to some of his other vassals who
were in the same plight as the Marshal,[2] and who may
perhaps have been allowed to accompany the latter partly
for the sake of still further obscuring the main object of
his mission.

The Marshal and the vice-chancellor found the French
king at Compiègne, and communicated to him their errand
from John.   Philip seemed disposed to entertain John's
proposals—we are not told what they were—and promised
to give them an answer a week later at Anet.[3]   Meanwhile
he reminded the Marshal that the time of their " covenant "
was nearly up, adding, " You may find it the worse for you
if you do not at once do me homage."   The Marshal assented
and performed the homage then and there, apparently
regarding it as a mere form necessary for the redemption of
his plighted word, but destined to be rendered void by
the peace which he trusted to conclude between the two

[1] *Hist. de G. le Mar.* vv. 12934-66.
[2] Gerv. Cant. vol. ii. p. 96.
[3] As a reason for Anet being chosen by Philip as the place of meeting, John
d'Erlée says :

" Quer s'ost out semonse por veir
          Por aler Caem aseeir " (vv. 12977-8).

But this is an anachronism : Caen had been surrendered to Philip in May or
June 1204 (see above, p. 102), and we are now in spring 1205.

sovereigns in a few days. By this time, however, Archbishop Hubert had discovered the fact of the secret negotiations, and was extremely wroth that the king should have
"plotted such a plot" without consulting him. He therefore sent a certain Ralf of Ardenne to tell the count of
Boulogne that the two English envoys had no power to
conclude a treaty. Boulogne at once communicated this
information to Philip, and when the meeting at Anet took
place, the taunt was flung in the Marshal's face, and the
negotiations were broken off. Ralf of Ardenne had already
hurried back to England and told John that the Marshal
had done homage and fealty to the French king and made
alliance with the latter against his own sovereign. When
the unlucky envoys came home, they met with a sorry
greeting. John at once charged the Marshal with having,
"against him and for his damage," sworn allegiance to his
enemy of France. The Marshal denied the charge, and
asserted that he had done only what John had given him
leave to do. On this John, in his rage, practically denied
his own words, and declared that "his barons and his men"
should judge between him and the Marshal—a judgement
which William retorted that he was quite ready to face.[1]

The fleet and the host were finally summoned to
assemble at Portsmouth at Whitsuntide.[2] The land forces
had probably received some increase by means of an order
issued by the king on April 15 that, "for the good of
his mother's soul," all prisoners, except those charged with
treason, should be set at liberty.[3] No doubt every prisoner
capable of bearing arms was, as he issued from confinement,
made to take the oath of allegiance and enrolled for
military service under the constable of his district. On the
Tuesday in Whitsun week (May 31) John arrived at
Porchester; there he stayed ten days, on the last five of
which he made daily excursions to Portsmouth,[4] probably
to watch the gathering of the fleet in its harbour.

---

[1] *Hist. de G. le Mar.* vv. 12967-13087. See the Marshal's charter to
Philip in *Cal. Doc. France*, vol. i. p. 475.
[2] R. Wendover, vol. iii. p. 182.
[3] *Rot. Pat.* vol. i. p. 54.
[4] *Itin.* a. 7.

It is doubtful how far the troops were aware of the king's real purpose in calling them together. The whole country was in a state of excitement, hourly expecting an invasion. It was reported that the duke of Louvain, in return for the French king's good offices in recovering for him from the count of Boulogne the share of the revenues of the latter county to which he was entitled in right of his wife, had done homage to Philip, and that the duke and the count had sworn in Philip's presence to be ready, each at the other's call, to proceed to England with all their forces and reclaim from John at the sword's point the English lands of which their wives—the grand-daughters of King Stephen and Maud of Boulogne—had been disinherited by Henry II.; whereupon Philip had sworn that he himself would follow them with his host within a month after their landing in England.[1]   John, in calling his people to arms, seems to have purposely expressed the object of the armament in general terms—" for the defence of the realm "—" for the king's service "[2]; terms which did not necessarily imply that he wanted his men to do anything more than stand on the defensive, ready to meet the expected invasion. He probably suspected that had he at the outset demanded more than this, he would have met with a flat refusal in certain quarters ; and the issue proved the suspicion to be correct. The rank and file of the host, indeed, were ready and willing not only for defence but for defiance, eager to carry the war into the enemy's country before the enemy could set foot in their own. To them John, at this stage of his career, was still the " king of the English," who had lost his continental possessions through the wiles of his foreign enemies and the disloyalty of his " French " subjects, and whom they, his faithful Englishmen, would gladly help to win those possessions back again. The heads of the baronage, however, and some at least of the innermost circle of the royal councillors, were of another mind. Those of the greater barons who had deserted or betrayed him in Normandy probably saw, or

---

[1] R. Coggeshall, p. 148.
[2] Gerv. Cant. vol. ii. pp. 96, 97 ; *Rot. Pat.* vol. i. p. 55.

thought they saw, the possibility of serving two masters,
one for their continental lands and the other for their
English lands, and of profiting by this division of service to
make themselves practically independent of both masters
alike.   This, indeed, was not a motive which could sway
such a noble soul as William the Marshal; nor could it
influence Hubert Walter, to whom the continuance or the
severance of the connexion between England and the rest
of the Angevin dominions made, either as an individual or
as archbishop, no difference at all.   Yet when the critical
moment came, these two men, who a few weeks before had
been in political as well as personal opposition to each
other, forgot their rivalry and united all their influence to
defeat the king's project of an expedition over sea.

On one of those days of waiting at Porchester, while the
host was gradually assembling, John, seated on the shore,
with his court around him, called the Marshal to his
presence and renewed his demand for "judgement" on the
question of William's alleged treason.   William quietly
repeated his former answer, that he had only acted upon
the king's own orders.   "I deny it," again said John.
"You will gain nothing in the end; but I will bide my
time; and meanwhile I will have you come with me to
Poitou and fight for the recovery of my heritage against the
king of France, to whom you have done homage."   The
Marshal remonstrated; he could not fight against a man
to whom he had done homage.   On this John declared his
treason to be manifest, and appealed to the judgement of the
barons present.   William faced them boldly, pointed to his
own forehead, and said: "Sirs, look at me, for, by my faith!
I am this day an example for you all.   You hear what the
king says; and what he proposes to do to me, that, and
more also, will he do to every one of you, if he can get the
upper hand."   The enraged king at these words called for
instant judgement upon the speaker; but the barons "looked
at each other and drew back."   "By God's teeth!" swore
John, "I see plainly that not one of my barons is with me
in this; I must take counsel with my bachelors about this
matter which is beginning to look so ugly"; and he with-

1205   drew to another place.   The barons seemingly followed
him, as did the " bachelors," and the Marshal was left alone,
save for two personal followers of his own.   The bachelors
as a body, when John appealed to them, gave it as their
opinion that there could be no essoign for failing to serve
the king on such an occasion as the present ; but one of
them, named Baldwin, added that there was in the whole
assembly no man worthy to judge such a good knight as
the Marshal, nor bold enough to undertake the proof (by
ordeal of battle) of the charge brought against him by the
king ;   and Baldwin's remark " was pleasing to many."
Finding that neither baron nor knight would challenge the
Marshal for him, John ended the scene by going to dinner ;
and after some further ineffectual endeavours to obtain a
champion he let the matter drop, and began once more to
treat the Marshal with civility, if not cordiality.[1]

By June 9 the tale of men and ships was complete.
It was a splendid array ; never before, folk said, had there
come together a greater host of brave fighting men, " all
ready and willing to go with the king over sea," nor had
there ever been assembled in any English harbour so large
a number of ships equipped for the crossing.[2]   To each of
the leaders of the host was assigned, by the king's orders,
a vessel or a number of vessels sufficient for the transport of
his following.   Each vessel had received her lading of arms
and provisions, and only the troops remained to be embarked, when the archbishop of Canterbury and the Earl
Marshal went to the king and " used every possible argument to dissuade him from crossing.   They represented
what great mischief might arise from his going over sea ;—
how perilous it would be for him to thrust himself among so
many battalions of enemies, when he had no safe place of
refuge in the transmarine lands ;—how the French king,
being now master of nearly all his territories, could bring
against him a force far outnumbering the English host ;—

---

[1] *Hist. de G. le Mar.* vv. 13103-270.
[2] R. Coggeshall, p. 154.   Gerv. Cant. vol. ii. p. 98, says that the ships were
said to number nearly fifteen hundred, and R. Coggeshall, p. 153, that the
shipmen were said to be fourteen thousand.

how great was the danger of putting himself into the hands
of the false and fickle Poitevins, whose wont was to be
always plotting some treachery against their lords ;—how
the count of Boulogne and his confederates would speedily
invade England if they heard that its chief men and its
brave army were away ;—and how it was much to be feared
that, while endeavouring to regain his lost dominions, he
might lose those which remained to him, especially as he
had no heir whom he could leave behind him to take up the
reins of government in case any misfortune should befall his
own person in the lands beyond the sea.   And when he
could not be moved by these and other like arguments, they
(the archbishop and the Marshal) fell down before him and
clasped his knees to restrain him from leaving them, declaring that of a surety, if he would not yield to their
prayers, they would detain him by force, lest by his departure the whole kingdom should be brought to confusion."
Such opposition as this, from two such men, implied a great
deal more than is expressed in their words as reported by
Ralph of Coggeshall.   John saw at once that his six months
of elaborate preparation had been wasted, and that his
hopes were ruined.   "Weeping and crying" with shame
and grief, he passionately demanded what, then, did the
archbishop advise as best to be done for the realm and for
the king's honour, as well as for the supporters who were
looking for him to join them beyond the sea?   After some
consultation, his counsellors agreed that a force of picked
knights should be sent, under the command of some English
noble, to the help of John's continental friends.   All the
rest of the host were bidden to return to their homes.

Bitter was the disappointment and vehement the indignation of the troops, especially the sailors, and loud and
deep were the curses which they hurled at the ministers
whose "detestable counsel" had thwarted the aspirations
and shattered the hopes of king and people alike.[1]   The
ministers hurried the unwilling king away to Winchester
(June 11) ; but next day he made his way back to Portsmouth, went on board a ship with a few comrades, and

[1] R. Coggeshall, pp. 152, 153.

1205

1205   crossed into the Isle of Wight, probably hoping that when
he was found to have actually set forth, the sailors and the
troops would compel the barons to follow, or intending to
throw himself alone, if need were, upon the honour of his
Aquitanian adherents.   At the end of two days, however,
his companions persuaded him to abandon this desperate
venture, and on June 15 he landed at Studland near
Wareham.[1]   His first act on landing was to claim " an
infinite sum of money " from the earls, barons, prelates and
knights, on the ground that they " had refused to follow him
over sea for the recovery of his lost heritage." [2]   In so far as
this exaction fell upon the shire'-levies and the country
knights, it was unjust, for the majority of these were clearly
in sympathy with the king, and as eager for the expedition
as he was himself.   But it was impossible for him, in the
actual circumstances, to distinguish between the willing and
the unwilling ; and there can be little doubt that so far as
the barons were concerned, his assertion was practically
correct.   The gathering of the mightiest armament that had
ever been seen in England had ended, not in a vigorous
effort to regain the lost dominions of England's sovereign,
but in the despatch of a handful of knights under the earl
of Salisbury to reinforce the garrison of La Rochelle.[3]
That it had so ended was directly owing to the action of the
primate and the Marshal.   But it would obviously have been
impossible for two men, however influential, to prevail
against the king, if his policy had been supported by the
whole body of the baronage on the spot and in arms.   The
most probable explanation of the matter is that Hubert and
William knew the majority of the barons to be, at best, half-
hearted in the cause.   Whether, in a military and political
point of view, the moment was really favourable or unfavour-
able for the undertaking which John contemplated and from
which they shrank, is a question on which speculation is
useless.   All we can say is that if an opportunity was thrown
away, the responsibility for its rejection does not lie upon John.

---

[1] Cf. R. Coggeshall, p. 154 ; Gerv. Cant. vol. ii. p. 98 ; and R. Wendover,
vol. iii. p. 182, with *Itin.* a. 7.   [2] R. Wendover, *l.c.*
[3] R. Coggeshall, p. 154.

John's own feeling about the scene at Portsmouth came 1205 out, brutally indeed, but very naturally, in the exclamation with which he received the tidings of Archbishop Hubert's death on July 13 : " Now for the first time I am King of England ! "[1]   He took up afresh the plan which Hubert had foiled.   Ten months, indeed, had to pass before he could bring his forces together again ; but when at last " a great host " gathered at Portsmouth once more, ready to sail on 1206
May 27 Whitsun Eve, 1206,[2] not a voice was raised to oppose its embarkation.   The year had passed without disturbance in England ; nothing had been seen, nothing further had even been heard, of the dreaded Flemish and French invasion. But on the other side of the sea the delay had told.   The fall of Loches, shortly after Easter 1205,[3] had been followed 1205 on June 23—scarcely a fortnight after the break-up of the English muster—by that of Chinon,[4] and this again by the submission of the viscount of Thouars to the French conqueror.[5]   Thus the last foothold of the Angevins in Touraine and on the northern frontier of Poitou were lost.   There remained to John only two fortresses on the northern border of Poitou—Niort [6] and La Rochelle, the " fair city of the waters," whose natural position made it almost impregnable even in those days, whither John had twice sent reinforcements,[7] and whose harbour offered a safe and commodious landing-place for him and his troops.

[1] M. Paris, *Hist. Angl.* vol. ii. p. 104.   R. Wendover, vol. iii. p. 183, and R. Coggeshall, p. 156, date Hubert's death July 13 ; Gerv. Cant., vol. ii. p. 98, dates it July 12.   They all mean the same ; from R. Coggeshall, p. 158, we learn that the archbishop died shortly after midnight.

[2] R. Wendover, vol. iii. p. 186 ; exact date from a writ (dated April 29, 1206) ordering the seizure of ships for transport ; they are to be at Portsmouth on Whitsun Eve, or before.   *Rot. Pat.* vol. i. pp. 62 b, 63.   A summons to the men of the Cinque Ports, for the same date, was issued on May 12 ; *ib.* p. 64.

[3] Rigord, c. 144 ; W. Armor. *Gesta P. A.* c. 134 ; R. Coggeshall, p. 152.

[4] R. Coggeshall, p. 154 ; R. Wendover, vol. iii. pp. 182, 183.

[5] W. Armor. *Gesta P. A.* c. 135.

[6] Niort had been taken by, or had surrendered to, Philip, but was regained in 1205 for John by a stratagem of Savaric de Mauléon, whom John had taken prisoner at Mirebeau and released on a promise of fealty—a promise which was immediately fulfilled and faithfully kept.   See *Hist. des Ducs de Normandie*, pp. 100-4 ; and cf. (as to Savaric) R. Coggeshall, p. 146.

[7] R. Coggeshall, p. 154.

1206   On June 7 John arrived at La Rochelle,[1] and met
with an eager welcome ; the vassals of the duchy of
Aquitaine flocked to the standard of Eleanor's heir.   Six
days after his landing he could venture as far into Poitou as
the abbey of St. Maixent, half-way between Niort and
Poitiers.   The Poitevin counts had for centuries been
benefactors to the abbey, and their descendant was no doubt
sure of a welcome within its walls.   He made, however, no
further advance northward ; it was needful, before doing so,
to be quite sure of his footing in the south.   From St.
Maixent he went back to Niort, and thence southward
through Saintonge[2] into Gascony.   Here there was known
to be a hostile party whose leaders had congregated in the
castle of Montauban, a mighty fortress which Charles the
Great was said to have besieged for seven years in vain.[3]
In the middle of July, John formed the siege of Montauban,
and then himself withdrew to Bourg-sur-Mer, a little seaport
at the mouth of the Garonne, while his engines hurled their
missiles against the fortress, till on the fifteenth day a
sufficient breach was made, when "the English soldiery, who
are specially admirable in this work, rushed to scale the
walls, and to give and receive intolerable blows.   At last the
Englishmen prevailed, the besieged gave way, and the castle
was taken."   John had probably come back to direct in
person the assault thus successfully made by his brave
"Englishmen," for he was at Montauban on the day of
its capture, August 1.[4]   With it there fell into his hands,
besides horses and arms and countless other spoil, a number
of prisoners of such importance that we are told he sent a
list of their names to his justiciars in England.[5]   They
evidently included all the Gascon barons whose hostility he
had had reason to fear ; and with them in his power, he
could turn his back upon the south without further anxiety.

[1] John crossed from Stoke to Yarmouth, Isle of Wight, on May 28, and thence
to La Rochelle on June 7.   Cf. R. Wendover, vol. iii. p. 186, where *Julii* is, of
course, in both places a mistake for *Junii* ; and *Itin.* a. 8.   [2] *Itin.* a. 8.
  [3] R. Wendover, vol. iii. p. 187.   The legend of the building of Montauban
by the "Four Sons of Aymon," and its siege by Charles, is told in the romance
of *Renaus de Montauban.*
  [4] Cf. R. Wendover, *l.c.*, and *Itin.* a. 8.
  [5] R. Wendover, *l.c.*   Unluckily the letter does not seem to be extant.

By August 21 John was back at Niort; after spending a week there, he proceeded to Montmorillon, on the borders of Poitou and Berry.[1] At this critical moment Almeric of Thouars reverted to his old allegiance.[2] John at once struck right across Poitou to Clisson,[3] on the borders of Anjou and Britanny ; Almeric joined him either there or on the way thither, and they marched together into Anjou. A chronicler writing in the abbey of S. Aubin at Angers, which had always been under the special patronage and protection of John's ancestors, tells how "when the king came to the river Loire, he found no boats for crossing. Therefore, on the Wednesday before the Nativity of the Blessed Mary, coming to the Port Alaschert, and making the sign of the cross over the water with his hand, he, relying on Divine aid, forded the river with all his host ; which is a marvellous thing to tell, and such as was never heard of in our time." With fire and sword the host fought its way into Angers, and for a whole week the heir of Fulk the Red held his court in the home of his forefathers.[4] He then marched up to Le Lude, on the border of Maine. On September 20 he was at Angers again, but left it next day.[5] On the two following days he was at Coudray, a few miles south of Saumur ; there, probably, he and Almeric divided their forces, Almeric moving westward through his own land to attack Britanny,[6] while John seems to have gone southward again.[7] On

---

[1] *Itin.* a. 8.

[2] Rigord, c. 147 ; W. Armor. *Gesta P. A.* c. 138.

[3] August 30, *Itin.* a. 8.

[4] Cf. *Chron. S. Albini*, a. 1206 ; Rigord, c. 147 ; W. Armor. *Gesta P. A.* c. 138, and *Itin.* a. 8. This last shows John on September 6 at Chalonnes, and on the 8th at Angers. "Portus Alaschert," therefore, must stand for Chalonnes or some place very near it.

[5] *Itin.* a. 8. The *Chron. S. Albini*, a. 1206, says that before he left the city he set fire to "the bridge" ; which of the two bridges then existing, we are not told, nor what was his object in destroying it.

[6] W. Armor. *l.c.*

[7] The next stage of his Itinerary is "Saint Alemand" (September 23-26), and the next after that (September 30, October 1) a place whose name is recorded only in a contracted form ("Bercer'," *Rot. Pat.* vol. i. p. 167 b ; "Berc'," *Rot. Claus.* vol. i. p. 74 b) which can hardly represent anything else than "Berchères" or "Bercières" (Sir T. D. Hardy made it *Bercy*, but this is surely impossible). Saint Alemand is probably one of two places now called Saint-Amand, in the Angoumois. "Tiebauts de Biaumont qui sires estoit de *Bierchières* [var. *Bercières*]" figures among the Aquitanian barons who besieged

1206   October 3 he was at Thouars, where he stayed a week,[1] perhaps to await Almeric's return.

Meanwhile, however, Philip Augustus had assembled the host of France, and led it as far as the Poitevin border.[2] With Philip's personal appearance on the scene of action, John knew that his own successes were at an end. Neither Almeric of Thouars, nor the many barons in the English host who had taken the oath of allegiance to Philip, would fight against that monarch in person. While John went on to secure his retreat over sea by another visit to Niort and La Rochelle,[3] therefore, negotiations were set on foot; and when he came back to Thouars once more, on October 26, it was to proclaim a truce which had been made between himself and Philip, to last from October 13 for two years. By its terms each sovereign was to retain during that period the homage and services of all those who had attached themselves to him during the recent war; and any disputes which might arise about the allegiance of such persons were to be decided by the judgement of four barons named, two to represent each of the kings.[4] Trade, and intercourse of every kind, between the dominions of John and Philip was to be free, save that no man, unless he were either a priest or a " known merchant," might go to the court of either without special licence, if he were a subject of the other. Thirteen sureties swore to the truce on behalf of John, and thirteen on behalf of Philip, who further undertook that it should be kept by four other barons whose oaths John had wished to have on his side, but had apparently been unable to obtain.[5] Philip's sureties were headed by " the count of Britanny," a title which can only represent Constance's widower, Guy of Thouars, and thus shows that Arthur's death was now, at any rate, regarded

---

Savaric de Mauléon at Niort in 1205 ; *Hist. des Ducs de Normandie*, p. 102.   I have failed to identify the place, but it was clearly in Aquitaine.

[1] *Itin.* a. 8.

[2] Rigord, c. 147 ; W. Armor. *Gesta P. A.* c. 139.

[3] *Itin.* a. 8.

[4] Ralf (of Lusignan), count of Eu, and Hugh, viscount of Châtelheraut, for Philip ; Savaric de Mauléon and William of Chantemerle for John.

[5] William des Roches, Maurice of Craon, William of Guerches, and Geoffrey of Ancenis.   This promise seems to have been made by Philip in person.

as certain. The first of John's sureties was Guy's brother,   1206
Almeric, the viscount of Thouars, whose action had' for
several years past generally turned the scale between the
rival sovereigns in Poitou, and who by the terms of the
truce was pledged to his present allegiance for the next two
years at least. The other sureties on both sides were nearly
all of them barons of Aquitaine ;[1] those of the Angevin
counties seem for the most part to have stood aloof. It is
clear, however, that John had secured a firm hold on the
southern provinces, and to a considerable extent regained a
hold upon Poitou. On the whole, therefore, his expedition
had been successful. The best proof of its success lies in
Philip's readiness to accept such a truce, without making
any attempt to regain the ground which he had lost in
Poitou, though he was actually in the land with an army
at his back. As for John, he was going home to his island
realm to prepare for a fight of another kind, and with an
adversary of a character very different from that of Philip
Augustus.

[1] See the truce in Duchesne, *Hist. Norm Scriptt.* pp. 1061-2, and *Foedera*,
vol. i. pt. i. p. 95.

CHAPTER IV

KING JOHN

1206–1210

Sed processu temporis mollities illa in tantam crudelitatem versa est, ut nulli praedecessorum suorum coaequari valeret, ut in sequentibus patebit.—GERV. CANT. ii. 93.

1205   THE first business wherein John had an opportunity of exercising the free kingship which he had, as he said, acquired by the death of Hubert Walter, was the appointment of Hubert's successor. Immediately after Hubert's funeral the king spent six days at Canterbury.[1] He "talked much and graciously with the monks" of Christ Church about the choice of a new archbishop, and even hinted that one might be found in their own ranks. At the same time, however, he took possession of a valuable set of church plate bequeathed by Hubert to his cathedral;[2] and before leaving Canterbury he issued orders that the election of the primate hould be made on November 30 by the monks and the bishops of the province conjointly.[3] A party in the chapter at once resolved to vindicate its independence both against the bishops, whose claim to share in the choice of their metropolitan was always opposed by the monks, and against the king, whose prerogative of designating the candidate to be chosen was in theory regarded by monks and bishops alike as uncanonical, though in practice they had been

---

[1] July 15-20, 1205, *Itin.* a. 7.
[2] Gerv. Cant. vol. ii. p. 98. Cf. *Rot. Pat.* vol. i. p. 60, 60 b.
[3] Cf. Innoc. III. *Epp.* l. viii. No. 161, and Gerv. Cant. *l.c.*

compelled to submit to it at every vacancy for a hundred   1205
years past at the least. The younger and more hot-headed
members of the chapter privately elected their sub-prior
Reginald, enthroned him at dead of night, and hurried him
off to seek confirmation from the Pope, pledging him to
secrecy till the confirmation should be secured.[1] The older
and more prudent brethren evidently connived at these
proceedings without taking part in them. Their policy was
to consent to Reginald's election after the fact, if the Pope's
sanction of it could be obtained ; but if this were refused,
they could repudiate the election as a matter in which they
had had no share. The convent was, however, unlucky in
its choice of a champion. Reginald was no sooner across the
sea than he began to announce himself publicly as " the elect
of Canterbury," and even to show the credentials which he
had received from his brethren for the Pope. Of course
this news soon reached England, and caused a great com-
motion in high places there. The bishops, indignant at
being tricked out of their share in the election, despatched
an appeal to Rome. The monks sent a counter-appeal ;[2]
but to them the wrath of the king was far more terrible than
the wrath of the bishops, or even the possible wrath of the
Pope. Long before the appeals could be decided, they sent
to John a deputation charged with a communication containing no allusion whatever to Reginald, but simply
requesting that the convent might be permitted to choose
for itself a pastor. John received the deputies graciously
and assented to their request ; then, taking them aside,
he " pointed out to them that the bishop of Norwich "
(John de Grey) " was attached to him by a great intimacy,
and the only one among the prelates of England who
knew his private affairs," wherefore it would be greatly
for the advantage of king and kingdom if he became
archbishop—a consummation which the king begged the
deputies would do their utmost to secure. He sent
back with them some confidential clerks of his own to
assist them in this task, and dismissed them with a

[1] R. Wendover, vol. iii. p. 183. Cf. Gerv. Cant. vol. ii. p. 99.
[2] Innoc. III. *Epp.* l. viii. No. 161.

1205   promise of bestowing great honour on their convent if it were accommodating in this matter.   The result was an unanimous election of John de Grey by the chapter of Christ Church.[1]

On December 6 the king obtained from both bishops and monks a withdrawal of their respective appeals.[2]   On December 11 John de Grey was enthroned at Canterbury in the king's presence, and invested by him with the temporalities of the See ; and on the 18th the king despatched a messenger to ask for the papal confirmation of the new primate's appointment.[3]   The Pope, however, at the end

1206   of March 1206, decided that the election of John de Grey was uncanonical ; on the validity of Reginald's election he suspended his judgement, ordering the Canterbury chapter to send sixteen of their number to him by October 1, with full powers to act on behalf of all, and if necessary to hold a new election in his court.   The suffragans of the province were desired to send proctors, and the king was invited to do the like.[4]   The king sent three proctors ;[5] the bishops seem to have contented themselves with writing a joint letter, of whose contents we know nothing, except that they had the royal approval.[6]   Of the sixteen monks who went as representatives of the chapter, twelve, before they sailed, secretly exchanged a promise with the king. He pledged himself to ratify whatever they should do at Rome ; they pledged themselves to do nothing there except re-elect John de Grey.[7]   The assembly at Rome, originally appointed for October 1, was postponed till the last week of Advent (December 17 to 24).   Then, in full consistory, the Pope, after examination, set aside the claim of the bishops to a voice in the election, and declared the monks to be the sole rightful electors ; but he also set aside, as informal and void, their election of their subprior, Reginald ; and he bade them elect, then and there,

---

[1] R. Wendover, vol. iii. pp. 184, 185.
[2] *Rot. Pat.* vol. i. p. 56 b.
[3] R. Wendover, vol. iii. p. 185 ; *Rot. Pat. l.c.*
[4] Innoc. III. *Epp.* l. ix. Nos. 34, 35, 36.
[5] *Rot. Pat.* vol. i. pp. 65 b, 67.   [6] *Ib.* p. 64.
[7] M. Paris, *Hist. Angl.* vol. ii. p. 111 ; *Chron. Mai.* vol. ii. p. 514.   Cf. W. Coventry, vol. ii. pp. 197, 198.

"whomsoever they would, so he were but an earnest and capable man, and above all, an Englishman." All eyes must have turned instinctively upon the English-born Cardinal-priest of S. Chrysogonus, the most illustrious teacher of theology in his day, "than whom there was no man greater in the Roman court, nor was there any equal to him in character and learning"—Stephen Langton. Innocent was but speaking the thought of the whole assembly when he added that the monks could not do better than choose Stephen. The unlucky twelve were as willing to do so as the other four, but felt tied by their compact with the king. After some shuffling, they confessed their difficulty to the Pope. He scornfully absolved them from their shameful promise, and the sixteen monks unanimously elected Stephen Langton. The king's proctors, however, refused to ratify the election in John's name; so Innocent at once wrote to request a formal ratification of it from John himself.[1]

These things were done in the week following John's return from La Rochelle to England, which took place on December 12.[2] His recent experiences had shown him that the recovery of his lost territories was by no means impossible, but that it could not, under existing political and social conditions, be achieved by means of the only forces which the military organization of his own realm could supply. Those forces must be supplemented, if not superseded, in any attempt at the reconquest of the Norman and Angevin dominions, by the employment of mercenaries on a large scale, and by an elaborate system of diplomacy, the gradual knitting together of a complicated scheme of foreign alliances. For both these purposes the first need was money; and the difficulties with which the king had to contend in his efforts to raise money were as much greater in John's case than in that of any of his predecessors, as his need was greater than theirs had ever been.

---

[1] Cf. Innoc. III. *Epp.* l. ix. No. 206; R. Wendover, vol. iii. pp. 212, 213; M. Paris, *Hist. Angl.* vol. ii. pp. 111, 112; W. Coventry, vol. ii. p. 198; *Ann. Burton,* a. 1211.

[2] R. Wendover, vol. iii. p. 188; R. Coggeshall, p. 156.

The financial difficulties of the Crown had been accumulating ever since Richard's captivity.   At John's accession
the arrears of taxes were enormous.   At Michaelmas 1201
arrears of all the three "scutages of Normandy" imposed
under Richard—in 1194, 1195 and 1196—were due from
almost every shire ; hidage "for the king's ransom" was
still owing from Dorset and Somerset, and there were many
arrears even of the "scutage of Wales," which dated from
1190.[1]   Some of these debts ran on as late as 1207, and
some much later still.   The king's claim to these unpaid
taxes, as well as to all other debts owed to his predecessor,
was, of course, never withdrawn.   A grotesque instance of
the way in which the principle of inheritance might sometimes work in such matters occurs in the treasury roll of
1201, where two men in Devon are set down as owing a
fine "because they had been with Count John"[2]—that is,
because they had supported, in his rebellion against Richard
in 1193, the very man for whom, as king, the fine was
now claimed.   The Crown had, however, no direct means
of enforcing payment of either fines or taxes, at any rate
in the case of the barons.   Its one remedy was to seize
the lands or castles of an obstinate and wilful defaulter ;
and this remedy was fraught with danger to the crown
itself.   Neither law nor custom defined the circumstances
or fixed the limits of time within which a defaulter was
not, and beyond which he was, liable to be treated as
obstinate and wilful ; in every case where the king exercised
his right of seizure on this ground, therefore, the defaulter
and his friends could always find a plea for denouncing its
exercise as arbitrary and unjust.   It seems probable that
at the close of Richard's reign his ministers may have thus
seized the castles or lands of certain barons in pledge for
the arrears of their dues to the crown, and that this may
have been one of the grievances referred to in the demand
of the barons that Richard's successor "should restore to
each of them his rights."   John's demand for the castles of
some of the barons in 1201 was in all likelihood a pro-

[1] Chancellor's Roll, 3 John (1201), *passim.*   [2] *Ib.* p. 18.

ceeding of the same kind, based on the same ground, and, 1199-1207 as it seems, equally ineffectual in compelling payment; all that the king obtained was the surrender not indeed of the castles, but of some of the barons' sons as hostages. The deadlock was probably inevitable; but every year of its continuance aggravated both the financial difficulties of the government, and the unfriendliness of the relations between the barons and the king; and this latter evil was yet further aggravated by the measures which had necessarily to be taken in order to meet the former one. Plunged as he was from the very moment of his accession in a costly struggle with France, John had been forced to lay continually fresh burdens upon that very class among his subjects who already were, or considered themselves to be, overburdened by the demands of his predecessor. The "first scutage of King John" seems to have been assessed immediately after his coronation; it appears in the Pipe Roll made up at Michaelmas 1199. In the financial year ending at Michaelmas 1201, and in every one of the five following years, there was another new scutage;[1] and these scutages were independent of the fines paid by the barons who did not accompany the king on his first return to Normandy in 1199, of the money taken from the host as a substitute for its service in 1201, of the equipment and payment of the "decimated" knights in 1205, and the

---

[1] A summary of the scutages was drawn up, from the Pipe Rolls, by Alexander Swereford, in the time of Henry III., and is printed in the Rolls edition of the *Red Book of the Exchequer*. The marginal dates added in that edition are wrong throughout John's reign. The true dates are as follows:—

First scutage of John,	"in rotulo primo"	(1198-1199), 2 marks.
Second scutage,	"in rotulo tertio"	(1200-1201), 2 marks.
Third scutage,	"in rotulo quarto"	(1201-1202), 2 marks.
Fourth scutage,	"in rotulo quinto"	(1202-1203), 2 marks.
Fifth scutage,	"in rotulo sexto"	(1203-1204), 2 marks.
Sixth scutage,	"in rotulo septimo"	(1204-1205), 2 marks.
Seventh scutage,	"in rotulo octavo"	(1205-1206), 20 s.
Eighth scutage,	"in rotulo duodecimo"	(1209-1210), 2 marks.
Ninth scutage (for Wales),	"in rotulo decimo tertio"	(1210-1211), 2 marks.
Tenth scutage (for Scotland),	"in rotulo decimo tertio"	(1210-1211), 20 s.
Eleventh scutage,	"in rotulo decimo sexto"	(1213-1214), 3 marks.

Red Book of the Exchequer, vol. i. pp. 11, 12.

1200-1207 fines claimed from all the tenants-in-chivalry after the dismissal of the host in the same year, as well as of the actual services which many of those who had paid the scutage rendered in the campaigns of 1202-1204 and 1206.

The other taxes levied during these years were a carucage in 1200[1] and a seventh of moveables in 1204.[2] But all the while arrears went on accumulating, and year after year a budget had to be made up by devices of the most miscellaneous character. The accession of a new king could, of course, easily be made a pretext for selling confirmations of existing rights and privileges, and John availed himself of this pretext to the uttermost of his power at the earliest opportunity——that is, on his visit to England in 1201. During that time nobody in England seems to have felt secure of anything that he possessed till he had bought it of the king. Individuals of various ranks bought the sovereign's " peace " or his " goodwill " ;[3] the cities of Winchester and Southampton and the county of Hants each gave him money "that they might be lovingly treated" ;[4] Wiltshire gave him twenty pounds "that it might be well treated."[5] The citizens of York offended him by omitting to welcome him with a procession when he visited their city, and to provide quarters for his cross-bowmen ; he demanded hostages for their future good behaviour, but afterwards changed his demand to a fine of a hundred pounds.[6] The sale of offices went on as of old ;[7] while the sale of charters to towns, which under Richard was already becoming a remarkable item in the royal accounts, was a transaction of yet greater frequency and importance under his successor.[8] On the other hand, John's treasury rolls contain many notices of persons who owe the king money "which he has lent them." These loans from the king to his barons and other

---

[1] R. Coggeshall, p. 100. See above, p. 73.
[2] R. Wendover, vol. iii. p. 173. See above, p. 101.
[3] Chancellor's Roll, 3 John, *passim.*
[4] *Ib.* p. 249.   [5] *Ib.* p. 228.   [6] *Ib.* p. 300.
[7] *E.g.* in 1201 William de Stuteville gave £1000 to be sheriff of Yorkshire ; *ib.* p. 299.
[8] See the printed *Rotuli Cartarum.*

subjects were probably made chiefly in the hope of securing 1200-1207
the fidelity of the borrowers. In one way or another the
speculation must have been in most cases a paying one for
John. The privilege of claiming interest in hard cash for
a loan was indeed reserved exclusively for the Jews, and
not shared even by the king ; but he could take from his
debtors ample security on their lands or castles, or by
means of hostages who were usually their sons or
other young members of their families, and whom it was
of the greater importance for him to hold in his power
as his relations with the barons grew more strained year
by year.

In 1206 the tension had reached such a point that John
did not venture to impose a scutage of the full amount—
two marks on the knight's fee—which had been usual since
his father's time, but contented himself with twenty shillings.[1]
In 1207 he evidently dared not attempt to levy any fresh   1207
scutage at all. Nor was a carucage likely to prove either
less unpopular or more productive ; for the agricultural
interest of the country was in a state of extreme depression,
owing to a long succession of bad seasons ; while the taxation of moveables was an expedient which seems to have
found, as yet, but little favour with either the people or
the government. John now put forth a suggestion which
was, so far as we can see, a novelty in English finance.
He "held a council in London on January 8, and there
requested the bishops and abbots that they would allow
parsons and others holding ecclesiastical benefices to give to
the king a fixed sum from their revenues."[2] Neither in
equity nor in policy was the idea a bad one. While the
military tenants and the socage tenants had each their own
peculiar burden—scutage in the one case, carucage in the
other—the beneficed clergy, as such, had never yet been
subjected to taxation. The king might well argue that it
was time for them to take their turn in making a special
contribution to the financial needs of the State ; and the
argument was sure to meet with the approval of the laity.
The prelates, however, were unwilling ; and the question

[1] *Red Book*, vol. i. p. 11.   [2] *Ann. Waverley*, a. 1207.

1207 was adjourned to another council, in which "an infinite multitude" of ecclesiastical and temporal magnates came together at Oxford on February 9.

At this second meeting the bishops of both provinces gave it as their final answer that "the English Church could by no means submit to a demand which had never been heard of in all previous ages."[1] The only approach to a precedent for it, indeed, had occurred in 1194, when Archbishop Geoffrey of York, eager to collect money for Richard's ransom, had asked the canons of his cathedral chapter to give for that purpose a fourth part of their revenues for the year, with the result that they accused him of "wanting to overthrow the liberties of their church," and shut its doors in his face.[2] Between the council in London and that at Oxford, Geoffrey and John, who had been more or less at variance ever since the latter's accession, were formally reconciled;[3] John therefore probably counted upon Geoffrey's support of his scheme, and he may have hoped that the suffragans of Canterbury, having no metropolitan of their own to lead them, would not venture to stand out against the northern primate and the king with the barons, for once, at his back. But what Geoffrey had himself asked of his own chapter as a special favour to Richard in a wholly exceptional emergency, he had no mind to give leave for John to claim from all the beneficed clergy of his province as a matter of right, and under entirely different circumstances. The king was prudent enough not to press his demand; but it may be doubted whether the lay barons agreed with the Waverley annalist in deeming its withdrawal a proof that he "had taken wiser counsel," since he substituted for it a demand for a thirteenth of the moveable goods of every layman throughout the realm.[4] This

---

[1] *Ann. Waverley*, a. 1207. [2] R. Howden, vol. iii. pp. 222, 223.
[3] On January 25, at Worcester. *Rot. Pat.* vol. i. p. 58 b.
[4] *Ann. Waverl.* a. 1207. R. Wendover (iii. 210) represents the thirteenth as exacted from both laity and clergy; the Waverley Annals say merely "omnis homo de cujuscunque feodo." But the writ for the assessment, issued from Oxford on February 17, says "concessum est quod quilibet *laicus* homo totius Angliae, de cujusque feodo sit," etc. (*Rot. Pat.* vol. i. p. 72 b). This would, of course, include laymen holding lands of ecclesiastical superiors (cf. *Rot. Claus,* vol. i. p. 84 b). Geoffrey's protest must therefore be interpreted accordingly.

they had no excuse for refusing. "All mu[...]
man dared contradict,"[1] except Geoffrey of [...]
seems, claimed exemption for laymen holding [...]
Church, or at least of his cathedral church. [...]
however, was disregarded ; whereupon he excor[...]
all spoilers of the Church in general, and of the [...]ce of
York in particular, and then withdrew over sea,[2] to spend
the rest of his life in exile.

Thus for the next eight years the vast diocese of York
was practically without a chief pastor and the province
without a metropolitan, while the temporalities of the see
were in the hand of the king. As for Canterbury, John had
answered the Pope's request that he would ratify the election
of Stephen Langton by a flat refusal to accept as primate a
man of whom he declared that he " knew nothing, save that
he had dwelt much among his enemies " ;[3] and when on June
17 Stephen was consecrated by Innocent,[4] the king seized
the estates of the Canterbury chapter, drove the monks into
exile,[5] and proclaimed that any one who acknowledged
Stephen as archbishop should be accounted a public enemy.[6]
In August Innocent bade the bishops of London, Ely and
Worcester threaten the king, if he continued obstinate, with
an interdict upon his realm, and hinted that this might be
followed by a papal excommunication of John himself.[7]
Negotiations went on throughout the winter, but without
result,[8] and on Passion Sunday, March 23, or Monday, March
24, 1208, the interdict was proclaimed.[9]   It seems that   1208

John, it seems, had not yet abandoned all hope of getting something from the
beneficed clergy ; on May 26 he asked those of the southern province for
something very like a " benevolence." *Rot. Pat.* vol. i. p. 72.

[1] R. Wendover, vol. iii. p. 210.

[2] *Ib.* Cf. *Ann. Waverl.* a 1207.

[3] Innoc. III. *Epp.* l. x. No. 219 ; R. Wendover, vol. iii. pp. 215-217.

[4] R. Wendover, vol. iii. p. 213.

[5] W. Coventry, vol. ii. p. 199 ; R. Wendover, vol. iii. p. 214.   The writ for
seizure of the estates was issued July 11, *Rot. Pat.* vol. i. p. 74 ; and executed
July 15, Gerv. Cant. vol. ii. p. 100.

[6] W. Coventry, vol. ii. p. 199.

[7] Innoc. III. *Epp.* l. x. No. 113.

[8] *Ib.* Nos. 159, 160 ; *Rot. Pat.* vol. i. pp. 78, 80 ; R. Wendover, vol. iii.
pp. 220, 221.

[9] Gerv. Cant. vol. ii. p. 101, and the Annals of Waverley, Worcester,
Bermondsey and Tewkesbury, a. 1207, date the publication of the interdict March

notice of the intended date of its publication was given about a week before, and that the king at first answered this notice by ordering all the property of the clergy, secular or monastic, to be confiscated on Monday, March 24; but that he immediately afterwards decided to anticipate, instead of returning, the blow, and caused the confiscation to be begun at once.[1]   For him the opportunity was a golden one.   The interdict enabled him to put the whole body of the clergy in a dilemma from which there was no escape.   They held their property—thus he evidently argued—on condition of performing certain functions : if they ceased from those functions, their property was forfeit, just as that of a layman was forfeit if he withheld the service with which it was charged.   The logical consequence in either case—from John's point of view —was confiscation ; difficult and dangerous to enforce on a wide scale against laymen, but easy and safe when the victims were clergy.   The barons made no objection to a proceeding which would fill the king's coffers without drawing a single penny from their own ; the chief justiciar himself, Geoffrey Fitz-Peter, earl of Essex, had no scruple in acting as *custos* for the Crown of all the Church property on his own estates, which were scattered through thirty-one counties, and also of the revenues and goods of the Templars throughout all England.[2]   The spoliation was indeed effected with a brutal violence which would have been impossible had there been any strong feeling against it among the influential

---

24 ; the *Ann. Winton.* date it "Monday in Passion Week," *i.e.* March 24 also.   The Annals of Margan and of Dunstable make it Passion Sunday, *i.e.* March 23, which is the date given by R. Wendover (iii. 222), W. Coventry (ii. 199) and T. Wykes (a. 1207).   Roger of Wendover, however, adds that it was the Monday in Passion Week, so his dates are self-contradictory.

[1] R. Coggeshall, p. 163, says the general confiscation of clerical property took place on March 24 ; and the king's orders (issued March 17 and 18) for the seizure of the sees of Bath and Ely are to take effect from that day (*Rot. Pat.* vol. i. p. 80, 80 b), which looks as if the confiscation was meant to be an immediate retort to the interdict.   But the see of Norwich—though its bishop was the king's favourite John de Grey—was evidently seized before March 23 (*ib.* p. 81) ; while the sheriffs of Derbyshire and Warwickshire were already holding for the king "all the manors of the bishop of Chester within their bailiwicks, and everything in them, and all the lands and goods of abbots, priors, religious, and clerks, within their bailiwicks," as early as March 21, for on that day they were ordered to hand them over to another custodian.   *Rot. Claus.* vol. i. p. 107.

[2] *Rot. Claus.* vol. i. pp. 107, 110.

classes of the laity,[1] and which so far outran
of the king that on April 11 he issued a
ordering that any man caught doing or even s
to a monk or a clerk, "contrary to our peace,"
hanged upon the nearest oak.[2]   The clergy, like the
to be ill-treated by no one save the king himself.   Many of
them made a compromise with their spoiler; within a very
few weeks five bishops, three cathedral chapters, the prior
of the Hospitallers, and the heads of fourteen important
monasteries, besides sundry individual priests, undertook
to farm their own benefices and other property for the
king.[3]   The Cistercians, asserting that the privileges of their
order exempted them from interdict, ceased from performing
the offices of religion for a few days only, and then resumed
them as usual;[4] whereupon their possessions, which had
been seized like those of the other orders, were restored to
them on April 4.[5]

At the same time John despatched an envoy to Rome
proposing terms on which he professed himself willing to let
Stephen take possession of his see ; and he contrived to spin
out the negotiations for six months before Innocent discovered
that the terms offered were merely a device for wasting time,
and that the king had never intended to fulfil them.[6]   On

---

[1] R. Coggeshall, p. 163 ; R. Wendover, vol. iii. p. 223.   The *Ann. Margan.*,
a. 1207, give a curious and not very intelligible account of the state of public
feeling on the question between John and the Pope : "Electus est Magister S. de
Langetone ad archiepiscopatum Cantuariensem . . . Pro cujus electione, quia
facta fuit contra profanas illas consuetudines quas vocant avitas leges et regias
libertates, orta est statim discordia inter Papam Innocentium et Johannem tyrannum
Angliae, faventibus *ei*" (Stephen, Innocent, or John ?) "et consentientibus
omnibus laicis et clericis fere universis, sed et viris cujuslibet professionis multis."

[2] *Rot. Claus.* vol. i. p. 111.   [3] *Rot. Claus.* vol. i. pp. 108-13 b.

[4] R. Wendover, vol. iii. p. 226.   [5] *Rot. Claus.* vol. i. p. 108 b.

[6] John proposed, instead of himself giving Langton the regalia of the see, to
place them in the Pope's hands and let him confer them on the archbishop, inasmuch as John "could not yet bring himself to receive Stephen as a friend."
The Pope, though he did not like the scheme, yet authorized the bishops of
London, Ely and Worcester to receive the regalia as his representatives and to
confer them as the king desired ; but whenever the bishops sought an interview
with the king on the subject, he put them off.   At last, in September (1208), he
gave Langton himself a safe-conduct for a week's visit to England, but addressed
it to "S. de Langton, Cardinal," thus showing that he did not yet intend to
recognize him as archbishop.   Langton of course declined to come on such terms.
See Innoc. III. *Epp.* l. xi. Nos. 89, 90 ; *Rot. Pat.* vol. i. pp. 82, 85, 86 ; *Ann.
Waverl.* a. 1208.

209 January 12, 1209, the Pope informed the bishops of London, Ely and Worcester that he had written to John a letter of which he sent them a copy, and bade them excommunicate the king if he did not repent within three months after its receipt.[1] John upon this began a fresh series of negotiations, which kept the three bishops—who had apparently gone over sea immediately after publishing the interdict—flitting to and fro between the continent and England, without any result, for nine more months. In October they finally withdrew, but without publishing the excommunication; and by the end of the year all possibility of its publication in England had vanished, for every English bishop had fled save two, Peter des Roches, bishop of Winchester, and John de Grey, bishop of Norwich, both of whom were creatures of the king; John de Grey, moreover, was now justiciar in Ireland, and the Poitevin Peter des Roches was thus left sole representative of the episcopal order in England.[2]

It was John's hour of triumph, not over the clergy alone, but over all his subjects and vassals within the four seas of Britain. The action of the Pope and the inaction of the barons had opened a way for him to make himself " King of England " in his own sense of the words. To all outward seeming his whole time, since his return from the continent, had been devoted to mere amusement and self-indulgence. He " haunted woods and streams, and greatly did he delight in the pleasure of them." [3] When he was not thus chasing

---

[1] Innoc. III. *Epp.* l. xi. No. 211.

[2] *Rot. Pat.* vol. i. pp. 89, 90; R. Wendover, vol. iii. pp. 222, 228, 229; Gerv. Cant. vol. ii. pp. 100, 103, 104; *Ann. Waverl.* and *Dunst.* a. 1208. All the chroniclers have confused the dates, which have to be rectified by the help of the Pope's letters, the Patent and Close Rolls (both of which, however, unluckily fail in 1209), and Bishop Stubbs's notes to Gerv. Cant. vol. ii. pp. 103, 104, appendix to preface, *ib.* pp. xci-cviii, and W. Coventry, vol. ii. preface, pp. lv, lvi. The sees of Chichester, Exeter, Lincoln and Durham were vacant; before June 21, 1209, Hugh of Wells was elected to Lincoln by desire of the king, who sent him to Normandy to be consecrated by the archbishop of Rouen, but he went to the archbishop of Canterbury instead, and was consecrated by him on December 20 (R. Wendover, vol. iii. p. 231; date from M. Paris, *Hist. Angl.* vol. ii. p. 120, note 4). Carlisle had been administered since 1203 by Bernard, the exiled archbishop of Ragusa. Coventry (or Chester) was vacated in October 1208 by the death of Geoffrey Muschamp, who is mentioned by Gervase among the bishops who went over sea.   [3] *Hist. des Ducs de Normandie*, p. 109.

the beasts of the forest, his yet more relentless pursuit of
other prey was making havoc of the domestic peace, and
rousing against him the deadly hatred, of some of the greatest
of his barons.[1]   But their hatred was futile ; they were para-
lyzed partly by their own mutual jealousies, which the king
was continually stirring up,[2] partly by the consequence of
their selfish shortsightedness with regard to his persecution
of the clergy.   The interdict had placed one whole estate of
the realm at John's mercy ; and the laity, having failed at
the critical moment to make common cause with their
clerical brethren, now found themselves in their turn without
a support against his tyranny.   His consciousness of power
broke out in the strangest freaks of wantonness ; in causing
the Michaelmas session of the Exchequer to be held at
Northampton instead of London, " out of hatred to the
Londoners " ;[3] in forbidding the capture of birds all over
England ;[4] in ordering that throughout the Forest districts
the hedges should be fired and the ditches made by
the people to protect their fields should be levelled, " so
that, while men starved, the beasts might fatten upon
the crops and fruits."[5]   It showed itself too in acts of graver
political significance.   A series of orders to the bailiffs of
the coast towns for the equipment and mustering of their
ships and the seizure of foreign vessels, issued in the spring
and summer of 1208, indicates that John was then either
meditating another expedition over sea, or, more probably,
expecting an attack from thence.   The muster, originally
fixed for Trinity Sunday, was postponed to S. Matthew's
day,[6] and the end of the matter was that John, finding he

[1] The two best known instances indeed are of doubtful authenticity ; see Note
II. at end.   But the general charge against John rests upon authorities which
there is no reason to question ; *Hist. des Ducs*, pp. 105, 200, and R. Wendover,
vol. iii. p. 240.   The list of John's children given by Pauli, *Gesch. von
England*, vol. iii. p. 475, is neither correct nor complete.

[2] *Hist. des Ducs*, p. 105.

[3] M. Paris records this twice, in 1208 (*Chron. Maj.* vol. ii. p. 524) and
1209 (*Hist. Angl.* vol. ii. p. 118).   One of the two dates is probably wrong, but
there is no means of deciding which.

[4] Christmas 1208, R. Wendover, vol. iii. p. 225.

[5] June 28, 1209; *ib.* p. 227 ; M. Paris, *Hist. Angl.* vol. ii. p. 119.   Cf.
Hist. des Ducs, p. 109.

[6] *Rot. Pat.* vol. i. pp. 80, 81 b, 83 b-86.

1208　had no immediate need for the services of the fleet, "took occasion"—no doubt on pretext of some deficiency in the contingent due from them—"to oppress the mariners of the Cinque Ports with great and heavy affliction. Some he hanged ; some he killed with the sword ; many were imprisoned and loaded with irons " ; the rest fled into exile, and it was only by giving him fines and hostages that they appeased his wrath and bought his leave to return to their homes.[1] The barons were again required to renew their homage ; the demand was made literally at the sword's point —for John's lavish hospitality and largesse [2] filled his court with mercenaries who were quite ready to enforce his will in such a matter—and they were compelled either to submit to it, or to give their sons and kinsmen as hostages for their

1209　fidelity.[3] The king seemed indeed, as Matthew Paris says, to be courting the hatred of every class of his subjects.[4] But hate him as much as they might, they feared him yet more than they hated him ; and " burdensome " as he was " to both rich and poor," [5] when he summoned all the free tenants throughout the realm, of whatever condition, who were above the age of twelve years, to swear fealty in person to him and his infant heir in the autumn of 1209, rich and poor alike durst not do otherwise than obey him.[6]

　　This ceremony took place at Marlborough in September,[7] just before the final rupture of the negotiations with Langton and the bishops. A few weeks earlier John had received the submission of the king of Scots. Twice or thrice in the last two years a visit of William the Lion to the English court had been projected.[8] It took place at length in the middle of April 1209 at Bolton, whence John and William proceeded together to Norham for a confer-

---

[1] Cf. Gerv. Cant. vol. ii. p. 102, and *Ann. Dunst.* a. 1208.

[2] *Hist. des Ducs*, p. 105.

[3] R. Wendover, vol. iii. p. 224.

[4] M. Paris, *Hist. Angl.* vol. ii. p. 118.

[5] R. Wendover, vol. iii. p. 227.

[6] Cf. *ib.*, Gerv. Cant. vol. ii. p. 104 (who makes the age fifteen years), and W. Coventry, vol. ii. p. 200.

[7] Gerv. Cant. *l.c.* The day must have been either the 13th or the 30th, *Itin.* a. 11.

[8] *Rot. Claus.* vol. i. p. 90 (Aug. 1207) ; *Rot. Pat.* vol. i. p. 76 (Oct. 1207) ; *ib.* p. 91 (April 1209).

ence.[1] The shelter given in Scotland to some of the bishops
and other persons who fled from John's persecution in con-
nection with the interdict [2] supplied the English king with
a pretext for demanding, once for all, security for William's
loyalty. He bade him surrender either three castles on
the border or his only son as a hostage. William refused
to do either.[3] John, on returning to the south, summoned
his host, and in July set out to take the three castles by
force. The papal excommunication was hanging over his
head, and its publication was hourly expected ; his troops
shrank alike from his leadership and from an encounter with
the Scot king, who was considered "eminent for his piety,"
the champion of the Church and the favourite of Heaven,
while they, being under interdict, were virtually outcasts
from the Christian fold. A dexterous renewal of negotiations with Innocent and Stephen, however, staved off the
excommunication and prevented the threatened desertion
of the English troops ; [4] and on August 4 John was at
Norham [5] at the head of a great host ready to do battle
with the Scots. On hearing this, William "greatly feared
his attack, knowing him to be given to every kind of
cruelty ; so he came to meet him and offered to treat for
peace ; but the king of the English flew into a rage and
insulted him bitterly, reproaching him with having received
his (John's) fugitives and public enemies into his realm, and
lent them countenance and help against him." At last
some "friends of both realms" arranged terms which pacified
John and which William dared not refuse. He sent his
son, not indeed as a hostage, but to do homage to the
English king "for the aforesaid castles and other lands
which he held " ; [6] he undertook to pay John by instalments
within the next two years fifteen thousand marks "to have

---

[1] *Chron. Mailros*, a. 1209.

[2] The *Ann. Dunst.*, a. 1208, say the bishops of Salisbury and Rochester
went to Scotland "cum Regis Angliae gratia"; but cf. Gerv. Cant. vol. ii. p.
100, and R. Wendover, vol. iii. p. 226. Langton's father had taken refuge at
St. Andrews in 1207. Gerv. Cant. vol. ii., appendix to preface, pp. lxii, lxiii.

[3] Gerv. Cant. vol. ii. p. 102.

[4] *Ib.* pp. 102-3. Cf. appendix to preface, *ib.* pp. c-ciii.

[5] *Itin.* a. 11.

[6] Gerv. Cant. vol. ii. p. 103.

1209   his goodwill"; he gave hostages for the fulfilment of this
undertaking; and he surrendered his two daughters to be
kept in John's custody as his wards and married at his
pleasure.[1] According to Gervase of Canterbury, one of
these ladies was to be married to John's son;[2] one of his
many illegitimate sons must be meant, for though John had
now two sons by his queen, the elder of them was not yet
two years old, while the younger of William's daughters was
thirteen at the least.[3] All that William obtained in return
for these concessions was the freedom of the port of Berwick, and leave to pull down a castle which the bishop of
Durham had built over against it.[4] Of his claim upon
Cumberland and Westmorland nothing further was ever
heard.

Two months later, Wales followed Scotland's example.
Over Wales, indeed, John's triumph was won without the
trouble even of a military demonstration on his part. The
anarchy of Wales had been growing worse and worse ever
since the death of Henry II. Its danger for England lay
mainly in the opportunities which it afforded to any of the
English barons of the border who might be treasonably
inclined, for making alliances with one or other of the
warring Welsh princes, and thus securing for themselves a
support which might enable them to set at defiance the
authority of the English crown. John himself had held the
position of a border baron for ten years, as earl of Gloucester and lord of Glamorgan, and had used it for his own
private ends as unscrupulously as any of his neighbours.[5]

---

[1] *Foedera*, vol. i. pt. i. p. 103. The Scottish authorities, *Chron. Mailros*
and *Chron. Lanercost*, a. 1209, make the sum thirteen thousand pounds. R.
Wendover, vol. iii. p. 227, says twelve thousand marks, and M. Paris, *Chron.
Maj.* vol. ii. p. 525, eleven thousand marks; the document in *Foedera* is the
best authority, although its original is lost and it is obviously not altogether an
accurate copy, its date, "*Northampton*, 7th August," being of course a tran-
scriber's mistake for "Norham."

[2] Gerv. Cant. vol. ii. p. 103.

[3] The first child of John and Isabel of Angoulême—the future Henry III.—
was born October 1, 1207; R. Wendover, vol. iii. p. 219. The second,
Richard, was born January 6, 1209; *Ann. Winton. ad ann.* Both the Scot
king's daughters were born before the end of 1195, when one of them was
betrothed to Otto of Saxony, R. Howden, vol. iii. pp. 299, 308.

[4] *Chron. Mailros* and *Chron. Lanercost*, a. 1209.

[5] See above, pp. 26, 32, 45.

The familiarity with Welsh politics which he had thus
acquired stood him in good stead when he became king.
At his accession, a struggle which had been going on for
two years between three rival claimants to the succession in
South Wales, Griffith and Maelgwyn, sons of the late prince
Rees ap Griffith, and Gwenwynwyn, son of Owen Cyveiliog,
prince of Powys, had just ended in the triumph of Griffith,
who, by the help of a force supplied to him by the English
government, overcame both his rivals at the close of 1198.
On Griffith's death in 1200 Gwenwynwyn for a moment
regained the ascendency in South Wales; but he found a
new and formidable rival in the prince of North Wales,
Llywelyn ap Jorwerth, who in a few years succeeded in
reducing most of the South Welsh princes to dependence
on himself.[1] Throughout these years John, amid all his
political and military occupations on the continent, watched
every vicissitude of the struggle in Wales, kept up constant
relations with both parties, and balanced the one against
the other [2] with a mingled unscrupulousness and dexterity
for which even the Welshmen were scarcely a match, and
which at last brought them all alike to his feet. In July
1202 Llywelyn promised to do homage to the English king
as soon as the latter should return from over sea ;[3] before
October 15, 1204, he was betrothed to John's illegitimate
daughter Joan,[4] and in 1206 she became his wife.[5] In
1208 his rival Gwenwynwyn was in an English prison,
whence he obtained his release by doing homage to John at
Shrewsbury on October 8.[6] Llywelyn's promised visit to
the English court seems to have not yet taken place ; but a
year later, on the king's return from the north, there befell,
say the chroniclers, " what had never been heard of in times
past : all the Welsh nobles "—that is, evidently, the princes
of both North and South Wales—" came to him and did

---

[1] *Ann. Cambriae* and *Brut y Tywysogion*, a. 1197-1209.

[2] *Rot. Chart.* vol. i. pp. 23, 44, 63, 100 b, 103, 103 b, 104; *Rot. Pat.*
vol. i. pp. 39, 40, 44 b, 51 b, 88, 89 b, 91 ; *Rot. Claus.* vol. i. pp. 23 b, 24.
Brut, a. 1207, 1209.

[3] *Rot. Pat.* vol. i. p. 8 b.

[4] *Rot. Claus.* vol. i. p. 12.

[5] *Ann. Wigorn.* a. 1206.

[6] *Foedera*, vol. i. pt. i. p. 101.

him homage," not on the border, but in the heart of his own realm, at Woodstock,[1] on October 18 or 19, 1209.[2]

The king's triumph was complete. The last date which had been fixed for the publication of the papal sentence was October 6 ;[3] the sentence was still unpublished, and the bishops who should have published it had fled. They proclaimed it indeed in France in November ;[4] but John took care that no official notification of the fact should reach England, and the sentence remained a dead letter. Its existence was known and talked of all over the country, but it was talked of with bated breath. The excommunicate king held his Christmas feast at Windsor surrounded by " all the great men of England," who sat at his table and held intercourse with him as usual, simply because they dared not do otherwise.[5] Of the fate in store for those who stood aloof, one terrible example sufficed. The archdeacon of Norwich quitted his place at the Exchequer table at Westminster, after warning his fellow - officers that they were perilling their souls by serving an excommunicate king. He was seized by a band of soldiers, loaded with chains, flung into prison, and there crushed to death beneath a cope of lead.[6] The whole body of the clergy, already stripped of their possessions, were now in peril of their lives. As the king was passing through one of the border counties he met some of the sheriff's officers in charge of a prisoner with his hands tied behind him. They said the man was a robber, and had robbed and slain a priest on the highway : what, they asked, should be done with him ? " Loose him and let him go," answered John, " he has slain one of my enemies ! " Nor was his persecution limited to the clergy ; the lay relatives and friends of Langton and of the other exiled bishops were hunted down and flung into prison, and their property

---

[1] R. Wendover, vol. iii. p. 227 ; M. Paris, *Hist. Angl.* vol. ii. p. 119. The event was not really so unprecedented as these writers imagined ; the princes of both North and South Wales had done homage to Henry II. at Oxford in 1177. The chroniclers' expressions about this Welsh homage to John, however, show the impression which it made and the importance which was attached to it.   [2] *Itin.* a. 11.

[3] Gerv. Cant. vol. ii. appendix to preface, p. cvi.

[4] *Ann. Dunst.* a. 1209.

[5] R. Wendover, vol. iii. p. 231.   [6] *Ib.* p. 229.

seized for the king.[1]   When he could plunder his Christian
subjects no more, he turned upon the Jews.   At the opening
of 1210 all the Jews in England, of both sexes, were by his
order arrested, imprisoned, and tortured to make them give
up their wealth.   It was said that the king wrung ten
thousand marks from one Jew at Bristol by causing seven of
his teeth to be torn out, one every day for a week,[2] and that
the total sum transferred from the coffers of the Jews to
the royal treasury amounted to sixty-six thousand marks.[3]
Never before—not even in the worst days of William the
Red—had England fallen so low as she now lay at the feet
of John.   "It was as if he alone were mighty upon earth,
and he neither feared God nor regarded man."[4]   John seems
in fact to have been one of the very few men of whom this
latter assertion can be made with literal truth ; and in this
utter recklessness and ruthlessness lay the secret of his
terrible strength.   "There was not a man in the land who
could resist his will in anything."[5]   The very few barons who
had dared openly to resist it since his return from Poitou in
1206 were now all in Ireland ; and it was Ireland that he
set himself to subdue in 1210.

John de Courcy had apparently ceased to be governor
of the Irish March in 1191.   The succession of governors
there during the next few years is obscure ; but we know
that, as John's chief ministers, they bore the same title which
was borne by the chief minister of the king in England, that
of justiciar.[6]   Owing to the paucity and obscurity of the
records it is difficult to gain any real understanding of
the vicissitudes of the English dominion in Ireland during
the twenty-five years which elapsed between John's two
visits to that country, and especially during the fourteen

---

[1] R. Wendover, vol. ii. pp. 223, 224.   [2] *Ib.* p. 232.
[3] *Ann. Waverl.* a. 1210.
[4] Gerv. Cant. vol. ii. p. 100.   [5] *Ib.*
[6] Ware, *Antiq.* p. 102, makes William Petit and William the Marshal
justiciars in 1191 ; but no authority is given.   R. Diceto, vol. ii. p. 99, says
that Roger de Planes was "in tota terra comitis [Johannis] justiciarius" when
he was slain in October 1191 ; see above, p. 29.   Peter Pippard was justiciar in
Ireland in 1194, according to Henry of Marlborough as quoted in Butler's *History
of Trim Castle*, p. 3 ; and Hamo de Valognes held the office c. 1196-1197 ; cf.
Gir. Cambr. vol. v. p. 342, and Ware, *l.c.*

1191-1200 years between his first visit there and his accession to the English crown. He granted a new and important charter to the city of Dublin in 1192.[1] In 1195 the intruders— neither for the first nor for the last time—fell out among themselves: "John de Courcy and the son of Hugh de Lacy marched with an army to conquer the English of Leinster and Munster."[2] They certainly did not succeed in wresting Leinster from William the Marshal. As for Munster, Richard de Cogan was apparently still holding his ground in Desmond; Raymond the Fat probably died in 1184 or 1185,[3] and as he had no direct heirs,[4] the share of that kingdom which had been originally allotted to Fitz-Stephen lapsed to John as overlord.[5] From the city of Cork the "English" are said to have been driven out in 1196;[6] but their expulsion was only momentary. Meanwhile they had at last begun to gain a footing in Thomond. By 1196 they had got possession of the city of Limerick; in that year or the next they lost it, but it was speedily recovered by Meiler Fitz-Henry,[7] who in 1199 or early in 1200 became chief justiciar in Ireland.[8] Limerick was put under the charge of William de Burgh, who apparently had won for himself some lands within the kingdom of Thomond, among them Ardpatrick, of which he received a grant from John in September 1199.[9]

[1] *Foedera*, vol. i. pt. i. p. 55; Gilbert, *Hist. Documents of Ireland*, pp. 51-55. Other Irish Charters of John before his accession to the crown—all dateless—are in *Rot. Canc. Hibern. Cal.* vol. i. pt. i. pp. 2, 4, 5, and *Hist. MSS. Comm.* 4th Report, pp. 574, 581.

[2] Four Masters, a. 1195.

[3] He certainly was not killed in 1182 as the Four Masters say; but he disappears after 1183. See *Dic. Nat. Biogr.* "Fitz-Gerald (Raymond)."

[4] Gir. Cambr. vol. v. pp. 345, 409.

[5] In 1207 John confirmed to William de Barri a sub-enfeoffment made by Fitz-Stephen to Philip de Barri, William's father and Fitz-Stephen's nephew. *Rot. Chart.* p. 172.

[6] Four Masters, a. 1196, note.

[7] Cf. Gir. Cambr. vol. v. p. 342, and Four Masters, a. 1196.

[8] *Rot. Chart.* p. 98.

[9] *Ib.* p. 19 b. John made at the same time several other grants of land within the honour, or kingdom, of Limerick, *ib.* All these grants, however, except the grant to William de Burgh, seem to have been cancelled by the later one to William de Braose; see below, p. 139. Half a cantred of land at "Tilra'ct in Kelsela" had been granted by John to De Burgh before King Henry's death, *Hist. MSS. Comm.*, 3rd Report, p. 231.

The last Irish Ard-Righ, Roderic O'Conor, died in 1198-1202
1198 ;[1] he had been dethroned sixteen years before, but
his death was the signal for renewed strife between his sons
for the possession of his kingdom of Connaught. The
foreign settlers in Ireland took sides for their own interest
in the struggle between the native princes ; John de Courcy
and the "English of Ulidia," with the De Lacys of Meath
and their followers, supported Cathal Crovderg O'Conor,
while his rival, Cathal Carrach, was helped by "William
Burke, with the English of Limerick." For a moment
Cathal Carrach's party was victorious ; but next year (1200)
he was attacked by "Meiler and the English of Leinster,"
while De Burgh changed sides and joined Cathal Crovderg.
In 1201 or 1202 the united forces of Cathal Crovderg and
De Burgh won a battle in which Cathal Carrach was slain.
Cathal Crovderg being thus master of Connaught, De Burgh
at once began to plot against his life ; but the men of Connaught slaughtered the followers of the double-dyed traitor,
and he himself escaped as best he could back to Limerick.[2]

The "honour of Limerick"—exclusive of the city and
the Ostmen's cantred, which the king retained in his own
hands, and the service due from the lands held within that
honour by William de Burgh, which was also reserved to
the Crown — had meanwhile been granted by John, on
January 12, 1201, to William de Braose, "as King Henry gave
it to his uncle, Philip de Braose."[3] These last words define
the extent of the "honour," as corresponding (with the excep-
tions specified) to the "kingdom of Limerick" (Thomond)
named in Henry's grant of 1177. Philip de Braose was
probably now dead. William was the son of Philip's elder
brother, another William who to the family estates of
Bramber in Sussex and Barnstaple and Totnes in Devon
had added, by his marriage with an heiress, the lordships of
Radnor, Brecon, and Abergavenny in Wales.[4] The younger

---

[1] Four Masters, a. 1198.
[2] Four Masters and *Ann. Loch Cé*, a. 1199-1202.
[3] *Rot. Chart.* p. 84 b.
[4] Dugdale, *Baronage*, pt. i. p. 414 ; who, however, has confused father and
son. See *Genealogist*, vol. iv. pp. 133-141, and *Dic. Nat. Biog.* "Braose,
William de."

1179-1201 William probably succeeded to all these possessions soon after 1179.[1] Before 1189 his sister Maud was married to Griffith Ap Rees, who from 1198 to 1201 was Prince of South Wales; and throughout the last ten years of the twelfth century William was constantly concerned in the quarrels of the South Welsh princes and people.[2] His daughter Margaret had before November 19, 1200 become the wife of Walter de Lacy,[3] the lord of Meath, who was already her father's neighbour on the Welsh border, where Ludlow formed part of the Lacy heritage; a younger daughter was married before 1210 to a son of another baron of the Welsh March, Roger Mortimer.[4] Count John of Mortain, as earl of Gloucester and lord of Glamorgan, was also for ten years a neighbour of William de Braose, and evidently made a friend of him, for in 1199 William was at the head of the party which most vigorously urged John's claim to the crown.[5] In June 1200 he received a royal grant of "all the lands which he had acquired or might at any future time acquire from our Welsh enemies, to the increase of his barony of Radnor."[6] As the king was at the same time in diplomatic relations with several of the "enemies" whom William was thus authorized to despoil, this grant was of doubtful value. The same may be said of the grant of Thomond; this, however, was a speculation on both sides; William covenanted to pay the king five thousand marks for it at the rate of five hundred marks a year.[7]

De Braose immediately went to Ireland;[8] and in process of time he succeeded in obtaining possession of the greater part of his new fief, though the difficulties with which he had to contend were many and great. The other persons who had previously received from John grants of land in

---

[1] His father was living in that year; *Monasticon*, vol. vi. pt. i. p. 457.

[2] *Ann. Camb.* a. 1189, 1192, 1195, 1196; *Brut y Tywysogion*, a. 1196, 1197. Maud died in 1209, *Brut, ad ann.*

[3] *Rot. Chart.* p. 80. Walter was the eldest son of Hugh de Lacy who was killed in 1186.

[4] *Foedera*, vol. i. pt. i. p. 107.

[5] *Ann. Margan.* a. 1199.   [6] *Rot. Chart.* p. 66 b.

[7] *Rot. Oblat.* p. 99, "ad quodlibet scaccarium quingentas marcas argenti."

[8] *Rot. Chart.* p. 100 b.

Thomond[1] no doubt resented and resisted the change in 1201-1204
their position from tenants-in-chief of the king to under-
tenants of William de Braose. It seems that they were
upheld in their resistance by the justiciar, Meiler Fitz-Henry,
and that John in consequence summoned Meiler to his
court, suspended him from his office, and put it into commission in December 1201. In August 1202 John issued
further orders for enforcing the claims of De Braose in
Thomond; in September he forgave him all the debts
which he owed to King Henry and King Richard; in
October he granted the entire custody of the lands and
castles of Glamorgan, Gwenllwg and Gower to " William de
Braose, whose service we greatly approve." [2] In the winter
William was with the king in Normandy, and had the
custody of the captive Arthur. This he resigned, seemingly
at the end of the year,[3] and in January 1203 he was in
charge of some matters connected with the fleet.[4]

Meanwhile the governor of Limerick city, William de
Burgh, had escaped from the vengeance of the Irish allies
whom he had betrayed, only to fall under that of the
English justiciar whom he had set at defiance. Meiler
Fitz-Henry had been restored to his post; in 1203 he and
Walter de Lacy joined with the Irish of Connaught in
expelling De Burgh from Limerick,[5] and on July 8
William de Braose was appointed by the king to succeed
De Burgh as constable of the city.[6] Meiler and De Burgh
had already appealed against each other to the king;[7] in
March 1204 a commission was appointed to hear their
reciprocal complaints;[8] in September all De Burgh's Irish
estates except those in Connaught were restored to him on

[1] Carte's *Life of Ormonde*, ed. 1851, vol. i. pp. xliv, xlv; *Rot. Chart.* pp. 19 b, 28.
[2] *Rot. Pat.* vol. i. pp. 4, 7, 16 b, 18 b, 19 b.
[3] W. Armor. *Philipp.* l. vi. vv. 478-492. The poet asserts that William resigned his charge because he suspected John's intentions towards his prisoner. This would be shortly before the attempt to blind Arthur, who was then in the custody of Hubert de Burgh.
[4] *Rot. Pat.* vol. i. p. 24 b.   [5] *Ann. Loch Cé*, a. 1203.
[6] *Rot. Chart.* p. 107 b.   [7] *Rot. Pat.* vol. i. p. 31 b.
[8] *Ib.* p. 39 b. On 29th April the commissioners are informed that De Burgh is respited, and Meiler is bidden to give him seisin of his lands again; *ib.* p. 41 b.

1204-1206 his promise of "standing to right in the King's Court of Ireland."[1]   There is no record of the trial, which may have been prevented by his death, for at the end of the year or in 1205 he died;[2] and on April 3, 1206 the justiciar was ordered to take all his Munster estates into the king's hand.[3]

The reservation of De Burgh's Connaught lands in 1204 may have been made in consequence of some negotiations which were at that moment going on between Meiler, as John's representative, and the King of Connaught, Cathal Crovderg.   Cathal, it seems, offered to cede two-thirds of Connaught to John, on condition that the remaining third should be secured to himself and his heirs for a yearly payment of one hundred marks.   John was willing to accept this offer, but he insisted that the portion of land to be ceded to him should be chosen by Meiler, and bade Meiler take care that it was "the best part, and that which contained the best towns, ports, and sites for castles."[4] Possibly this claim of John's to choose the land for himself was refused by Cathal; the negotiations certainly came to nothing, for in December 1206 Cathal made another proposition.   He would hold one-third of Connaught of King John for a hundred marks a year; out of the other two-thirds he would cede to John two cantreds, and for the remainder he would pay him a tribute of three hundred marks.   John authorized Meiler to accept these terms, if he could get no better.[5]   Whether the agreement was ever actually made, there is nothing to show; it was not likely to have any practical result.   The invaders had evidently already gained some slight and precarious footing in eastern Connaught; but they had too much to do within their own March—as the dominions of the English crown in Ireland were called in those days[6]—to make any real progress westward for some years to come.

---

[1] *Rot. Pat.* vol. i. p. 46.

[2] *Ann. Loch Cé* a. 1205 ; Four Masters, a. 1204.

[3] *Rot. Pat.* p. 60 b.   They seem to have been restored to his son Richard before July 11, 1214 ; *ib.* pp. 118 b, 119.

[4] *Foedera*, vol. i. pt. i. p. 91.   Cf. *Rot. Claus.* vol. i. p. 6 b.

[5] *Rot. Claus.* vol. i. p. 62.

[6] *Rot. Chart.* p. 68 b (a. 1200) ; *Rot. Claus.* vol. i. p. 40 (a. 1205).   I am indebted to Mr. G. H. Orpen for the information that the districts held by the

The turbulence and lawlessness which prevailed in the 1199-1205 Irish March reflected that of the Welsh March whence most of its original settlers had come. William de Braose and William de Burgh were far from being the only barons at feud with Meiler Fitz-Henry, either simply as a fellow-baron, or in his official capacity of representative of the king. In September 1199 John de Courcy and Walter de Lacy are mentioned in a royal writ as having acted together " for the destruction of our realm of Ireland." [1] The reference probably is to their joint attack upon Leinster in 1195, which had been followed by the forfeiture of Lacy's English and Welsh lands ; these, however, he had regained in 1198.[2] In 1203, as has been seen, he helped Meiler to expel William de Burgh from Limerick ; and in February 1204 he was appointed one of four commissioners to assist Meiler in dealing with escheats.[3] His former ally, John de Courcy, had a safe-conduct to and from the king's court in July 1202 ;[4] but he evidently did not come to terms with the king ; and next year the Lacys turned against him ; Hugh de Lacy, Walter's younger brother, defeated him in a battle near Down and drove him out of Ulidia.[5] In September he had another safe-conduct to go to the king and return " if he does not make peace with us." [6] This time it seems that he did " make peace," but failed to fulfil its conditions. On August 31, 1204, he was summoned, on pain of forfeiture, to come to the king's service " as he swore to come " ; and Meiler was instructed, if the forfeiture should take place, to give to the two De Lacys the eight cantreds of De Courcy's land which lay nearest to Meath.[7] De Courcy incurred the forfeiture ; Meiler seemingly committed its execution to the De Lacys ; they again attacked De Courcy, and drove him to take refuge in Tyrone ;[8] and on May 2, 1205, King

English crown in Ireland were not known as " the Pale " till after Poynings's Act (1494), when the colonists were ordered to maintain a ditch " six feet high on the side which neared next to the Irishmen " (Joyce, *Hist. of Ireland*, p. 351).

[1] *Rot. Oblat.* p. 74.
[2] Eyton, *Hist. of Shropshire*, vol. v. pp. 257, 258.
[3] *Rot. Chart.* p. 133 b.
[4] *Rot. Pat.* p. 15.   [5] Four Masters, a. 1203.
[6] *Rot. Pat.* p. 34 b.   [7] *Ib.* pp. 45, 45 b.
[8] Four Masters, a. 1204.

1205　John granted Ulster to Hugh de Lacy, to hold "as John de Courcy held it on the day when Hugh defeated him."[1] A few weeks later Hugh was belted earl of Ulster;[2] and at the end of June the triumph of the Lacys was completed by a royal order forbidding the chief justiciar to "move war against any man of the March" without the consent of Earl Hugh and his brother Walter.[3]

　　With the colleagues thus forced upon him Meiler was soon at strife. His strife with Walter de Lacy, indeed, had recommenced already. Walter's appointment as a com-
1204　missioner of escheats in 1204 had been made in connexion with a demand which John—anxious to prepare for an attack upon France, as well as to guard against an expected French invasion of England, and scarcely daring to ask his English subjects for more money — addressed to all his vassals in Ireland, that they would furnish him with an aid.[4] They undertook to do so; on September 1 the king thanked them for their services and their promises, and desired that the latter might be fulfilled.[5] At the same time he was taking measures for the security of the March and of his own authority there; on August 31 he had ordered Meiler to build a castle at Dublin,[6] and in September he bade the citizens do every man his part in helping to fortify the city.[7] In November he decided upon taking back into his own hands the city of Limerick and its cantred, being, as he said, advised by his barons of England that this step was necessary for the security of his domains in Connaught and Cork. It appears that William de Braose had called in the help of his son-in-law, the lord of Meath, for the keeping of this important border-post; the king's orders for its surrender to the justiciar were addressed to Walter de Lacy and the bailiffs of William de Braose.[8] Walter seemingly refused to obey the order; Meiler, however, succeeded in

---

[1] *Rot. Pat.* p. 54.

[2] *Rot. Chart.* p. 151—"de qua [*i.e.* Ultonia] ipsum cinximus in comitem." Date, May 29, 1205.

[3] *Rot. Claus.* vol. i. p. 40.　　　[4] *Rot. Chart.* pp. 133 b, 134.

[5] *Rot. Pat.* p. 45 b.

[6] *Rot. Claus.* vol. i. p. 6 b.

[7] *Rot. Pat.* p. 45 b. John had granted another charter to Dublin on November 7, 1200; *Rot. Chart.* pp. 78 b, 79.　　　[8] *Rot. Pat.* p. 47.

taking possession of the city, "on account of which there
arose a great war" between him and De Lacy,[1] with the result
that John, to end their strife, took away the custody of
Limerick from both of them, and restored it in August
1205 to William de Braose.[2]   Nineteen months later
Walter de Lacy's castle of Ludlow was seized for the Crown,
and Walter was bidden to come and "stand to right" in the
English court.[3]

By that time Meiler was at strife with William de
Braose again, and also with another Marcher lord of very
different character from any of those with whom he had as
yet had to deal.   Meiler Fitz-Henry, though loyal to the
king, was evidently not quite the man for the post of chief
justiciar in Ireland.   He was one of the few survivors of the
first band of Norman-Welsh adventurers who had taken part
in the invasion under Robert Fitz-Stephen.   The royal blood
of England and of Wales was mingled in his veins; he was
in fact, though not in law, first cousin to Henry II.[4]   The
two young Lacys, now so often opposed to him, were cousins
of his wife, a niece of the elder Hugh de Lacy.[5]   He was,
however, not one of the great barons of the March; he
seems to have held in chief of the Crown nothing except
three cantreds in Desmond granted to him by John in
October 1200;[6] his principal possession was the barony of
Leix in Ossory,[7] for which he owed homage to William the
Marshal as lord of Leinster.   In the spring of 1207 William
the Marshal asked leave of John to visit his Irish lands,
which he had never yet seen.   The leave was given, though

---

[1] The Four Masters, a. 1205, describe the war as "between the English of
Meath and the English of Meiler"; but the only "English of Meath" who took
part in it seem to have been Walter de Lacy and his personal followers.   See
Rot. Pat. p. 69 (February 21, 1206), where John commends the barons of
Meath and Leinster for not having supported Walter in his strife with Meiler
about Limerick.

[2] *Rot. Claus.* vol. i. p. 47 b.

[3] *Rot. Pat.* pp. 69 b, 70 b.

[4] His father was son of Henry I. by Nest, daughter of Rees ap Griffith,
prince of North Wales.   Gir. Cambr. vol. i. p. 59.

[5] Gir. Cambr. vol. v. p. 356.

[6] Two cantreds in Kerry—"Akunkerry" and "Hyerba"—and one "in
terra de Corch"—"Yogenacht Lokhelen quae est terra de Humurierdach"—to
be holden by the service of fifteen knights.   *Rot. Chart.* p. 77 b.

[7] Gir. Cambr. vol. v. pp. 355, 356.

1207 unwillingly ; but as William was on the point of setting out from Striguil, he was overtaken by a message from the king, bidding him either remain in England, or give his second son as a hostage. William sent the boy back with the messenger, saying that the king might have all his children as hostages if he pleased,[1] but as for himself, he was determined to go to Ireland ; and next day he sailed. His coming was far from welcome to the justiciar, who till then had been without a superior in the country, and who resented alike the necessity of doing homage to the Marshal for the land which he held under him, and the probability of his own importance being overshadowed by the presence of a man whose territorial and personal weight was so much greater than his own. Meiler therefore wrote to the king urging him to recall the Marshal. John did so, but bade Meiler himself come over at the same time. The Marshal, though feeling that mischief was in prospect, obeyed the king's summons with his usual readiness, and returned to England at Michaelmas, leaving his wife with a band of trusty followers to defend Leinster in his stead. Meiler also came, after secretly bidding his kinsmen and friends attack the Marshal's lands as soon as he was gone, which they did the very next week. The king gave Meiler a warm welcome, but treated the Marshal with coldness and displeasure,[2] which Meiler soon found a way to increase.

At the beginning of the year the justiciar had seized for the Crown some of the lands, men and goods of William de Braose.[3] His excuse for this proceeding was probably the fact that De Braose was in debt to the Crown for the ferm of the city of Limerick, and also for no less than four thousand two hundred and ninety-eight marks of the five thousand which he had in January 1201 covenanted to pay, by instalments of five hundred every year, for the grant of the honour of Limerick.[4] Meiler, however, had acted without instructions from the king ; and when De Braose complained of the

---

[1] He had had the eldest son ever since July 1205 ; *Hist. G. le Mar.* vv. 13271-6.

[2] *Ib.* vv. 13311-20, 13350-584.

[3] *Rot. Claus.* vol. i. p. 77 b.   [4] See Note I. at end.

treatment which he had received, John declared that he "found no fault in him," and bade Meiler restore everything that had been taken from him, unless indeed the city of Limerick was included ; if that had been seized for the Crown, Meiler was to retain it till further orders.[1] The mingled feelings of the king are reflected in his letter. John had found in William de Braose a useful servant and friend ; he knew that he might find in him a dangerous enemy ; he was therefore reluctant to take any measures which might drive William into opposition. On the other hand, William's neglect of his pecuniary obligations to the Crown had reached such a pass that it could hardly be ignored much longer ; and William was further suspected of being in secret alliance against the king, both with the Welsh and with the De Lacys.[2] Of this suspicion the king seems to have known nothing till after the middle of July, when he reappointed "our beloved and faithful William de Braose" custodian of Ludlow Castle.[3] It had, however, reached his ears by the time of Meiler's coming to England, and Meiler turned it to account for a double purpose of his own. One day, as the king and his chief counsellors sat talking together after dinner, something was said about William the Marshal and his friendly relations with William de Braose. Meiler wrought upon the king's jealousy of the one and his suspicions of the other, till he persuaded him to join in a plot for bringing them both to ruin.

At the justiciar's instigation John secretly despatched letters to all those of the Marshal's followers in Ireland who held lands in England, bidding them, on pain of forfeiting these, to be at his court within a fortnight. At the same time Meiler, with the king's licence, returned to Ireland.

1207
Feb. 12

---

[1] *Rot. Claus.* p. 77 b.

[2] W. Coventry, vol. ii. p. 202.

[3] *Rot. Pat.* p. 74. Walter de Lacy, on his marriage with Margaret de Braose, had promised that he would never give, sell, or pledge any part of his land in England or Normandy without his father-in-law's consent; and this engagement had been embodied in a charter and confirmed by the king. *Rot. Obl.* (a. 2 Joh.), p. 81. One of its results seems to have been that De Braose took charge of Ludlow Castle ; it was he who on March 5, 1206, was summoned to deliver it up to Philip d'Aubigné for the king ; *Rot. Pat.* p. 69 b. · On July 13, 1207, John transferred its custody from D'Aubigné back to De Braose.

1207 The Marshal asked permission to do the same; but this
was refused.   Meiler on his arrival found that hitherto his
men had, on the whole, been worsted in their strife with
those of Leinster.   He now summoned the Marshal's men to
a "parliament," at which the king's messenger read out the
secret letters.   The men to whom these letters were addressed
saw but too plainly what would be the result of their
obedience: the Marshal's lands would be left without
defence against Meiler.   They unanimously resolved to
sacrifice their own English estates, disobey the king for
their lord's sake, and resist Meiler to the uttermost; and
with the help of two powerful neighbours whom they called
to their aid, Ralph Fitz-Payne and Hugh de Lacy, they
succeeded, as one of them says, in doing to Meiler as much
mischief as he had thought to do to their lord.[1]   The
Marshal, meanwhile, was compelled to remain at court, but
so discountenanced by the king that hardly any one dared
to speak to him.   At last, one winter day, as they rode out
from Guildford,[2] John called to him: " Marshal, have you
had any news from Ireland that pleases you?"   " No, sire."
" I can tell you some news," said the king, laughing; and
he told him that his wife, the Countess Isabel, had been
besieged in Kilkenny by Meiler, who had indeed been at
length worsted and even captured by her people, but with
very heavy losses on her side, three of the Marshal's chief
friends being among the slain.   The story was a sheer
invention of John's; in reality he had received no news
from Ireland at all.   The Marshal, though perplexed and
1208 troubled, retained his outward composure; and early in the
spring he himself received from Ireland a very different
account of what had happened there.   The justiciar had
not only been captured, but had made submission to the
countess and given his son as a hostage till he himself
should stand to right in her husband's court for the wrong
which he had done to him as his lord.

These tidings were sent at the same time to the king,

---

[1] *Hist. de G. le Mar.* vv. 13589-786.
[2] John was at Guildford December 27 to 28, 1207, and January 25 to 27,
1208; *Itin.* a. 9.

who was by no means pleased with them, but characteristically changed his policy at once to meet the turn of the
tide.   He called the Marshal to his presence, greeted him
with unusual courtesy, and asked him if he had heard anything from Ireland.   " No, sire ; I have no news from
thence."   " Then I will tell you some good news, of which I
wish you joy "—and thereupon John related the truth, which
William knew already, though he had not chosen to say so.
From that time forth " the king made him as good cheer as
he had made him evil cheer before " ; and when the Marshal
soon afterwards again asked leave to go to Ireland, it was
granted at once.[1]   On March 7 Meiler was ordered to
refrain from interfering with the lands of the Marshal, who
had instructed his men to keep the peace towards Meiler in
return ;[2] on March 20 John informed the justiciar that
" the Marshal has done our will," and despatched to Ireland
four commissioners by whose instructions Meiler was to act,
and who, if he failed to do so, were empowered to act in his
stead.[3]   On the 28th, a new grant of Leinster, on the terms
of the original grant to Richard de Clare, was made by the
king to the Marshal.[4]   A month later Meath was in like
manner granted afresh to Walter de Lacy ;[5] and at the end
of the next year, 1209, Meiler was removed from his office of
justiciar, and replaced by the bishop of Norwich, John de Grey.[6]

On one point, however, Meiler was justified by the king.
In the spring of 1208 John made up his mind to bear with
William de Braose no longer, and ordered a distraint upon
his Welsh lands.   William's wife, Maud of Saint-Valery,[7]

---

[1] *Hist. de G. le Mar.* vv. 13787-936.
[2] *Rot. Claus.* vol. i. p. 105.   [3] *Ib.* p. 106 b.
[4] *Rot. Chart.* p. 176.
[5] *Ib.* p. 178.   Cf. *Rot. Claus.* vol. i. p. 106.
[6] The bishop of Norwich was in Ireland before January 2, 1210 (*Rot. Misæ*,
p. 144) ; Meiler had ceased to be justiciar before February 16 of the same year
(*ib.* p. 149) ; and the bishop was in office as justiciar when the De Braoses
arrived in Ireland towards the end of 1209, as appears from *Hist. de G. le Mar.*
vv. 14119-172.   The Four Masters' account of Bishop John's appointment
and its consequences is too amusing to be omitted.   They say under the year
1208 : " John, bishop of Norwich, was sent by the king of England into Ireland
as lord justice ; and the English were excommunicated by the successor of S.
Peter for sending the bishop to carry on war in Ireland."
[7] The king speaks of her as Maud de la Haye, *Foedera*, vol. i. pt. i. p. 107.
But she witnesses a charter of her husband by the title of " domina Matiltis de

1208   his nephew, Earl William of Ferrars, and his sister's husband, Adam de Port, met the king at Gloucester and
persuaded him to grant an interview to William himself at
Hereford. William promised to pay his debts to the treasury within a certain time, pledged some of his castles for
the payment, and gave three of his grandsons and four other
persons as hostages.[1] Roger of Wendover relates that when
the king's officers went to fetch the hostages, Maud refused
to deliver up her grandchildren to the king, "because," said
she, "he has murdered his captive nephew"; that her
husband reproved her, and declared himself willing to answer
according to law for anything in which he had offended the
king; and that John, on hearing what Maud had said, was
"greatly perturbed," and ordered the whole family of De
Braose to be arrested.[2] John himself, in a public statement
attested by the chief justiciar of England and twelve other
men of high position, among whom were De Braose's own
nephew and brother-in-law, asserted that shortly after the
meeting at Hereford De Braose and his sons attempted to
regain the pledged castles by force, and when they had
failed in this attempt, attacked and burned Leominster.[3]
Thereupon it seems that William was proclaimed a traitor;
on September 21 John empowered Gerald of Athies to
make an agreement with all who were or had been homagers
of William de Braose, so that they should "come to the
king's service and not return to the service of William."[4]

1209   De Braose was chased by the king's officers,[5] till in the
following year, 1209, he escaped, with his wife and two of
their sons, from some Welsh seaport, intending to go to
Ireland. A violent storm kept them tossing on the sea for

Sancto Walerico," Round, *Cal. Doc. France*, vol. i. p. 461. See the curious
account of her—"fille fu Bernard de Saint Waleri," etc.—in *Hist. des Ducs de
Normandie*, pp. 111, 112.

   [1] *Foedera*, vol. i. pt. i. p. 107. John was at Gloucester in 1208 April
22 and 23, and at Hereford April 24 to 28 ; *Itin.* a. 9.

   [2] R. Wendover, vol. iii. p. 225. He brings in this story in connexion with
the general demand for hostages from the barons in 1208 ; but his own account
of the words used by William de Braose shows that he was aware there was a
special ground for the demand in De Braose's case.

   [3] *Foedera*, vol. i. pt. i. p. 108.

   [4] *Rot. Pat.* p. 86 b.   [5] *Foedera, l.c.*

IRELAND

A.D. 1210.

ULSTER

R. Foyle

R. Bann

Carrick fergus

Holywood

R. Erne

Armagh

Down

Banbridge

Carlingford

CONNAUGHT

Louth

Louth

Drogheda

R. Boyne

Duleek

Granard

Kells

MEATH

Fowre

Trim

Tuam

Greenoge

Dublin

Kildare

Naas

LEINSTER

LIMERICK

Kilkenny

Limerick

Thomastown

R. Shannon

R. Suir

Wexford

R. Blackwater

Lismore

Waterford

CORK

WATERFORD

Waterford

R. Barrow

Cork

Dungarvan

R. Lee

London: Macmillan & Co. Ltd.

Stanford's Geog.¹ Estab.ᵗ London.

three days and three nights ; at last they landed at Wicklow.
William the Marshal chanced to be there ; he received them
kindly and sheltered them for three weeks.   Then their
presence was discovered by the new justiciar, Bishop John
de Grey, who at once taxed the Marshal with harbouring
" the king's traitors," and bade him give them up to justice.
The Marshal refused, saying he had only received " his lord," [1]
as he was bound to do, and without knowing that De Braose
had incurred the king's displeasure ; and he added that he
himself would not act like a traitor towards De Braose at
the justiciar's bidding.   Thereupon he sent the refugees
safely on to their destination, the home of De Braose's son-
in-law, Walter de Lacy.   The justiciar complained to the
king, who summoned his host for an expedition to Ireland ; [2]
both the Marshal and the Lacys having positively refused
to give up De Braose, though they offered to be answerable
for his going to England to satisfy the king within a fixed
time, and promised that, if he failed to do so, they would
then harbour him no more.   At last—seemingly in the
spring of 1210—De Braose was allowed to go on these
conditions back to Wales.   John had apparently consented
to meet him at Hereford ; but when De Braose reached
Hereford, " he," says the king, " regarded us not," but began
to collect all the forces he could muster against the Crown.
His nephew, the earl of Ferrars, however, managed to bring
him to a meeting with the king at Pembroke.   He offered
a fine of forty thousand marks.   " We," says John, " told him
we knew well that he was not in his own power at all, but
in that of his wife, who was in Ireland ; and we proposed
that he should go to Ireland with us, and the matter should
be settled there ; but he chose rather to remain in Wales," [3]
and was suffered to do so—John being determined now to
settle matters not only with Maud de Braose, but with all

---

[1] " Mès j'ai herbergié mon seignor, Si comme faire le deveie," *Hist. de G. le
Mar.* vv. 14214-15.   How De Braose was "lord" of the Marshal, I can find
nothing to show.

[2] *Ib.* vv. 14137-52.

[3] *Foedera*, vol. i. pt. i. p. 108.   John was at Cross-by-the-Sea, close to
Pembroke, from June 3 to June 16 inclusive, and at Crook on June 20.   *Itin.*
a. 12.

1210   the barons of the Irish March, according to his own will and
pleasure.

At some date between June 16 and 20 John crossed
from Pembroke to Crook, near Waterford.   Thence he
proceeded by way of Newbridge and Thomastown to
Kilkenny, where he and all his host were received and entertained for two days (June 23 and 24) by William the
Marshal.[1]   On June 28 the king reached Dublin ; thence
he led his host into Meath.[2]   Walter de Lacy and the De
Braoses fled, evidently into Ulster ; thither John marched in
pursuit of them, but before he could overtake them they
had escaped over sea into Galloway.[3]   Hugh de Lacy had
retired into the stronghold of Carrickfergus ; at the king's
approach, however, he, too, slipped away in a little boat to
Scotland.[4]   Carrickfergus was provisioned for a siege, but
its garrison was soon frightened into surrender.[5]   While
John was at Carrickfergus, his "friend and cousin," Duncan
of Carrick, sent him word that he had captured Maud de
Braose, one of her daughters, her eldest son, his wife and
their two children ; her younger son, Reginald, had escaped,
and so had the Lacys.   The king despatched John de
Courcy (whom he had taken back into favour, and brought
with him to Ireland, as likely to be a willing and useful
helper against the De Lacys) to fetch the captives from
Galloway.   When they were brought before him, Maud
offered the surrender of all her husband's lands and a fine
of forty thousand marks, which John accepted ; but three
days later she repudiated her agreement.[6]   Taking his
prisoners with him, the king turned southward again, and
soon completed the subjugation of the Lacys' territories.
Most of the lesser barons fled before him as their lords
had done, "fearing to fall into his hands."[7]   A week's stay

[1] Cf. *Itin.* a. 12 and *Hist. de G. le Mar.* vv. 14259-66.
[2] June 30, Greenoge ; July 2 and 3, Trim ; July 4 and 5, Kells. *Itin.* a. 12.
[3] *Foedera*, vol. i. pt. i. p. 108.
[4] *Ann. Cambr.* a. 1210, Rolls edition, pp. 66, 67, note.
[5] *Hist. de G. le Mar.* vv. 14270-78.   John was at Carrickfergus July 19 to 28 ; *Itin.* a. 12.
[6] *Foedera, l.c.*
[7] R. Wendover, vol. iii. p. 234.

in Dublin (August 18 to 24) brought his expedition to
a close.[1]

It was probably during this second stay of John's at
Dublin that, as Roger of Wendover says, "there came to
him there more than twenty kinglets [2] of that country, who
all, terrified with a very great fear, did him homage and
fealty ; yet a few kinglets neglected to come, who scorned
to do so, because they dwelt in impregnable places. Also
he caused to be set up there English laws and customs,
establishing sheriffs and other officers who should judge the
people of that realm according to English laws." [3] This
latter statement of Roger's may have given rise to the later
belief that it was John who organized the administration of
the March in Ireland after the English model, by dividing
the whole of the conquered territory into counties, each
under its own sheriff.[4] It appears, however, that there were
sheriffs in Ireland in the days of Henry II.[5] The earliest
known mention of a sheriff's district there occurs in 1205,
when we hear of the "county of Waterford." [6] Ten years
later the same county is mentioned again, and also that of
Cork ; [7] and before the end of the century ten counties, at
least, were recognized by the English government in Ireland.[8]

[1] His itinerary from Carrickfergus is : July 29, Holywood ; July 31,
Ballymore ; August 2, 3, Down ; 4, Banbridge ; 5, Carlingford ; 8, 9, Drogheda ;
9, 10, Duleek ; 10, 11, Kells ; 11, Fowre ; 12, Granard ; 14, Rathwire ; 16,
Castle Bret ; 18-24, Dublin. *Itin.* a. 12.

[2] " *Reguli.*" The *Hist. des Ducs de Normandie*, pp. 112, 113, tells how the
king of Connaught came to John's "service" at Dublin, and how John while at
Carrickfergus tried to catch the king of "Kenelyon" in a trap, but was out-
witted by the Irishman.

[3] R. Wendover, vol. iii. pp. 233, 234.

[4] This assertion, adopted by many modern writers, seems to have been first
definitely made by Sir John Davies, in his *Discoverie of the true causes why
Ireland was never entirely subdued*, etc. (1612), p. 121 : "King John made xii.
shires in Leinster and Mounster ; namely, Dublin, Kildare, Meth, Uriel, Cather-
logh, Kilkenny, Wexford, Waterford, Corke, Limeric, Kerrie, and Tipperary."

[5] Ware, *Antiq.* c. v. p. 33.

[6] Patent granted by John to the citizens of Waterford, July 3, a. r. 7 (1205),
according to Ware, *l.c.*

[7] *Rot. Claus.* vol. i. p. 218.

[8] Writs for a parliament held at some date between 1293 and 1298 were
addressed to the *sheriffs* of Dublin, Louth, Kildare, Waterford, Tipperary, Cork,
Limerick, Kerry, "Connaught," and Roscommon, and to the seneschals of the
liberties of Meath, Wexford, Carlow, Kilkenny and Ulster. *Irish Archæological
Society's Miscellany*, p. 15.

1210   The names of the earliest Irish counties thus known to us
        and the circumstances of John's visit to Ireland in 1210 may
        suggest a clue to the rise and growth of the shire-system
        in that country.   The district which forms the present county
        of Waterford had never been enfeoffed either by Henry II.
        or by John, but remained directly in the hands of the supreme
        ruler of the March.   Of the present county Cork, the eastern
        half, at least, escheated together with the rest of Raymond
        FitzGerald's share of the "kingdom of Cork" on his death
        about 1185.   No notice of a new enfeoffment of any of the
        lands which had been his occurs till 1208, and then they
        were not granted as a whole; so far as we know, only a
        portion of them was enfeoffed, and that portion was dis-
        tributed among several feoffees.[1]   It seems probable that
        the system of county administration may have been first
        established in Ireland in those districts which were under
        the direct rule of the English Crown (or, to speak more
        exactly, of the "English," or Angevin, "Lord of Ireland"),
        and of which the continuous extent was too great for them
        to be left, like the single cantreds attached to the other sea-
        port towns, under the control of a mere military governor
        or constable, and that it was only by degrees introduced
        into the great fiefs.   If this were so, the events of 1210
        would furnish an excellent opportunity for its extension.
        Of the four great fiefs which, together with the royal
        domains and the lately redistributed honour of Cork, made
        up the "English" March in Ireland, Leinster was, when
        John sailed from Dublin for England at the end of August,[2]
        practically the only one left.   Meath, Ulster, and Limerick
        were all forfeit to the Crown; and the Crown kept the greater
        part of them for many years after.   Meath was not restored
        to Walter de Lacy till 1215;[3]   Walter's brother, the earl of
        Ulster, did not return from exile till after John's death;[4]

        ---

        [1] *Rot. Chart.* pp. 171 b, 172, 172 b.   Cf. an inquisition ordered April 3, 1206
        (*Rot. Pat.* p. 60 b), which clearly implies that the eastern half of the "kingdom
        of Cork" was then in the king's hands.
        [2] He is last mentioned as being in Dublin on August 24, and he was at
        Fishguard on August 26; *Itin.* a. 12.
        [3] *Rot. Pat.* pp. 131, 132 b, 151, 181.
        [4] *Dict. Nat. Biog.* "Lacy, Hugh de (d. 1242)."

and the honour of Limerick was never again bestowed as a whole upon a single grantee. Under these circumstances a system of administrative division into counties placed under sheriffs appointed by the king, or by the justiciar in his name, might be established without difficulty in territories where its introduction in earlier years, if ever attempted, would probably have been rendered ineffectual by the power of the great barons. The one great baron who in the autumn of 1210 still held his ground in the March—Earl William the Marshal, the lord of Leinster—had no hesitation in withstanding the king to his face in the cause of honour and justice ; but he was not a man to throw obstacles in the way of the royal authority when it was exercised within the sphere of its rights and in the interest of public order.

On the king's return to Dublin William the Marshal came to the court. John at once accused him of having "harboured a traitor" in the person of William de Braose. The Marshal answered the king as he had answered the justiciar, and added that if any other man dared to utter such a charge against him, he was ready to disprove it there and then. As usual, no one would take up his challenge ; nevertheless, John again required hostages and pledges for the Marshal's fidelity, and again they were given at once.[1] Meanwhile, the sheriff of Hereford sent word that William de Braose was stirring up trouble in Wales, and urged that he should be outlawed ; but the king ordered that the matter should await his own return to England. When he was about to sail, Maud de Braose offered to fine with him for forty thousand marks, and ten thousand in addition, as amends for having withdrawn from her former agreement. John accepted these terms ; the fine was signed and sealed, and it was agreed that Maud, and also, it seems, the other members of her family who had been captured with her, should remain in custody till it was paid. John carried his prisoners back with him to England, put Maud in prison at Bristol, and at her request gave an audience to her husband, who ratified the fine

[1] *Hist. de G. le Mar.* vv. 14286-372.

1210   which she had made, but fled secretly just before the day
fixed for paying the first instalment.   The king asked
Maud what she now proposed to do, and she answered
plainly that she had no intention, and no means, of paying.
Then it was ordered that "the judgement of our realm
should be carried out against William," and he was outlawed.[1]   Thus far the king tells his own story, and there
is no reason to doubt its truth.   What he does not tell is
the end of the story.   He sent Maud and her son to a
dungeon at Windsor, and there starved them to death.[2]

<hr>

[1] *Foedera*, vol. i. pt. i. p. 108.   [2] See Note I. at end.

CHAPTER V

JOHN AND THE POPE

1210–1214

[Rex] prudenter sane sibi et suis providens in hoc facto, licet id multis ignominiosum videretur, et enorme servitutis jugum. Cum enim res in arto esset, et undique timor vehemens, nulla erat via compendiosior imminens evadendi periculum, nec forsitan alia ; quoniam ex quo se in protectione posuit apostolica, et regna sua beati Petri patrimonium fecit, non erat in orbe Romano princeps qui in sedis apostolicae injuriam vel illum infestare, vel illa invadere praesumeret.   W. COVENTRY, ii. 210.

DURING John's absence in Ireland, England had been disquieted by rumours of a threatened Welsh invasion. His ministers, however, faced the peril boldly ; the justiciar, the treasurer (Bishop Peter of Winchester), and the earl of Chester marched into Wales with "a great host" and built three castles on Welsh soil,[1] and on the king's return the Welsh "vanished," as a chronicler says, into their mountains, "and the land kept silence before him."[2] John, however, was in no mood, now that England, Scotland and Ireland were all at his feet, to be content with mere silence on the part of the Welsh princes, and especially of his own son-in-law, Llywelyn, who, having secured the hand of the king's daughter and the mastery over the greater part of Wales, was now openly turning against the power by whose help he had risen. The case is frankly stated by a Welsh chronicler : " Llywelyn, son of Jorwerth, made cruel attacks upon the English ; and on that account King John became enraged, and formed a design of entirely divesting Llywelyn

1210

---

[1] *Ann. Dunst.* a. 1210.   [2] W. Coventry, vol. ii p. 202.

1210

of his dominion." [1] The native rivals whom Llywelyn had forced into submission were always on the watch for a chance of flinging off the North-Welsh yoke; and when John assembled his host at Chester, seemingly in the third

1211

week of May 1211,[2] he was joined by most of the chieftains of the south.[3] At the tidings of his approach, "Llywelyn," says the same chronicler, "moved with his forces into the middle of the country, and his property to the mountain of Eryri (Snowdon); and the forces of Mona, with their property, in the same manner. Then the king, with his army, came to the castle of Dyganwy. And there the army was in so great a want of provisions that an egg was sold for a penny halfpenny, and it was a delicious feast to them to get horseflesh; and on that account the king returned to England, after disgracefully losing many of his men and much property." [4]

Whatever military "disgrace" there may have been was speedily wiped out; John had only gone home to collect fresh supplies and larger forces.[5] Setting forth again from Whitchurch in July,[6] "the king"—again it is a Welsh chronicler who tells the story—"returned to Wales, his mind being more cruel and his army larger; and he built many [7] castles in Gwynedd. And he proceeded over the river Conway towards the mountain of Eryri, and incited some of his troops to burn Bangor. And there Robert, bishop of Bangor, was seized in his church, and was afterwards ransomed for two hundred hawks." Llywelyn sent his wife to make terms for him with her father, and was

---

[1] *Brut y Tywysogion*, a. 1210.

[2] The *Brut* (a. 1210) says that the host assembled at "Caerleon," and returned to England "about Whitsuntide." It places the campaign in 1210, but this is obviously a year too early. Cf. *Ann. Cambr.* a. 1211, and W. Coventry, vol. ii. p. 203. John was at Chester (*i.e.* "Caerleon") on May 16 and 17, 1211, the Tuesday and Wednesday before Whitsunday; *Itin.* a. 13. The Itinerary shows that the expedition had not taken place earlier than this; and from May 17 to August 29 there is a blank.

[3] *Ann. Cambr.* a. 1211. Cf. *Brut*, a. 1210.

[4] *Brut*, a. 1210.

[5] W. Coventry, vol. ii. p. 203.

[6] July 8, R. Wendover, vol. iii. p. 235. The *Brut*, *l.c.*, says he "returned to Wales about the calends of August."

[7] Fourteen "or more," according to *Ann. Cambr.* a. 1211.

received into the king's peace on delivering up to him a
large number of hostages, paying a heavy indemnity in
cattle and horses, "and consigning also the midland district
to the king for ever.   And thereupon all the Welsh princes,
except Rhys and Owain, the sons of Gruffydd, son of
Rhys, made peace with the king; and the king returned
victoriously, and with extreme joy, to England."[1]   Of
course the peace was a hollow one, like every other peace
with the Welsh; but for the moment John's success was
complete.   "In Ireland, Scotland, and Wales there was no
man who did not obey the nod of the king of England—
a thing which, it is well known, had never happened to
any of his forefathers; and he would have appeared happy
indeed, and successful to the utmost of his desires, had he
not been despoiled of his territories beyond the sea, and
under the ban of the Church."[2]

To neither of these drawbacks was John altogether
indifferent.   He was only biding his time to make a great
effort for the removal of the first; and although the second
appeared, as yet, to have made no difference to his political
position, he was not insensible to the dangers which it
might involve.   He was still playing with both primate and
Pope.   In the spring of 1210 he had made another feint
of renewing negotiations with Stephen Langton, had sent
him a safe-conduct for a conference to be held at Dover,
and had actually gone thither (May 4), ostensibly for the
purpose of meeting him.   But the safe-conduct was irregular
in form; and this circumstance, coupled with a warning
from some English barons, made Stephen refuse to trust
himself in John's power.[3]   The king vented his wrath by
cutting down the woods on all the archbishop's manors.[4]
On his return from Ireland he dealt a heavy blow at the
religious orders.   Towards the end of October he called

[1] *Brut*, a. 1210.   Cf. *Ann. Cambr.*, *Margan.*, *Tewkesb.*, *Winton.*, *Waverl.*
a. 1211; W. Coventry, vol. ii. p. 203, and R. Wendover, vol. iii. p. 235.
Roger says John was back at Whitchurch on August 15.
[2] W. Coventry, vol. ii. p. 203.
[3] Cf. *Canterbury Chronicle*, in Stubbs's Gerv. Cant. vol. ii. pp. cvi., cvii.,
cxi., cxii.; Gerv. Cant. vol. ii. p. 106; R. Coggeshall, p. 164; *Ann. Winton.*,
Waverl., and *Dunst.* a. 1210.   The date comes from *Itin.* a. 11.
[4] *Ann. Waverl.* a. 1211.

1210   together in London the heads of all the religious houses in England, and compelled them to give him sums of money, of which the total is said to have amounted to one hundred thousand pounds.[1] The Cistercians, whom he had spared in the earlier days of the Interdict, had to bear the brunt of his exactions now ; they "were forced to find him chariots with horses and men,"[2] or, as another writer explains it, their privileges were quashed, and they had to give the king forty thousand pounds ;[3] moreover, their abbots were forbidden to attend the triennial chapter of the order at Cîteaux, "lest their piteous complaints should exasperate the whole world against such an oppressor."[4]

1211   In June or July 1211[5] the cardinal subdeacon Pandulf, who was much in the Pope's confidence, and a Templar named Durand came to England "that they might restore peace between the Crown and the clergy."[6] They seem to have been sent at the king's request. The terms of the commission which they had received from the Pope are known from a reissue of it two years later. They were to exhort John to make satisfaction "according to a form subscribed between ourself" (the Pope) "and his envoys." If he would publicly take an oath of absolute obedience to the Pope's mandates on all matters for which he was under excommunication, they were to give him absolution ; and when they had obtained from him security for the reinstatement of the archbishop of Canterbury, they were to withdraw the interdict.[7] John met them on his return from Wales, at North-

---

1 R. Wendover, vol. iii. pp. 234, 235. He gives no date ; but John was in London, seemingly for the only time in 1210, at the end of October ; he dates from the Tower on October 27. *Itin.* a. 12.

2 *Ann. Dunst.* a. 1210. Cf. R. Coggeshall, p. 164, and *Ann. Waverl.* a. 1210.

3 R. Wendover, vol. iii. p. 235.

4 M. Paris, *Hist. Angl.* vol. ii. p. 12. Cf. W. Coventry, vol. ii. p. 201, and R. Coggeshall, p. 163.

5 Cf. *Ann. Winton.* and *Waverl.* a. 1211.

6 R. Wendover, vol. iii. pp. 235, 236.

7 The second appendix to Innoc. III. *Epp.* l. xv. No. 234—"Forma quidem est talis" (printed also, under the heading "Instructiones legato traditae," in *Foedera*, vol. i. pt. i. p. 109)—is obviously a copy, enclosed in a letter of 1213, of the original commission issued to Pandulf and Durand in 1211. See below, p. 179.

ampton, on August 30,[1] and received them publicly in a great assembly of the barons.   The details of the conference rest only upon the authority of two comparatively late monastic chronicles ; but there is no reason for doubting the correctness of the main outlines of their story.   The envoys called upon John to make satisfaction to the Church, restore the property which he had taken from her ministers, and receive Archbishop Stephen, the exiled bishops, their kins- folk and their friends " fairly and in peace."   The king answèred that they might make him swear to restore every- thing, and he would do whatever else they liked, " but if that fellow Stephen sets foot in my land, I will have him hanged." A discussion followed as to the circumstances of Stephen's election and the respective rights of Pope and King in such matters.   John ended by offering to receive as archbishop any one whom the Pope might choose except Stephen, and to give Stephen another see if he would resign all claims upon Canterbury.   Pandulf scornfully rejected this proposal. At last, in presence of the whole council, he pronounced to John's face the papal sentence of excommunication, of which, he said, the publication had only been delayed till his own arrival in England and that of his colleagues ; he absolved all John's subjects from their allegiance, bade them be ready to join the ranks and obey the leader of any host which the Pope might send to England, and denounced not only John himself, but also all his posterity, as for ever incapacitated for the office of king.   It is said that on this John bade the sheriffs and foresters who were present bring in whatever prisoners they had in their charge, and gave orders for the hanging of some and the blinding or mutila- tion of others, to show the papal envoys his own absolute power and his ruthlessness in the exercise of it ; that among the prisoners was a clerk charged with forgery, whom he ordered to be hanged ; that Pandulf wanted to excommuni- cate at once any one who should lay hands on this man, and

---

[1] The day comes from *Ann. Burton.* a. 1211, and we know from the *Itiner- ary*, a. 13, that John was at Northampton on August 29.   The *Ann. Waverl.* date this conference a year too late, viz. 1212.   Cf. W. Coventry, vol. ii. p. 204 ; R. Wendover, vol. iii. p. 235, and *Ann. Margan., Tewkesb., Winton., Oseney*, and *Worcester*, a. 1211.

M

1211   went out of the hall to fetch a candle for the purpose, but
that the king followed him and gave up the accused clerk
"to his judgement"—which of course meant, to be set at
liberty.[1]   Whether or not the mock tragedy enacted between
king and cardinal really ended in this strange fashion, the
result of the conference was clearly the same as that of all
previous diplomacy between Innocent III. and John : the
Pope gained nothing and the king lost nothing.   Pandulf
and Durand went back to Rome accompanied by envoys
from John ; [2] an order was issued for the recall of the exiles,
but it seems to have taken the form of a writ bidding all
bishops and beneficed clergy return before next mid-summer,
"on pain of losing their property." [3]   The excommunicate
sovereign kept his Christmas feast at Windsor,[4] and found
a new triumph awaiting him at the opening of the new
year.

1212   King William of Scotland, stricken in years and with no
male heir save one young son, the child of his old age, was
hard pressed by a party in his realm who rallied round a
certain Cuthred MacWilliam, a descendant of the older line
of Scottish kings which the house of Malcolm and Margaret
had ousted from the succession.   In despair of overcoming
these rebels, William turned to England for succour, and
early in 1212 " committed himself, his kingdom and his son
to the care " of his English overlord.[5]   Before Ash Wednesday (February 7) he had formally granted to John the
right to dispose of young Alexander in marriage, " as his
liegeman," within six years from that date.[6]   On Mid-Lent
Sunday, March 4, the boy was knighted by John, " as the
king held a festival in the Hospital of S. Bridget at Clerken-
well." [7]   Later in the year an English army marched to
William's aid.   John himself probably led his troops as far
as Hexham, where he was on June 27,[8] and then sent

1   *Ann. Burton*, a. 1211.   Cf. *Ann. Waverl.* a. 1212.
2   *Ann. Burton*, a. 1211.
3   *Ann. Waverl.* a. 1211.   Cf. R. Coggeshall, p. 164.
4   R. Wendover, vol. iii. p. 238.
5   W. Coventry, vol. ii. p. 206.
6   *Foedera*, vol. i. pt. i. p. 104.
7   R. Wendover, vol. iii. p. 238.   Cf. *Chronn. Mailros* and *Lanercost*, a.
1212.   8 *Itin.* a. 14.

them on to Scotland with instructions which proved sufficient
to secure the object of their expedition. They scoured the
country till Cuthred fell into their power ; and the struggle
of the old Scottish royal house against the " modern kings "
ended, for a time at least, with the hanging of its champion
by English hands.[1]

Meanwhile, John had never lost sight of his plans for a
renewal of the war with France. The first need of course
was money. It was probably in the hope of finding some
additional sources of revenue which could be claimed for the
Crown that on his return from Ireland he ordered an inquiry
into all assizes of novel disseisin which had been held during
his absence, and also into the right of presentation to, and
actual tenancy of, all ecclesiastical benefices throughout the
country.[2] An inquest into the services due from the knights
and other tenants-in-chief in every shire was ordered in the
same year or early in the next ;[3] and an inquest concerning
escheated honours and the services due from them was set
on foot shortly afterwards.[4] In 1211 " the king of France
seized all the English ships that touched his shores, and
therefore "—says the Dunstable annalist—" the king of
England seized many men of the Cinque Ports " ;[5] a statement which we can only suppose to mean one of two things :
either that John suspected some of the ships to have been
willing prizes, or that he was dissatisfied with the way in
which his sailors had executed, or failed to execute, some
order which he had given for retaliation. In either case,
however, it is clear that he made his displeasure a ground for
further exactions from the leading men of the southern coast
towns.

Of far greater moment than the desultory skirmishes
between the sailors of England and France was the scheme
of European coalition against Philip which John had been
gradually building up during the past ten years. One of

---

[1] W. Coventry, vol. ii. p. 206.
[2] *Ann. Dunst.* a. 1210.
[3] This inquest was taken *a. r.* 12 and 13 (*i.e.* May 1210-May 1212); *Red
Book*, vol. ii. pp. 469-574.
[4] *A.* 13 John (May 1211-May 1212) ; *Red Book*, vol. ii. pp. 575-621.
[5] *Ann. Dunst.* a. 1211.

1197-1200 the most important elements in his political calculations throughout those years was the course of events in Germany. The death of the Emperor Henry VI. in September 1197 had been followed by a disputed election to the imperial crown, the late Emperor's brother, Philip of Suabia, claiming it for himself against the candidate chosen by the majority of the electors, Otto of Saxony, a son of Duke Henry the Lion and Maud, daughter of Henry II. of England.[1] The Suabian prince was backed by his powerful family connexions, including the duke of Austria, son and successor of Richard Cœur-de-Lion's old enemy Leopold. Otto's youth had been passed in exile at the court of his Angevin grandfather, and he was a special favourite of his uncle Richard, who granted him first the earldom of York and afterwards the county of Poitou, and whose influence with some of the princes of the empire had had a share in procuring him their votes. It was, therefore, obvious policy for his rival and the king of France to make common cause against him and his kinsman of England. A treaty of alliance between the two Philips was signed on June 29, 1198.[2] In 1200 Otto sent his two brothers to demand for him from John a renewal of the investiture of York and of Poitou, and also—if we may belief Roger of Howden—two-thirds of Richard's treasure and all his jewels, which he said Richard had bequeathed to him. His assertion was correct with regard to the jewels, but the other claims are so unreasonable that it is difficult to believe that they can have had any justification.[3] John, however, had an answer ready

---

[1] R. Howden, vol. iv. pp. 31, 37-9 ; R. Diceto, vol. ii. p. 163.

[2] *Foedera*, vol. i. pt. i. p. 70.

[3] Cf. R. Howden, vol. iv. pp. 83 and 116. The account of Richard's testamentary dispositions in the former place is open to two interpretations. Richard, says Roger, " divisit Johanni fratri suo regnum Angliae . . . et praecepit ut traderentür ei castella sua, et tres partes " [in p. 116 Otto claims only " duas partes "] " thesauri sui, et omnia baubella sua divisit Othoni nepoti suo regi Alamannorum; et quartam partem thesauri sui praecepit servientibus suis et pauperibus distribui." Grammatically, there is nothing to show whether " tres partes thesauri sui " is meant to be connected with " praecepit ut traderentur ei [Johanni]" or with " divisit Othoni," but common sense strongly supports the former interpretation ; however anxious Richard may have been to help his nephew, he could not possibly mean deliberately to leave his own chosen successor literally without a penny. The actual wording of Richard's will may, indeed, have been as ambiguous as Roger's summary of it, and Otto may have tried to take advantage

for all these demands.   The envoys did not reach him till
after the treaty of Gouleton (May 1200) was signed, and
by that treaty he was pledged to give no help of any kind
to Otto without the consent of the French king.[1]   This
excuse, indeed, was only temporary; in June 1201 the
Pope recognized Otto as lawful emperor-elect;[2] and though
John was at that very moment renewing his treaty with
France, the uncle and nephew speedily drew together.
Throughout the vicissitudes of the next six years John
never lost sight of the community of their interests; he
constantly showed his sense of it by letters and presents, by
loans and gifts of money, and by grants of trading and
other privileges in England to the German and Flemish
cities which supported Otto,[3] as well as by undertaking the
custody of at least one prisoner of importance who belonged
to the party of Otto's rival.[4]   Otto, whose fortunes were
gradually rising throughout these years, was so fully alive to
the value of the English alliance that in May 1207 he
came to London for a personal interview with John.   It is
said that on this occasion Otto promised to conquer the
realm of France and make it over to his uncle, all except
three cities, Paris, Etampes and Orléans, which Philip
Augustus had once jestingly said he would bestow upon
Otto himself if ever the latter became emperor.   John gave
his nephew six thousand marks,[5] and received from him the

of its ambiguity.   His claim to the earldoms seems somewhat unreasonable; he
had never really held the earldom of York, and it was for that very reason that
Richard had granted him Poitou; but it was clearly preposterous to expect John
to renew this latter grant after Otto had accepted the German Crown.

[1] R. Howden, vol. iv. p. 116; *Foedera*, vol. i. pt. i. p. 80.

[2] Leibnitz and Scheidt, *Origines Guelficae*, vol. iii. pp. 281, 282.

[3] *Rot. Chart.* p. 133 (1204); *Rot. Pat.* vol. i. pp. 11 b (1202), 40, 44
(1204), 48 (1205).

[4] The young countess of Holland, Ada, daughter and heiress of Count
Theodoric who died in 1203; see *Art de Vérifier les Dates*, vol. xiv. pp. 261,
430.   Her mother at once married her to Louis, count of Los; her father's
brother, William, claimed Holland against the young couple; he and Louis took
opposite sides on the Imperial question, William holding for Otto, Louis for
Philip of Suabia; and eighteen days after the wedding William drove Ada's
mother and husband out of Holland, captured Ada herself, and sent her to
England to be kept in prison by John.   She was still there in 1207, and was
only released when her husband had done homage to both John and Otto, *Rot.
Pat.* vol. i. p. 82, 82 b.

[5] Cf. M. Paris, *Hist. Angl.* vol. iii. p. 109, and *Rot. Claus.* vol. i. p. 82 b.

1207 symbolical gift of a great golden crown.[1] As yet, indeed,
Otto was only emperor-elect, and had the conquest of his
own realms to complete ere he could attempt that of
France. But his fortunes were steadily rising; his rival,
1208 Philip of Suabia, was slain in the following summer;[2] and
1209 on October 4, 1209, just at the moment of his uncle's
triumph over the English Church, he was crowned by the
Pope at Rome.[3]

1210   Within a year, however, Pope and Emperor had
quarrelled, and Otto was excommunicated.[4] This was, of
course, an additional bond of union between him and John.
At the same time, a kinsman of both princes was setting
the Pope and the French king alike at defiance. Count
Raymond of Toulouse, the husband of John's sister Joan,
had from the outset favoured the heretics who for the last
1211 two years had kept southern Gaul in turmoil; in 1211 he
openly allowed them to concentrate in his capital city, and
headed their resistance to the forces which Innocent and
Philip had sent against them under Simon de Montfort.
Toulouse was besieged, but John and Otto kept their
kinsman so well supplied with the means of defence and
sustenance that the "crusaders" at last grew hopeless of
taking it and raised the siege. Otto had answered the
Pope's excommunication by conquering Tuscia, Apulia and
Calabria; whereupon Innocent published another sentence,
deposing him from his imperial office and his German
kingdom, and bidding the princes of the empire elect a new
sovereign in his stead.

John, "with such a comrade," grew bolder than ever.[5]
The common interest of the three excommunicate kinsmen
obviously lay in crushing France, the ally of the Pope; and
the moment seemed at hand for the fulfilment of John's
highest hopes. John and Raymond in the south, John and
Otto in the north and east, might hem in Philip Augustus
completely, if the princes of the border-land of France and

[1] *Rot. Pat.* vol. i. p. 77.
[2] W. Coventry, vol. ii. p. 200.
[3] R. Wendover, vol. iii. p. 227.
[4] W. Coventry, vol. ii. p. 202; R. Wendover, vol. iii. pp. 232, 233.
[5] W. Coventry, vol. ii. pp. 202, 203.

Germany—Boulogne, Flanders, the Netherlands, L⟨
could be so won over as to insure their co-operatic⟨
plans of the uncle and nephew for the conquest a⟨
memberment of the French kingdom.   To this end ⟨ohn's
utmost powers of diplomacy had been devoted for many
years past ; and in the case of most of these princes the end
was now gained.   In the autumn of 1211 Reginald of
Boulogne, whose policy had long been wavering, quarrelled
openly with Philip and took refuge with his kinsman the
count of Bar ;[1] in May 1212 he was in England, pledging
his homage and his service to John.   By the middle of
August the counts of Bar, Limburg, Flanders and Louvain
were all pledged to John's side.[2]   John himself was meanwhile preparing for an expedition to Gascony ; on June
15 thirty-nine English towns were ordered to furnish
contingents of men " ready to cross the sea with the king in
his service when he should require them."[3]

A month later, however, the destination of his armament
was changed.   Just as his plans were ripe for an attack
upon France, they were checked once more by the necessity
of guarding his realm against the Welsh.   Before the close
of 1211 Llywelyn—provoked, as he declared, by " the many
insults done to him by the men of the king "—had leagued
himself with his former rivals in South Wales and taken
" all the castles which John had made in Gwynedd, except
Dyganwy and Rhuddlan."[4]   And this time the league was
more likely to hold together than was usually the case with
alliances formed by the Welsh princes either with their
neighbours or with each other ; for a new hope had
dawned upon the Welsh people.   The tidings of John's
excommunication and deposition by the Pope had penetrated
into Wales ; and in this matter the Welsh, although of all
Christian nations probably the least amenable to ecclesiastical

---

[1] W. Armor. *Gesta P. A.* c. 162.   The date there given is a year too late,
as the English Rolls show.
[2] Boulogne, *Foedera*, vol. i. pt. i. p. 104 ; *Rot. Claus.* vol. i. pp. 116, 117 ;
Chart. p. 186 ; *Pat.* p. 93 ; Bar and Limburg, *Pat.* p. 92 b ; *Foedera*, p. 106 ;
Flanders, *Pat.* pp. 93, 94 ; Louvain, *Foedera*, pp. 106, 107.
[3] *Rot. Claus.* vol. i. p. 130 b.
[4] *Brut y Tywysogion*, a. 1211.   Cf. *Ann. Cambr.* a. 1213.

1212   discipline and the least submissive to ecclesiastical authority, became full of zeal to do the utmost that in them lay towards carrying out the Papal sentence against their overlord and conqueror. "They with one consent," says their own chronicler, " rose against the king, and bravely wrested from him the midland district which he had previously taken from Llywelyn." [1]   The version of the English chroniclers is that the Welsh invaded the English border, took some castles and beheaded their garrisons, carried off a mass of plunder, and then burned everything and slew every man that they could lay their hands on.[2]

It was clear that an end must be made of this Welsh trouble before John could venture across the Channel. He changed his plans with his usual promptitude. In July the king's escheators throughout England were ordered to see that the escheats in their custody should furnish each a certain number of carpenters and other labourers provided with proper tools, and with money enough to carry them to Chester. Writs were also issued to Alan of Galloway bidding him send a thousand of his "best and bravest men," to William the Marshal, Bishop John of Norwich, and others of the king's liegemen in Ireland, and to the tenants by serjeanty throughout England, requiring their personal attendance ; the place of muster for all alike being Chester, and the appointed date Sunday, August 19.[3]   On August 16, however, the king sent out from Nottingham a notice that he was unable to be at Chester on the day fixed, and that the muster would not take place.[4]   The orders which he issued next day indicate that he was contemplating a diversion by sea, part of the fleet being ordered to sail from Chester, coast along North Wales, and " do as much harm to the enemy as possible," while another part was to assemble at Bristol.[5]   He probably meant to await the result of these movements, as well as of some negotiations which he was carrying on with the South Welsh

---

[1] *Brut*, a. 1212.
[2] R. Wendover, vol. iii. p. 238 ; R. Coggeshall, p. 164.
[3] *Rot. Claus.* vol. i. p. 131, 131 b.
[4] *Rot. Pat.* vol. i. p. 94.
[5] *Rot. Claus.* vol. i. pp. 121 b, 122.

chieftains,[1] before deciding whether his main advance should   1212
be made by way of North or South Wales.

The host finally mustered at Nottingham in the second
week of September.[2]   The chivalry of England gathered Sept. 9-15
round the king " in such array and in such numbers," says
a contemporary, " that no man of our day remembers the
like." [3]   John's first act on reaching the muster-place, " before
he tasted food," was to hang twenty-eight of the hostages
whom he had taken from the Welsh in the previous year.[4]
But " suddenly God brought his counsel to nought." [5]   As
he sat at table there came to him a breathless messenger
from the king of Scots, followed by one from the Princess
Joan of Wales, John's daughter and Llywelyn's wife.   Both
messengers brought letters whose contents, they said, were
weighty and secret.   When the two letters were read, their
purport proved to be almost identical.   William and Joan
alike warned the king that his barons were preparing to act
upon the papal sentence which absolved them from their
allegiance, and, if he persisted in leading them to war, either
to turn and slay him themselves, or deliver him up to death
at the hands of his Welsh enemies.[6]   Such a warning, coming at the same instant from two such different quarters,
was not to be lightly put aside.   It was emphasized by the
sudden disappearance of two barons, Eustace de Vesci and
Robert FitzWalter, who at once secretly withdrew from the
host.[7]   John could hardly doubt the significance of their
departure at such a moment.   He dismissed his army and
moved by slow stages back to London.[8]

The month which had elapsed between John's order
countermanding the muster at Chester and his return to

---

[1] *Rot. Claus.* vol. i. p. 123 b.
[2] Cf. R. Wendover, vol. iii. p. 239, and *Itin.* a. 14.
[3] W. Coventry, vol. ii. p. 207.
[4] Cf. *ib.* and R. Wendover, as above.
[5] W. Coventry, *l.c.*   [6] R. Wendover, *l.c.*
[7] *Ann. Waverl.* a. 1212.   See Note II. at end.
[8] R. Wendover, vol. iii. p. 239 ; W. Coventry, vol. ii. p. 207.   John was at
Nottingham September 9-15, and reached London on the 20th, after passing
through "Salvata," Geddington, Northampton, and St. Albans, *Itin.* a. 14.
The assertion of the *Ann. Margan.* (a. 1211 for 1212) that in his terror at the
discovery of the meditated treason he " shut himself up for fifteen days in Nottingham castle " is thus shown to be false.

1212 Nottingham had been spent by him in a progress through
the north ;[1] and it was probably during this time that there
came to his ears a prediction concerning him spoken by one
Peter, variously described as "of Pontefract" or "of Wakefield." This Peter was "a simple countryman," who lived
on bread and water, and was counted among the people for
a prophet. He foretold that on the next Ascension Day
John should cease to be king. Whether John was to die,
or to be driven from the land, or to abdicate, Peter could
not say ; he only knew that it had been revealed to him in
a vision that after the king had reigned prosperously for
fourteen years, neither he nor his heirs should rule any
more, "but one who is pleasing to God."[2] John, on hearing of this prophecy, laughed it to scorn ; but when Peter
was found to be wandering all over the north country
publishing his supposed vision wherever he went, some of
the king's friends deemed it prudent to take the prophet
into custody.[3] He was brought before John himself, who
asked for more explicit information as to his own impending
fate. Peter only replied, "Know thou of a surety that on
the day which I have named, thou shalt be king no more ;
and if I be proved a liar, do with me as thou wilt."
"According to thy word, so be it," answered John ; and he
sent the man to be imprisoned at Corfe.[4] This precaution,
however, defeated its own end ; Peter's captivity in a royal
dungeon gave to him and his prophecy a new importance in
popular estimation ; his words were repeated far and wide,
and believed "as if they had been spoken by a voice from
Heaven"[5] The dread which they are said to have inspired
in the king himself[6] proves nothing as to whether, or how
far, he shared the superstitious credulity of his people.
Apart from all such questions, he had obviously a sufficient
reason for alarm in the fact that the general acceptance of a
political prophecy naturally tends to work its fulfilment.

[1] *Itin.* a. 14.
[2] W. Coventry, vol. ii. p. 208. Cf. R. Wendover, vol. iii. p. 240; *Hist.
des Ducs*, pp. 122, 123; *Ann. Tewkesbury*, a. 1212, and *Chron. Lanercost*, a.
1213.   [3] W. Coventry, *l.c.*
[4] R. Wendover, vol. iii. p. 240.   [5] *Ib.* Cf. W. Coventry, vol. ii. p. 208.
[6] R. Wendover, vol. iii. p. 248.

Other influences were working in the same direction. Even without the special warnings which he had received at Nottingham, John must have been well aware that he had, as Roger of Wendover says, "almost as many enemies as he had barons."[1] The question was only how soon their silent hate would break out in open defiance, and whether he could once more terrify or beguile them into submission before the smouldering embers of their discontent were kindled into a general conflagration by Innocent's anathema and Peter's prophecy. On reaching London he addressed to all those whose fidelity he suspected a new demand for hostages, "that he might prove who would and who would not obey his orders." The response showed that he was even yet stronger than he himself had dared to believe. From many of these men he had already had hostages in his keeping for years; several of them had suffered in their family relations a far deeper injury at his hands; yet once again, at his bidding, they gave up to him sons, nephews, kinsmen, "as many as he would, not daring to resist his commands."[2] Eustace de Vesci and Robert Fitz-Walter alone refused all purgation, and fled, the one to Scotland, the other to France; their castles were seized, their lands confiscated, and themselves outlawed.[3] With his own servants and clerks the king dealt in yet more summary fashion; those among them whom he suspected were arrested and cast into prison.[4] Fresh humiliations were heaped upon the clergy. The Cistercians are said to have been mulcted of twenty-two thousand pounds in punishment for the help which they were supposed to have given to the enemies of Raymond of Toulouse;[5] and all the English clergy, both regular and secular,

[1] R. Wendover, vol. iii. p. 241.   [2] *Ib.* pp. 238, 239.
[3] *Ib.* p. 240 ; R. Coggeshall, p. 165 ; W. Coventry, vol. ii. p. 207. The entry in *Ann. Dunst.* a. 1211 about the razing of Fitz-Walter's castles and the cutting down of his woods is probably misplaced, and should be referred to 1212. See Note II. at end.
[4] W. Coventry, *l.c.* R. Coggeshall, *l.c.*, and *Ann. Dunst.* a. 1211 (for 1212) name as one of these victims a clerk called Geoffrey of Norwich, whom M. Paris, *Hist. Angl.* vol. ii. p. 126 and *Chron. Maj.* vol. ii. p. 527, confuses with the archdeacon whose fate is related by Roger of Wendover, vol. iii. p. 229. See above, p. 136.
[5] R. Coggeshall, p. 164.

1212   were forced to set their hands to a deed whereby they renounced all pecuniary claims against the king, and declared
that all the money which he had had from them since his
accession was a free and voluntary gift.[1] On the other
hand, John was taking some pains to conciliate the people.
He checked the severity of the Forest administration.
He forbade the extortions practised by his officers on merchants and pilgrims. " Moreover, he is said to have showed
mercy on widows, and done what in him lay to promote
peace in temporal affairs." Sternness and conciliation alike
did their work. Again " the land kept silence " ;[2] and it
seems that the first sound which broke the silence was a
declaration of the barons in favour of the king.

Some time between the summer of 1212 and the spring
of 1213 two remarkable letters were written by John, the
one to his chief justiciar in Ireland, Bishop John of Norwich,
the other to Earl William the Marshal.[3] Both letters deal
with the same subjects, and they were evidently despatched
both at once. The king greatly commends the bishop's
discretion in the matter of " the oath of fealty lately sworn
to us by our barons of Ireland, for the greater safety of
ourself and our realm," for which, he says, he is sending
letters of thanks to them all. He expresses the warmest
gratitude to William the Marshal, " as their spokesman in
this matter, and also as the one from whose suggestion and
sole desire we doubt not this thing took its rise, and to
whom we are indebted for the ready disposition and devotion
of all the rest." He states further that he is sending to the
bishop, the earl, and the other barons of the March " copies
of the letters patent which our magnates of England have
drawn up for us," and he requests that the barons of Ireland
will " set their seals to letters of similar tenour, and send

[1] Cf. *Rot. Chart.* pp. 191 b, 192 ; *Ann. Waverl.* a. 1212 ; W. Coventry,
vol. ii. p. 207 ; R. Coggeshall, p. 165, and M. Paris, *Hist. Angl.* vol. ii. p. 132,
and *Chron. Maj.* vol. ii. p. 537.

[2] W. Coventry, *l.c.*

[3] From the tenour of these letters it is clear that neither of the persons
addressed had been in England recently. We must therefore suppose that an order
countermanding the muster at Chester had reached the barons in Ireland before
they set out to obey the royal summons, and that for the muster at Nottingham
their presence had not been required.

them to us." Lastly, he alludes to some advice which the
Marshal and the other lay barons in Ireland "have sent to
us about making peace with the Church," and desires that
they will "provide, by the common counsel of our faithful
subjects in those parts, a form whereby peace may be made
sure without injury to our liberties and rights," and transmit
it to him. "See you to it," he adds to the justiciar, "that
this be done."[1]

We can hardly doubt that there is some connexion
between these letters and another yet more remarkable document, whose date must lie between Pandulf's visit in August
1211 and the spring of 1213. This is a manifesto addressed
"to all faithful Christians" by "the whole of the magnates of
Ireland," with Willam the Marshal and Meiler Fitz-Henry at
their head, expressing their "grief and astonishment" that
the Pope should propose to absolve the subjects of the
king of England from their allegiance, and declaring their
approval of John's political conduct and their determination
to "live and die with their king."[2] This manifesto may
have been drawn up when the barons of the Irish March, at
the Marshal's suggestion, renewed their fealty to John; or it
may have been their answer to John's request that they
would set their hands to and transmit to him letters patent
similar to those which, he says, had been "made for him"
by the magnates of England. There is, indeed, another
possible alternative. On more than one occasion, and by
more than one chronicler, John is charged with forging
letters and other like documents. The letter ascribed to
the magnates of Ireland and the letters—of which nothing
is now known—sent to them by John as having been issued
by the magnates of England may therefore have been both
alike forgeries. There is, however, nothing to indicate
that such was the case. If it was not, then it seems that
the barons of England, who in the autumn of 1212 were
believed to be on the verge of rebellion or something worse,
were yet so weak, as well as so false, that John could force

---

[1] *Rot. Claus.* vol. i. p. 132 b (*a. r.* 14).
[2] Hunter, *Three Catalogues*, pp. 42, 43; Sweetman, *Cal. Doc. Ireland*,
vol. i. pp. 73, 74 (No. 448).

1212   from them a collective declaration in writing which, whatever its precise import may have been, was evidently a declaration in his interest and for his advantage; and that in the same crisis the barons of the Irish March, acting under the guidance of the noblest and wisest man in their whole order, ranged themselves boldly on the side of John against all his enemies. The king, to whom for a moment ruin had seemed so near that he himself gave way to despair, was within a few months, perhaps even a few weeks, outwardly more than ever supreme.

On the other hand, those same loyal barons in Ireland who seem to have so emphatically declared their resolve to stand by the king in resistance to the papal sentence of deposition had yet urged upon him the importance of procuring a withdrawal of that sentence by endeavouring to make peace with the Church. Whether they did, according to John's request, draft a form of proposals to be laid before the Pope, there is nothing to show; but it is certain that in November John despatched to Rome four envoys charged to offer his acceptance of the terms which Pandulf and Durand had proposed fifteen months before.[1]

John, in fact, knew well how unsubstantial his apparent supremacy was, and how hollow were the foundations on which it rested. He knew that if he wished to prevent the fulfilment of Peter's prophecy, he must now disarm once for all, and secure permanently for his own interest, some one at least of the various enemies, or groups of enemies, against whom he had been struggling for six years at such overwhelming odds. By the end of 1212 the signs of the times were beginning to point out who this one must be; by the early spring of 1213 there could no longer be any doubt on the point. The fortunes of war in Germany and in southern Gaul had shattered John's hopes of crushing Innocent and Philip Augustus both at once. In Aquitaine Simon de Montfort and his "crusaders" were gradually winning their way against the Albigenses, and Raymond of Toulouse was practically ruined. In Germany the young King Frederic

---

[1] Cf. *Rot. Claus.* vol. i. p. 126; Innoc. III. *Epp.* l. xv. No. 234, and *Ann. Burton*, a. 1211, 1214.

of Sicily had at the Pope's instigation been elected to the
empire in Otto's stead.   Otto sought to regain his footing in
the country by marrying the daughter of his former rival,
Duke Philip of Suabia ; but the bride died a few days after
her marriage ;[1] and in November (1212) the political league
which Innocent was building up against Otto and John was
completed by a treaty of alliance between Frederic and
Philip Augustus.[2]   Triumphant everywhere on the continent, Innocent resolved to make an end of matters with
John.   In the winter of 1212 Stephen Langton and the
bishops of Ely and London carried to Rome in person their
complaints against their sovereign, and their entreaties that
such a state of things should be suffered to continue no
longer.   In January 1213 they returned to the French
court accompanied by Pandulf, and bringing with them a
letter from the Pope to the French king.[3]   Innocent in this
letter solemnly laid upon Philip, for his soul's health, the
task of expelling the English king from his realm, and bade
him assume in John's stead the sovereignty of England for
himself and his heirs for ever.[4]   It is said that the Pope
wrote at the same time to the other sovereigns and princes
of Europe, bidding them join under Philip's leadership in a
sort of crusade against John, and granting to all who should
take part in this expedition the same privileges, temporal
and spiritual, which were conferred on pilgrims to the Holy
Sepulchre.[5]

These letters and the papal decree for John's deposition
were publicly read to the French bishops, clergy and people
in a council assembled for that purpose at Soissons on the
Monday in Holy Week, April 8.[6]   It was no new idea
that the papal mandate suggested to Philip Augustus.   For
a whole year at least he had been contemplating the conquest of England and the establishment of his eldest son,
Louis, upon its throne ; in April 1212 Louis had already

---

[1] *Orig. Guelficae*, vol. iii. pp. 340, 341 ; W. Coventry, vol. ii. pp. 204, 205.
[2] Martène, *Ampliss. Collectio*, vol. i. col. 1111. Cf. W. Armor. *Gesta
P. A.* cc. 158, 159.
[3] Cf. R. Wendover, vol. iii. pp. 241, 242, and R. Coggeshall, p. 165.
[4] R. Wendover, *l.c.*   [5] R. Wendover, vol. iii. pp. 241, 242.
[6] W. Armor. *Gesta P. A.* c. 165.

1213   arranged the terms on which he would receive the homage
of the English barons and the political relation in which he
was to stand towards his father after his own coronation in
England.[1]   To Philip and Louis the Pope's commission was
merely the signal that their longed-for hour had come.
" Then the king of the French, hearing and receiving the
thing which he had long desired, girded himself up for the
fight," and bade all his men, on pain of " culvertage," be
ready to meet him at Rouen on April 21, the first Sunday
after Easter ;[2] and ships, victuals, arms and men were
rapidly gathered together in answer to his call.[3]

Still more prompt and vigorous were John's preparations
for defence.   He seems to have begun by ordering that all
English ships should return to the ports to which they
severally belonged not later than the first Sunday in Lent,
March 3.   On that day he despatched writs to the bailiffs
of the seaport towns, bidding them make out a list of the
vessels which they found in their respective ports capable of
carrying six horses or more, and direct the captains and
owners of all such vessels, in his name, to bring them to
Portsmouth at Mid-Lent (March 21), "well manned with
good and brave mariners, well armed, who shall go on our
service at our expense."[4]   He next bade the sheriffs summon
all earls, barons, knights, freemen and sergeants, whosoever
they were and of whomsoever they held, who ought to have
arms or could get them, and who had done him homage and
fealty, to the intent that, "as they love us and themselves
and all that is theirs, they be at Dover at the close of Easter
next, well prepared with horses and arms and with all their
might to defend our head, and their own heads, and the land
of England.   And let no man who can bear arms stay behind,
on pain of culvertage and perpetual servitude ; and let each
man follow his own lord ; and let those who have no land
and can carry arms come thither to take our pay."   Each

---

[1] *Foedera*, vol. i. pt. i. p. 104.
[2] R. Wendover, vol. iii. p. 243.   Cf. W. Coventry, vol. ii. p. 209.   W.
Armor. *Philipp.* l. ix. v. 235, makes the day April 22.   " Culvertage " was the
penalty for treason—forfeiture and perpetual servitude.
[3] W. Coventry, *l.c.*
[4] Writ given by R. Wendover, vol. iii. p. 244.

sheriff was to see that all sales of victuals and all markets
within his sheriffdom "followed the host," and that none were
held elsewhere within his jurisdiction.   He himself was to
come to the muster "in force, with horses and arms," and to
bring his roll, whereby the king might be certified who had
obeyed his summons and who had stayed behind.[1]

England responded as quickly and readily as France to
the call of her king; the threat of "culvertage" seems to
have acted upon the Englishmen of John's day as the threat
of being accounted "nithing" had acted upon their forefathers in the days of William Rufus and Henry I.; they
came together at the appointed places—Dover, Faversham
and Ipswich—in such crowds that in a few days, despite
John's precautions, the supply of food became insufficient,
and the marshals of the host found it needful to dismiss the
greater part of the light-armed troops, retaining only the
knights, sergeants and better-armed freemen, with the cross-
bowmen and archers.   The picked body thus left, which was
finally reviewed by the king on Barham Down, near Canterbury, was still so numerous that a patriotic chronicler declares,
"If they had been all of one heart and mind for king and
country, there was no prince under heaven against whom
they could not have defended the realm of England." [2]   How
many of the barons in the host had come to it with the
intention of going over to Philip as soon as he landed, it is
useless to inquire; perhaps the only one whom we can with
full confidence acquit of any such suspicion is William the
Marshal.[3]   The king's plan, however, was that his fleet should

---

[1] Writ in R. Wendover, vol. iii. p. 245.

[2] R. Wendover, vol. iii. pp. 245, 246.   Cf. *Ann. Dunst.* a. 1212 (evidently
meant for 1213).   John was at Canterbury May 4-6, 1213; *Itin.* a. 14.

[3] John, who in his prosperous days made almost a parade of disbelief in
William's loyalty, and delighted in straining it to the uttermost by saying and
doing everything he could think of to insult and provoke William, nevertheless
knew well that in moments of peril William was the one counsellor to whose dis-
interestedness he could safely trust, the one follower on whom he could count
unreservedly, the one friend whom he could not do without.   So at the close of
1212 or early in 1213 he had recalled the Marshal to his side, and proved his
confidence in him by giving him back his two sons who were in England as
hostages (*Hist. de G. le Mar.* vv. 14492-598).   The bishop of Norwich had
also come over from Ireland with five hundred knights and other horsemen to
join the muster (R. Wendover, vol. iii. p. 245).   It tells something of the success of
John's measures for the settlement of the Irish March that the simultaneous

intercept the invaders and "drown them in the sea before ever they could set foot on the land"; and as his ships were more numerous than Philip's, the plan had a good chance of success.[1]

But the first check to Philip's enterprise was to come from another quarter. Even if we could perceive no outward indication of the Pope's motives in giving his commission to the French king, we should still find it hard to believe that so far-seeing a statesman as Innocent III. seriously contemplated with approval the prospect of a French conquest of England. At the moment, indeed, France was the most efficient political instrument of the Papacy; but it could scarcely be a part of the papal policy to give her such an overwhelming predominance as she would have acquired by the annexation of England to her crown. England, no less than France, had her place in the European political system, of which Innocent looked upon himself as the director and the guardian; and the extinction of England as an independent state would have destroyed the balance of powers which it was a special function of the Papacy to maintain with the utmost care, and whose preservation was of great importance to Innocent for carrying into effect his own political designs. There can hardly be a reasonable doubt that he made use of Philip's ambition for a purpose of his own, a purpose which was really the direct opposite of that which Philip had in view—the purpose, not of crushing England, but of winning her back to the Roman alliance, and thus securing her as a counterpoise, in case of need, to the power of Philip himself.[2] In a word, Innocent and John had simultaneously recognized the fact that, in the interest of both alike, the time for their reconciliation had come.

John, as we have seen, had paved the way by offering, at the close of 1212, his acceptance of the terms proposed by the Pope in 1211. Innocent's reply to this offer was written on February 27, 1213. Although, he said, he considered

---

absence of the justiciar and the Marshal, at such a crisis in the king's fortunes, appears to have been followed by no disturbance in the country which they thus left without a ruler.

[1] R. Wendover, vol. iii. p. 246.
[2] See Petit-Dutaillis, *Hist. de Louis VIII.* pp. 37, 38.

himself no longer bound by his own terms, since the king
had rejected them, yet for the sake of peace he was willing
to abide by the form of agreement thus again proposed, if
before June 1 the king would, by an oath sworn in his
presence by four barons, and by letters patent addressed to
the archbishop of Canterbury and the other exiled bishops,
promise to keep it faithfully and fulfil it effectually, " according to the expositions and explanations which we have
thought good to be set forth for the removal of all scruple
and doubt." In May, when all England was expecting the
attack of Philip Augustus, three of John's messengers brought
back from Rome this letter, together with a copy of the form
originally committed to Pandulf and Durand, and the
"expositions and explanations" of the arrangements now
required on both sides to insure its execution.[1] All these
documents seem to have been communicated to Pandulf in
a private interview which he had with the Pope on the eve
of his departure from Rome in January;[2] at any rate he
was well aware of their contents and fully instructed how to
act in consequence. Just as the French fleet was ready to
sail, he in the Pope's name forbade all further proceedings
against England till he should have once more appealed to
John and learned whether he would yet repent.[3] Close upon
the return of the English envoys from Rome followed two
Templars, who landed at Dover with a message from Pandulf
to the king, requesting an interview. It took place at Dover
on May 13. In presence of king and legate, the earls of
Salisbury, Warren, and Ferrars and the count of Boulogne
swore in John's behalf the oath of security required by
Innocent; and on the same day John published by letters
patent the agreement concluded between himself and Pandulf in the form which the Pope had prescribed.[4]

[1] The Pope's letter, the "Forma," and the "Expositiones" are given in
Innoc. III. *Epp.* l. xv. No. 234. The two former are also in *Ann. Burton.*
a. 1214. I think there can be no doubt that the three documents together
constitute the "quasi peremptorium mandatum" brought by the three envoys
mentioned in W. Coventry, vol. ii. p. 209. Cf. above, p. 160.
[2] R. Wendover, vol. iii. p. 242.   [3] R. Coggeshall, p. 166.
[4] Cf. W. Coventry, vol. ii. p. 210, and the letter patent in R. Wendover,
vol. iii. pp. 248-52, Innoc. III. *Epp.* l. xvi. No. 76, and *Foedera*, vol. i. pt. i.
p. 111.

1213   Two days later—on Wednesday, May 15—king and legate met again, " with the great men of the realm," in the house of the Knights Templars at Ewell, near Dover.   There, by a charter attested by himself, the archbishop of Dublin, the chief justiciars of England and Ireland, seven earls (of whom the Marshal was one), and three barons, the king " granted and freely surrendered to God and His holy Apostles Peter and Paul, and to the Holy Mother Church of Rome, and to Pope Innocent and his Catholic successors," the whole realm of England and " the whole realm of Ireland," with all rights thereunto appertaining, to receive them back and hold them thenceforth as a feudatary of God and the Roman Church.   He swore fealty to the Pope for both realms in Pandulf's presence, promised to perform liege homage to the Pope in person if he should ever have an opportunity of so doing, and pledged all his successors to a like engagement, besides undertaking to furnish the Roman see with a yearly sum of one thousand marks—seven hundred for England and three hundred for Ireland.[1]

One English chronicler says that John, in performing this homage, acted " according to what had been decreed at Rome." [2]   Another, not less generally accurate and well informed, says that John " added it of his own accord " to the agreement already completed.[3]   On the whole, it is probable that this latter account of the matter is the correct one, at least thus far, that the scheme originated not at Rome, but in England.   Not much weight can indeed be attached to the king's own assertion, made in the charter of homage itself, that the act was a voluntary one, which he had done by way of penance and humiliation for his offences, " not urged by force nor compelled.by fear, but of our own good free will and by the common counsel of our barons " ; [4]

[1] Innoc. III. *Epp.* l. xvi. No. 77 ; R. Wendover, vol. iii. pp. 252-4 ; *Foedera*, vol. i. pt. i. pp. 111, 112.   The oath of fealty is given by R. Wendover, p. 255, and in *Foedera*, p. 112.   Roger makes the date Ascension Eve, but it was really the Wednesday in the week before Rogation Sunday.

[2] R. Wendover, vol. iii. p. 252.

[3] " Addidit autem hoc ex suo," W. Coventry, vol. ii. p. 210.

[4] In a private letter which he wrote to the Pope on the same day, John says he did it "inspirante gratia Sancti Spiritus, ad perpetuam Ecclesiae pacem et exaltationem," Innoc. III. *Epp.* l. xvi. No. 78.

nor is the accuracy of this version of the transaction proved
by the fact that Innocent accepted it without remark in his
reply to John's letters on the subject,[1] and that no extant
document emanating from the court of Rome contains the
slightest indication that the Pope had ever demanded or
suggested any proceeding of the kind. There is, however,
no perceptible reason why Innocent should have required of
John a penance of so extraordinary a character, nor why, if
he did require it, either he or his royal penitent should make
a secret of his having done so. On the other hand, John
had a very cogent reason for "adding something of his
own" to the agreement between himself and Innocent. If
he was to give up all for which he had been fighting—and
fighting successfully—against the Pope and the Church for
the last six years, he must make quite sure of gaining such
an advantage as would be worth the sacrifice. Mere
release from excommunication and interdict was certainly,
in his eyes, not worth any sacrifice at all. To change the
Pope from an enemy into a political friend was worth it, but
—from John's point of view—only if the friendship could
be made something much more close and indissoluble than
the ordinary official relation between the Pope and every
Christian sovereign. He must bind the Pope to his personal
interest by some special tie of such a nature that the
interest of the Papacy itself would prevent Innocent from
casting it off or breaking it. For a sovereign of John's
character no additional sacrifice would be involved in the
device which he actually employed for this purpose. To
outward personal humiliation of any kind John was absolutely indifferent, when there was any advantage to be
gained by undergoing it. To any humiliation which the
Crown or the nation might suffer in his person, he was
indifferent under all circumstances. His plighted faith he
had never had a moment's hesitation in breaking, whether it
were sworn to his father, his brother, his allies, or his people,
and which he would break with equal facility when sworn
to the supreme Pontiff; moreover, he took the precaution of

---

[1] Innoc. III. *Epp.* l. xvi. No. 79.

1213   inserting in his charter a saving clause which he could easily
have interpreted, had occasion ever arisen, so as to reduce
the whole transaction to a mere empty form.[1]   There seems,
in short, to be good reason for believing that John's homage
to the Pope was offered without any pressure from Rome,
and on grounds of deliberate policy.[2]

How far the credit or discredit—whichever it be—of
that policy belongs to John is, however, a question not
easily solved.   Two years later, the English barons seem to
have claimed the credit for themselves.   We are told that
they besought the Pope, "as he was lord of England," to
take their part against John, "since he well knew that they
had at his command boldly opposed the king in behalf of
the Church's liberty, and that the king had granted an
annual revenue to Rome, and bestowed other honours on
the Pope and the Roman Church, not of his own accord,
but only out of fear and under compulsion from them." [3]

[1] "Salvis nobis et haeredibus nostris justitiis, libertatibus et regalibus nostris,"
R. Wendover, vol. iii. p. 254.

[2] If we may believe Matthew Paris, the Pope was not the only potentate to
whom John about this time offered homage and tribute.   In Matthew's *Gesta
Abbatum S. Albani*, vol. i. pp. 236-40, and in his *Chronica Majora*, vol. ii.
pp. 559-62, is a long account of an embassy which John is said to have sent to
the emir of Morocco, Al Moumenim (Mohammed al Nassir), "significans eidem
quod se et regnum suum libenter redderet eidem et dederet, et deditum teneret
ab ipso, si placeret ei, sub tributum.   Necnon et legem Christianam, quam
vanam censuit, relinquens, legi Machomet fideliter adhaereret."   Matthew proceeds
to give a lively account of the ambassadors' adventures, and of the rebuke which
the emir administered, through them, to the sovereign who had sent them on so
shameful an errand ; all of which Matthew professes to have heard from one of
the envoys themselves.   Unluckily for him, he has given two contradictory dates
for the embassy.   In the *Gesta Abbatum* he represents it as taking place during
the Interdict ; and Dr. Lingard has shown, by evidence drawn from Matthew
himself, that if it was sent at all, it must have been sent in 1212 (Lingard, *Hist.
England*, vol. ii. p. 325 ; cf. M. Paris, *Chron. Maj.* vol. ii. p. 566).   But in
Chron. Maj. Matthew puts it after the reconciliation with Rome, representing it
as despatched by John in his disappointment at finding that transaction profit him
less than he had expected.   The story of the interview between the envoys and
the emir, as Matthew tells it, has therefore a very strong appearance of having
been invented by that writer, as a kind of satire on John's submission to the
Pope ; though the mere fact of some overture on John's part for an alliance with
the emir is neither impossible nor unlikely.

[3] In March 1215 William Mauclerc, John's agent at Rome, writes to John
that there have come thither some envoys sent by the barons to complain to the
Pope, "cum ipse sit Dominus Angliae," that John refuses them their rights, etc.,
and he continues : "Supplicant autem Domino Papae quod super his eis provideret,
cum satis constet ei quod ipsi audacter pro libertate Ecclesiae ad mandatum suum

This, if correctly reported, is a distinct assertion by the malcontent barons that they had deliberately chosen to set up the Pope as temporal overlord of their country, and that it was pressure from them which had compelled John to do him homage as such. The truth probably lies half-way between this version and that of the king. Whether the "common counsel of the barons" was given spontaneously to John and accepted by him, or whether it was merely a response to a proposal which he had laid before them, there can be little doubt that each party adopted the scheme in the hope of turning it to account against the other party. That on the side of the barons this hope proved utterly delusive, while on the side of John it was completely realized, simply shows once more how far less than a match was the collective sagacity of the barons for the single-handed dexterity of the king.

It was not till many years later that a great historian, who was also a vehement partisan, denounced John's homage to the Pope as "a thing to be detested for all time."[1] The Barnwell annalist, writing at the time of the event, tells us indeed that "to many it seemed ignominious, and a heavy yoke of servitude." But the action of all parties at the moment was a practical acknowledgement of their consciousness that, as the same annalist says, John "by this act provided prudently both for himself and for his people; for matters were in such a strait, and so great was the fear on all sides, that there was no more ready way of evading the imminent peril—perhaps no other way at all. For when once he had put himself under Apostolical protection, and made his realms a part of the patrimony of S. Peter, there was not in the Roman world a sovereign who durst attack him, or invade them; inasmuch as Pope Innocent was universally held in awe above all his predecessors for many years past."[2]

---

se vobis opponerent, et quod vos annuum redditum Domino Papae et Ecclesiae Romanae concessistis, et alios honores quos ei et Romanae Ecclesiae exhibuistis, non sponte nec ex devotione, imo ex timore *et per eos coactus* fecistis." *Foedera.* vol. i. pt. i. p. 120. See Lingard, *Hist. Eng.* vol. i. p. 333.

[1] M. Paris, *Hist. Angl.* vol. ii. p. 135.

[2] W. Coventry, vol. ii. p. 211.

1213

May 23

John had, in fact, at one stroke cut the ground from under the feet of all his enemies both at home and abroad. The people resumed their ordinary attitude of loyalty on Pandulf's assurance that it was once more, and more than ever, sanctioned by the Church. The traitor barons found themselves without a cloak for their treason, and were reduced to send out letters patent repudiating all connexion with the French king.[1] Philip found himself without an ally, and without an excuse for his enterprise. The believers in Peter of Wakefield, indeed, still looked forward with a vague expectation to Ascension Day. But the king himself could meet its dawn without fear. He had ordered his royal tent to be set up in a large open field, and caused his heralds to proclaim a general invitation to all who were within reach, to come and spend the festival day in stately festivities with him. " And a right joyous day it was, the king taking his pleasure and making merry with the bishops and nobles who had come together at his call." [2] Still Peter's disciples were not convinced ; some of them took up the idea that the prediction might refer not to the ecclesiastical but to the civil anniversary of John's coronation, May 27, which in 1213 was four days after Ascension Day. This anniversary, however, passed over likewise without any mishap. Then the wise and the foolish alike began to see that John had prevented a literal fulfilment of the prophecy by lending himself to a figurative one. He had " ceased to be king " by laying his crown at the feet of Pandulf, to take it back again on conditions which unquestionably helped to fix it, for the time at least, more securely than ever on his brow. The scapegoat of all parties was the unlucky prophet himself. Next day he and his son, who had been imprisoned with him, were tied each to a horse's tail, dragged thus from Corfe to Wareham, and there hanged.[3]

Pandulf meanwhile had returned to France, and com-

---

[1] W. Coventry, vol. ii. p. 211.

[2] *Ib.* p. 212. Cf. R. Wendover, vol. iii. pp. 255, 256.

[3] W. Coventry and R. Wendover, *ll.cc.* Cf. *Hist. des Ducs,* pp. 125, 126 ; and R. Coggeshall, p. 167. The date, May 28, is given in *Ann. Waverl.* a. 1213.

manded Philip, on pain of the Pope's displeasure, to lay aside
all thoughts of invading England and go home in peace.
Philip at first indignantly refused to abandon a scheme
which, he said, he had planned at the Pope's instigation, and
for which he had already spent more than sixty thousand
pounds.[1]   But he dared not go on in the teeth of the papal
prohibition ; so he turned his wrath upon the one great
feudatary of his realm who had refused to take part in the
projected invasion, Count Ferrand of Flanders.   Ordering
his fleet to sail round as quickly as possible to Swine, the
king dashed into Flanders at the head of all his forces.
Ferrand besought help of John, with whom he was already
in alliance ; and John at once despatched five hundred ships,
carrying a large body of horse and foot under the command
of his half-brother Earl William of Salisbury and the counts
of Holland and Boulogne.[2]   They sailed on Tuesday, May
28, intending to land at Swine and march across the country
to join Ferrand ; but a contrary wind delayed them so that
they did not reach Swine till Thursday, the 30th ; and then,
to their amazement, they found the harbour occupied by the
French fleet, which, however, they soon discovered to be
unguarded save by a few seamen, all the troops having gone
ashore to ravage the neighbourhood.   Salisbury at once
ordered an attack ; the French sailors were speedily
overcome ; three hundred ships laden with provisions were
set drifting towards England, a hundred more were rifled of
their contents and then set on fire.   " Never came so much
wealth into England since King Arthur went to conquer it,"
says a contemporary poet.[3]   Next day Count Ferrand came
to meet his allies, and renewed his league with John.[4]   On
the Saturday—Whitsun Eve—the earls disembarked their
troops and advanced to attack the French at Dam.   The
overwhelming numbers of the enemy, who were headed by

[1] R. Wendover, vol. iii. p. 256 ; *Foedera,* vol. i. pt. i. p. 112.

[2] R. Wendover, vol. iii. p. 257.   Cf. W. Armor. *Gesta P. A.* cc. 169, 170 ;
and *Rot. Pat.* vol. i. p. 99.

[3] *Hist. de G. le Mar.* vv. 14612-40 ;   *Hist. des Ducs,* p. 130 (the dates are
from this writer) ; R. Wendover, vol. iii. p. 258 ; and W. Coventry, vol. ii.
p. 211.

[4] *Hist. des Ducs,* p. 131.   Cf. *Rot. Pat.* vol. i. p. 100.

1213 King Philip himself, compelled them to retreat. Salisbury, however, not only escaped to his ships, but brought all his prizes safe to England ;[1] while Philip was so mad with rage at the disaster to his fleet that he ordered the remnant of it to be burnt.[2] So far as England was concerned, his expedition was at an end.

John at once resolved that the fleet and the host which had been gathered for the defence of England should be used for an attack upon France. His plan was, while strengthening Ferrand's hands so as to keep Philip busy in Flanders, himself to land with an army in Poitou, and thus place the French kingdom between two fires. At the end of June he reassembled his forces at Porchester, and again despatched William of Salisbury to Flanders with further reinforcements and large sums of money. The magnates, however, refused to accompany the king over sea till he was absolved from excommunication.[3] Their excuse was transparently false ; his public absolution was indeed committed to Archbishop Stephen, and therefore deferred till Stephen's arrival in England ; but Pandulf had, in the Pope's name, declared him reconciled to the Church. It could only be from political motives that men who had without protest marched with the excommunicate king against Scotland, Ireland and Wales, and gathered year after year at his festival banquets, now suddenly became more punctilious about a matter of ecclesiastical discipline than Innocent III. himself. It was, however, no moment for quarrelling with them openly ; and their excuse, such as it was, soon ceased to exist.

King and legate had been rapidly pushing on the arrangements for the return of the exiles ;[4] and in June or July Archbishop Stephen and four of the bishops

[1] *Hist. des Ducs*, pp. 131-3 ; W. Coventry, vol. ii. p. 211 ; R. Wendover, vol. iii. p. 258. Salisbury was wrecked on the Northumberland coast on his return, but nothing was lost, *Hist. de G. le Mar.* vv. 14649-58.

[2] W. Coventry, *l.c.* ; *Hist. de G. le Mar.* vv. 14641-6.

[3] Cf. R. Wendover, vol. iii. p. 259, and W. Coventry, vol. ii. p. 212. John was at Porchester June 16, and at Bishopstoke June 17-20 and June 29-July 1 ; *Itin.* a. 15. For Salisbury's mission, see *Rot. Pat.* vol. i. pp. 100 b, 101 (June 22 and 26).

[4] R. Wendover, vol. iii. pp. 259, 260 ; W. Coventry, vol. ii. p. 211 ; *Rot. Pat.* vol. i. pp. 98 b, 99, 99 b, 100, 100 b ; *Rot. Chart.* pp. 193 b, 194.

landed at Dover.[1] On S. Margaret's Day, Saturday, July
20, they were received by the king at Winchester.[2] He
seems to have gone forth to meet them on the crest of the
hill which lies to the east of the city.[3] He threw himself at
the primate's feet, bidding him welcome, and with tears
imploring his mercy ; " and the prelates and all the rest,
when they saw this, could not refrain from weeping." The
procession made its way to the Old Minster and entered the
chapter-house ; the king swore on the Gospels " that he
would cherish, defend and maintain the holy Church and
her ordained ministers ; that he would restore the good laws
of his forefathers, especially S. Edward's, rendering to all
men their rights ; and that before the next Easter he would
make full restitution of all property which had been taken
away in connexion with the Interdict." This oath he seems
to have repeated publicly at the door of the church ; Stephen
then formally absolved him, led him into the church, and
celebrated mass in his presence, accepting his offering and
giving him the kiss of peace ; " and there was great joy
among the people." [4]

Having at last made up his mind to a formal reconciliation with both Pope and primate, John showed no signs of
a wish to evade any part of its terms. During the past
three months order after order had been issued in his name
for carrying into effect the provisions of his agreement with
Pandulf. The outlawry of the clergy had been revoked at
once, on May 15, and this revocation was repeated on
June 13.[5] Two laymen—Eustace de Vesci and Robert Fitz-
Walter—who had gone into exile, not in company with any of
the bishops nor for their sake, but on independent grounds,

---

[1] W. Coventry, vol. ii. p. 213, says " mense Junio " ; R. Wendover, vol.
iii. p. 260, July 16 ; Gerv. Cant. vol. ii. p. 108, and *Ann. Worc.* a. 1213,
say July 9.

[2] R. Wendover, *l.c.* Cf. *Ann. Tewkesb.* and *Worc.* a. 1213, and *Itin.*
a. 15.

[3] The *Ann. Dunst.*, which place the return of the exiles under a wrong year,
1212, say the king met them " in monte juxta *Porecestre.*" This is surely an
error for Winchester. Nothing is more likely than that John should have gone
to meet them on S. Giles's Hill.

[4] Cf. R. Wendover, vol. iii. p. 261; *Ann. Dunst.* a. 1212 ; and W. Coventry,
vol. ii. p. 213.

[5] *Rot. Pat.* vol. i. p. 100, 100 b.

1213 in the autumn of 1212, had been specially mentioned by name in John's agreement with the Pope, and promised reinstatement in their lands and in the king's favour. Safe-conducts were issued to these two barons on May 27, and orders for the restitution of their property on July 17, 19, and 21.[1] For the bishops something more than mere restitution was required ; they, or the Pope and Pandulf for them, claimed indemnification as well ; and the terms of the indemnity were difficult to decide. John seems to have proposed that they should be decided by a kind of general July 21 inquest ; on the day after his absolution he bade all the sheriffs in England cause a deputation of four men and the reeve from each township to be at S. Albans on August 4, "that through them and his other ministers he might ascertain the truth concerning the damages suffered by the several bishops, and what had been taken from them, and how much was due to each." Whether such an inquisition was actually held does not appear ; but early in August the justiciar and the bishop of Winchester met the primate, the other bishops and the magnates in a great council at S. Albans ; there, in the king's name, peace was proclaimed to all ; the observance of King Henry's laws and the disuse of evil customs were strictly enjoined ; and the sheriffs, foresters, and other officers of the Crown were warned, "as they valued their limbs and their lives," to commit no more extortions and wrongs, "as they had been wont to do."[2]

John meanwhile had returned to the coast of Dorset, where the host had apparently been ordered to reassemble, with the intention of sailing for Poitou. In view of his own expected absence from England, he is said to have committed the government to the justiciar and the bishop of Winchester, bidding them "order all its affairs with the advice of the archbishop of Canterbury."[3] The king's departure, however, now met with a new series of checks. First the knights came to him in a body and protested that

---

[1] *Rot. Pat.* vol. i. pp. 99, 101 b ; *Rot. Claus.* vol. i. p. 146.

[2] R. Wendover, vol. iii. pp. 261, 262.

[3] *Ib.* p. 261. Roger says John went to Portsmouth ; but the *Itinerary* shows him hovering about between Studland, Corfe, Dorchester, Poorstock, and Gillingham.

the months which had elapsed since they assembled for
defence against the French had consumed all their money,
so that they could not possibly follow him any farther
unless he would pay their expenses.   This he refused to do.[1]
The barons of the north were the next recalcitrants;
when called upon to accompany him over sea, they "with
one mind and determination refused, asserting that according
to the tenure of their lands they were not bound to him in
this; besides that they were already too much worn out and
impoverished by expeditions within the realm."[2]   The angry
king embarked with his household on August 5 or 6, and
sailed to Jersey; but finding that no one followed him thither
he soon came back,[3] in a mighty rage, "cursing the day and
hour when he had consented to the peace, and declaring that
he had been deceived, and made a gazing-stock for nothing."[4]
His mercenaries and foreign auxiliaries were still a formidable host; and with these he set out for the north, "to
bring back the rebels to their obedience."[5]   He seems to
have landed at Corfe on August 9; he began his northward
march from Winchester on the 16th, reached Wallingford
on the 25th, and Northampton on the 28th.[6]   On the 25th
Archbishop Stephen was in London, presiding over a great
council in S. Paul's Cathedral.[7]   Thence he hurried away in
pursuit of the king; he overtook him at Northampton, and
remonstrated vigorously against John's plans of vengeance
upon the northern barons, telling him he would bring
contempt upon the oath which he had sworn before his
absolution if he made war upon any man without a legal
sentence.   John "with a great clamour" declared that he
would not put off the business of his realm for the archbishop, who had no concern with matters of lay jurisdiction;
and early next morning he set out, "in a furious temper," for
Nottingham.   The archbishop followed him, and threatened
that unless the project were at once given up he would
excommunicate every man, save the king himself, who

---

[1] R. Wendover, vol. iii. pp. 261, 262.   [2] R. Coggeshall, p. 167.
[3] R. Wendover, vol. iii. p. 261 ; for dates see *Itin.* a. 15.
[4] M. Paris, *Hist. Angl.* vol. ii. p. 141.
[5] R. Wendover, vol. iii. p. 262.   [6] *Itin.* a. 15.
[7] R. Wendover, vol. iii. p. 263.

1213 should take part in any military expedition so long as the
interdict continued in force ; nor could John shake him off
till he had appointed a day for the accused barons to come
and stand their trial in his court.[1]

Characteristically, John behaved as if unconscious of
defeat. He carried out his progress through the north in
peaceable instead of warlike guise, and did not return to
London till the end of September.[2] His arrival there was
timed to coincide with that of the papal legate who came as
the specially appointed minister of England's restoration to
the communion of the Church, and whose authority would
for the time supersede that of the primate. On September 27 Cardinal Nicolas of Tusculum landed in England.[3]
On the 30th he met the king, bishops and barons at a
council in London, to discuss plans for a pecuniary settlement between the Crown and the clergy. John offered the
bishops one hundred thousand marks down, with security for
the payment before next Easter of any damages in excess of
that sum which might be discovered on further investigation.
The legate urged the bishops to accept this offer ; but they
preferred to accept nothing till they had prepared their own
estimate and could demand the sum total at once ; and the
king readily consented to the delay. Three days had been
spent in the discussion. On the fourth day, October 3, the
council reassembled in S. Paul's. At the foot of the high
altar, in the sight of clergy and people, the ceremony which
John and Pandulf had gone through at Ewell was repeated
by John and Nicolas. John resigned his crown into the
legate's hands, received it back from him, and swore fealty
to him as the Pope's representative ; and the charter of
homage and tribute, which had been temporarily sealed with
wax and delivered to Pandulf, was sealed with gold and
finally made over to Nicolas, " for the benefit of the Pope
and the Roman Church." [4]

Still the interdict could not be raised till the settlement

[1] R. Wendover, vol. iii. pp. 262, 263. John was at Northampton August
28-31, at "Salvata" September 2, and at Nottingham September 3 ; *Itin.* a. 15.
[2] *Itin.* a. 15.   [3] *Ann. Waverl.* a. 1213.
[4] R. Wendover, vol. iii. pp. 275, 276 ; *Foedera*, vol. i. pt. i. p. 115. Cf.
W. Coventry, vol. ii. p. 214.

between the Crown and the bishops was completed ; and
another meeting for this purpose was appointed to take
place at Reading on November 3.   To this meeting all the
interested parties came, except the king,[1] who was at
Wallingford, where it seems he had appointed the northern
barons to appear before his court on All Saints' Day.   The
legate was there too, and through his mediation the barons
were reconciled to the king and admitted to the kiss of
peace.[2] As John did not show himself at Reading, the
bishops went to Wallingford in their turn.   By that time
John had moved on to Woodstock ; but he seems to have
returned to Wallingford to meet them for a few hours on
November 5,[3] and repeated his former proposals.   These,
however, " seemed little to those who had had their castles
razed, their houses levelled with the ground, and their woods
cut down " ; so that it was decided to refer the matter to the
arbitration of four barons.   But this arbitration never took
place.   " All the parties concerned in the matter of the interdict " came together again at Reading on December 6,[4] and
each of the injured persons brought forth a schedule of the
amount of his losses and damages ; the legate, however,
supported the king in his refusal to pay the whole sum at
once ; and after three days' deliberation no one received
anything at all, except the archbishop and the five bishops
who had been in exile beyond the sea, to whom John on
December 12 ordered the payment of fifteen thousand marks.[5]
At last it seems to have been agreed that the damages
should be investigated by two sets of commissioners acting
together, one set appointed by the king, the other by the
primate, and that the sum to be paid by the Crown should
be fixed—doubtless on the report of these commissioners—
by the Pope ; and this scheme was carried out in the
following year.[6]

[1] R. Wendover, vol. iii. p. 276.

[2] *Ann. Dunst.* a. 1212 (*i.e.* 1213).   " Quae pax non tenuit, quia promissa
non fuerant hinc inde soluta," adds the chronicler.

[3] Cf. R. Wendover, *l.c.*, and *Itin.* a. 15.

[4] R. Wendover, *l.c.*

[5] *Ib.*   John's order for this payment is in *Rot. Pat.* vol. i. p. 106.

[6] Such an investigation by joint commissions was going on in the diocese of
Durham in January 1214, *Rot. Claus.* vol. i. p. 106 b.

questions had arisen in connexion with the
...t between Church and king. There were no less
: vacant sees and thirteen vacant abbeys,[1] all, of
in the king's hands. In July 1213 John issued
orders for filling these vacancies in the manner which had
been customary under Henry II.; the several chapters were
bidden to send delegates, by whom an election was to be
made in the king's presence, wherever he might chance to
be.[2] This arrangement implied a tacit understanding that
the delegates were to elect a candidate designated by the
king. The bishops seized their opportunity to protest
against this practice and claim for the churches their
canonical right of free election, subject only to the royal
assent, signified by the grant of the regalia. The legate
seems to have been, passively at least, on the side of the
Crown; but John was anxious to avoid any fresh quarrel
with the primate, and he therefore allowed the elections to
be left in abeyance till Nicolas should receive instructions
about the matter from the Pope. These came at last in
a somewhat ambiguous form. Innocent bade Nicolas cause
the vacant sees and abbeys to be filled with men "not only
distinguished for their good life and learning, but also
faithful to the king and useful as helpers and advisers for
the welfare of the realm, and appointed by means of
canonical election or postulation, the king's assent being
sought thereunto."[3] It was obviously possible to interpret
this letter as sanctioning, by implication at least, the claims
of the Crown; and Nicolas was quite willing thus to
interpret it in John's favour. John, however, knew that no
such interpretation would ever be accepted by Langton;
and with Langton he had no mind to quarrel at that
moment, even though he might have the legate on his own
1214   side. He did indeed issue on January 2, 1214, orders for

---

[1] York, Durham, Chester, Worcester, Exeter, Chichester, Whitby, S.
Edmund's, S. Augustine's at Canterbury, Reading, S. Benet's at Hulme, Battle,
Ramsey, Peterborough, Cirencester, Eynsham (W. Coventry, vol. ii. p. 213),
Grimsby, Wherwell and Sherborne (*Rot. Claus.* vol. i. pp. 147, 148, 150).

[2] *Rot. Claus.* vol. i. pp. 146 b, 148, 150, 150 b.

[3] Date, November 1, 1213; R. Wendover, vol. iii. p. 277. Cf. W.
Coventry, vol. ii. p. 216.

the election of a bishop to Worcester and an abbot to
Eynsham, "according to the customs of the realm";[1] but
he seems to have immediately afterwards made an arrangement with the archbishop which satisfied the latter for the
time being. On the 12th John signified to Stephen his
acceptance of "the form known to us concerning the
making of elections, saving our right in all things"; he
abandoned his claim to have the elections held only in his
own presence, and delegated the power of giving them the
royal assent to the ministers who were to have the charge
of the realm during his absence beyond the sea; and he
closed his letter to the archbishop with the words: "Be
assured that there is no controversy between us."[2] On the
26th he wrote again to Stephen, requesting him to confirm
the election of the vice-chancellor, Walter de Gray, to the
see of Worcester, and issued orders for elections to five
bishoprics and three great abbeys.[3]

What made both John and Stephen anxious for an
agreement on this point was the king's approaching departure for the Continent. Soon after Stephen's arrival in
England John had made up his mind that his expedition
to Poitou must be postponed till the spring,[4] and in August
(1213) he fixed February 2, 1214, as its approximate date.[5]
Throughout the autumn and winter the fleet was preparing
at Portsmouth under the superintendence of William de
Wrotham, archdeacon of Taunton.[6] Arrangements were
also in progress for securing the tranquillity of the realm
during the king's absence. On June 3 John—according to
his own account at Pandulf's desire—had made a truce with
the Welsh to last till August 1.[7] By August 25 he had
enlisted the aid of the newly arrived primate as a peace-
maker between the English realm and these troublesome
neighbours; the wardens of the Marches were authorized
to agree to a prolongation of the truce till November 1,

---

[1] *Rot. Pat.* vol. i. p. 107. The name of the abbey is there printed as
Evesham; but cf. W. Coventry, vol. ii. p. 213.
[2] *Rot. Claus.* vol. i. p. 160.   [3] *Rot. Pat.* vol. i. p. 109, 109 b.
[4] *Foedera,* vol. i. pt. i. p. 114.   [5] *Rot. Pat.* vol. i. p. 103 b.
[6] *Ib.* p. 106 b; *Rot. Claus.* vol. i. pp. 156, 158.
[7] *Rot. Pat.* p. 100.

1213   on the understanding that at its expiration the archbishop
of Canterbury would negotiate with the Welsh on the king's
behalf.[1]   Of these negotiations there is no further record ;
but they seem to have resulted in keeping the Welsh in
check for some months at least.

In Ireland and in England John had to provide himself
with new vicegerents.   In July Bishop John of Norwich
resigned the justiciarship of the Irish March to go to Rome
on a mission for the king; the archbishop of Dublin was
appointed justiciar in his stead.[2]   On October 14 the office
of chief justiciar of England was vacated by the death of
Geoffrey Fitz-Peter,[3] who had held it ever since 1198, when
he was appointed to it by Richard on the resignation of
Hubert Walter.   It is impossible to regard Geoffrey as a
patriot; had he been one, he could scarcely have held the
reins of government under John for fourteen years without
coming into open conflict with his master.   He was, however, a man of much weight in the land by reason of his
noble birth, his great wealth, and his knowledge of law, and
also because he was connected by kindred, affinity or friendship with all the great baronial houses.   Such a man was
necessarily somewhat of a check upon the self-will of John.
The king's personal feeling towards his minister found a
characteristic expression when he heard of Geoffrey's death :
"When he gets to hell," laughed John, "he may greet
Archbishop Hubert, whom he is sure to meet there ! "[4]
So long as the king was himself in England he could do
without any justiciar at all ; and accordingly no successor
was appointed to Geoffrey for more than three months.
John was, however, too cautious to venture upon any
glaring abuse of his newly acquired freedom of action[5] at
a moment when it was of the utmost importance for him
to conciliate all parties and all classes by every means in
his power.   The one recorded incident of this period of

---

[1] *Rot. Pat.* vol. i. p. 103 b.   [2] *Ib.* p. 102.
[3] R. Wendover, vol. iii. p. 271.
[4] M. Paris, *Chron. Maj.* vol. ii. p. 558.
[5] M. Paris, *l.c.* p. 559, makes John repeat on the death of Geoffrey Fitz-
Peter the remark which he has previously recorded as having been made by the
king on the death of Hubert Walter.   See above, p. 113.

John's personal government, indeed, looks almost like a dim foreshadowing of one of the most weighty innovations which were to be made by the constitutional reformers of the latter part of the century.

It seems that at the end of October or early in November the tenants by knight-service were ordered to meet the king at Oxford on November 15. On November 7 John sent letters to the sheriffs bidding each one of them cause the knights within his shire to appear as previously directed, with their arms, the barons also in person but without arms, " and "——so ran the writ——" that thou cause to come thither at the same time four discreet men of the shire, to speak with us concerning the affairs of our realm." [1] This writ is the earliest known instance of an attempt to call into council on " the affairs of the realm " representatives of the freemen of the shire, as distinguished from the tenants-in-chivalry. Representatives in the strict sense of the word, indeed, they were not ; the writ says nothing of how they were to be chosen, and there can be little doubt that they would be selected by the sheriff. Still, the fact remains that——so far as extant evidence goes——John Lackland seems to have been the first English statesman who proposed to give some place, however subordinate, in the great council of the realm to laymen who were neither barons nor knights, but simple freemen. His motive is plain ; he was seeking to win the support of the yeomen as a counterpoise to the hostility of the barons. Unluckily we know nothing of the results of his experiment, and cannot even be sure that it was actually tried ; for though the king was certainly at Oxford in that year on November 15 and the two following days,[2] no mention occurs, in either chronicle or record, of any council holden there at that date.

At Christmas John held his court at Windsor, " where he distributed robes of state to a multitude of his nobles." [3]

---

[1] *First Report on Dignity of a Peer* (1826), vol. ii. appendix i. p. 2, from Close Roll 15 John ; see Hardy's edition of the Close Rolls, vol. i. p. 165. In *Foedera*, vol. i. pt. i. p. 117, the document is printed with an obviously wrong date.

[2] *Itin.* a. 15.   [3] R. Wendover, vol. iii. p. 278.

1214   Immediately afterwards Count Ferrand of Flanders came over to cement his alliance with the English king by performing his homage to him in person, at Canterbury, in the second week of January 1214.[1] Raymond of Toulouse had been over shortly before; the fortunes of war had gone utterly against him, and nothing but prompt succour from John, in some shape or other, could enable him to hold out any longer in his capital city, the sole refuge now left to him. He is said to have gone back, after doing homage to John, with a subsidy of ten thousand marks.[2] Early in January the king announced to the primate and the bishops that he himself was about to depart over sea, and begged that they would lend their support to Bishop Peter of Winchester and the other persons in whose charge he intended to leave the kingdom during his absence.[3] At the end of the month he put in train a scheme for con-ciliating the eldest son of the late justiciar by marrying him to the greatest heiress in England—that same Countess Isabel of Gloucester who had once been married to John himself.[4] On February 1 John by letters patent appointed Peter des Roches, the bishop of Winchester, to the office of justiciar of England, and committed his realm to the custody and protection of the Holy Roman Church, the Pope and the Legate, leaving Peter as keeper of the peace in his stead.[5] Next day he embarked at Portsmouth with his queen, his son Richard,[6] his niece Eleanor of Britanny, and a quantity of treasure; he spent a few days at Yar-mouth in the Isle of Wight, and thence sailed to Poitou.[7]

---

[1] Cf. R. Coggeshall, p. 168; *Hist. des Ducs*, pp. 139-41, and *Itin.* a. 15. The Flemish authority says "li cuens . . . li fist houmage de la tierre ke il devoit avoir en Engletierre"; the English chronicler says the homage was for "all Flanders." Unluckily there seems to be no charter extant to settle the point.

[2] R. Coggeshall, p. 168. Raymond seems to have been on his way home, and travelling at John's expense, in January 1214; *Rot. Pat.* vol. i. pp. 106 b, 108 b.

[3] *Rot. Claus.* vol. i. p. 160.

[4] *Rot. Pat.* vol. i. p. 109 b.

[5] *Ib.* p. 110, 110 b.

[6] It is a question whether this means the queen's child so named, or that elder son Richard who figures actively in his father's struggle with the barons a year or two later.

[7] Cf. R. Wendover, vol. iii. p. 280; R. Coggeshall, p. 163; and *Itin.* a. 15.

It was evidently of set purpose that the appointment of a
new chief justiciar had been delayed till the very eve of
the king's departure.   When it came to the knowledge of
the barons, they all grumbled at having a foreigner set over
them ;[1] but they did not know it till the expedition had
sailed, and their discontent could vent itself only in useless
words.

Over sea the king's partisans were ready to welcome
him.   At La Rochelle the barons of Aquitaine came
crowding to offer him their allegiance.[2]   Leaving La
Rochelle on February 20, he moved northward to Mervant,
in the middle of Lower Poitou.   Mervant belonged to
Geoffrey de Lusignan ; and the king's visit to this place
may have been connected with some negotiations between
him and the Lusignan family which were certainly begun
soon after his landing in Aquitaine.   He next proceeded
southward, to the abbey of La Grâce-Dieu on the border
of Saintonge ; on February 25 he was at Niort.[3]   Meanwhile
he had opened communications with the men of Périgord
and the viscounts of Limoges and Turenne.[4]   On March 6
he was back at La Rochelle, whence he sent on the 8th, in
letters patent addressed to the "good men" of all the chief
cities of England, the following account of his expedition :
"Know ye that we and our faithful followers whom we
brought with us to Poitou are safe and well, and by God's
grace we have already begun to expedite our affairs to the
joy and gladness of our friends and the confusion of our
foes.   For on the Sunday before Mid-Lent we laid siege to
the castle of Milécu, which Porteclin de Mausé had fortified
against us, and on the following Tuesday we took it."[5]
Moving across Saintonge and up the Charente, he reached
Angoulême on the 13th, stayed there two days, then
advanced eastward to Saint-Junien and Aixe in the Limousin ;[6]
at Aixe, on March 22, he granted the seneschalship of
Limoges to Emeric de Roche, and that of Périgord to

---

[1] R. Coggeshall, p. 168.
[2] R. Wendover, vol. iii. p. 280.   John was at La Rochelle February 15-20,
Itin. a. 15.
[3] *Itin.* a. 15.   [4] *Rot. Pat.* vol. i. p. 111.
[5] *Ib.* p. 111 b.   [6] *Itin.* a. 15.

Geoffrey Teyson.[1]   On Palm Sunday, March 23, he left
Aixe, and thence he struck right across the county of La
Marche to Saint-Vaury and La Souterraine, on the southern
border of Berry ; he spent Good Friday and Easter at La
Souterraine,[2] and there, on Easter Day (March 30), he
received the homage of the count of Périgord.[3]   He then
re-crossed La Marche and the Limousin—stopping this time
for two days at Grandmont, where the monks evidently still
had a ready welcome for the son of their old friend King
Henry — back to Limoges and Angoulême, Cognac and
Saintes ; thence, turning southward, he proceeded through
Périgord as far as La Réole in the county of Agen.   On
April 20 he was back at Mausé in Saintonge, and for the
next fortnight he was never far from either La Rochelle or
Niort ; but on May 6 he was at Saint-Léger in Anjou, and it
was there that he spent Ascension Day, May 8.   Two days
later he was again at Niort.[4]

The panegyrist of Philip Augustus asserts that John's
sudden dash into the lands south of Périgord was prompted
by dread of Philip, who, " being desirous to meet him " in
the field, had hurried to the Poitevin border, and was
preparing to cut him off from his fleet.   The same writer,
however, owns almost in the same breath that " no one
knows, ever has known, or ever will know, the way of a
serpent, of a ship on the deep, of a feather in the wind, or of
a deceiver " such as John ; and that Philip dared neither
attempt to follow him nor await his return, but hurried back
—after burning the rural districts of Poitou—to protect his
own interests in Flanders.[5]   John's erratic movements had
probably a double purpose : to baffle Philip, and to ascertain
the extent of his own resources in the south.   Of more real
importance than these tentative excursions was a negotiation
which he had set on foot with the house of Lusignan, whose
alliance and allegiance he proposed to regain by giving the
infant Joan, his eldest daughter by Isabel of Angoulême, in

[1] *Rot. Pat.* p. 112 b.   [2] *Itin.* a. 15.
[3] *Rot. Pat. l.c.*   [4] *Itin.* a. 15.
[5] W. Armor. *Philipp.* l. x. vv. 99-115.   Cf. Peter of Blois's complaint (*Ep.*
xli.) of the impossibility of tracking the movements of Henry II.

marriage to young Hugh of La Marche, as compensation for   1214
the loss of Isabel herself. The first preliminary was a truce
with the counts of La Marche and Eu; and it was probably
this truce which enabled John to pass unmolested through
La Marche on his way to and from La Souterraine. The
third Lusignan brother, Geoffrey, seems not to have been
included in the truce; and when it expired no terms of
peace had been agreed upon. "We therefore"—so wrote
John to his representatives in England—"on the Friday
next before Pentecost transported ourself and our army to   May 16
Geoffrey's castle of Mervant; and although many believed
it impregnable by assault, yet on Whitsun Eve, by one   May 17
assault lasting from daybreak to the hour of prime, we took
it by force. On Whitsunday we laid siege to another of   May 18
Geoffrey's castles, Vouvant, in which was he himself with his
two sons; and when we had plied our slings against it
continually for three days, so that its fall was imminent, the   May 20
count of La Marche came to us and caused the said Geoffrey
to surrender himself to our mercy, with his two sons, his
castle, and all that was in it." Another of Geoffrey's castles,
Montcontour, which lay farther east, close to the Angevin
border, was at the same time besieged by Louis of France.
The French king seems to have discovered the negotiations
of the Lusignans with his rival, and to have been so much
alarmed at the prospect of a reconciliation which would
deprive him of his best helpers in Aquitaine that he tried to
prevent it by offering a son of his own as bridegroom for
little Joan; but Joan's father was too wary to take the
French bait. On learning that Louis was at Montcontour,
"we," says John, "at once turned thitherward to meet him;
so that on Trinity Sunday we were at Parthenay, where the   May 25
count of La Marche and the count of Eu came to us with
the said Geoffrey of Lusignan and did us homage and fealty.
And as it had been under discussion between ourself and the
count of La Marche that we should give our daughter Joan
in marriage to his son, we did so grant it to him, although
the king of France asked for her for his own son; but that
demand was a trick; for we remembered how our niece was
given to the French king's son Louis, and what was the

consequence of that ; but may God grant us more profit from this marriage than we have had from that one ! And now," ends the king with a burst of eager anticipation, "by God's grace there is given us an opportunity to carry our attack upon our chief enemy, the king of France, beyond the limits of Poitou." [1]

He made good use of his opportunity. Louis had apparently retired from Montcontour at his approach, for we hear nothing of any encounter between them, and within twenty-four hours of his departure from Parthenay John was at Cissé, only a few miles from Poitiers. On Poitiers he made no attempt, but passed on into Berry, into which he penetrated as far north as Chezelles (June 7). Four days later he was at Ancenis, on the border of Anjou and Britanny. The next week was spent in feeling his way towards Angers. From Ancenis, on June 12, he moved up the Loire to St. Florent and Rochefort,[2] thus securing the approach to the city from the west and south. Then, by a master stroke of audacity, he seems to have suddenly made a rapid march westward again, to draw up his forces on June 13 [3] within sight of Nantes. The citizens and the French garrison came forth to meet him at the bridge outside the city ; in the fight which ensued John's troops were completely victorious, and twenty French knights were taken prisoners, among them a cousin of the French king, the eldest son of Count Robert of Dreux whose second son, Peter, was now recognized by the French as "count of Britanny" in right of his wife Alice, the half-sister of Arthur and Eleanor.[4] Whether this victory struck terror into the men of Angers, and whether they opened their gates to the victor in consequence, we cannot tell ; we only know that on June 17 and 18 John was once more in the original capital

---

[1] R. Wendover, vol. iii. pp. 280, 281. The treaty with the Lusignans is in *Rot. Chart.* p. 197 b ; it has no date.　　　　[2] *Itin.* a. 16.

[3] M. Petit-Dutaillis (*Hist. de Louis VIII.* p. 48) thinks this affair at Nantes occurred "dans les premiers jours de juin." The only blank days in John's itinerary during this month are June 2-4, 8, 9 and 13. From the relative positions of the places where he was on the other days, I cannot but think that the 13th is the most likely date.

[4] R. Wendover, vol. iii. pp. 285, 286. Cf. R. Coggeshall, p. 169 ; W. Armor. *Gesta P. A.* c. 172 ; and *Hist. des Ducs*, p. 143.

of his forefathers.[1]   But once more he was compelled by the   1214
untrustworthiness of his followers to turn his back upon it,
and this time for ever.

The castles in the immediate neighbourhood of Angers
were mostly in the hands of John or his friends ; there was,
however, one important exception—La Roche-au-Moine,[2]
where William des Roches, now seneschal of Anjou for
Philip Augustus, had lately built a fortress to protect the
road between Angers and Nantes against the garrison of
Rochefort, whose commandant was a partisan of John.[3]   To
La Roche-au-Moine John laid siege with all his forces on
June 19.   The siege had lasted a fortnight [4] when Louis
advanced from Chinon to relieve the place, then on the verge
of surrender.   At the tidings of his approach John sent out
scouts to ascertain the strength of the enemy ; they returned
with the assurance that the English king had an overwhelming advantage in numbers, and was certain to be
victorious if he engaged the French in a pitched battle.
John was eager for the fight ;[5] so, according to the French
historiographer-royal, was Louis, who sent to his rival a
public challenge, which John as publicly accepted.[6]   But
the "wonted treachery"—as an exasperated English writer
calls it—of the Poitevins overthrew his hopes.   According
to one account, "the barons of Poitou, disdaining to follow
the king, said that they were not ready for a fight in the
open field."[7]   According to the French version of the story,
the immediate author of John's discomfiture was the veteran
turncoat Almeric of Thouars, who, it seems, addressed John
in a most insulting manner, mocking at his eagerness for
battle, insinuating that it was mere boastfulness which the
king would never carry out in act, and then made it impossible for him to do so, by withdrawing himself and all his

---

[1] *Itin.* a. 16.

[2] M. Petit-Dutaillis (*Louis VIII.* p. 49) remarks that the modern post-office
spelling, "La Roche-aux-Moines," is wrong, the Latin form being "Rupes
Monachi," not "Monachorum."

[3] W. Armor. *Gesta P. A.* c. 178.

[4] Dates from *Itin.* a. 16.

[5] R. Wendover, vol. iii. p. 286.

[6] W. Armor. *Philipp.* l. x. vv. 202-18.

[7] R. Wendover, *l.c.*

1214

July 2

followers from the host.[1]   Whichever version be the correct
one, the consequences were inevitable ; John could not risk
an encounter with Louis after such a revelation of treason
in his own ranks.   In rage and grief he broke up the siege,
and hurried away to the south side of the Loire.[2]

His retreat, however, implied no abandonment of the
design which had brought him across the sea.   His expedition was only a part of the great combination whereby he
hoped to bring Philip Augustus to ruin.   Through long
years of diplomacy he had knit together a league which
included all the powers on the northern and eastern borders
of France, and, now that it was at last ready for united
action, threatened the very existence of the French monarchy.
While John was scouring the country between the Loire and
the Dordogne, a formidable host was gathering in Flanders.
Earl William of Salisbury was there with a picked band of
Englishmen ; the Flemish troops under Hugh de Boves who
had been serving John as mercenaries in England had been
recalled to swell the muster in their native land ; Count
Reginald of Boulogne and Count William of Holland had
joined their forces to those of Ferrand ; all alike were
soldiers of the king of England, receiving his pay through
William of Salisbury, who as John's representative was
Marshal of the whole host.   While that host ravaged
Ponthieu, the dukes of Brabant and Louvain " with all their
might " attacked the north-eastern extremity of the French
border, in concert with a certain German count " whom the
French called *Pelu*."   The Emperor Otto was in full
sympathy with the allies, helping them indirectly by his
" counsel and favour " ; at last, when the eastern and western
divisions of the composite host had effected a junction, he
himself came with a small body of knights to join their
ranks.[3]

So skilfully and secretly had the combination been
planned that Philip was quite unprepared to meet it.   He
had sent the greater part of his available forces southward

---

[1] W. Armor. *Philipp.* l. x. vv. 243-65.
[2] W. Armor. *Gesta P. A.* c. 179.   Cf. *Itin.* a. 16.
[3] Cf. R. Wendover, vol. iii. p. 287, and M. Paris, *Hist. Angl.* vol. ii. p. 150.

under Louis to check the progress of John. For the
moment this had been achieved, not so much by Louis as
by the Poitevin traitors.   But the check was only momentary ; Louis made no attempt to follow John across the
Loire ; and John was already taking steps to fill the places
of the Poitevin deserters with more trustworthy troops.   On
July 9 he wrote from La Rochelle to " all his faithful men "
in England, telling them that he was safe and prosperous,
thanking them for the support which they had given him
hitherto, and desiring that all those who had not accompanied him over sea would come to his aid now, unless
their presence at home was specially required by his representatives in the government.   " And if," he added, " any
one of you should think that we have been displeased with
him, his surest way to set that matter right is by coming at
our call." [1]   France was caught between two fires.   The
most imminent danger was from the allies who were ready
to pour into the realm from the north and east ; but Philip,
though conscious that the troops which he had at hand
were insufficient to cope with this danger, dared not recall
Louis while John was still threatening attack from the
south.   Gathering courage from the extremity of the peril,
the French king hastily collected what forces he could—
counts, barons, knights, men-at-arms, horse and foot, with
the communes of the towns and villages—bade the bishops
and clergy, monks and nuns, offer up masses, prayers and
alms for the safety of the realm, and marched boldly against
the invaders.   He met them at the bridge of Bouvines on
Sunday, July 27, and routed them completely.   Hugh de
Boves fled ; Otto fled likewise, or was driven from the field ;
the earl of Salisbury, the counts of Flanders and Boulogne
and the German count were made prisoners, together with
Otto's seneschal and a crowd of other knights.   The great
coalition which had cost John so many years of diplomacy
and such vast sums of money to build up was shivered into
fragments at a single blow. [2]

[1] *Rot. Pat.* p. 118 b.
[2] Cf. R. Wendover, vol. iii. pp. 288-91 ; M. Paris, *Hist. Angl.* vol. ii. p.
151 ; W. Armor. *Gesta P. A.* cc. 181-97 ; R. Coggeshall, p. 169 (wrong
date), and W. Coventry, vol. ii. p. 216.

⸝ re-entered Paris in triumph with his captives,[1]
⸝ᴧ marched southward to unite his victorious army
⸝ₐt of his son.[2] Against the whole military forces of
ᵣ. ⸝e, thus concentrated and in their present mood of
exalted patriotism and enthusiastic loyalty, John was still
eager to continue the war; in the middle of August Peter
des Roches was trying to secure the fulfilment of an order
from the king for three hundred Welshmen to join him
over sea before the end of the month.[3] But another
power stepped in to check the hostilities between the kings.
Innocent III. was planning a new crusade, and the first
necessity for his purpose was the restoration of peace in
Europe. As early as April 22 he had urged both the
kings, on pain of ecclesiastical censures, to cease from the
strife which was hindering the work to be done in the Holy
Land and imperilling the safety of Christendom, and to
make at least a truce till after the meeting of a general
council,[4] the date of which he had already fixed for All
Saints' Day 1215.[5] The English-born cardinal who was
now legate in France, Robert Curson, seems to have urged
the barons who were with John to persuade him to agree to
a truce for nine days, with a view to arranging a personal
interview between John and Philip.[6] The French king had
advanced as far as Loudun, where he received the submission of Almeric of Thouars and several other Poitevin
barons. John was some seventeen miles off, at Parthenay,
"having," says Philip's biographer, "no place to flee unto,
and not daring either to stay where he was, or to offer
battle."[7] To offer battle at that moment, with the legate
and the barons all urgent for peace, would indeed have been
madness; so on August 30 John signified his assent to a
cessation of hostilities for a fortnight from the next day, if
the legate would ensure its observance on the French side.[8]
On September 3 John withdrew to Saint-Maixent; thence

---

[1] M. Paris, *Hist. Angl.* vol. ii. p. 151.
[2] R. Coggeshall, p. 170; W. Coventry, vol. ii. p. 216.
[3] *Rot. Claus.* vol. i. p. 210 b.   [4] *Rot. Pat.* vol. i. p. 139.
[5] R. Coggeshall, p. 167. Cf. W. Coventry, vol. ii. p. 214.
[6] *Foedera*, vol. i. pt. i. p. 124.   [7] W. Armor. *Gesta P. A.* c. 204.
[8] *Foedera, l.c.*

he went on the 9th to Niort; on the 12th he returned to
Parthenay,[1] and there, on the 13th, he, by letters patent,
pledged himself to ratify whatever terms nine envoys, whom
he named, should agree upon with Philip.[2]

These envoys were supported by the legate in person;
"and," says William the Breton, "although the high-souled
King Philip, having in his army two thousand knights and
more, besides a multitude of other troops, could easily have
seized the whole land and the person of the king of England, yet with his wonted benignity he granted a truce."[3]
In England Philip was reported to have yielded either to
the authority of the Pope, or to the attraction of sixty
thousand marks offered to him by John.[4] We may doubt
whether either of these motives, or all of them united,
would have proved effectual, if the complete overthrow and
capture of his rival had really been as easy as the Breton
court-historian imagined. The truce was dated from September 18, and was to last for five years from the next
Easter, 1215. The conditions were that each party should
retain its prisoners; that the oath sworn to Philip by the
towns of Flanders and Hainaut should be recognized as
valid; that Philip, his men, and his adherents should hold
throughout the time of the truce whatever they held on the
day of its commencement; and that any disputes which
might arise should be settled at certain appointed places by
the sworn arbitrators of the truce, who were eight in number,
each of the kings being represented by two laymen, an
abbot and a secular priest. The *maltôte* or tax levied by
each king on the adherents of his rival was to be given up
if John, its originator, consented to renounce it; if not,
Philip claimed the right to continue it likewise. Frederic
of Sicily was to be included in the truce as an ally of
Philip, and Otto as a friend of John, if they chose to be so
included; if otherwise, then Philip was to be at liberty to
assist Frederic and John to assist Otto, within the boundaries
of the empire, without violating the peace between themselves.

---

[1] *Itin.* a. 16.   [2] *Rot. Pat.* p. 140 b.
[3] W. Armor. *Gesta P. A.* c. 204.   [4] R. Coggeshall, p. 170.

Philip's proclamation of the truce was issued on September 18 from Chinon.[1] John seems to have been then still at Parthenay. The terms secured to him the very utmost that he could possibly hope to attain, now that he was deprived of the co-operation of his allies in the north. He had in fact, as an English writer says, " completed what he had to do over sea," [2] as well as his share of the work could be completed when that work as a whole was ruined by the disaster of Bouvines. On September 21 he was again at Niort, on the 30th at Saintes, and at some date between October 2 and 13 he sailed from La Rochelle to England.[3]

To all outward seeming England was at peace. The Pope's letter containing his decision as to the conditions on which the interdict was to be withdrawn had reached John on March 4, at the siege of Milécu, and he had at once sent it on to Peter des Roches for delivery to the legate Nicolas,[4] whom he had, before leaving England, empowered to settle the matter in conjunction with William the Marshal. A council was summoned at S. Paul's; the Pope's decision was communicated to the assembled prelates and barons, and the legate asked for an account of the sums already paid by the Crown in connexion with the interdict, that he might know how much was still wanting to complete the forty thousand marks which the Pope had fixed as the total of the indemnity. When this was ascertained, it was agreed that the remainder—thirteen thousand marks—should stand over on the security of the bishops of Winchester and Norwich and of the king himself.[5] This last John gave by

---

[1] *Foedera*, vol. i. pt. i. p. 125. There is a mutilated version of this document in R. Wendover, vol. iii. pp. 292, 293.

[2] " Expletis agendis suis in partibus transmarinis, rediit in Angliam," R. Wendover, vol. iii. p. 293.

[3] *Itin.* a. 16; for the last date see *Memorials of S. Edmund's*, vol. ii. p. 92.

[4] *Rot. Pat.* p. 111 b.

[5] R. Wendover, vol. iii. pp. 283, 284. The terms are stated in a very confused way, both in the Pope's letter (given *l.c.*; also in *Rot. Chart.* pp. 208, 209), in a letter of Earl William of Ferrars (*Rot. Pat.* p. 139; Ferrars was one of those who swore as sureties for the king), and in that of John himself (*Rot. Chart.* p. 199); but a comparison of the three documents with Roger's own account of the matter makes it tolerably clear that Nicolas was authorized to

letters patent issued from Angers on June 17[1]; and as soon
as these letters reached England, Nicolas solemnly withdrew
the interdict.[2]

Serious grievances connected with it, however, still
remained. A special tax seems to have been levied throughout the realm, under the title of " aid for the relaxation of
the interdict " [3]—either to pay the remainder of the indemnity
to the bishops or to furnish the tribute due to Rome. No
indemnification was provided for the losses of any one except
the bishops ; the multitude of lower clergy, the monks, nuns
and lay people of both sexes whose property had been
seized or damaged " on occasion of the interdict " were
ignored in the settlement. When they applied to the legate
for redress, he told them that he had no instructions to deal
with their case, but that they might appeal to the Pope.[4]
For the great majority of individual victims, ruined as they
were, such an appeal was impracticable. The greater
religious houses might have been able to attempt it ; but
regulars and seculars alike were apparently in too much
dread of the king to attempt anything at all. Within two
months after his return to England John put forth a demand
to the clergy of at least one diocese, and to several religious
houses, in the shape of a courteous request that they would
waive all claim to the return of " those things which you
gave to us in the time of the interdict, and which are now
described as having been taken from you." A form of
renunciation or quit-claim was issued, evidently intended for
distribution throughout the country, to be signed by the
parties concerned.[5] John in fact seems to have again asked
all the English clergy, as he had asked them two years
before, for a quit-claim on the plea that their contributions

---

raise the interdict as soon as he had obtained security for the payment of twelve
thousand marks a year, in half-yearly instalments, till the total of forty thousand
should be complete.

[1] *Rot. Chart.* p. 199.

[2] R. Wendover, vol. iii. p. 284, makes the date June 29 ; W. Coventry,
vol. ii. p. 217, R. Coggeshall, p. 169, and *Ann. Waverl.* a. 1214, make it
July 2.

[3] *Rot. Claus.* vol. i. pp. 208, 208 b, 209.

[4] R. Wendover, vol. iii. pp. 284, 285.

[5] *Rot. Pat.* pp. 124, 140 b, 141.

1214   had been voluntary ; and though we have no statement of
the result, there seems no reason to doubt that in 1214, as
in 1212, the audacious demand was complied with.

The weakness of the clergy was partly owing to the fact
that they were disappointed in their hopes of finding a
champion in the legate.   At his coming he had been hailed
as a reformer both in Church and State [1] ; but the year
1214 had scarcely begun when Archbishop Stephen, after
consultation with his suffragans,[2] addressed to him a solemn
protest, threatening to appeal against him to the Pope unless
he desisted from instituting prelates to vacant churches,
contrary to the rights of the metropolitan.   Nicolas disregarded the protest, and commissioned Pandulf—who had
just gone back to Rome—to defend him against the appeal.[3]
For nine months Nicolas continued to exercise his influence
as he chose, without remonstrance from the Pope.   He was
an instrument which could not be dispensed with until its
special work—the removal of the interdict—was done ;
moreover, the king was on the Continent, and in the doubtful
state of political affairs it would scarcely have been prudent,
during his absence, for Innocent to withdraw his own
representative from England.   No sooner, however, had
John returned than Nicolas was summoned back to Rome.[4]
It is clear that Stephen's protest and appeal had been really
directed not merely against legatine intrusion into his own
metropolitical rights, but also, and chiefly, against the legate's
interpretation of the papal letter concerning elections to
churches, and his action in making himself the medium
of royal interference in this matter.[4]   Stephen indeed seems
to have looked upon Nicolas as the chief obstacle to a
settlement, between himself and the king, of this question of
elections ; and a formal settlement, wholly in the Church's

[1] W. Coventry, vol. ii. p. 215.
[2] At Dunstable, "after the octave of Epiphany," R. Wendover, vol. iii.
p. 278.
[3] R. Wendover, vol. iii. pp. 278, 279, says that Nicolas, with the king's
assent, sent Pandulf specially to plead for him at Rome against the archbishop ;
but Pandulf's approaching departure over sea "in nuncium nostrum" was
announced by John on January 4 (*Rot. Claus.* vol. i. p. 141), ten days at least
before Stephen's appeal was made or even threatened.
[4] Cf. R. Wendover, vol. iii. pp. 278, 279, and R. Coggeshall, p. 170.

favour, was in fact made as soon as king and archbishop
were once more face to face. On November 21 John published
a grant of free and canonical election to all the churches in
his realm.[1]   This grant, like every other acknowledgement
made by the Crown, before or since, of the Church's right
on this point, was of course destined never to be anything
but a dead letter.   But it served John's purpose.   It saved
him from a fresh quarrel with the Church at a moment
when the struggle with the barons in which he had been
engaged almost ever since his accession to the Crown had
entered upon a new phase and assumed a new character
which made it, alike for them and for him, a matter of life
and death.

---

[1] *Statutes of the Realm*, Charters of Liberties, p. 5.   A copy of this grant,
with the date January 15, is printed in *Foedera*, vol. i. pt. i. pp. 126-7.

CHAPTER VI

JOHN AND THE BARONS

1214–1215

Ki ore vaurroit oïr l'ocoison de la guerre dont li rois Jehans moru deshiretés de la plus grant partie d'Engletierre, bien le poroit oïr en cest escrit.

Hist. des Ducs de Normandie, p. 145.

Intervenientibus itaque archiepiscopo Cantuariensi cum pluribus coepiscopis et baronibus nonnullis, quasi pax inter regem et barones formata est.

R. COGGESHALL, p. 172.

1214   ON May 26, 1214, John had issued writs for the collection of a scutage of three marks per fee from all tenants-in-chief, royal demesnes, vacant bishoprics, lands in royal wardship, and escheats, except those fees which were personally represented in the army in Poitou ; on these the scutage was, as usual, to be remitted by royal warrant.[1] Those northern barons who had refused to serve now refused to pay. They adhered to their contention that they were by their tenure exempt from the obligation to foreign service, and they argued that, in consequence, they were also exempt from the obligation to payment in substitution for such service.[2] Whether they claimed this double exemption as a privilege peculiar to themselves, or as common to the whole baronage, is not quite clear. In either case the claim would have been difficult, if not impossible, to prove. There is nothing to indicate that the fiefs in northern England had been originally granted on different conditions from those in the south. On the other hand, there are, indeed, some slight indications of the possible existence in some quarters, in the

[1] *Rot. Claus.* vol. i. p. 166 b.   [2] W. Coventry, vol. ii. p. 217.

days of both Richard and Henry, of a theory that the obligation to foreign service—and therefore to payment of scutage
for a foreign war—did not form part of the regular obligations of military tenure ; in other words, that tenants-in-
chivalry were not legally bound to serve in, or to pay for,
any war save one of defence.   But no general attempt had
ever been made even to formulate such a theory, far less to
carry it out to its logical consequences ; and it is obvious
that those consequences would have made it practically impossible for the kings of England to carry on any continental
warfare at all.   When John in reply to the northern recalcitrants insisted that " it always used to be so done "—that
is, foreign service had been rendered or scutage paid in its
stead—in his father's and brother's days,[1] he was unquestionably right ; and he might have added that it had also been
so done, over and over again, in the early years of his own
reign.   The protest of the northern barons seems to have
been made to him in a personal meeting very soon after his
return to England ; we are told that " the matter would
have gone further, had it not been checked by the presence
of the legate."   It seems indeed to have gone further notwithstanding that obstacle, for the same chronicler adds :
" There was brought forth a certain charter of liberties given
to the English by Henry I., which the said barons asked the
king to confirm." [2]

If we may believe a report which was current a few
years later, this demand had been first suggested to the
barons, more than a year before, by Archbishop Stephen of
Canterbury.   On August 25, 1213 ; he had gathered the
bishops, abbots and other ecclesiastical dignitaries, with
some of the lay magnates, around him in S. Paul's cathedral
that they might receive his instructions concerning a partial
relaxation of the interdict, which he was empowered to
grant, pending the arrival of the legate.   It was said [3] that
he had afterwards called aside the lay members of the
assembly to a secret meeting in which he laid before them
a yet weightier matter.   " Ye have heard "—thus he was

---

[1] W. Coventry, vol. ii. p. 217.   [2] *Ib.* p. 218.
[3] " Ut fama refert," R. Wendover, vol. iii. p. 263.

1213 reported to have addressed them—"how, when I absolved the king at Winchester, I made him swear to put down bad laws and enforce throughout his realm the good laws of Edward. Now, there has been found also a certain charter of King Henry I. by which, if ye will, ye may recall to their former estate the liberties which ye have so long lost":— and he caused the document in question—the coronation-charter of Henry I.—to be read aloud before them. "And when this charter had been read through and interpreted to the barons, they rejoiced with very great joy, and all swore in the archbishop's presence that when they saw a fitting time they would fight for those liberties, if it were needful, even unto death; the archbishop, too, promised them his most faithful help to the utmost of his power. And, a confederacy being thus made between them, the conference was dissolved."[1] This story is given by Roger of Wendover only as a rumour; but whether the rumour were literally true or not, it was at any rate founded upon a fact: the fact that the movement which was to result in the Great Charter owed its true impulse to the patriotism, as it owed its success to the statesmanship, not of any of the barons, but of Stephen Langton.

During eight months out of the fourteen which elapsed between the archbishop's return and that of the king, the administration of government was in the hands of Peter des Roches, and he ruled the country with a rod of iron.[2] But Peter's vice-regal tyranny was only the final outcome of a state of things which had been growing worse from year to year for more than a quarter of a century. England in the sixteenth year of King John was suffering under an accumulation of grievances consisting, as Ralph of Coggeshall truly says, of all "the evil customs which the king's father and brother had raised up for the oppression of the Church and realm, together with the abuses which the king himself had added thereto."[3] No doubt these last formed the worst

[1] R. Wendover, vol. iii. pp. 263-6.

[2] *Ann. Waverl.* a. 1214; "potestate sua non bene utens, iram baronum converti fecerat contra regem."

[3] R. Coggeshall, p. 170.

part of the evil, and it was the addition of them that gave
such an increase of bitterness to all the rest.   The obligation laid upon all men to attend the Forest courts, when
summoned, whether subject to their jurisdiction or not, had
been a hardship ever since it was imposed by Henry II. in
1184 ; the working of the Forest laws had been a source
of suffering from a period much earlier still ; but the area of
the hardship and the suffering was rendered more extensive
by the new afforestations made by John.[1]   The inconvenience
caused by the old practice of making common pleas " follow
the king "—that is, of holding trials of civil causes only
before the justices who accompanied the king, wheresoever
he might be—had been felt in Henry's time, and Henry had
tried to remedy it by setting up a permanent bench of
justices in a fixed place to deal with such causes.   But the
right retained by the sovereign of calling up suits from this
tribunal to his own presence was exercised by John to a
degree which his restless and erratic movements—almost
more restless and erratic than those of his father—seem to
have rendered extremely vexatious to litigants.[2]   The
precise limits of the king's rights over his tenants-in-chief
as to military service, scutage, control over their castles,
and such-like matters, had been more or less in dispute
throughout the two preceding reigns ; but the bitterness of
such disputes was intensified by John's personal dealings
with his barons, his subtle contrivances for stealing from
them their rights over their own tenants and their own
lands, his interference with their domestic life by his con-
tinual demands for hostages, and, above all, in many cases,
by a desecration of their homes which blood alone could
expiate.

Again, the corrupt administration of the sheriffs had
been matter of complaint under Henry ; but it was far
worse under John ; for whereas Henry, and after him
Hubert Walter acting for Richard, had endeavoured by
various means to check the independent action and curtail
the powers of the sheriffs, now the king himself was almost

---

[1] Articles of the Barons, 1215 cc. 39, 47.
[2] *Ib.* c. 8.

1214　openly in league with those officers, and their usurpations and extortions were not merely condoned, but encouraged, if not even directly instigated, by him for his own interest. Owing to the rise in the value of land and a variety of other causes, the sheriffs' annual receipts had for many years past been generally in considerable excess of the sum—fixed under the Norman kings on the basis of the Domesday Survey—for which they were accountable to the royal treasury as ferm of the shire. Whatever they received beyond this fixed sum seems to have been originally, in theory at least, their own profit. But a share of it was naturally soon claimed by the Crown ; and this was done, not by putting the ferm at a higher figure, but by charging the sheriff with an additional lump sum under the title of *crementum*, or, in John's time, *proficuum*.[1] Whatever proportion the increment thus paid to the Crown may have borne to the actual receipts of the sheriffs, it is clear that under a sovereign of John's character an arrangement which made king and sheriff partners in gain would make them also partners in extortion. The partnership began when the sheriff entered upon his office ; he was appointed to it by the king alone, he held it during the king's pleasure ; John had no trouble in finding sheriffs after his own heart. As the improvement of the royal demesnes and the legitimate proceeds of royal jurisdiction were inadequate to produce increment on a scale such as is shown in some of the Pipe Rolls of the reign, these men fleeced the people of their shire by every means they could devise, for the joint profit of the king and themselves ; and the king connived at and abetted every possible usurpation of the sheriffs, that they might wring out of the shire a larger amount of money for him. They set at nought the restrictions which John's predecessors had placed upon their action. They took upon

---

[1] Of the value to which these profits had risen some idea may be gathered from the fact that a *proficuum* of £336 : 18 : 8 was accounted for as due to the Treasury in 1205 by the sheriff of Staffordshire and Shropshire, of which two counties the united ferm was £413 : 12 : 4, *Salt Archaeol. Soc. Publications*, vol. ii. pp. 129, 133. It must, however, be added that this *proficuum* was reduced next year to £266 : 13 : 4, and went down further year by year, till in 1212 it was only about £155 : 11s., *ib.* pp. 136, 138, 142, 145, 147, 151, 159. After that year the Pipe Rolls are in confusion till 1218.

themselves to keep the pleas of the Crown, without reference
to the coroners to whom that duty had been specially
intrusted under Richard.[1] They accused men of offences
and sent them to the ordeal without more ado, in defiance
of Henry's ordinance limiting the employment of that mode
of trial to cases in which the charge was made on the pre-
sentment of a sworn jury.[2] The corrupt and extortionate
rule of the sheriffs had been strongly condemned by the
bishops and magnates in the king's name at the council at
S. Albans in August 1213, and it is said that after the
coming of the legate some attempt was made to check these
abuses by removing the most glaring offenders from office ;[3]
but a mere change of officers was of little avail ; the fault
lay not only in the persons who worked the system, but also
in the system itself ; and the evil extended far beyond the
sphere of the sheriffs' activity.

The whole judicial administration of the realm was
corrupt. There was very distinctly one law for the rich and
another for the poor.[4] Justice was sold, delayed, or refused
altogether, at the king's will.[5] Proceedings for which the
presence of only the parties concerned in the suit, and a
certain number of jurors, was legally necessary, were made a
pretext for summoning other persons,[6] evidently for the sake
of exacting fines from them if they failed to attend, and
were protracted [7] so as to make attendance as vexatious
as possible, that there might be the more defaulters and the
more fines. The course of justice was subjected to constant
interference through the summary evocation of causes from
the lower courts to that of the king, at the instance of any
suitor who could afford to pay for the writ of "*praecipe*"
whereby the sheriff was authorized to effect the transfer.[8]
Fines were imposed without regard either to the scale of the
offence or the offender's means of paying, so that men of all
classes were reduced by them to ruin, being unable to make
up the required sum except by selling their sole means of
livelihood—the free yeoman his tenement, the villein his

---

[1] Art. Bar. c. 14.   [2] *Ib.* c. 28.
[3] W. Coventry, vol. ii. pp. 214, 215.   [4] Art. Bar. c. 26.
[5] *Ib.* c. 30.   [6] *Ib.* c. 8.   [7] *Ib.* c. 13.   [8] *Ib.* c. 24.

cart, the merchant his stock in trade ;[1] clerks were amerced to the full value not only of any lay tenement which they possessed, but also of their ecclesiastical benefices.[2]   Henry's Assize had given to the Crown only the chattels of a convicted felon ; but now the Crown took his land also, without compensation to the mesne lord to whom it ought to have reverted.[3]

The exactions and usurpations of the Crown were of the most various kinds, and affected every class of society. Reliefs of arbitrary and unreasonable amount were again, as in the Red King's days, exacted from tenants-in-chief on succession to their estates.[4]   Sub-tenants holding land which formed part of an escheated honour were made to pay relief not as other sub-tenants paid to their immediate lord, but as if they held in chief of the Crown.[5]   The widows of tenants-in-chief could not obtain the dowry to which they were legally entitled without payment to the king for its assignment,[6] and were forced into second marriages against their will.[7]   The wardship and marriage of minor heirs was given, or sold, by the king to his friends without regard to the honesty or dishonesty of the guardian and the interests of the minor and his family.[8]   By an ingenious piece of intentional confusion the Crown arrogated to itself the right of wardship in cases where it had no such right.   If a man held land of the Crown by a non-feudal tenure, and also held other land under another lord by knight-service, the distinction between his holding in chief and his holding in chivalry was ignored for the king's benefit, and the custody of all the man's lands was appropriated to the Crown.[9] Distraints for debt to the Crown were made in the most arbitrary way ; the king's bailiffs would, if it so pleased them or their master, seize a debtor's land instead of his chattels, though the value of these latter sufficed to discharge his debt ; or they would distrain a debtor's sureties, although he himself was able to pay.[10]   When a freeman died, they assumed as matter of course that he was in debt to the

[1] Art. Bar. c. 9.   [2] *Ib.* c. 10.   [3] *Ib.* c. 22.
[4] *Ib.* c. 1.   [5] *Ib.* c. 36.   [6] *Ib.* c. 4.
[7] *Ib.* c. 17.   [8] *Ib.* c. 3.   [9] *Ib.* c. 27.   [10] *Ib.* c. 5.

king, and without inquiring to what amount, they seized his
chattels, to be restored to his executors or next-of-kin only
when the royal claim was satisfied, and not always then.[1]
John, like William Rufus, "would be every man's heir." If
a man died in debt to the Jews, and leaving an heir under
age, those usurers were suffered to exact interest upon their
debt during the minority of the heir, so that if through the
death of the Jewish creditor the debt should fall into the
king's hand (the Crown being the legal heir of all Jews),
there should be as much for the king as possible ; and in
such cases he claimed payment of the uttermost farthing
that was set down in the Jew's account-book, although he
might thereby leave the Christian debtor's widow and
children to starve.[2]   Exorbitant tolls were exacted from
merchants.[3]   Fines were laid upon towns for the making of
bridges, in places where no such obligation had existed in
times past.[4]   Weirs were placed in the rivers that the king
might keep to himself the profits of fishing.[5]   Monasteries
not of royal foundation were taken into the king's custody
during vacancy, in defiance of the rights of their founders'
representatives.[6]   The king's bailiffs compelled men to give
their corn and other goods for the use of the king or his
servants, their horses and carts for the carriage of burdens
in his service, their wood for the construction of his buildings,
whether the owners were willing or not, and seemingly
without payment.[7]   Free men were arrested, imprisoned,
ejected from their lands, even exiled or outlawed, without
legal warrant or fair trial.[8]   Individuals were forbidden to
enter or quit the realm at the mere will of the king.[9]   Some
barons whom he specially favoured, or wanted to propitiate,
received licences to impose arbitrary taxes on their sub-
tenants, without regard to the limits of feudal custom,[10]
just as the king himself imposed taxes on his subjects
according to his will and pleasure.   In a word, the entire
system of government and administration set up under the
Norman kings and developed under Henry and Richard

---

[1] Art. Bar. c. 15.   [2] *Ib.* cc. 34, 35.   [3] *Ib.* c. 31.
[4] *Ib.* c. 11.   [5] *Ib.* c. 23.   [6] *Ib.* c. 43.
[7] *Ib.* cc. 18, 20.   [8] *Ib.* c. 29.   [9] *Ib.* c. 33.   [10] *Ib.* c. 6.

1214 had been converted by the ingenuity of John into a most
subtle and effective engine of royal extortion, oppression
and tyranny over all classes of the nation, from earl to
villein.

The only class which was as yet capable of making any
corporate opposition or protest was the baronage ; and
hitherto the discontent of the barons had shown itself only
in the resistance of some of their number to the king's
demands on certain special occasions and in reference to
certain special points which affected them personally as
tenants-in-chief.   But there was now one man in England
who looked at the questions at issue between them and the
king from a higher standpoint than theirs, and in whose
eyes those questions were only small parts of a much wider
and deeper question, on the solution of which he had set his
mind from the very hour of his landing in the realm.   One
chronicler relates that John's first impulse on hearing of
Archbishop Stephen's arrival in England had been to withdraw himself to some remote place and put off their meeting
as long as possible, and that he had only been induced to
abandon this intention by the remonstrances of some of the
barons.[1]   Whether this particular story be true or not, it
seems plain that John's conduct throughout his quarrel with
the Church was to a great extent dictated by personal dis-
like to the archbishop.   This feeling must have been mainly
instinctive ; for the two men had never seen each other till
they met at Winchester on July 20, 1213.   The instinct,
however, was a true one : it was Stephen Langton who was to
give the first impulse to the work which was destined—
though not till long after he had passed away—to make the
rule of such a king as John impossible in England for
evermore.

The archbishop was determined to be satisfied with
nothing short of a literal fulfilment of the promise on which
he had insisted as a condition of the king's absolution, the
promise that to " *all* men " their rights should be restored.
He saw that this end could be gained only by the instru-

---

[1] *Ann. Waverl.* a. 1213.

mentality of the barons ; he also saw that it could be gained
only by a policy based on clearer and firmer, as well as
broader and nobler, lines than any of them were capable of
designing.   They, indeed, had no definite scheme of policy ;
nor had they any leader able to furnish them with such a
scheme.   The men of highest standing among the magnates,
such as the earls of Salisbury, Chester, Albemarle, Warren,
Cornwall and William the Marshal,—the men of highest
standing among the official class, such as the heads of the
houses of Aubigny, Vipont, De Lucy, Basset, Cantelupe,
Neville, Brewer [1]—had either gone to the war or paid their
scutage for it without a murmur, and stood utterly aloof from
the group of "Northerners," among whom the most conspicuous were two barons of secondary rank, Eustace de
Vesci and Robert Fitz-Walter.   Both Eustace and Robert
are said to have had just grounds for bitter personal resentment against John ; but Robert Fitz-Walter had twice already
shown himself to be both a traitor and a coward ; and on
the second occasion, in 1212, Eustace de Vesci had done
the like.   The pardon and restoration of both these men in
the following year was a matter of policy, but was not due
to any merits of their own.[2]   It was not under the inspiration and guidance of such men as these that the liberties of
the English people could be won, nor even that the barons
could succeed in their struggle for the privileges, pretended
or real, of their own order.   Another guide offered himself
to them in the person of Stephen Langton, and offered to
them at the same time a definite basis of action in the
charter of Henry I.   Whether the offer was made at the
meeting in S. Paul's in August 1213, or at some later date
and in some other way, is of little consequence ; it is enough
that antecedent probability and after-history alike justify the
general belief of which Roger of Wendover is the spokesman :—that it was Langton who brought to light the charter
of which the very existence seems to have been forgotten,
and it was from him that the barons adopted it as the basis
of their demands.

[1] R. Wendover, vol. iii. pp. 300, 301.
[2] See Note II. at end.

The step which they took in so doing was weightier than, probably, they themselves had any idea of.   At first glance the charter seems to have little or no bearing upon the immediate subject of dispute between them and the king ; it contains no mention whatever of either scutage or military service beyond sea.   But it does contain a series of clauses regulating the relations between the tenants-in-chief and the Crown ; and thus it furnished them with a substantial ground for insisting that all violations of its provisions on the part of the Crown must be redressed before any further burdens could be binding upon them.   It was even possible for them to argue that any demands on the king's part other than those expressly sanctioned in the charter were an encroach-ment on their privileges as therein defined.   For the greater purpose which Langton had in view, the value of the charter lay in its opening of the way to wider reforms by the incidental clauses which bound the tenants-in-chief to extend to their sub-tenants the same benefits which they themselves received from the king, and in the comprehensive sentence which declared the abolition of "all evil customs whereby the realm was unjustly oppressed."[1]   The more thoughtful among the confederate barons may perhaps by this time have begun to see that, even from a selfish point of view, they had nothing to lose, and might have something to gain, by identifying their cause with that of the nation as a whole.   Many of the grievances which touched the lower classes touched the higher also, though not always in the same way.   Moreover, although the people were as yet powerless to initiate any corporate action in their own behalf, their support had saved more than one earlier sovereign in a struggle against the barons ; it might prove no less useful to the barons in a struggle against the king.   But whatever the barons may have thought about these matters, the king was statesman enough to see as clearly as the primate how weighty and far-reaching might be the consequences involved in the demand for a renewal of the charter.   He therefore postponed its discussion till after Christmas.[2]

[1] Charter of Henry I. cc. 2, 4, 1.
[2] W. Coventry, vol. ii. p. 218.

Such is the brief statement of the Barnwell annalist. In its stead, Roger of Wendover gives us a dramatic scene in S. Edmund's abbey. "The earls and barons of England," he tells us, came together in that sanctuary, "as if for prayer; but there was something else in the matter, for after they had held much secret discourse, there was brought forth in their midst the charter of King Henry I., which the same barons had received in London, as hath been before said, from Archbishop Stephen of Canterbury. Then they went all together to the church of S. Edmund the King and Martyr, and beginning with the eldest, they swore on the high altar that if the king sought to evade their demand for the laws and liberties which that charter contained, they would make war upon him and withdraw from fealty to him till he should, by a charter furnished with his seal, confirm to them all that they demanded. They also agreed that after Christmas they would go all together to the king, and ask him for a confirmation of the aforesaid liberties; and that meanwhile they would so provide themselves with horses and arms that if the king should seek to break his oath, they might by seizing his castles compel him to make satisfaction. And when these things were done they returned every man to his own home." [1]

John was at S. Edmund's on November 4; [2] it is possible therefore that his meeting with the barons may have been held there, and that the scene described by Roger may have taken place after the king's departure. He kept Christmas at Worcester, and returned to London at the opening of the new year. [3] There, at Epiphany, the confederate barons came to him in a body, "in somewhat showy military array," and prayed him "that certain laws and liberties of King Edward, with other liberties granted to them and to the English Church and realm, might be confirmed, as they were written in the charter of King Henry I. and the laws aforesaid; moreover they declared that at the time of his absolution at

---

[1] R. Wendover, vol. iii. pp. 293, 294.   Cf. R. Coggeshall, p. 170.
[2] *Itin.* a. 16.
[3] He was at Worcester December 25-27; Tewkesbury, 27, 28; Geddington, December 31, 1214; and at the New Temple in London January 7-15, 1215. *Itin.* a. 16.

1215   Winchester, he had promised those ancient laws and liberties,
and thus he was bound by his own oath to the observance of
the same." John cautiously answered that "the matter which
they sought was great and difficult, wherefore he asked for
a delay till the close of Easter, that he might consider how
to satisfy both their demands and the dignity of his crown."[1]
He then seems to have tried to persuade them—no doubt
each man singly—into giving him a written promise "never
again to demand such liberties from him or his successors";
but to this no one would consent except the bishop of
Winchester, the earl of Chester, and William Brewer.[2] At
last the proposed adjournment till the close of Easter was
agreed upon, but not till the king had, "against his will,"
pledged himself by three sureties to fulfill his promise by
giving reasonable satisfaction to all parties at the date thus
appointed.[3]

The king's sureties were the archbishop of Canterbury,
the bishop of Ely, and William the Marshal. The choice
of the archbishop as one of them was good policy on John's
part; and Langton's acceptance of the office implies no
wavering or double-dealing on his side. In so far as it was
his inspiration that gave a new force to the enterprise of the
barons, by raising it from a struggle for their own privileges
into a struggle for the liberties of the English nation, he
was in truth, as Roger of Wendover says, their "chief ally";[4]
and for the achievement of its end as he himself conceived
it, he did indeed "give them his most faithful help to the
utmost of his power." But the help which he gave them
was not that of a partisan; Stephen Langton was at once
too true a churchman and too great a statesman, and held
too lofty a conception of his proper constitutional functions
as primate of all England, to identify himself with any party.
The right and the duty of the archbishop of Canterbury
was to be the partisan of neither king nor people, but the
guide and monitor of both, so far as they would accept his

---

[1] R. Wendover, vol. iii. p. 296.   Cf. W. Coventry, vol. ii. p. 218.

[2] *Foedera*, vol. i. pt. i. p. 120.

[3] R. Wendover, *l.c.*

[4] "Isti omnes conjurati Stephanum Cantuariensem archiepiscopum capitalem
consentaneum habuerunt," *ib.* p. 298.

guidance and listen to his admonitions, and the mediator
between them whenever mediation was needed.   He was by
virtue of his office the first adviser of the Crown as well as
the guardian of the nation's rights ; and it was only by
standing firmly at his post by the king's side in the former
capacity that he could be truly efficient in the latter.
Langton's attitude was evidently understood by both parties
at the time.   From the moment when the northern barons
first asked the king to confirm his great-grandfather's charter,
if not before, John must have known that the hand of the
primate was with them in the matter.   But he was quite as
much alive as they were to the value of such a helper ;
moreover, he seems to have had the somewhat rare gift of
being able to recognize in another man qualities which were
conspicuously absent from his own character.   Much as he
hated Langton, he evidently trusted to his honour and
loyalty as implicitly as he trusted to that of William the
Marshal.   He therefore continued to the end the policy
which he had pursued ever since the archbishop's coming to
England.   He treated Langton with every mark of confidence
and respect ; he carefully avoided any step which might
have forced him into opposition on ecclesiastical grounds ;
and in his diplomatic dealings with the barons it was
Langton whom he employed as his chief commissioner and
representative.

The king, however, was even more prompt than the
barons in preparing to back diplomacy by force.   Immediately after the Epiphany meeting he ordered a renewal of
the oath of allegiance throughout the country ; and this time
it was to be taken in the form of an oath of liege homage,
binding his subjects to "stand by him against all men."
This, it is said, was an unwonted addition, which was generally opposed as being "contrary to the charter" — the
standard by which all things were now tried.[1]   It may
have been in connexion with this matter that the king sent   Feb. 10

---

[1] W. Coventry, vol. ii. p. 218.   It need scarcely be remarked that the
charter contains not a word on the subject.   The argument evidently was "whatever is not in the charter is contrary to it " ; in other words, " omission is prohibition."   The fact that such an argument might be used on both sides was of
course conveniently ignored.

1215 to the men of sixteen southern and midland shires commissioners "to explain his business" to them ;[1] but he ended by withdrawing his demand, "not deeming the time opportune for exciting a tumult among the people."[2] That tumults would nevertheless arise before long he knew full well ; and to meet this danger he had already called to his aid the loyal "barons and bachelors" of Poitou.[3] The summons must have been issued immediately after, if not even in anticipation of, his meeting with the English malcontents at Epiphany, and the response must have been as prompt as the summons, for on February 8 he had already heard of the arrival in Ireland of some troops sent to him by Savaric de Mauléon, and was issuing orders to the archbishop of Dublin for the payment of their passage to England.[4] On February 19 the king gave a safe-conduct to "the barons of the North" that they might come to Oxford to speak with the primate, the other bishops and the Earl Marshal on Sunday the 22nd.[5] Whether this conference took place, or what came of it, we are not told ; but on March 13 John wrote to the barons and bachelors of Poitou that the matter for which he had summoned them was now settled, and he therefore, thanking them for their readiness to obey his call, bade those of them who had not yet set out remain at home, and those who had started go home again, with the assurance that he would indemnify them for their expenses.[6]

It is possible that the barons may have asked for the conference at Oxford in order to remonstrate against the warlike preparations of the king, and that it may have resulted in some temporary arrangement which compelled him to dismiss the Poitevins. It is also possible that this dismissal may have been prompted by tidings from Rome. The prospect of some such crisis as the present one had almost certainly been in the minds of king and barons alike when John performed his homage to the Pope ; and both alike now sought to make their profit out of that transaction, each side appealing to the Pope, as the common overlord of

---

[1] *Rot. Pat.* vol. i. p. 128.
[2] W. Coventry, vol. ii. p. 218.
[3] *Rot. Pat.* p. 130.
[4] *Rot. Claus.* vol. i. p. 187 b.
[5] *Rot. Pat.* p. 129.
[6] *Ib.* p. 130.

both, to use his authority in compelling the other
An envoy from John, William Mauclerc, had reached
on February 17.   Eleven days later Eustace de Vesc
two other representatives of the malcontent party an
with letters for the Pope.   In these letters—so Mauc...c
reported to his master—the confederate barons besought
Innocent, "since he was lord of England," to urge and, if
needful, compel the king to restore the ancient liberties
granted by his predecessors and confirmed by his own oath.
They recited how at the meeting in London at Epiphany
John had not only refused to grant these liberties, but had
endeavoured to make the petitioners promise never to ask
for them again.   They begged that the Pope would take
measures to help them in this matter, " forasmuch as he well
knew that they had at his command boldly opposed the king
in behalf of the Church's liberty, and that the king's grant
of an annual revenue and other honours to the Pope and the
Roman Church had been made not of free will and devotion,
but from fear and under compulsion from them." [1]   Of what
John wrote, or charged his envoy to say, to Innocent in his
behalf, no record remains ; but Innocent's letters show what
the tenour of John's argument must have been.   With his
usual dexterity the king made capital out of the secret
meetings held, or said to have been held, by the malcontents ;
and he also brought into special prominence the one point of
discussion which was quite clearly defined, and in which he
unmistakeably had precedent on his side—the question of the
scutage.   On March 19 Innocent wrote to the archbishop
of Canterbury and the other English bishops, expressing his
surprise that they had not checked the quarrel between the
king and " certain magnates and barons," and reproving them
for their failure to do so ; he strongly condemned the " conspiracies and conjurations " which the barons were reported
to have made, and ordered the bishops to quash all such conspiracies and urge the barons to proceed only by fair and
lawful means.   On the other hand, he besought the king " to
treat the aforesaid nobles graciously, and mercifully to grant

[1] *Foedera*, vol. i. pt. i. p. 120.   See above, p. 182.

1215   their just petitions." On the same day he wrote to the
barons, informing them of the contents of his letter to the
bishops.[1] On April 1 he wrote to the barons again,
avowedly in consequence of the king's complaint of their
refusal to pay the scutage for the Poitevin war ; he reproved
them for their contumacy in this matter, and "warned and
exhorted" them to satisfy the king's claims without further
delay.[2]

By the middle of April the two former of these letters
must have reached England, the second being probably
brought back by Eustace de Vesci and his companions.
The third letter was scarcely needed to show the barons that
their cause was lost at Rome. John, moreover, had secured
its ruin in that quarter by taking the Cross[3]—partly, no
doubt, as a protection against personal violence, but still
more as a means of enlisting the Pope's strongest sympathies
in his behalf, and holding up his enemies to execration as
hinderers of the crusade. They grew desperate ; they held
another council among themselves, at which they determined,
without waiting for their promised interview with the king,
that they "would deal civilly with him no longer" ;[4] and
April 19-26   in Easter week they assembled at Stamford in arms.

Five earls and forty barons are mentioned by name as
present at the muster, "with many others" ; they all came
with horses and arms, and brought with them "a countless
host," estimated to comprise about two thousand knights,
besides other horsemen, sergeants-at-arms, and foot soldiers.[5]
"And because for the most part they came from the north,
they were all called Northerners." From Stamford they
marched to Northampton, but without doing any act of

---

[1] *Foedera*, vol. i. pt. i. p. 127.   [2] *Ib.* p. 128.

[3] On February 2, according to R. Wendover, vol. iii. p. 296 ; on Ash
Wednesday (March 4), according to W. Coventry, vol. ii. p. 219, and *Ann.
Winton.* a. 1215. This latter is the likelier date ; if the fact had been known at
Rome before the Pope's letters were written, they would almost certainly have
contained some reference to it.

[4] W. Coventry, *l.c.*

[5] R. Wendover, vol. iii. pp. 297, 298 ; M. Paris, *Chron. Maj.* vol. ii. p.
585. W. Coventry, vol. ii. p. 219, adds a bishop, Giles of Hereford. Giles,
however, was there not as bishop, but as the avenger of his father, mother and
brother—William, Maud, and the younger William de Braose.

violence.[1]   John, who had spent Easter in London,[2] sent the   1215
primate and some other bishops and magnates to parley with
them.[3]   Several meetings appear to have taken place.   The
deliberations evidently turned chiefly on the Pope's letters.
No allusion is made by the chroniclers to the letter about the
scutage, which perhaps had not yet arrived ; but, on the one
hand, Innocent's condemnation of secret conspiracies could
not be ignored ; and on the other, the barons urged his
injunction to the king to hearken to their " just petitions." [4]
At length John—secure in the consciousness that he could
refuse every petition on the plea that it was not just—authorized his commissioners to demand of the barons, in his name,
a categorical statement of the laws and liberties which they
desired.

This message was delivered to the insurgents by the
primate and the Marshal, at Brackley, on Monday April 27
—the day after that originally fixed for the meeting of the
barons and the king.   " Then they [the barons] presented to
the envoys a certain schedule, which consisted for the most part
of ancient laws and customs of the realm, declaring that if
the king did not at once grant these things and confirm them
with his seal, they would compel him by force." [5]   This
" schedule " was no doubt a kind of first draft, prepared under
the direction of Langton himself in his conferences with the
insurgents during the previous week, of those " Articles of the
Barons " from which we chiefly learn the grievances of the
time, and most of which were ultimately embodied in the
Great Charter.   Langton and the Marshal carried it back to
the king, who was now in Wiltshire.[6]   One by one the
articles were read out to him by the primate.   John listened

---

[1] W. Coventry, vol. ii. p. 219.   [2] *Itin.* a. 16.
[3] W. Coventry, *l.c.*   [4] *Ib.*
[5] R. Wendover, vol. iii. p. 298.
[6] Roger of Wendover, Walter of Coventry, and several other annalists
absurdly say that in Easter week (April 19-26) John was at, or near, Oxford,
where he was to have met the barons.   John had not been at Oxford since the
Tuesday before Easter, April 13 ; from the 16th to the 23rd he was in London :
on the 23rd he went to Kingston, Reading and Alton, and thence on the 26th
to Clarendon ; *Itin.* a. 16.   On the day he left London he granted a general
safe-conduct to all persons who should come to him in the suite of or with letters
patent from the archbishop (*Rot. Pat.* p. 134) ; none of the barons, however, seem
to have availed themselves of this offer.

1215   with a scornful smile : " Why do these barons not ask for
my kingdom at once ? " he said.   " Their demands are idle
dreams, without a shadow of reason."   Then he burst into a
fury, and swore that he would never grant to them liberties
which would make himself a slave.   In vain the archbishop
and the Marshal endeavoured to persuade him to yield ; he
only bade them go back to the barons and repeat every word
that he had said.   They performed their errand ;[1] and the
barons immediately sent to the king a formal renunciation
of their homage and fealty,[2] and chose for themselves a
captain-general in the person of Robert Fitz-Walter, to whom
they gave the title of " Marshal of the army of God and
Holy Church." [3]   They then marched back to Northampton,
occupied the town and laid siege to the castle.[4]

   The king was not behindhand in his preparations for
war.   His friends were already mustering at Gloucester ; on
April 30 he requested them to proceed thence on the
following Monday (May 3), well furnished with horses and
arms, and with " all the men they could get," to Cirencester,
there to await his further commands.[5]   Orders were issued
for strengthening the fortifications of London, Oxford,
Norwich, Bristol and Salisbury.[6]   The earls of Salisbury,
Warren, Pembroke and others perambulated the country to
see that the royal castles were properly fortified and
manned ;[7] help was summoned from Flanders[8] and from
Poitou.[9]   Early in May the king returned for a couple of
days to London ;[10] and as fourteen years before he had won
the support of its citizens in his struggle with Richard's
chancellor by granting to them the " commune " which they
desired, so now he endeavoured to secure their adhesion by
confirming their liberties and adding to them the crowning
privilege of a fully constituted municipality, the right to

---

[1] R. Wendover, vol. iii. p. 299.
[2] W. Coventry, vol. ii. p. 219.   [3] R. Wendover, *l.c.*
[4] Cf. R. Wendover, *l.c.*, and R. Coggeshall, p. 171.
[5] *Rot. Pat.* p. 134 b.
[6] *Rot. Claus.* vol. i. p. 198, 198 b ; *Rot. Pat.* p. 135.
[7] *Rot. Pat.* p. 135, 135 b.
[8] On May 8 John announces that some horse and foot are coming over under
Gerard of Gravelines ; *Rot. Pat.* p. 141.
[9] *Ib.* p. 135 (May 11).   [10] May 7-9 ; *Itin.* a. 16.

elect their own mayor every year.[1]   Meanwhile the
"northern" barons had found Northampton castle too
strong to be taken without military engines which they did
not possess; so at the end of a fortnight they had raised the
siege and moved on to Bedford.   Here the castle was given
up to them by its commandant, William de Beauchamp.[2]
Their forces were rapidly increasing in number; the younger
men especially, sons and nephews of the greater barons,
joined them readily, "wishing to make for themselves a
name in war"; the elder magnates, for the most part, clave
to the king "as their lord."[3]

On May 9 the king—now at Windsor—proposed that
the quarrel should be decided by eight arbitrators, four to
be chosen by himself and four by "the barons who are
against us," with the Pope as "superior" over them; he
offered the earl of Warren and four bishops as sureties for
his own acceptance of the award, and promised that until it
was delivered he would take no forcible measures against
the insurgents, "save according to the law of the realm and
the judgement of their peers in his court."[4]   This proposal
seems to have been rejected at once, for two days later
John ordered the sheriffs to seize the lands, goods and
chattels of "his enemies" in their several shires and apply
them to his benefit.[5]   Almost immediately afterwards he
seems to have commissioned the archbishop of Canterbury
to negotiate a truce for a few days.   On the 16th he
appointed his brother, Earl William of Salisbury, to act as
his representative in London.[6]   The object of William's
mission evidently was to secure, if possible, the loyalty of
the "mayor, aldermen and other barons of London," which
John suspected to be wavering.   His suspicion was correct;
a plot for the betrayal of the city was already ripe, and on
the very next morning—Sunday, May 17—the insurgents
were masters of the capital.[7]   The first use they made of

---

[1] *Rot. Chart.* p. 207.   [2] R. Wendover, vol. iii. p. 299.
[3] W. Coventry, vol. ii. p. 220.   [4] *Rot. Pat.* p. 141.
[5] *Rot. Chart.* p. 209; *Rot. Claus.* vol. i. p. 204.
[6] *Rot. Pat.* p. 136 b.
[7] R. Wendover, vol. iii. pp. 299, 300; W. Coventry, vol. ii. p. 220; R.
Coggeshall, p. 171; for date see *Rot. Pat.* vol. i. p. 137 b.

1215   this success was to fill their pockets with plunder taken
        from the king's partisans in the city, and from the Jews;
        the next was to pull down the Jews' houses and use the
        stones for repairing the city walls.   They then sent letters
        to all the earls, barons and knights who still adhered to the
        king, " bidding them, if they cared to retain their property
        and goods, forsake a king who was perjured and in rebellion
        against his barons, and join with them in standing firmly
        and fighting strongly for the peace and liberty of the realm;
        threatening that if they neglected so to do, they, the writers,
        would direct their banners and their arms against them as
        against public enemies, and do their utmost to overthrow
        their castles, burn their dwellings, and destroy their fish-
        ponds, orchards and parks."   These invitations and threats
        brought over to the winning side all who had been waiting
        to see which way the tide would turn, and they, of course,
        made a right goodly company.[1]

        Still the king did not lose heart.   He had gone from
        Berkshire into Wiltshire,[2] and was at his hunting seat of
        Fremantle—" a house which stands on a height, and in the
        heart of a forest "—when, on May 18 or 19, a party of
        Flemish knights under Robert de Béthune found their way
        to him and offered themselves for his service.   He gave
        them a joyous welcome, and hearing that a sudden rising
        had taken place in Devon, despatched them under the
        command of the earl of Salisbury to deal with it.   The
        insurgents were reported to be besieging Exeter, whence
        the earl was bidden to dislodge them; but they had, in fact,
        already taken it; and when Earl William reached Sher-
        borne, he was told that they were lying hidden in a wood
        through which his road lay, in such numbers that he and
        his followers had no chance of escape if they fell into the
        ambush; whereupon he went back to the king at Win-
        chester.[3]   "You are not good at taking fortresses!" said
        John scornfully when he heard the tale.   A few days later

        ---

        [1] R. Wendover, vol. iii. pp. 300, 301.
        [2] *Itin.* a. 16, May 10-17.
        [3] *Hist. des Ducs*, pp. 147, 148.   John was at Fremantle May 17-19; thence
        he went to Silchester, May 19; Winchester, 19, 20; Odiham, 21, 22; Windsor,
        22, 23; Winchester again, 23; *Itin.* a. 16.

he again bade the same party go and drive the " Northerners "
out of Exeter.   Again they were met at Sherborne by
alarming accounts of the increased numbers of the enemy ;
but this time the Flemings, stung by the king's taunt,
insisted upon going forward to " conquer or die " ; and the
" Northerners," though they are said by the contemporary
Flemish chronicler to have been ten to one, evacuated
Exeter at the mere tidings of their approach.[1]

This second expedition to Exeter probably started from
Winchester on the same day (May 24) on which John
issued a notice that any persons who came to his service
from over sea were to place themselves under the orders of
his chamberlain, Hubert de Burgh.[2]   He had summoned a
part of his forces to muster on May 26 at Marlborough ;
but on the 25th they were bidden to proceed to " the parts
of Odiham and Farnham," there to receive his commands ;
while others, who were to have come to Reading, were to
await his orders sent through Jordan de Sackville.   On the
same day John wrote to the archbishop of Canterbury,
urgently, but very courteously, entreating that he would
temporarily waive his right to the custody of Rochester
castle and allow the king to garrison it with men of his
own.[3]   To this request Langton acceded.[4]   By this time he
had negotiated another truce, and two days later John gave   May 27
him a safe-conduct for himself and for whatever persons he
might bring with him to Staines " to treat of peace between
ourself and our barons." [5]

The object of all these changes of front on the king's
part was to gain time for assembling new forces and
devising a new policy.   On the same day on which he gave
the safe-conduct to the archbishop, he despatched an urgent
appeal to all " his knights, men-at-arms, and friends who were
coming to join him " from over sea, entreating them to come
as speedily as possible, and promising that they should be

[1] *Hist. des Ducs*, pp. 148, 149.
[2] *Rot. Pat.* p. 138.
[3] *Ib.* p. 138 b.
[4] Rochester castle was restored to the archbishop after the "peace" in June.
R. Wendover, vol. iii. p. 319.
[5] *Rot. Pat.* p. 142.

1215   well rewarded for so doing.[1]   On May 29 he again wrote
to the Pope, complaining of the rebellious attitude of the
barons, which made it impossible for him to fulfil his vow of
crusade.[2]   On Whitsun Eve, June 6, he bade his favourite
captain of mercenaries, Falkes de Bréauté, send four
hundred Welshmen to Salisbury to meet its earl by the
following Tuesday,[3] seemingly to be ready for action on
the Thursday, when the truce would expire.

John knew, however, that the game was lost.   Four
bodies of insurgents were now in the field, and none of
them seem to have paid any regard to the truce.   The
townsfolk of Northampton had risen against the royal
garrison of the castle and slain several of them.   The force
which occupied London was besieging the Tower ; and now,
in this Whitsun week, another body seized Lincoln.[4]   The
king was almost deserted ; at one moment he is said to
have had only seven knights left in his suite ; the sessions
of the Exchequer and of the sheriffs' courts throughout the
country had ceased, because no one would pay him anything or obey him in any matter.[5]   He had come up on
May 31 from Odiham to Windsor, doubtless to meet the
archbishop at Staines ; on June 4 he went back into Hampshire.[6]   On Whit-Monday, June 8, he issued from Merton
a safe-conduct for envoys from the barons to proceed to and
from Staines from Tuesday the 9th till Thursday the 11th.
On Wednesday the 10th he returned to Windsor, and the
truce was prolonged from Thursday to the following Monday, the 15th.[7]   Finally, he despatched William the Marshal
and some other trusty envoys to tell the barons in London
" that for the sake of peace and for the welfare and honour
of his realm, he would freely concede to them the laws and

---

[1] *Rot. Pat.* p. 141 b.
[2] *Foedera*, vol. i. pt. i. p. 129.
[3] *Rot. Claus.* vol. i. p. 214.
[4] W. Coventry, vol. ii. pp. 220, 221.   Cf. R. Coggeshall, p. 171.
[5] R. Wendover, vol. iii. p. 301.
[6] *Itin.* a. 17.   The authentic details of John's movements at this time are of
some importance in view of Ralph of Coggeshall's assertion (p. 172) that he was
just then so overcome with terror " ut jam extra Windleshoram nusquam progredi
auderet."
[7] *Rot. Pat.* pp. 142 b, 143.

liberties which they asked ; and that they might appoint a   1215
place and day for him and them to meet, for the settlement
of all these things." The messengers "guilelessly performed
the errand which had been guilefully imposed on them " ;
and the barons, "buoyed up with immense joy," fixed the
meeting to take place on June 15 in a meadow between
Staines and Windsor,[1] called Runnimead.[2]

There, on the appointed morning, the two parties   June 15
pitched their tents at a little distance from each other on
the long reach of level grass-land which stretched along the
river-bank. The barons came "with a multitude of most
illustrious knights, all thoroughly well armed."[3] "It is
useless," says another chronicler, "to enumerate those who
were present on the side of the barons, for they comprised
well-nigh all the nobility of England." With the king
were the archbishops of Canterbury and Dublin, seven
bishops, Pandulf—who had been sent back to England as
the Pope's representative instead of Nicolas—the Master of
the English Templars, the earls of Pembroke, Salisbury,
Warren and Arundel, and about a dozen barons of lesser
degree, including Hubert de Burgh.[4] It was to these
chosen few, and above all to the first of them, that John
really capitulated. His declaration that he granted the
Great Charter by their counsel may well have been true of
them all ; his most devoted adherents could, if they had any
political sagacity, advise him nothing else for his own
interest. The terms of capitulation, however, imply more
than this. Nominally, the treaty—for it was nothing less[5]
—was based upon a set of forty-nine articles "which the
barons demanded and the lord king granted."[6] But those
articles are obviously not the composition of "the barons"
mustered under Robert Fitz-Walter. Every step of the proceedings of these insurgents up to that moment, every step

[1] R. Wendover, vol. iii. p. 301.
[2] "In prato qui vocatur Runemad," R. Coggeshall, p. 172.
[3] *Ib.*
[4] R. Wendover, vol. iii. p. 302.
[5] Stubbs, *Const. Hist.* vol. i. p. 530.
[6] Heading of Articles of the Barons : "Ista sunt capitula quae Barones petunt
et Dominus Rex concedit."

1215   of their proceedings afterwards, as well as everything that is
known of the character of their leaders, goes to show that
they were no more capable of rising to the lofty conception
embodied in the Charter—the conception of a contract
between king and people which should secure equal rights
to every class and every individual in the nation—than
they were capable of formulating it in the minute detail and
the carefully chosen phraseology of the Charter or even of
the Articles. The true history of the treaty of Runnimead
is told in one brief sentence by Ralph of Coggeshall: " By
the intervention of the archbishop of Canterbury, with
several of his fellow-bishops and some barons, a sort of
peace was made." [1]   In other words, the terms were drawn
up by Stephen Langton with the concurrence of the other
bishops who were at hand, and of the few lay barons, on
either side, who were statesmen enough to look at the crisis
from a higher standpoint than that of personal interest;
they were adopted—for the moment—by the mass of the
insurgents as being a weapon, far more effective than any
that they could have forged for themselves, for bringing the
struggle with the king (so at least they hoped) to an easy
and a speedy end; and they were accepted—also for the
moment—by John, as his readiest and surest way of escape
from a position of extreme difficulty and peril. Thus
before nightfall the Great Charter was sealed; and in return
John received anew the homage of the barons who had
defied him.[2]

It was, however, one thing to make the treaty, and
quite another to carry it into effect. The framers of the
Articles and of the Charter had done what they could
towards that end by a carefully planned " form of security
for the observance of the peace and liberties between the
king and the kingdom." [3] Out of the whole baronage of
England the barons present at Runnimead were to choose
twenty-five, who should " observe, keep, and cause to be

---

[1] R. Coggeshall, p. 172. Cf. Gerv. Cant. vol. ii. p. 96.
[2] *Rot. Pat.* p. 143. The " die Veneris " which occurs three times in this
writ is in each case an unquestionable, though unaccountable, error for " die
Lunae."   [3] Art. Bar. c. 49.

observed, with all their might," the provisions of the
Charter.   If the king failed to do his part, these twenty-
five were to compel him thereto by force if necessary.   For
this purpose they were authorized to claim assistance from
"the community of the whole country," and they were
therefore to receive an oath of obedience from every man in
the realm.[1]   King and barons alike swore that they would
keep all the provisions of the Charter "in good faith and
without deceit."[2]   The king was made to promise that he
would not procure "from any one" anything whereby his
concessions might be revoked or diminished, and that if
such revocation should be obtained it should be accounted
void and never used.[3]   That John's promises were worthless
every one knew ; it was not likely that all the pressure
which could be brought to bear upon him by "five-and-
twenty over-kings"—as his foreign mercenaries sarcastically
called the elected barons[4]—would more than suffice, if even
it should suffice, to compel him to keep his word.   Still the
check thus set over him was a very strong one.   It was
in fact the strongest that could be devised ; and it was
made of indisputable authority by its incorporation in the
Charter.[5]

On the other hand, the Charter contained no provision
for compelling the barons in general to fulfil their part of
its obligations, either towards their sub-tenants[6] or towards
the Crown, except what might be implied in the authority
given to the twenty-five ; while for securing the loyalty and
good faith of the twenty-five themselves it contained no
provision at all.   If we look at the text of the Charter
alone, we can but endorse the verdict of its foreign soldier-
critics : England was exchanging one king for five-and-
twenty.   This defect in the treaty seems to have been
noticed as soon as it was passed, and a remedy was sought
in the appointment of another body of barons, thirty-eight

---

[1] Art. Bar. c. 49 ; Magna Charta, c. 61.
[2] M. Charta, c. 63.   [3] *Ib.* c. 61.
[4] M. Paris, *Chron. Maj.* vol. ii. p. 611, "Ecce vigesimus quintus" [it
should have been "sextus"] "rex in Anglia ; ecce jam non rex, nec etiam
regulus, sed regum opprobrium," etc.
[5] M. Charta, c. 61.   [6] *Ib.* cc. 15, 16, 60.

1215   in number, chosen from both parties,[1] and including the Earl
Marshal and the other chief adherents of the king ; these,
after swearing obedience to the twenty-five, took another oath
which bound them to compel both the king and the twenty-
five to deal justly with one another.[2]   This precaution may
perhaps have been suggested by Langton and the other
bishops when a significant incident had shown them that
the promise of the insurgent barons was worth no more
than that of the king.   This incident rests upon the
authority of a joint statement purporting to be issued, evidently by way of protest and warning and for the clearing
of their own consciences, by ten eye-witnesses—the archbishops of Canterbury and Dublin, seven English bishops,
and Pandulf.   In a letter-patent addressed to " all Christian
people," these ten persons (if the document be genuine)
recite how in their sight and hearing the barons had made
to the king—seemingly before the Charter was sealed—a
verbal promise that they would give him, for their observance of the agreement between him and themselves, any
security which he might choose, except castles or hostages.
" Afterwards " John called upon them to fulfil this promise
by giving him in their turn a charter, whereby they should
acknowledge themselves bound to him by oath and homage
as his liegemen, and for the preservation of his rights and
those of his heirs and the defence of his realm.   " But," say
the witnesses, " this they would not do." [3]   Such, it seems,
was the earnest of the loyalty to their plighted word which
England, as well as John, had to expect from the men who
posed as the champions of justice and right.

For ten days the nominally reconciled enemies sat
watching each other, the king at Windsor, the barons still

[1] The twenty-five were of course all " Northerners " in the political sense ;
see the list in M. Paris, *Chron. Maj.* vol. ii. p. 604.
[2] The list of these thirty-eight is headed " Obsecutores et Observatores,"
and ends thus : " Isti omnes juraverunt quod obsequerentur mandato viginti
quinque baronum."   Another MS. adds : " Omnes isti juraverunt cogere si
opus esset ipsos xxv barones ut rectificarent regem.   Et etiam cogere ipsum si
mutato animo forte recalcitraret," M. Paris, *Chron. Maj.* vol. ii. pp. 605, 606.
Considering the whole context, I think there can be little doubt that " rectificare
regem "—though an odd way of expressing it—really means here " to do right to
the king."   [3] *Rot. Pat.* p. 181.

encamped in the surrounding meadows.   In private, John's   1215
feelings broke out in wild paroxysms of fury characteristic
of his race ; he " gnashed his teeth, rolled his eyes, caught
up sticks and straws and gnawed them like a madman, or
tore them into shreds with his fingers." [1]   But to the
outside world he wore a calm and smiling face, chatting
familiarly and gaily with every one whom he met, and
declaring himself perfectly satisfied with the settlement of
affairs.[2]   Within the next seven days he despatched copies June 19-22
of the Charter to the sheriffs, foresters and other royal
bailiffs in every shire, with letters patent ordering them to
make the men under their jurisdiction swear obedience to the
twenty-five barons in whatever form these latter might
prescribe, and cause twelve sworn knights to be elected in
the next county court for the purpose of inquiring into evil
customs with a view to their extirpation as promised in the
Charter.[3]   He also sent to his mercenary captains orders to   June 18
desist from hostilities and amend any damage which they
might have done to the barons since the peace was made.[4]
On the following Tuesday, June 23, he ordered the foreign
soldiers at Dover to be sent home at once.[5]   On the 25th
a number of sheriffs were removed from office and replaced
by new ones.[6]   Before that date the king had appointed a
new chief justiciar, Hubert de Burgh,[7] a faithful adherent of
his own, who was also an honourable man, respected by all
parties, and a member of the committee of thirty-eight.   On
the 27th the sheriffs and the knights elected in every shire
to inquire into evil customs were ordered to punish summarily
all persons who refused the oath of obedience to the twenty-
five.[8]

The king was then at Winchester ; he had left Windsor
on the night of the 25th.[9]   Illness—seemingly a severe
attack of gout—had made him unable to move sooner, and
the barons had taken advantage of his physical helplessness
to heap upon him every insult in their power.   One day the

[1] M. Paris, *Chron. Maj.* vol. ii. p. 611.
[2] M. Paris, *Hist. Angl.* vol. ii. p. 159.
[3] *Rot. Pat.* p. 180 b.   [4] *Ib.* p. 143 b.   [5] *Ib.* p. 144.
[6] *Ib.* pp. 144 b, 145.   [7] *Ib.* p. 144 b.
[8] *Ib.* p. 145 b.   [9] *Itin.* a. 17.

1215　twenty-five required his presence to confirm a judgement in
the Curia Regis ; he was in bed, unable to set a foot to the
ground, so he sent them word that they must come and
deliver the judgement in his chamber, as he could not go to
them.　They " answered that they would not go, for it would
be against their right ; but if he could not walk, he must
cause himself to be carried."　He did so, and when he was
brought into their presence " they did not rise to meet him,
for it was their saying that if they had risen, they should
have done contrary to their right." [1]　This scene probably
occurred in connexion with one of the cases dealt with in
the fifty-second article of the Charter, the cases of persons
who were, or asserted that they were, deprived of their lands,
castles, privileges or rights by an arbitrary act of John or
of his predecessors, without judgement of their peers.　Some
of these cases, in which there was no doubt about the circumstances of the deprivation, were settled without delay,
and immediate restitution was made to the claimants by the
Crown.[2]　But there were others which required investigation.
Such was the claim of the earl of Essex to the custody of
the Tower of London.[3]　The chief justiciar of England had
been recognized as entitled by virtue of his office to the
custody of the Tower ever since the accession of Henry II. ;
but Henry's mother, the Empress Maud, had granted it by
charter to Geoffrey de Mandeville and his heirs ; [4] and it
was now claimed as an hereditary right by the earl of Essex,
as eldest son of the late justiciar Geoffrey Fitz-Peter by his
marriage with Beatrice de Say, on whom the representation
of the Mandeville family had devolved.[5]　This matter was
too delicate and too important to be decided in haste ;
pending its decision, the Tower was temporarily placed in

---

[1] *Hist. des Ducs*, p. 151.
[2] W. Coventry, vol. ii. p. 221 ; *Rot. Claus.* vol. i. pp. 215-18.
[3] W. Coventry, *l.c.*
[4] Round, *Geoffrey de Mandeville*, pp. 89, 166.
[5] W. Coventry, vol. ii. p. 225, sums up the earl's position and character
very suggestively : " In parte adversa erat Gaufridus de Maundevilla comes
Essexae, quem rex cingulo militari donaverat, quique regi in XIX millibus
marcarum obligatus erat pro comitissa Gloucestriae quondam uxore sua, quam iste
nuper acceperat." See above, p. 196.　Geoffrey's first wife had been a daughter
of Robert Fitz-Walter ; see Note I at end.

neutral hands, the hands of the archbishop of Canterbury,[1] to whom Rochester castle was at the same time restored.[2] Finally, John proposed that the other questions in dispute between himself and individual barons should all be determined at Westminster on July 16. This being agreed, the barons withdrew to London [3] and the king to Winchester, whence at the beginning of July he proceeded into Wiltshire.[4]

King and barons alike knew that the " peace " had been made only to be broken. The barons were the first to break it. Some of those " Northerners " from beyond the Humber by whom the strife had been originally begun had actually left Runnimead in the middle of the conference, and were now openly preparing for war, on the pretext that they " had not been present " at the settlement.[5] Their southern allies were really doing the same ; only they veiled their preparations under the guise of a tournament to be held, ostensibly in celebration of the peace, at Stamford on July 6. Robert Fitz-Walter and his companions, however, quickly discovered that if they wished to keep their hold upon London they must not venture far away from the city ; they therefore postponed the tournament for a week, and transferred it from Stamford to Staines. The victor's prize was to be " a bear, which a lady was going to send." [6] Meanwhile the new sheriffs—appointed since the peace, and specially charged to enforce its provisions—were meeting with a very rough reception in every shire where the " Northern " influence predominated. All over the country the barons were fortifying their castles ; some were even building new ones.[7] A more scrupulous king than John might well have deemed himself justified, under such circumstances, in doing what John did—following their example in preparing to fling the treaty to the winds and renew the war.

---

[1] W. Coventry, vol. ii. p. 221 ; *Ann. Dunst.* a. 1215. Cf. R. Wendover, vol. iii. p. 319.   [2] R. Wendover, *l.c.*

[3] *Ib.* ; R. Coggeshall, p. 172.

[4] *Itin.* a. 17.   [5] W. Coventry, vol. ii. p. 222.

[6] R. Wendover, vol. iii. pp. 321, 322.

[7] W. Coventry, *l.c.*

The meeting which had been appointed for July 15 was postponed till the 16th, and the place for it changed from Westminster to Oxford. On the 15th the king came up from Clarendon into Berkshire, and on his way from Newbury to Abingdon despatched a letter to the barons stating that he " could not " meet them in person at Oxford on the morrow, but that the archbishop of Dublin, the bishop of Winchester, Pandulf, the earls Marshal, Warren, and Arundel, and the justiciar, would be there in his stead, " to do to you what we ought to do to you, and to receive from you what you ought to do to us." [1] The archbishop of Dublin was no longer justiciar in Ireland ; Geoffrey Marsh had been, on July 6, appointed to succeed him in that office.[2] On the same day Walter de Lacy had been reinstated in all his Irish lands.[3] Throughout the summer of this year John, busy as he was with English affairs, had found time to pay even more attention than usual to those of his Irish dominion. From May to July the Close and Charter Rolls are full of letters and writs relating to the Irish March ; charters to towns, to religious houses, to individual barons, orders concerning military arrangements and other matters of local administration,[4] all show such constant intervention and such personal interest on the king's part as to convey an impression that he was specially endeavouring to win for himself the support of the nobles, clergy and people of the Irish March as a counterpoise to the hostility and disaffection which surrounded him in his English realm. It was, however, to the Continent that he mainly looked for aid. " After much reflection," says Roger of Wendover, " he chose, like the Apostle Peter, to seek vengeance upon his enemies by means of two swords, that is, by a spiritual sword and a material one, so that if he could not triumph by the one, he might safely count upon doing so by the other." [5]

The spiritual weapon was the first to be actually drawn ; but even before its first stroke fell, swords of the other kind

---

[1] *Rot. Pat.* p. 149. [2] *Ib.* p. 148.
[3] *Ib.* p. 148 b.
[4] *Rot. Claus.* vol. i. pp. 218, 218 b, 219, 219 b ; *Rot. Chart.* pp. 210-13.
[5] R. Wendover, vol. iii. p. 319.

were making ready for the king's service. Emissaries from
him were soon busy in "all the neighbouring lands beyond
the sea," gathering troops by promises of rich pay and ample
endowments in English land, to be confirmed by charters if
the recipients desired it.[1]   The chancellor, Richard Marsh,
was thus raising troops in Aquitaine ;[2] Hugh de Boves was
doing the like in Flanders.   Those whom they enlisted were
to be ready to come to the king at Dover by Michaelmas
Day.[3] John was also seeking allies in France.   On August
12 he wrote to Count Peter of Britanny, offering him a grant
of the honour of Richmond if he would come " with all speed,
and with all the knights he could bring," ready for service
against the insurgents in England.[4]   He is even said to have
tried hard, " by enormous promises," to gain help from Philip
Augustus ; but in this quarter " others had been beforehand
with him," says the chronicler significantly.[5]   It was not
without a cause that the barons at Runnimead had refused
to write themselves John's liegemen.

Within the realm, the royal castles were being re-
victualled and made ready to stand a siege at any moment.[6]
As yet no further attempt had been made upon any of them ;
but in the north the barons, or their followers and partizans,
had begun to lay waste the royal manors and overrun the
forests, cutting down and selling the timber, and killing the
deer.   Again the archbishop and bishops came forward as
peacemakers, and it was arranged that the king should meet
them on August 16 at Oxford, while the barons should
assemble at Brackley, there to await the result of the church-
men's mediation.   When the day arrived, however, the king
was still in Wiltshire, and excused his absence on the ground
that he had been so ill-treated since the conclusion of the
peace, and moreover at the last conference the barons had
come together in such menacing array, that he deemed it
neither safe nor prudent to risk himself in their midst ; an
excuse which was practically justified by the action of the

---

[1] R. Wendover, vol. iii. p. 320 ; where, however, the list of emissaries is
obviously incorrect.   [2] *Rot. Pat.* p. 153, 153 b.
   [3] R. Wendover, *l.c.*   [4] *Rot. Pat.* vol. i. p. 152 b.
   [5] W. Coventry, vol. ii. p. 222.   [6] R. Wendover, *l.c.*

themselves, who, instead of waiting at Brackley as ι̇ad agreed to do, came "with a numerous following" ̇eet the bishops at Oxford.[1]

The bishops had now received from Rome a communication which made their position, or at least that of the Primate, an exceedingly anxious and painful one. In consequence, it seems, of John's letter of May 29 Innocent had issued a commission to the bishop of Winchester, the abbot of Reading and Pandulf, whereby he declared excommunicate all "disturbers of the king and kingdom of England, with their accomplices and abettors," laid their lands under interdict, and ordered the archbishop and his episcopal brethren, on pain of suspension from their office, to cause this excommunication to be published throughout the realm every Sunday and holiday till the offenders should have made satisfaction to the king and returned to their obedience.[2] Ill-fitted as the barons had proved to be for the great work in which Langton had sought to enlist them, the cause of England's freedom was yet too closely bound up with theirs for him to be willing to launch at them such a sentence as this, and he had sympathized too keenly with his country's misery under a former interdict not to recoil from the prospect of another. The barons, on the other hand, had been heedless of interdict and excommunication so long as their material interests coincided with those of the king against the Church; but the matter would wear a different aspect in their eyes now that the situation was reversed and their one hope was in the aid of the Church against the king. The Pope's mandate was shown to them and the bishops

Aug.
16·18

in conference at Oxford; after three days' deliberation the bishops agreed to delay the publication of the sentence till they had seen the king again and made one more effort to bring him to a colloquy in London or at Staines. It was rumoured that he had gone to the coast with the intention of quitting England altogether; and the bishops are said to have followed him to Portsmouth, and there found that he was

[1] W. Coventry, vol. ii. p. 222.
[2] R. Wendover, vol. iii. pp. 336-8; misplaced, as may be seen by comparing W. Coventry, vol. ii. p. 223.

actually on shipboard. He came ashore again, however,
to speak with them ; but he absolutely refused to hold any
more personal conferences with the barons. The bishops
returned to meet the barons at Staines on August 26,
accompanied by envoys from the king, who were charged
with a protest, to be delivered in his name in the hearing of
the whole assembly, that " it was not his fault if the peace
was not carried out according to the agreement." After long
deliberation the papal sentence was proclaimed, but with a
taçit understanding that it was to be, for the present at least,
a dead letter, on the ground that as no names were mentioned
in it, the phrase " disturbers of the king and kingdom " need
not be applied to any person or group of persons in particular,
but might be interpreted by every man as he pleased. The
more violent partizans immediately applied it to the king
himself, since in their eyes he was the chief troubler of the
land, and therefore also his own worst enemy.[1]

After placing his queen and his eldest son in safety in
Corfe castle,[2] John had taken ship, seemingly about August
24, at Southampton or Portsmouth, and sailed round the
coast to Sandwich, where he appears to have landed on
the 28th.[3] The barons in London, if we may believe the
report of the chroniclers, were foolish enough to imagine
that he would never land again at all.[4] They were now
taking upon themselves, in all those counties where their
power was strong enough, to supersede both the sheriffs and
the justices and usurp their functions, parcelling out the
country among members of their own body, each of whom
was to act as the chief judicial and administrative authority
in the district committed to him.[5] In their premature

---

[1] W. Coventry, vol. ii. p. 224. Cf. R. Wendover, vol. iii. p. 341.

[2] *Hist. des Ducs*, p. 152.

[3] John's Itinerary, a. 17, is blank from August 22, when he was at Wareham,
to August 28, when he appears at Sandwich. The *Hist. des Ducs*, p. 153,
accounts for this blank by stating that he went by sea from Southampton to Dover
(whither he did proceed on August 31 or September 1 ; *Itin. l.c.*). W. Coventry
(vol. ii. p. 224) says the bishops who left Oxford on August 19 to seek him
found him just embarked at Portsmouth, which comes to the same thing.

[4] The absurdity of the reports given in R. Wendover (vol. iii. pp. 320, 321)
and M. Paris (*Hist. Angl.* vol. ii. pp. 160, 161) about John's movements at this
time was pointed out long ago by Dr. Lingard, *Hist. England*, vol. ii. p. 362.

[5] Earl Geoffrey de Mandeville took Essex ; Robert Fitz-Walter, Northampton-

1215　triumph they were even beginning to talk of choosing a new
sovereign, and of calling the whole baronage of England
to a council for that purpose, " since this ought to be done
by the common consent of the whole realm." [1]　Early in
September, however, the revolutionists awoke from their
dreams to find that the king was safe in Dover castle,
surrounded by a little band of foreign soldiers who had
already joined him there, and awaiting the coming of the
host which was gathering for him beyond the sea.[2]　The
three executors of the papal mandate were meanwhile
insisting that now, at any rate, the barons had unquestionably fallen under its terms, by endeavouring to expel the
king from his realm ; and they excommunicated by name
several of the revolutionary leaders, together with the citizens
of London, whom they placed under interdict.　These
sentences, however, were disregarded, on the plea that they
were barred by a previous appeal to the general council [3]
which was to be held at Rome on All Saints' Day, and
which most of the English bishops were preparing to attend.
Archbishop Stephen was about to set forth, in the middle of
September, when two of the papal commissioners—Pandulf
and Bishop Peter of Winchester—went to him in person
and insisted that he should enforce the publication of the
Pope's sentence throughout his own diocese on all the
appointed days, and order his suffragans to do the same.
Stephen answered that he would take no further steps in the
matter till he had spoken of it with the Pope himself, since
he believed the sentence to be grounded on a misunder-
standing of the facts of the case.　On this Pandulf and Peter
denounced him as disobedient to the Pope's mandate, and,
in accordance with its terms, suspended him from his office.[4]

Stephen accepted his suspension without protest.　He
was indeed so grievously disappointed at the turn which

shire ; Roger de Cresci, Norfolk and Suffolk ; the earl of Winchester, Cambridge-
shire and Huntingdonshire ; William of Aubigny, Lincolnshire ; John de Lacy,
Yorkshire and Nottinghamshire ; Robert de Ros, Northumberland.　W.
Coventry, vol. ii. p. 224.　　　　　[1] *Ib.*

[2] *Ib.*　Cf. *Hist. des Ducs*, p. 153.

[3] W. Coventry, *l.c.*

[4] R. Wendover, vol. iii. p. 340.　Cf. R. Coggeshall, p. 174, and W. Coventry,
vol. ii. p. 225.

affairs in England had taken, and so hopeless of doing any
further good there, that he had almost determined not only
to resign his see, but to retire altogether from the world and
bury himself in a hermitage or a Carthusian cell.[1]   Several
of the bishops visited the king before they went over sea ;[2]
we are not told whether Stephen did so ; but he certainly
had the king's permission for his journey to Rome, for on
September 10 John by letters patent took under his protection all the archbishop's men, goods, lands and other
possessions, and forbade his own men to do them any
injury.[3]   On the 13th the king wrote again to the Pope,
asking for his counsel and aid, and complaining that
" whereas before we subjected our land to you as overlord,
our barons were obedient to us, now they have risen up
violently against us, specially on account, as they publicly
declare, of that very thing."   This letter was carried by the
archbishops of Bordeaux and Dublin and seven other
envoys.[4]   Pandulf—now bishop-elect of Norwich—seems to
have gone to Rome about the same time, charged with
another letter to the Pope.[5]   But before any of these travellers
had set out on their way the Pope had drawn his sword
again ; and this time the sword was a two-handed one.   It
was the sword of the temporal overlord of England, as well
as of the spiritual head of Christendom.

The sixty-first article of the Charter enacted, as we have
seen, that if the king should procure " from any one " a
revocation or cassation of that document, such revocation
should be accounted void.   The only person, however, from
whom such a thing could possibly be sought was of course
the Pope ; and in so far as the Pope was concerned, the
clause was itself in feudal law null and void from the beginning, owing to the action of the barons before the Charter
was drawn up or thought of.   Whatever may have been
their real share in the surrender of the kingdom to the Pope
in May 1213, they had at any rate in February 1215,

[1] Gir. Cambr. vol. i. p. 401.
[2] W. Coventry, vol. ii. pp. 224, 225.
[3] *Rot. Pat.* p. 154 b.   This disposes of R. Coggeshall's assertion (p. 174)
that Stephen went "rege invito et ei minas intentante."
[4] *Rot. Pat.* p. 182.   [5] *Ib.* p. 182 b (dateless).

e may believe William Mauclerc (and there is no reason for disbelieving him), put on record their full concurrence in that transaction after it was accomplished, and even taken voluntarily upon themselves the whole responsibility both for its accomplishment and for its initiation.[1] Thereby they had deprived themselves of whatever legal pretexts they might otherwise have had for repudiating its consequences; and foremost of those consequences was the fact that the Pope was now legally the supreme arbiter of political affairs in England, by a right which had been given to him by the joint action of the king and the barons, and against which no later reservation made between those two parties themselves (such as the sixty-first article of the Charter) was of any force in feudal law. The framers of the Charter seem to have been conscious of this;[2] John, indeed, had pointedly reminded them of it before he consented to the Charter, telling the barons, in answer to their demands, that nothing in the government and constitution of England ought to be, or lawfully could be, altered without the knowledge and sanction of the Pope, now that he was overlord of the realm; and he had publicly appealed to the Pope, as overlord, against them and all their doings. As soon as the Charter was sealed, he had despatched envoys to Rome to prosecute his appeal, and to lay before Innocent a statement of his case, together with such extracts from the Charter as were most likely to influence the Pope in his favour. The result was that on August 24—two days before the papal denunciation of the " disturbers of the realm " was published by the English bishops at Staines— Innocent as temporal overlord of England quashed the Charter, and as Pope forbade its observance by either king or people, on pain of excommunication.[3]

---

[1] See above, pp. 182 and 225.

[2] In the " Articles of the Barons," c. 49, this reservation-clause ran : " Rex faciet eos securos per cartas archiepiscopi et episcoporum et magistri Pandulfi quod nihil impetrabit *a domino Papa*," etc.   In the Charter, c. 61, " *ab aliquo* " was substituted for " a domino Papa," and the security to be given by letters patent of Pandulf and the bishops was made to refer to the keeping of the Charter in general (*ib.* c. 62), instead of to that one particular point.

[3] R. Wendover, vol. iii. pp. 322-7.

CHAPTER VII

JOHN LACKLAND

1215–1216

Dicitur . . . "Sine Terra," quia moriturus nil terrae in pace possedit.
M. Paris, *Hist. Angl.* vol. ii. p. 191.

THE Pope's letters evidently did not reach England till after the primate and the bishops had set out for Rome, so that there was no one left to publish the new sentence ; and it seems, in fact, never to have been published in England at all.   But its existence soon became known there ; and when once the barons knew of it, they knew, too, that they must make their choice between unconditional surrender and war to the uttermost with both king and Pope ; for there was no one left to act as their mediator with either.   They chose war ; but they were not ready for war, and the king was. Poitevins, Gascons, Brabantines, Flemings, were flocking to him from over sea.[1]   On October 2 he ordered his brother, Earl William of Salisbury, to visit ten royal castles and select from their garrisons troops for service in the field. On the 4th he committed the superintendence of military affairs in mid-England and the west to Falkes de Bréauté, and issued a general safe-conduct to " all who may wish to return to our fealty and service" through the medium of Falkes or the earl.[2]   He himself had, towards the end of September, advanced as far inland as Malling ;[3] but this seems to have been merely a sort of reconnoitring expedition ; his plan evidently was to wait till all his expected

[1] R. Wendover, vol. iii. p. 331 ; W. Coventry, vol. ii. p. 226.
[2] *Rot. Pat.* vol. i. p. 156 b.   [3] *Itin.* a. 17.

1215 reinforcements had arrived from over sea, and then march
with them upon London, while William and Falkes did the
same with the troops which they could bring up from the
west, so as to place the capital between two fires.   While
his forces were concentrating, those of the barons were
scattering ; they had no scheme of united action ; one party
had renewed the siege of Northampton castle, another was
engaged in that of Oxford.[1]   At last the leaders in London
decided that something must be done to bar John's way to
the capital ; and they advanced into Kent as far as Ospring.
When they reached it John was at Canterbury ; having only
a small escort he, on hearing of his enemies' approach,
hurriedly fell back to Dover ; they, however, were so scared
by a report that he had set out from Canterbury to offer
them battle that they beat an equally hasty retreat towards
Rochester.[2]   Their great fear was lest he should gain
possession of Rochester castle, which he had vainly tried
to induce the archbishop to give up to him two months
before.[3]   On October 11 Reginald of Cornhill, in whose
charge Stephen had left it, suffered it to be occupied by a
band of picked knights under William of Aubigny.   But the
triumph of the intruders was shortlived ; two days later the
king was at the gates of Rochester.[4]

"Certes, sire," said one of John's Flemish allies as the
royal host set out for Rochester, "you make little account
of your enemies if you go to fight them with so small a
force !"   "I know them too well," answered John ; "they
are to be nothing accounted of or feared.   With fewer men
than we have we might safely fight them.   Certes, one
thing I may tell you truly, I grieve not so much for the
evil which the men of my land are doing to me, as that

[1] W. Coventry, vol. ii. p. 226.
[2] *Hist. des Ducs*, p. 157.   The date seems to be either September 20 to 22
or October 5 to 6 ; see *Itin.* a. 17.
[3] *Rot. Pat.* vol. i. p. 181 b.
[4] R. Wendover, vol. iii. pp. 330, 331.   The dates are not quite clear.
Roger gives none, but says John laid siege to the castle " on the third day " after
the barons entered it ; Ralph of Coggeshall, p. 175, says John entered the city
on Sunday October 11.   But the *Itinerary* shows that John was on the 11th
at Ospring and on the 12th at Gillingham, and he does not date from Rochester
till the 13th.   I have therefore ventured to suppose that Ralph has given the
date of the barons' arrival by mistake for that of the king's.

their wickedness should be seen by strangers." [1]   The king
knew what the stranger did not know, that so long as he
could keep the Medway between himself and the main
body of the barons he was safe.   He therefore began his
operations by an attempt to destroy the bridge, and thus to
cut off the communications between Rochester and London.
It seems that he sent a party up the river in boats to fire
the bridge from beneath, and that they succeeded in so
doing, but that Robert Fitz-Walter, with a picked body of
knights and men-at-arms, was guarding the bridge at the
time and managed to extinguish the flames and drive off
the assailants.[2]   Fitz-Walter, however, appears to have
immediately returned to London; [3] and in a second attack
on the bridge John was completely successful; the bridge
was destroyed, and the king proceeded to invest the castle [4]
and assault the town.

On his first approach the citizens had manned their
walls and "made a great show of defending themselves";
but "when they saw he was preparing to assault them they
broke into a rout, left the battlements, and fled on all sides.
Then his men entered through the gates, and began to chase
them through the town to the bridge so vigorously that they
drove all the knights by force into the castle; of whom"—
sarcastically adds the Flemish soldier of fortune who tells
the tale—"many would gladly have fled to London if they
could." [5]   But they could not, the bridge being now gone.
The whole party thus gathered in the castle numbered about
ninety-five knights and forty-five men-at-arms.[6]   The castle
when given to William of Aubigny and his followers was
destitute of provisions; they had had no time to procure
any, save what little they could get in the town; [7] and they
saw before them an imminent prospect of starvation.   John
pressed the siege vigorously; on the day after its commencement he ordered "all the smiths in Canterbury" to
devote their whole time, "day and night," to making pick-

---

[1] *Hist. des Ducs*, pp. 158, 159.   [2] R. Coggeshall, p. 175.
[3] See below, p. 250.   [4] W. Coventry, vol. ii. p. 226.
[5] *Hist. des Ducs*, p. 159.
[6] Cf. *ib.* p. 157; W. Coventry, vol. ii. p. 226; R. Wendover, vol. iii. p.
330; and R. Coggeshall, p. 176.   [7] R. Wendover, *l.c.*

1215 axes, which were to be sent to him at Rochester as fast
as they were made.[1]   His forces increased daily till they
became "such a multitude that they struck fear and horror
into all who beheld them."[2]   They ravaged all over Kent,
and wrought havoc in Rochester, stabling their horses in the
cathedral and committing every kind of sacrilege in the
holy places.[3]

At all this the barons in London looked on in helpless
consternation.   They had plighted a solemn oath to William
of Aubigny, when he undertook the expedition to Rochester,
that if the king besieged him there they would succour him
without fail.[4]   A fortnight passed before they made any
movement to redeem their promise; then, on October 26,
some seven hundred knights[5] set out under the command of
Robert Fitz-Walter; but they got no farther than Dartford.
One chronicler says they "retreated before the breath of a
very soft south wind as if beaten back by swords";[6] another,
that they turned back in dismay on hearing how numerous
were the forces of the king;[7] a third, that they were misled
on this point by an exaggerated account given them by
a Templar sent to meet them for that purpose by John
himself.[8]   In any case, they returned to London, and having
taken care to provide themselves with ample stores, they sat
down to "play at the fatal dice and drink the best wine,
according to each man's taste, and do it is needless to say
what besides,"[9] till S. Andrew's Day.   By that time they

---

[1] *Rot. Claus.* vol. i. p. 231 b.

[2] R. Wendover, vol. iii. p. 331. Cf. *Hist. des Ducs*, p. 160.   One party
under Hugh de Boves was wrecked in a storm on the Norfolk coast, September
26; their leader was drowned, so were many others, and a large quantity of
money also went down; but the survivors made their way to the king in time to
join him at Rochester and help in the siege, *Hist. des Ducs*, pp. 155, 156;
Chron. Mailros, a. 1215; R. Coggeshall, pp. 174, 175; R. Wendover, vol. iii.
p. 332.

[3] R. Coggeshall, p. 176.

[4] W. Coventry, vol. ii. p. 226; R. Wendover, vol. iii. p. 333.

[5] W. Coventry, *l.c.*   [6] R. Wendover, *l.c.*

[7] W. Coventry, *l.c.*

[8] M. Paris, *Hist. Angl.* vol. ii. p. 165.   It is Matthew alone who gives the
name of the leader of the party.   His version of the expedition is important, as
he—notwithstanding his strong anti-royalist feeling—shows up the cowardice of
the barons, and especially of Fitz-Walter, on this occasion, quite as strongly,
and is quite as sarcastic upon it, as the royalist Roger of Wendover.

[9] R. Wendover, vol. iii. p. 333.

expected important reinforcements ; and they reckoned that   1215
the besieged could hold out till then.[1]

William of Aubigny and his comrades did hold out, but
at desperate odds.   Every possible mode of attack—mining,
battery, assault—was tried in turn upon the fortress.   Five
great slinging engines were plied incessantly, day and night,
against its walls.   The garrison, already short of food, and
expecting no mercy from the king if they surrendered, were
minded to sell their lives dearly ; they fought like heroes ;
" nor," says the Barnwell annalist, " does living memory recall
any siege so urgently carried on and so manfully resisted." [2]
A strange contrivance at last shattered the mighty keep.
On November 25 John ordered the justiciar to send him
with all possible speed " forty bacon-pigs of the fattest, and
of those which are least good for eating, to be put to set fire
to the stuff that we have got together under the tower." [3]
Of the results of the blaze thus kindled a token remains to
this day, in the round tower which at the south-west angle
of the keep contrasts so markedly with the square towers at
the other corners, and which replaces the original square
one thus destroyed by John.   Even after its fall the garrison
fought on until their last morsel of food was gone ; then at
last they surrendered on S. Andrew's Day.[4]   The king set
up a gallows in front of the army and declared he would
hang them all ; but he yielded to Savaric de Mauléon's warning that if he hanged brave knights such as these, the barons
would surely do the like to any friends of his who might fall
into their hands, and that in view of such a prospect no man
would remain in his service.[5]   On this he contented himself
with sending the knights to prison, leaving the men-at-arms
to ransom themselves as best they could, and hanging only
a few cross-bowmen.[6]

[1] W. Coventry, vol. ii. p. 226.   R. Coggeshall, p. 177, says that John had
contrived to prevent some of the northern barons from joining them by means of
forged letters purporting to come from Fitz-Walter and his comrades, telling the
Northerners that their help was no longer needed.
[2] W. Coventry, vol. ii. p. 227.
[3] R. Wendover, vol. iii. pp. 334, 335.
[4] *Hist. des Ducs*, p. 163 ; R. Wend. vol. iii. p. 335.
[5] R. Wend. vol. iii. p. 336.   In W. Coventry, *l.c.*, John is said to have
hanged only one cross-bowman, whom he had had in his service from boyhood.

Three times since the siege began the barons in London,
or some of them, had opened negotiations with the king.
On October 17 Richard of Argentan and others had a safe-
conduct " to treat with us for peace between ourself and our
barons " ; [1] on October 22 Roger de Jarpeville and Robert
de Coleville had a safe-conduct till the 27th to treat with
the king concerning peace between him and " the barons who
may come with the Master of the Temple and the Prior of
the Hospital " ; [2] and on November 9 a safe-conduct till the
12th was given to Earl Richard of Clare, Robert Fitz-Walter,
Geoffrey de Say, and the mayor and two, three or four citizens
of London, that they might go and speak with the bishop of
Winchester, the earls of Warenne and Arundel, and Hubert
de Burgh, " to treat of peace between ourself and our
barons." [3]   On the side of the barons these overtures were
nothing but a cloak for the cowardice and incapacity which
kept them from taking any active steps for the relief of their
besieged comrades.   They were all the while pushing on
negotiations for bringing in a foreign power to aid them in
their selfish scheme of revolution.

One chronicler asserts that as long ago as the year 1210
some of the barons had contemplated driving John from his
throne and setting up as king in his stead a man who,
though born on foreign soil and engaged throughout his
whole life in the service of foreign powers, had yet a claim
to rank as one of themselves, and certainly not as the least
distinguished among them—Simon, count of Montfort and
titular earl of Leicester.[4]   To modern eyes the cruelties of
the war against the Albigenses, in which Simon was the
leader of the " crusading " host, have somewhat obscured the
nobler aspects of a character which was not without a heroic
side.   It was indeed by a strange instinct that—if the
Dunstable annalist's tale be true—the chiefs of the English
revolutionary party fixed their hopes for a moment on the
father of that other Simon de Montfort, at that time still but

See the names of the knights made prisoners, in R. Wend. vol. iii. pp. 335, 336,
Rot. Claus. vol. i. p. 241 b, and *Rot. Pat.* p. 161.
 [1] *Rot. Pat.* p. 157.   [2] *Ib.* p. 157 b.
 [3] *Ib.* p. 158.   [4] *Ann. Dunst.* a. 1210.

a boy, who was one day to seal with his blood the work of
England's deliverance which they professed to have at heart,
but which in their narrow and short-sighted selfishness they
were alike unworthy and incapable of achieving. The instinct was at any rate a loftier one than that which guided
them in their choice of a rival to John five years later. The
scheme put forth by the group of barons in London in the
summer of 1215 for electing a new king "by the common
consent of the whole realm" of course came to nothing ; the
magnates would have none of it, and the northern barons who
had separated from the other malcontents before the sealing
of the Charter had, as will be seen later, made an independent choice of their own. The mad little faction in London,
headed now by Earl Geoffrey de Mandeville, acted by themselves and for themselves alone when they "chose for their
lord" the eldest son of the king of France, "begging and
praying him that he would come with a mighty arm to pluck
them out of the hand of this tyrant." [1]

Only one English chronicler gives or even pretends to
give any hint of the grounds on which this choice was, either
really or nominally, based. In no English writer of the time
do we find any indication that the connexion of Louis of
France with the reigning royal house of England, through
his marriage with John's sister's daughter, had, or was supposed to have, anything to do with it. The claim to the
English crown which Louis afterwards put forth on this
ground seems to have been an idea of purely French origin,
which not only had never suggested itself to any English
mind, but, when it was suggested, failed to meet with general
recognition even among Louis's partizans in England. The
intricate rules of succession, and especially of female succession, which it pre-supposed were as yet, when applied to the
Crown at least, completely strange to English statesmen.
Moreover, it is by no means clear that the barons who offered
the Crown to Louis had any real intention of transferring it
to him and his heirs for ever. Roger of Wendover tells us
that "after hesitating for some time whom they should
choose, they at length agreed upon this, that they would set

<hr>

[1] W. Coventry, vol. ii. p. 225.

1215 over themselves Louis, the son of King Philip of France, and raise him up to be king of England. Their reason was that if through the agency of Louis and his father King John could be deprived of the host of foreign soldiers who surrounded him, most of whom were subjects of Louis [1] or Philip, he, being without support from either side of the sea, would be left alone and unable to fight." [2] In other words, they wanted Louis as a tool wherewith to crush John ; and to gain him for their tool they offered him the bribe of the crown, thinking that when their immediate purpose should be accomplished it would be time enough to consider whether the annexation of England to France would or would not really profit them better than to break faith with their new lord as they had broken it with their old one.

The first direct overtures of the barons to Louis seem to have been made before the outbreak of hostilities, in September or October 1215 ; [3] and these overtures were renewed at some time after the commencement of the siege of Rochester, when the earls of Winchester and Hereford went over with a message from their comrades in London to Louis, that " if he would pack up his clothes and come, they would give him the kingdom and make him their lord." [4] These envoys were at once confronted by Philip with a letter which he had just received, purporting to come from the same barons and informing him that his son's intervention was no longer needed, as peace had been made between them and their own sovereign. The earl of Winchester offered to pledge his head that the letter was forged by John.[5] The French king accepted this assurance ; but he was too wary to commit himself hastily to a scheme so full of perils and difficulties as that which the earls so lightly proposed, and he merely gave it a negative countenance by standing altogether aloof from their negotiations with his son. Louis promised that he would at once send to England as many knights as he

---

[1] Louis had inherited the county of Artois from his mother.

[2] R. Wendover, vol. iii. p. 359.

[3] W. Coventry, vol. ii. pp. 225, 226.

[4] " S'il voloit venir en Engletierre sa cape toursée, il li donroient le règne en boine pais et le feroient seigneur d'eus," *Hist. des Ducs*, p. 160. Cf. W. Coventry, *l.c.*   [5] R. Coggeshall, pp. 176, 177.

could get, and would himself follow them at Easter. He   1215
then called his own vassals together at Hesdin, and at the
end of November some hundred and forty of his knights
with their followers—in all about seven thousand men—
landed at the mouth of the Orwell [1] and made their way to
London, " where they were very well received and led a
sumptuous life ; only they were there in great discomfort
because they ran short of wine and had only beer to drink,
to which they were not accustomed. Thus they remained
all the winter." [2]

John spent the winter in other fashion. On November
28—two days before the surrender of Rochester—Tonbridge
castle, which belonged to the rebel earl of Clare, had
surrendered to Robert de Béthune, one of John's Flemish
allies, and on the same day the castle of Bedford yielded
to Falkes de Bréauté. In each case the garrison had sent
to their lord for help, and in each case no help had been
given them.[3] John left Rochester on December 6, marched
through Essex and Surrey into Hampshire, and thence
proceeded to Windsor.[4] On the 20th he held a council at
S. Albans.[5] Two of his envoys had recently come back
from Rome with a papal confirmation of the suspension of
Archbishop Stephen.[6] This was read to the convent
assembled in the chapter-house, and committed to them
for transmission to all cathedral and conventual churches
throughout England. The king then retired with his
counsellors into the cloister "to arrange how he might
confound the magnates of England who were his enemies,
and how he might find pay for the foreigners who were
fighting under him." He decided upon dividing his host
into two bodies ; one was placed under the command of
Earl William of Salisbury, assisted by Falkes de Bréauté,
Savaric de Mauléon, William Brewer, and a Brabantine
captain known as Walter Buck, with orders to check the

---

[1] Cf. *Hist. des Ducs*, p. 160, and R. Coggeshall, p. 176.

[2] *Hist. des Ducs*, pp. 160, 161.

[3] R. Wendover, vol. iii. pp. 349, 350 ; *Hist. des Ducs*, pp. 161, 162. John
had granted the earldom of Clare to Robert de Béthune ; *Hist.*, *l.c.*

[4] *Itin.* a. 17.

[5] R. Wendover, vol. iii. p. 347.   [6] *Ib.* pp. 344-6.

1215 irruptions of the barons who were in London; of the other the king himself took the command, " intending to go through the northern provinces of England, and destroy with fire and sword everything that came in his way." [1]

Dec. 20 That same night John, with his division, moved on to Dunstable; before daybreak on the morrow he set out for Northampton, and by Christmas he was at Nottingham.[2] All along his route he sent out parties in every direction to burn the houses of the hostile barons and seize their cattle and their goods; every obstacle that stood in his path was destroyed; and as if the day were not long enough to satiate his love of destruction, he would send men out at night to fire the hedges and the villages along his line of march, that he might rejoice his eyes with the damage done to his enemies; while the other question which had occupied his deliberations at S. Albans, the remuneration of his followers, was solved with the produce of the rapine in which they were not merely indulged but encouraged. Every human being, of whatever rank, sex or age, who crossed the path of this terrible host was seized, tortured, and put to heavy ransom. The constables of the baronial castles dared not trust to the protection of their walls; at the report of the king's approach they fled, leaving their fortresses to be occupied by him and his troops.[3] Thus, "not in the usual manner, but as one on the war-path,"

Dec. 26 he kept Christmas at Nottingham.[4] On the following day
Dec. 27 he moved on to Langar, and thence, next morning, despatched a notice to the garrison of William of Aubigny's castle of Belvoir that if they did not surrender at once, their lord should be starved to death. To this threat they yielded.[5]

Meanwhile, the barons in London had made no use of the reinforcements sent to them by Louis. They seem to

[1] R. Wendover, vol. iii. p. 347. Cf. R. Coggeshall, p. 177. Ralf substitutes Gerard of Sotteghem for William Brewer; but in R. Wendover, p. 348, Gerard is named among those who accompanied the king.
[2] R. Wendover, vol. iii. pp. 348, 350; confirmed by *Itin.* a. 17.
[3] R. Wendover, vol. iii. p. 348.
[4] W. Coventry, vol. ii. p. 228.
[5] R. Wendover, vol. iii. p. 350.

have despaired of overcoming John by any means short of an invasion headed by Louis in person with the whole forces of the French kingdom at his back. Towards the close of the year Saher de Quincy and Robert Fitz-Walter went on another embassy to Philip and Louis, "urgently imploring the father that he would send his son to reign in England, and the son that he would come thither to be crowned." How or by whom he was to be crowned, when the only prelate competent to perform the rite was in exile and under suspension, and the rival sovereign was under the direct protection of the Pope, they did not explain. Philip refused to entertain their proposals without further security, and demanded "twenty-four hostages at least, of the noblest of the whole land." The hostages were sent under the charge of the earls of Gloucester and Hereford. When they arrived, Louis began to prepare eagerly for his expedition ; but there were still weighty reasons why, as an English chronicler says, "he himself could not hastily set out to undertake so arduous a matter." So, "to raise the hopes of the barons and try their fidelity,"[1] he sent his marshal and some others of his vassals with a second contingent, some three hundred knights and cross-bowmen and a proportionate number of foot soldiers, all of whom, together with the English earls, sailed up the Thames and arrived in London just after Epiphany 1216; he himself promising on oath that he would be at the coast, ready to cross, "with a great multitude of people," at latest on the octave of S. Hilary, January 20.[2]

So, while John was pursuing his northward march, the barons sat still and waited. The southern division of John's host meanwhile was far from idle. Between Christmas and the middle of January detachments of it overran the whole of Essex, Hertfordshire, Middlesex, Cambridgeshire and Huntingdonshire, while the main body marched to S. Edmund's, drove the insurgents who had taken refuge

---

[1] R. Wendover, vol. iii. pp. 359, 360.
[2] R. Howden, vol. iv. p. 189, note 4. Cf. R. Coggeshall, p. 178, and *Hist. des Ducs*, p. 162. R. Wendover, vol. iii. p. 360, has confused this second French contingent with the first, which had come in November 1215, and seemingly also with a third. See below, pp. 261, 262.

1216　there to seek another shelter in the Isle of Ely, followed them thither, and sacked, burned and ravaged the patrimony of S. Etheldreda as they did every other place to which they came.[1] Their leaders, before setting out, had charged the constables of Windsor, Hertford and Berkhamsted to keep a watch upon all who went into and out of London, and if possible to stop the supplies of the barons there. This latter charge either proved impossible to execute, or the constables deemed its execution impolitic, and deliberately preferred to let the king's enemies in London ruin themselves by " lying there like delicate women, anxiously considering what variety of food and drink could be set before them to renew their wearied appetites."[2]　The advance of Savaric de Mauléon on Colchester, on January 29, perhaps roused them at last, for a report reached him that they were hastening to relieve it, and caused him to retire towards S. Edmunds,[3] probably to rejoin the other royalist leaders who had been doing the work of destruction at Ely. But the barons, still vainly waiting for their foreign ally who came not, made no further movement ; and even when the royalists fired a suburb of London itself, and carried off " plunder of inestimable value,"[4] no retaliation seems to have been attempted.

While the barons slumbered—as a chronicler says—the king was not asleep ;[5] he was wreaking his long-delayed vengeance on the north. The malcontents in the land beyond the Humber had been quicker than their southern comrades to recognize their need of foreign help in their struggle against John, and they had taken a short and easy way of obtaining it for themselves. No sooner had civil

1215　war broken out in England in the autumn of 1215 than the young Scottish king, Alexander, who owed his throne and almost his life to the timely help which John had given to his father four years before, marched into Northumberland and laid siege, on October 19, to Norham castle.

---

[1] Cf. R. Wendover, vol. iii. pp. 349, 358 ; W. Coventry, vol. ii. p. 229, and R. Coggeshall, pp. 177, 178.

[2] R. Wendover, vol. iii. pp. 349, 352.

[3] R. Coggeshall, p. 178.

[4] R. Wendover, vol. iii. p. 349.　　　　　[5] *Ib.* p. 352.

Three days later the Northumbrian barons did homage to   1215
him at Felton.   No immediate results, indeed, followed from
this new league ; the garrison of Norham seem to have been
as loyal as their castle was strong ; at the end of forty days   Nov. 28
Alexander raised the siege and returned home,[1] just as
John was on the point of receiving the surrender of
Rochester ; and for more than a month no further movement took place in the north except an obscure rising at
York.[2]   When at the opening of 1216 John entered York-   1216
shire, the terror of his march to Nottingham had gone
before him and all thought of resistance was abandoned.
He reached Pontefract on January 2 ; its constable " came
there to his mercy." [3]   He went on to " his city of York,"
and " wrought all his will with it." [4]   On January 7 and 8
he was at Darlington.[5]   The horrors wrought by his troops
seem to have equalled, if not surpassed, those which the
Scots had been wont to perpetrate in their raids upon
Northumbria in their days of savage heathenism before the
conversion of Malcolm Canmore.[6]   A few barons " submitted
themselves to the mercy of the merciless one " ; the rest
" fled before his face." [7]   From Darlington he seems to
have advanced on the 8th to Durham ; thence he was
about to turn southward again, when he learned that
Alexander had set fire to Newcastle-on-Tyne.   Swearing
" by God's teeth " that he would " run the little sandy fox-
cub to his earth," [8] John dashed forward to Newcastle ; the
place was indeed burnt, but Alexander had withdrawn into
his own territory,[9] and on the 11th the English refugees
gathered round him in the chapter-house at Melrose and
renewed their oath to him on the relics of the saints.   John
was on their track, burning and ravaging what little there was

---

[1] *Chron. Mailros*, a. 1216.
[2] See note 4 below.
[3] *Hist. des Ducs*, p. 163 ; date from *Itin.* a. 17.
[4] " Puis s'en ala-il à Wrewic [*var.* Euerwic] sa cité, qui encontre lui s'iert
revelée ; si en fist toute sa volenté." *Hist. des Ducs*, *l.c.*   John was at York on
January 4, *Itin.* a. 17.   [5] *Itin.* a. 17.
[6] R. Wendover, vol. iii. pp. 351, 352.   [7] R. Coggeshall, pp. 178, 179.
[8] *Hist. des Ducs*, pp. 163, 164.   Cf. M. Paris, *Chron. Maj.* vol. ii. pp.
641, 642, and *Hist. Angl.* vol. ii. p. 172.
[9] *Hist. des Ducs*, p. 164 ; for dates see *Itin.* a. 17.

1216　left to ravage—little enough, for the fugitives had set fire
to their own fields and villages that he might get no benefit
from them.[1]　On the day of the homage at Melrose John
reached Alnwick.[2]　On the 14th he assaulted Berwick;
town and castle were taken next day,[3] and the population
butchered, after horrible tortures, by his mercenaries.　From
Berwick he made, in the following week, a series of raids
across the Tweed, and swept the country as far as Dunbar
and Haddington, both of which he burned.　At last, seeing
that the " fox-cub " was not worth a longer chase and that
there was more important work to be done elsewhere, he
ordered Berwick to be burnt, fired with his own hand—so
the Scottish story runs—the house in which he had himself
been lodging,[4] and on January 23 or 24 began to move
southward.　After stopping two days at Newcastle[5] and
granting a new charter to its citizens,[6] he made his way
slowly back through Yorkshire.　When at the end of
February he reached Fotheringay,[7] all the castles in the
shire save two were in his power and garrisoned by followers
of his own, who were charged to hold the country and
continue the work of destruction on the lands of the rebels
wherever there was anything left to destroy.[8]　Alexander's
dreams of conquest, the Northumbrian barons' dream of
independence — if subjection to their country's hereditary
foe could be called independence—were alike at an end.
Alexander, indeed, made a raid upon Carlisle as soon as
John's back was turned;[9] but it was a mere raid which led
to nothing.　Far more significant is the string of safe-
conducts which shows how throughout the winter and the
spring the terror-stricken English rebels came crowding in
to make their peace with John.[10]

John had now regained the mastery over the whole
eastern side of England, from the south coast to the Scottish

---

[1] *Chron. Mailros*, a. 1216.

[2] *Itin.* a. 17.

[3] Cf. *ll.cc.* and *Hist. des Ducs*, p. 164.

[4] *Chron. Mailros* and *Hist. des Ducs*, *ll.cc.*

[5] *Itin.* a. 17.

[6] *Rot. Chart.* p. 219.

[7] *Itin.* a. 17.

[8] R. Wendover, vol. iii. pp. 352, 353.

[9] February, *Chron. Mailros*, a. 1216.

[10] *Rot. Pat.* pp. 162, 162 b, 168, 169.

border,[1] except a few castles in Norfolk, Suffolk and Essex.   1216
After spending a week in Bedfordshire,[2] probably to concert
measures with Falkes de Bréauté, he marched into East
Anglia.   On March 12 he was at the gates of Roger
Bigod's castle of Framlingham; it surrendered at once.[3]
Next day he moved on to Ipswich; on the 14th he laid
siege to Colchester.[4]   Here the garrison had been reinforced by a detachment of Louis's Frenchmen, who agreed to
surrender on condition that they should be suffered to march
out free and their English comrades held to ransom.   John,
however, broke his promise to the Englishmen and put them
in chains.   The Frenchmen on reaching London were
accused by the barons of having betrayed their comrades by
making separate terms for themselves ; they were arrested and
even threatened with death, but it was finally determined to
keep them in custody till Louis should arrive.[5]   On the 25th
John proceeded to Hedingham, which belonged to the earl
of Oxford, Robert de Vere ; three days later it surrendered,
and the earl himself " came there to the king's mercy, and
swore that he would thenceforth serve him loyally."   Robert's
oath was soon broken ;[6] but his submission, insincere though
it was, indicates that the barons were losing heart.   So, too,
does an application made at the same time by the earl of
Clare and his son for a safe-conduct to and from the king's
court.[7]   A yet more important result of John's recent
campaign was the supply of money which he had acquired
by the plunder of his enemies.   This enabled him during
his stay at Hedingham to satisfy his mercenaries by a
general distribution of pay and gifts.   Thus secured against
the risk of their desertion, he prepared to march upon
London.[8]

A third body of troops sent by Louis had arrived in

[1] R. Wendover, vol. iii. p. 352.
[2] February 29–March 8, *Itin.* a. 17.
[3] Cf. *Itin.* a. 17, and *Hist. des Ducs*, p. 165.
[4] Cf. *ib.* and R. Coggeshall, p. 179.
[5] R. Coggeshall, pp. 179, 180 ; for dates see *Itin.* a. 17.   The king's safe-
conduct to the French soldiers (names given) from Colchester to London is
dated March 24, *Rot. Pat.* pp. 171 b, 172.
[6] *Hist. des Ducs*, p. 165.
[7] *Rot. Pat.* vol. i. p. 172 b.   [8] R. Coggeshall, p. 180.

ᵢn at the end of February,[1] and a letter had been
ᵥed from Louis himself, announcing that "by God's
ᵤe" he would "most certainly" be at Calais ready to
cross on Easter Day, April 10.[2] Encouraged on the one
hand by this assurance, on the other the Londoners had
been stirred into a mood of dangerous defiance by tidings
from Rome. On December 16, 1215, the Pope renewed his
condemnation of the barons in such a manner that it could
no longer remain what circumstances had made it hitherto,
a dead letter. He excommunicated the rebels, this time
not merely in general terms, but mentioning thirty-one of
them by name; he also placed the city of London under
interdict, and he appointed the abbot of Abingdon and two
other commissioners to execute this mandate.[3] It seems to
have reached England about the end of February 1216.[4]
The commissioners sent it to all the cathedral and conventual churches for immediate publication, and it was soon
published everywhere except in London. There the clergy
of S. Paul's, the barons and the citizens all alike rejected it
and appealed against it, declaring that it had been obtained
by "false suggestions, and was therefore of no account, more
especially as the ordering of lay affairs pertained not to the
Pope."[5] This last assertion seems ridiculous in the mouths
of the barons, who scarce twelve months before had professed
pride in having compelled the king to surrender to the Pope
the temporal overlordship of England. It was in a spirit of
mingled rage at the downfall of the expectations which they
had once founded upon that surrender, and revived hope of
speedy help from France, that the revolutionists who held
the capital met the king's threat of attack. The citizens
opened their gates and arrayed themselves "ready to go
forth and fight with him if he should approach within ten
leagues of the city."[6] Advancing slowly and cautiously, he

1215

1216

[1] R. Wendover, vol. iii. p. 360, who, however, has confused this contingent
with the former ones.
[2] *Ib.* p. 363.
[3] R. Wendover, vol. iii. pp. 354-6.
[4] R. Coggeshall, p. 179, mentions its arrival just after the death of Geoffrey
de Mandeville, which occurred on February 22.
[5] R. Wendover, vol. iii. p. 357.
[6] R. Coggeshall, p. 180.

reached Enfield on the last day of March ;[1] on the following night he seems to have slept at Waltham Abbey, "seven little English leagues from London."[2] But he came no nearer. Savaric de Mauléon, venturing on a closer approach, was caught at unawares and barely escaped with heavy loss of men and with a wound of which he all but died ; a band of "pirates" who attempted to block the Thames were all either slain, drowned or captured by the Londoners ; and evil tidings came from the north how the rebels there had risen anew, laid siege to York, and pressed it so hard that the citizens had been compelled to purchase for a thousand marks a truce till Trinity Sunday.[3] From Enfield the king passed round by Berkhamsted to Windsor and Reading, and thence went south into Hampshire.[4]

Of the northern rising we hear no more, but it seems to have proved a failure, for before April 12 three of the chief northern barons, Eustace de Vesci, Robert de Ros and Peter de Brus, offered to return to the king's service on one condition—that he would allow them to do so without a fine. John's answer was as politic as it was dignified. "What we desire to have from our barons," he wrote, "is not so much money as their good and faithful service" ; and he sent the three petitioners a safe-conduct to come and speak with him on their own terms.[5] On the previous day he had given orders that the mayor of York should be "competently provided" out of the lands of the king's enemies "for his good and faithful service which he did to the king,"[6] no doubt in the defence of the city during the recent siege. The mayor's loyalty and the king's promptitude in rewarding it illustrate a feature of John's home policy which is traceable through all the vicissitudes of his career : his interest in the towns and the trading classes, and his constant endeavours to cultivate their friendship. All the while that he was harrying the open country, burning villages and plundering castles, he was making

---

[1] *Itin.* a. 17.
[2] Cf. *Hist. des Ducs*, p. 165, and *Itin.* a. 17.
[3] R. Coggeshall, p. 180.   [4] *Itin.* a. 17.
[5] *Rot. Pat.* p. 176.   [6] *Rot. Claus.* vol. i. p. 260.

provision for the furtherance of trade, the security of
g merchants[1] and the preservation of foreign com-
merce from disturbance or interruption. With a French
invasion close at hand, he was still issuing safe-conducts to
French merchants in London and elsewhere.[2] For this,
indeed, there may have been a political reason; John was
anxious to keep on good terms with France in order to
counterwork the schemes of the barons in that quarter. He
had lately sent an embassy to try whether Philip Augustus
could by any means be induced to forbid his son's proposed
expedition.[3] One of the envoys at least, William the
Marshal, was back by Easter,[4] the day which Louis had
fixed for his own departure. That day passed and Louis
came not—hindered, it seems, by contrary winds.[5] About
this time John sent a letter to Louis himself, signifying his
willingness to amend any injury which Louis might have
received at his hands;[6] and on April 28 he wrote to the
guardians of the truce in France proposing that they should
hold a meeting with his proctors for the settlement of all
disputes which had arisen from infractions of the truce.[7]

By that time the projected expedition of Louis had
assumed an aspect very different from that which it had
worn when first suggested by the English barons in the
previous autumn. Philip as well as Louis was naturally
tempted by what looked like a golden opportunity for
annexing England to France; but he was held back by the
dread of offending the Pope, who had no sooner heard of
the scheme than he despatched a legate, Gualo, with instructions to proceed to France and England for the express
purpose of forbidding it. Philip saw that to make his son's
project tolerable in the Pope's eyes, and therefore safe in
those of his own feudatories, he must invent for it some more
plausible excuse than the flimsy pretence of election by the
excommunicate English barons. He had made out an
elaborate case in behalf of Louis and planned his own

---

[1] *Rot. Pat.* pp. 170, 170 b, 171.   [2] *Ib.* p. 172 b.
[3] R. Coggeshall, pp. 180, 181.   [4] *Rot. Pat.* vol. i. p. 175 b.
[5] W. Coventry, vol. ii. p. 229.
[6] *Rot. Pat.* p. 176.   [7] *Ib.* p. 179.

course of action with characteristic wariness and skill, by the
time that Gualo arrived in the spring of 1216.   On April 25
the legate was publicly received at Melun[1] by the French
king, to whom he presented the Pope's letters desiring that
Philip would not permit his son to invade England or to
molest the English king in any way, but rather that he
would protect and assist John as a vassal of the Roman
Church.   Philip answered at once : "The realm of England
never was S. Peter's patrimony ; it is not so now, and never
shall be.   John was convicted long ago of treason against
his brother Richard, and condemned by the judgement of
Richard's court ; therefore John was never rightfully king,
and had no power to surrender the kingdom.   Moreover, if
he ever was rightfully king, he afterwards forfeited his right
to the crown by the murder of Arthur, for which he was
condemned in our court.   And in any case no king or
prince can give away his realm without the consent of his
barons, who are bound to defend it."   This last proposition
was loudly applauded by the French magnates.   Next day
a second meeting took place.   Louis, according to a previous arrangement with his father, came in after the rest of
the assembly and seated himself by his father's side,
scowling at the legate.   Gualo, without appearing to notice
his discourtesy, besought him "not to go to England to
invade or seize the patrimony of the Roman Church," and
again begged Philip to forbid his doing so.   "I have always
been devoted and faithful," answered Philip, "to the Pope
and the Roman Church, and by my counsel and help my
son will not now attempt aught against them ; yet if Louis
claims to have any rights in the realm of England, let him
be heard, and let justice be done."   On this a knight
whom Louis had appointed as his proctor rose and set forth
the case thus : "My Lord King, it is well known that John,
who is called king of England, was in your court by sentence
of his peers condemned to death for treason against his
nephew Arthur, whom he had slain with his own hands,
and that he was afterwards rejected by the barons of
England from reigning over them by reason of the many

[1] See *Revue historique*, vol. xxxii. p. 49, note 2.

1216 murders and other enormities which he had committed there ; wherefore they began war against him, that they might drive him from the throne without hope of restoration. Moreover, the said king, without the consent of his magnates, made over the realm of England to the Pope and the Roman Church, to receive it back from them for an annual tribute of a thousand marks. Although he could not give the crown of England to any one without consent of the barons, yet he could resign it ; and when he resigned it he ceased to be king, and the throne was vacant. Now a vacant throne ought not to be filled save by consent of the barons ; wherefore the barons elected the Lord Louis on account of his wife, whose mother, the queen of Castille, was the sole survivor of all the brothers and sisters of the English king."

With this ingeniously-woven tissue of perverted truths and dressed-up lies it was obviously impossible for Gualo to deal on the spur of the moment. He evaded the point at issue by pointing out that John had taken the cross, and was therefore entitled to be left unmolested till his vow of crusade was fulfilled. Louis's proctor retorted that John had made war upon Louis both before and after taking the cross, and that Louis was therefore justified in retaliating. Gualo, without further argument, again forbade Louis to invade England, and his father to suffer him to do so, under pain of excommunication. Louis turned to his father : " Sire, although I am your liegeman for the fief which you have given me on this side of the sea, yet concerning the realm of England it appertaineth not to you to decree anything ; wherefore I submit me to the judgement of my peers whether you ought to forbid me to prosecute my right, and especially a right concerning which you cannot yourself do me justice. I beseech you therefore not to hinder me, since for my wife's heritage I will fight, if need be, even unto death." With these words he left the assembly. Gualo made no remark, but simply asked the king for a safe-conduct to the sea, that he might proceed on his mission to England. " I will gladly give you a safe-conduct through my own domains," answered Philip ; " but should you chance to fall into the hands of any of my son's men who are guarding the coast, blame me not if evil befall you." The legate departed in a rage. As soon as he was gone, Louis returned, asked and received his father's blessing on his enterprize, despatched messengers to Rome to lay his case before the Pope, and himself went to collect his forces at Calais.[1]

On April 14 John had ordered twenty-one coast towns to send all their ships to the mouth of the Thames.[2] On the 17th he bade the sheriffs throughout England make a proclamation calling upon all persons who had been in arms against the king to join him within a month after the close of Easter (April 24), on pain of forfeiture for ever.[3] On the 20th he returned to Windsor; thence he went through Surrey back to Rochester;[4] on the 25th—the day of the council at Melun—he issued from Canterbury orders to the soldiers then at Rochester to follow him immediately "wheresoever he might be."[5] He reached Canterbury that night, Dover on the morrow, and spent the next three weeks flitting up and down along the coast of Kent,[6] watching for the arrival of both Gualo and Louis, and superintending the gathering of the fleet and the preparation of the coast towns for defence. The Cinque Ports were again pledged, by oaths and hostages, to his service. Yarmouth, Lynn, Dunwich and other sea-ports sent their ships to the muster[7] at Dover. As soon as it was complete, the king intended to sail with his whole fleet to Calais and block up Louis in the harbour, "for he well knew," says a contemporary, "that the little vessels which Louis had could not defend themselves against his ships, which were so large; one of his ships was well worth four of those of Louis." But towards evening on May 18 a storm arose and swept over the fleet as it lay off Dover, and by the morning the ships were so broken and scattered that all hope of bringing them together again was

[1] R. Wendover, vol. iii. pp. 364-7. The version of M. Paris, *Hist. Angl.* vol. ii. pp. 176, 177, is as M. Petit-Dutaillis says (*Louis VIII.* p. 95, note), obviously nothing but an oratorical amplification.
[2] *Rot. Claus.* vol. i. p. 270.
[3] *Ib.* p. 270 b.   [4] *Itin.* a. 17.
[5] *Rpt. Pat.* p. 178 b.   [6] *Itin.* a. 17.
[7] R. Coggeshall, p. 181.

1216   lost.[1]   On the night of the 20th Louis set sail from Calais.
Next morning the watchmen on the shore of Thanet saw
some of his ships in the distance ; they sent word to the
king, who was at Canterbury, on the point of setting out to
meet the legate, of whose arrival at Romney he had just
been apprised.   He told the messengers from Thanet that
what had been seen were not the enemy's ships, but some of
his own which the storm had driven out to sea.   But his
words were only spoken to encourage his followers ; in his
heart he knew that the watchmen were not mistaken.   He
seems to have ridden only a few miles towards Romney
when he met Gualo, clad in his scarlet robes as cardinal, and
mounted on a white palfrey, as beseemed the representative
of the Pope.   King and legate dismounted and embraced.
John at once told Gualo that Louis had arrived ; Gualo
pronounced the invader excommunicate, and rode with John
into Canterbury.[2]

Louis meanwhile had landed at Stonor almost alone ;
the greater part of his fleet did not even come in sight till
the next day, Sunday, May 22.   John had now hurried to
Sandwich ; thence he saw with his own eyes the approach
of the hostile fleet as it sailed past the mouth of Pegwell
Bay.   To prevent its reaching the shore was impossible ;
the only question was whether he should encounter the
French host as soon as it had disembarked and stake everything upon a pitched battle.   The trumpets were sounded, the
troops arrayed ; but as he rode up and down along the shore
surveying their ranks his heart sank within him.[3]   They
were, almost to a man, mercenaries and foreigners, most of
them born subjects of the French king ; what if, when the
fight was at the hottest, they should go over in a body to
their fellow-countrymen and their own king's son ?   The

---

[1] *Hist. des Ducs*, pp. 167, 168.   Cf. R. Coggeshall, p. 181.

[2] *Hist. des Ducs*, pp. 168, 169.   Cf. R. Wendover, vol. iii. p. 368, and
Ann. Winton. a. 1216, both of which give the same date for Louis's arrival.
R. Coggeshall, p. 181, gives a date which, though self-contradictory, is, I think,
meant for the same—" die sabbati post Ascensionem Domini, scilicet xiiii kalen-
das Junii."   W. Coventry, p. 229, is quite wrong.   John had gone on May 19
(Ascension Day) to Folkestone ; on the 20th and 21st he was at Canterbury.
Itin. a. 17, 18.

[3] *Hist. des Ducs*, p. 169.

1216

risk was too grave to be faced ; it was better to withdraw
than to court an encounter so likely to prove fatal.[1] Such
was the counsel given to John by one of the few Englishmen
still at his side, the wisest and truest of them all, William
the Marshal.[2] For a while John hesitated ; then, as was his
wont in moments of disappointment and distress, he stole
away in silence, and had galloped a league on the road to
Dover before the greater part of his men knew that he was
gone.[3] Leaving Dover under the charge of Hubert de
Burgh, with a strong garrison and ample provisions,[4] and
appointing the earl of Warren warden of the Cinque Ports,[5]
he made his way through Sussex to Winchester, where he
remained watching the course of events during the next ten
days.[6]

The first act of Louis after landing his troops was to
issue a manifesto to the English clergy, setting forth, in
somewhat more blunt terms than he had ventured to use
in presence of the legate at Melun, his pretensions to the
English Crown, and exhorting those whom he addressed not
to be persuaded into thwarting his endeavours " for the good
of the English Church and realm " by anything that they
might hear from Gualo, whom he represented as having no
just grounds for opposition to him, and as having been
brought to England " by the suggestions and bribes " of
John.[7] He then, after seizing a few English ships which had
put in at Sandwich after the storm, and plundering the

[1] R. Wendover, vol. iii. p. 368 ; W. Coventry, vol. ii. pp. 229, 230.
[2] *Ann. Dunst.* a. 1215.
[3] *Hist. des Ducs*, p. 170. The assertion of William the Breton, *Gesta P. A.*
c. 221, that John actually did await the attack of the French, and was driven
away by their vigorous onset, certainly is, as M. Petit-Dutaillis says (*Louis VIII.*
p. 100), an error. That error is grounded, like the sneering comments of Ralf of
Coggeshall (p. 181), the *Ann. Winton.* (a. 1216), and some later writers, on the
mistaken idea that John was on the spot when Louis first landed on the 21st.
[4] *Hist. des Ducs*, p. 170.
[5] *Rot. Pat.* p. 184.   [6] *Itin.* a. 18.
[7] Thorne, *Gesta Abb. S. Aug. Cant.* in Twysden, *X Scriptt.* cols. 1868-70.
The letter as there given is addressed to the abbot and convent of S. Augustine's,
but it was evidently a manifesto of which copies were sent, or intended to be
sent, to all the religious houses of note, probably also to the secular clergy, and
perhaps to be distributed among the laity as well. The character of Louis's
"case" as set forth in this letter, and in the arguments of his envoys at Rome
(R. Wendover, vol. iii. pp. 371-8), has been sufficiently exposed by M. Petit-
Dutaillis, *Louis VIII.* pp. 75-87.

1216   town, marched upon Canterbury.   The citizens admitted
him without resistance;[1] Gualo fled from his lodgings in
S. Augustine's abbey; the abbot, who was John's foster-
brother, alone refused all submission to the invader.[2]   From
Canterbury Louis proceeded to Rochester, where he was
joined by his men from London.[3]   The mighty fortress which
had cost John a siege of nearly two months surrendered to
Louis in less than a week, on Whit Monday, May 30.[4]
Already the forebodings of the king and the Marshal were
more than justified ; John's mercenaries were deserting, and
not only those barons who had been recently preparing, or
pretending to prepare, to return to their allegiance, but even
many of those who had hitherto seemed loyal to him, now
joined the leaders of the revolution in doing homage to the
invader.[5]   On Whitsun Eve (May 28) Gualo had rejoined
the king at Winchester,[6] after issuing a citation to the
English bishops and clergy to meet him there "in aid of the
king and the kingdom."   On Whit Sunday, in their presence,
he excommunicated Louis by name, together with all his
followers and adherents, whose lands, as well as the city of
London, he laid under interdict.[7]   The sentence was disregarded ; on June 2 Louis entered London ;[8] the citizens
welcomed him joyously, and the canons of S. Paul's received
him with a procession in their cathedral church.[9]   Next day
he received the homage of the barons and citizens, headed
respectively by Robert Fitz-Walter and the mayor, William
Hardel.[10]   He then swore on the Gospels "that he would
restore to all of them their good laws and their lost heritages,"
and wrote to the king of Scots and all the English magnates

---

   [1] *Hist. des Ducs*, pp. 170, 171 ; cf. R. Coggeshall, p. 181, and *Ann. Dunst.*
a. 1216.   [2] Thorne, *l.c.* cols. 1864, 1870.
   [3] *Hist des Ducs*, p. 171.
   [4] *Chron. Merton.* in Petit-Dutaillis, *Louis VIII.* p. 514.
   [5] W. Coventry, vol. ii. p. 230 ; R. Wendover, vol. iii. p. 370.
   [6] *Ann. Winton.* a. 1216.
   [7] W. Coventry, vol. ii. p. 230.   Cf. R. Wendover, vol. iii. pp. 369, 370.
   [8] *Hist. des Ducs*, p. 171 ; W. Coventry, *l.c.* ; *Liber de Antiq. Legibu-*,
Appendix, p. 202.
   [9] *Hist. des Ducs*, *l.c. Liber de Antiq. Legibus*, *l.c.*
   [10] *Chron. Merton.* in Petit-Dutaillis, *Louis VIII.* p. 514.   Cf. *Hist. des Ducs*,
pp. 171, 172 ; R. Coggeshall, pp. 181, 182, and R. Wendover, vol. iii. pp.
368, 369.

who had not yet joined him "bidding them either come and do him homage, or quit the realm of England without delay."[1]

On June 6 Louis started from London[2] to seek out his rival at Winchester,[3] but he was already too late ; John had quitted Winchester the day before,[4] leaving it, with its two castles, under the command of Savaric de Mauléon.[5] Louis's first day's march from London brought him to Reigate, which he entered without opposition, the earl of Warren having withdrawn his garrison from the castle. The royal castle of Guildford surrendered on the 8th, Farnham, which belonged to the see of Canterbury, on the 10th.[6] On the 14th Louis reached Winchester.[7] Savaric de Mauléon was, it seems, under orders to rejoin the king when he saw the enemy approaching the city and had completed his preparations for its defence. With the idea, doubtless, of checking the entrance of the foe, he, or some of his followers, set fire to the suburb before he left it. Unluckily the flames spread into the city and laid half of it in ashes. Defence became impossible, and the French marched in to take undisputed possession.[8] John and Savaric had, however, left a strong garrison in the "chief castle"[9] at the west end of the city; the bishop's stronghold of Wolvesey too, at the eastern end, was well provided with defenders, among whom was one of the king's sons, a young squire named Oliver.[10] For ten days Louis plied his engines against the "chief castle"; then on June 24 Savaric returned with a licence from the king to negotiate for its surrender and that of Wolvesey. The garrisons were suffered to withdraw,

---

[1] R. Wendover, vol. iii. p. 369.
[2] *Hist. des Ducs*, pp. 171, 172.
[3] R. Coggeshall, p. 182.
[4] *Itin.* a. 18.   This disposes of R. Coggeshall's story (*l.c.*) that John "cognito ejus adventu, draconem suum deposuit et aufugit."
[5] *Ann. Winton.* a. 1216.
[6] *Ann. Waverl.* a. 1216.
[7] *Ib.* a. 1216.   The *Ann. Winton.* a. 1216 give a wrong date.
[8] Cf. *Ann. Winton.* a. 1216, and *Hist. des Ducs*, p. 173.   Whichever version be the correct one, both alike show that Ralf of Coggeshall (*l.c.*) is wrong in attributing the fire to John himself.
[9] "Li grans castiaus le roi," "le maistre castiel," *Hist. des Ducs*, p. 173.
[10] *L.c.*

1216   and Louis gave the city into the custody of the count of
Nevers.[1]

In the ten days of the siege Louis had gained something
besides Winchester.   Before the castles surrendered "there
came thither to his will" four of "the greatest and most
powerful men in England of those who stood by the king"
—the earls of Warren, Arundel, Albemarle and Salisbury.[2]
Albemarle was a turncoat whose adhesion was too uncertain
to be of much value to either party;[3] but the other three
had hitherto been steadfast in their loyalty, and Salisbury,
moreover, was half-brother to the king.[4]   Still the invader
did not seem much nearer to the attainment of the crown
which he coveted.   From Winchester he went to Porchester,[5]
and thence to Odiham ; both places surrendered to him, but
the latter cost him a week's siege, though its garrison consisted only of three knights and ten men-at-arms, who of
July 9   course marched out with the honours of war, "amid the
great admiration of the French."[6]   The conflicting claims
and mutual jealousies of his French and English followers
were already a source of trouble.   The office of marshal of
the host, held by Adam de Beaumont, who was marshal to
Louis in France, was claimed as an hereditary right by
Earl William of Pembroke's eldest son ; Louis transferred it
to him "as one who durst not do otherwise, for if he gave it
him not, he deemed he should lose the hearts of the English."
Young William the Marshal further claimed the castle of
Marlborough, which had been voluntarily surrendered to
Louis by Hugh de Neville.   Louis, however, bestowed it

---

[1] Cf. *Hist. des Ducs*, p. 174 ; *Rot Pat.* p. 188 b, and *Ann. Waverl.* a. 1216.

[2] *Hist. des Ducs, l.c.*   Cf. R. Coggeshall, p. 182, and W. Coventry, vol. ii.
p. 231.

[3] "Qui tamen cito rediit," W. Coventry, vol. ii. p. 231.

[4] William of Armorica, *Gesta Phil. Aug.* c. 222, says that Salisbury changed
sides because "ei certo innotuit relatore" that during his own captivity in France
his royal brother had made an attempt on the honour of his wife (the well-known
Countess Ela).   As, however, we shall see that Salisbury "went back" almost
as promptly as Albemarle, and the story seems quite unknown to the English
chroniclers, its truth may be doubted, though the mere fact that such a story
could be told of John with reference to his own sister-in-law illustrates the character for reckless wickedness which he had earned for himself.

[5] *Hist. des Ducs*, p. 174.

[6] R. Wendover, vol. iii. p. 371.   Odiham surrendered July 9, *Ann. Waverl.*
a. 1216.

on his own cousin, Robert of Dreux ; whereat the young   1216
Marshal "was very angry." The French followers and
continental allies of Louis were already weary of an expedition which they doubtless saw would bring them little honour
and less gain. The count of Holland had taken the cross
and hurried home to prepare for his crusade. Soon afterwards a number of the men of Artois departed to London
and thence took ship for their own land ; and before they
could reach it they had to beat off "the English in their
boats" who attacked them at the mouth of the Thames.
Louis himself, after an unsuccessful attempt to make terms
with the legate, returned to London,[1] seemingly about the
middle of July.

While Louis was in Hampshire, the barons whom he
had left in London, with some of his French troops, overran
the eastern counties ; they sacked some of the towns,
ravaged the country, exacted "tenseries" everywhere, and
returned "laden with countless booty and spoils."[2] Another
party, under Gilbert de Gant and Robert de Ropesley, had
been charged by Louis to check the excursions whereby the
baronial castles in the neighbourhood of Nottingham and
Newark were being reduced to ashes, and the baronial lands
around them to subjection, by the garrisons of those two
royal fortresses. Gilbert and Robert took the city of Lincoln
and laid a tax on the whole of Lindsey ; but Lincoln castle
was too strong for them, so they went on to invade Holland,
which they ravaged and likewise placed under tribute. A
third body of troops under Robert de Ros, Peter de Brus
and Richard de Percy was meanwhile conquering Yorkshire
for Louis ;[3] and Alexander of Scotland had again set out
"with all his host, except the Scots from whom he took
money," to renew the siege of Carlisle.[4] This, like all other
sieges of that famous fortress, proved a long and weari-
some business ; Alexander, however, relieved its tediousness
by expeditions into the counties of Northumberland and

---

[1] *Hist. des Ducs*, pp. 175-7.
[2] Cf. R. Wendover, vol. iii. pp. 371, 378-81, *Hist. des Ducs*, p. 172, and
M. Paris, *Hist. Angl.* vol. ii. p. 182.
[3] R. Wendover, vol. iii. p. 379.
[4] *Chron. Mailros*, a. 1216.

T

1216   Durham.   He had no purpose now of conquering them for
himself; his aim was simply to join hands with the other
invader.   The Scot king was the natural ally of the English
king's adversary.

Thus by the end of July the power of Louis extended
from the Channel to the Scottish border, but not without
some important breaks.   The castles of the bishopric of
Durham were still held for John by Hugh de Balliol and
Philip de Ulecotes.[1]   The stranger's hold upon the south
coast was precarious in the extreme so long as Dover, the
"key of England," defied him under Hubert de Burgh; and
Windsor at once threatened his hold upon London, and
barred his way to the Midlands and the West.   These were
the districts in which John counted upon making good his
defence.   Throughout June, while Louis was in Hampshire,
John was perambulating Wiltshire and Dorset, personally
seeing to the fortification and replenishing of the fortresses
in those two shires, planning schemes and giving orders for
the security of the royal castles in all parts of his realm,
and issuing instructions to their custodians how to act in
every possible contingency.[2]   Diplomacy went hand in
hand with military precautions.   Overtures were made to
Reginald de Braose, the deadliest of John's personal foes,
and one of those who had most influence on the western
border, for his return to allegiance at the price of the restoration of his heritage.[3]   Safe-conducts were offered to "all
who might choose to return to the king's service" through
the intervention of certain appointed persons.[4]   A temporary
submission to the invader's demand of "tenserie" was
formally sanctioned in special cases where it was clear that
resistance would be ineffectual at the moment.[5]   Help
was again sought from over sea; on June 2 the town of
Bayonne was desired to send its galleys "for the annoyance
and confusion of our enemies."[6]   John's own movements
indicate that he, very naturally, expected Louis to follow up

[1] R. Wendover, vol. iii. p. 379.
[2] *Rot. Pat.* pp. 184 b, 185 b, 186, 186 b, 187 b, 188, 193-5.
[3] *Ib.* p. 184.   Cf. *ib.* p. 192.
[4] *Ib.* pp. 185, 187, 187 b, 188 b, 189, 189 b, etc.
[5] *Ib.* pp. 187, 188.   [6] *Ib.* p. 185 b.

his conquest of Hampshire by an attack on the western shires. It was obviously with this expectation, and with the double purpose of putting the border in a state of defence and securing for himself a refuge at need, that soon after the middle of July he began to advance northward from Sherborne to Bristol, Berkeley, Gloucester, Tewkesbury and Hereford, reaching Leominster on the last day of the month.[1] He was at the same time negotiating with some of the Welsh chieftains for their aid and support ;[2] and on August 2 he was actually on Welsh soil, at Radnor. That night, however, he was again in England, at Kingsmead ; thence he moved on to Clun, Shrewsbury and Whitchurch. On the 11th he turned southward again ; he reached Bridge-north on the 14th, and stayed there till the 16th, when he went back to Worcester for one night ; next day he was at Gloucester.[3] A letter written on the 19th from Berkeley shows that these movements were dictated by the belief that Louis was preparing an attack upon Worcester and Here-ford.[4] This fact illustrates one of the greatest difficulties of medieval warfare, the difficulty of obtaining correct informa-tion as to the whereabouts and movements of the adversary. Louis, at the moment when John was thus anxiously look-ing out for him in the west, had been for nearly four weeks absorbed in the siege of Dover.

According to Matthew Paris, Philip Augustus had taunted his son with not understanding his business as a commander-in-chief, because he was attempting to conquer England without first securing its key.[5] At any rate Louis, soon after his return to London, perceived that his hold on the country would never be assured till Dover and Windsor were both in his hands. On July 25 he set out for

---

[1] *Itin.* a. 18.

[2] *Rot. Pat.* p. 191 b ; *Brut y Tywysogion*, p. 293.

[3] *Itin.* a. 18.

[4] *Rot. Pat.* p. 194. Worcester had been surrendered to the younger William Marshal, for Louis, early in July, but was retaken on the 17th by the earl of Chester and Falkes de Bréauté ; *Ann. Wigorn.* a. 1215. The castle, according to *Ann. Dunst.* a. 1215, was taken by " the old Marshal " at some unspecified date. (In both the Worcester and the Dunstable Annals the history of 1216 is placed under the year 1215.)

[5] M. Paris, *Chron. Maj.* vol. ii. p. 664.

1216   Dover,[1] and a day or two later the counts of Dreux and
Nevers, with some English barons, laid siege to Windsor.[2]   Of
this latter party the Flemish soldier-chronicler of the war says,
" Long were they there, and little did they gain." [3]   They
in fact sat before the place for nearly two months in vain.[4]
The siege of Dover proved longer still, and for many weeks
bade fair to be equally unprofitable.   Many of Louis's
followers went back over sea to their homes, " so that the
host dwindled marvellously." [5]   On August 8, however, the
town—not the castle—of Carlisle surrendered to Alexander;[6]
and he at once began to move southward for the purpose
of joining Louis.   Still a whole month elapsed before the
junction was effected.   On his way the Scot king stopped
to besiege Barnard castle, held by Hugh de Balliol for John.
The siege appears to have been unsuccessful, and it cost the
life of one of the foremost leaders of the baronial party in
the north, Eustace de Vesci.[7]   Some of the other northerners
were now helping Gilbert de Gant at the siege of Lincoln
castle.   This time its constable, Dame Nicola de Haye,[8]
bought off her assailants, who thereupon united their forces
to those of Alexander.[9]   The combined host seems to have
reached Kent about the second week in September.[10]   Louis
went to meet Alexander at Canterbury, brought him back
to Dover,[11] and there received his homage for the lands
which he held of the English crown.[12]

---

[1] *Liber de Antiq. Legibus*, appendix, p. 202 ; *Ann. Waverl.* a. 1216.   R.
Wendover, vol. iii. p. 380, gives a wrong date.
[2] *Hist. des Ducs*, p. 177.   Cf. R. Coggeshall, p. 182 ; R. Wendover, vol.
iii. p. 381, and W. Coventry, vol. ii. p. 230.
[3] *Hist. des Ducs*, *l.c.*   [4] R. Coggeshall, *l.c.*
[5] *Hist. des Ducs*, *l.c.*   [6] *Chron. Mailros*, a. 1216.
[7] *Ib.* ; R. Wendover, vol. iii. pp. 382, 383.
[8] Widow of John's old friend Gerard de Camville ; see above, p. 31.
[9] W. Coventry, vol. ii. p. 230.
[10] *Hist. des Ducs*, p. 179, relates John's advance to Reading, which took
place on September 6 (*Itin.* a. 18), and then goes on " *Puis* vint li rois d'Escoce,"
etc.   [11] *Ib.*
[12] " Fecit [Alexander] ei [*i.e.* Ludovico] homagium de jure suo, quod de
rege Anglorum tenere debuit," R. Wendover, vol. iii. p. 382.   " Lendemain
fist li rois son houmage à Looys de la tierre de Loonnois," *Hist. des Ducs*, p.
179.   (M. Francisque-Michel and M. Petit-Dutaillis render the last word
" Lennox " ; does it not rather represent " Lothian " ?)   The Chronicle of
Melrose, a. 1216, says cautiously, " Alexander rex . . . humagium fecit dicto
Laodowico, ut dicitur."

Meanwhile John had at last learned the truth as to his   1216
adversary's movements, and was acting on the information.
Gathering a numerous host from the garrisons of the western
castles, which he now saw to be out of danger, and from his
old allies the Welsh,[1] he marched up on September 2 from
Cirencester to Burford, spent the three following days at
Oxford, then struck across the Thames to Wallingford, and
on the 6th appeared at Reading.   From the 8th to the 13th
he fixed his quarters at Sonning.[2]   His advance looked as
if intended for the relief of Windsor ; he did in fact approach
so near that castle that its besiegers " thought they were
going to have a battle."   His Welshmen " came by night to
shoot into the host, and gave them a great fright.   They
were a long time armed to await the battle, but they did not
get it, for the king retired, I know not by what counsel,"
says the Flemish chronicler.[3]   John had in truth never
intended to attack them ; his real " counsel " is given us by
the English writers—his aim was the eastern counties, where
he purposed to intercept the Scot king on his homeward
journey, and to punish the local landholders and owners of
castles for their submission to the invader.[4]   The relief of
Windsor he probably hoped to effect by other means, if
there is any truth in the assertion of some English chroniclers that the count of Nevers was secretly in his pay.[5]   It
may have been for the purpose of communicating with
Nevers, as well as for that of frightening Nevers's companions
and reconnoitring the district, that the king lingered in
Berkshire.   On September 15 he suddenly struck northward from Walton-on-Thames to Aylesbury and Bedford ;
next day he went on to Cambridge.[6]   The immediate consequence was the relief of Windsor ; its besiegers were no
sooner assured of his departure from their neighbourhood
than they struck their tents, set fire to their military engines,
and hurried in pursuit of him.   They hoped to overtake

[1] Cf. R. Wendover, vol. iii. p. 381, and *Hist. des Ducs*, pp. 178, 179.
[2] *Itin.* a. 18.
[3] *Hist. des Ducs*, p. 179.
[4] Cf. W. Coventry, vol. ii. p. 231, and R. Coggeshall, p. 182.
[5] Cf. R. Wendover, vol. iii. p. 382 ; M. Paris, *Hist. Angl.* vol. ii. p. 185 ;
and *Ann. Dunst.* a. 1215.   [6] *Itin.* a. 18.

1216 him at Cambridge ; but, warned by his scouts, he escaped in time, on the night of September 17. A dexterous move-ment southward to Clare and Hedingham threw his pursuers off the track, and another rapid march brought him to Stamford before they reached Cambridge.[1] They avenged their disappointment by harrying Cambridgeshire—this was the second, if not the third, harrying which that unhappy county had suffered within four months—carried their spoils back to London, and then proceeded to join Louis at the siege of Dover.[2]

The count of Nevers was immediately sent off again to escort the Scot king safely homeward as far as Cambridge.[3] Thence Alexander made his way towards Lincoln, which Gilbert de Gant, with a few followers, had continued to occupy after the other barons had abandoned the siege of the castle.[4] John meanwhile had gone from Stamford to Rockingham ; thence, on September 21,[5] he set out to begin the work for which he had come from the west. The story of that day and the next, as told by Matthew Paris—how the king went first to Oundle and thence to the other manors of the abbey of Peterborough, burning the houses and barns ; how he passed on to Crowland and bade Savaric de Mauléon fire the abbey church and the village while he himself stood at a distance to watch the blaze ; how Savaric yielded to the monks' prayer for mercy, and accepted from them, as the price of their escape, a sum of money which he brought back to John, and how the furious king, after over-whelming his too placable lieutenant with abuse, helped with his own hands to fire the harvest-fields, running up and down amid the smoke and the flames till the whole territory of S. Guthlac was a blackened desert [6]—whether its details be literally exact or not, pictures vividly the mood of the

---

[1] Cf. R. Wendover, vol. iii. p. 382 ; R. Coggeshall, p. 183 ; W. Coventry, vol. ii. p. 231 ; *Itin.* a. 18 ; and *Rot. Pat.* p. 197 b.

[2] R. Wendover, vol. iii. p. 382.

[3] *Hist. des Ducs*, p. 179. [4] R. Wendover, *l.c.*

[5] *Itin.* a. 18.

[6] M. Paris, *Hist. Angl.* vol. ii. pp. 189-190. Cf. *Chron. Maj.* vol. ii. p. 667. Matthew gives no precise date ; but he implies that it was before Michaelmas ; and the *Itinerary* shows that the only possible date is September 21-22, on the way from Rockingham to Lincoln.

tyrant.   It is little wonder that when the tidings of his   1216
advance reached Lincoln, Gilbert and his men "fled before   Sept. 22
his face, dreading his presence like lightning."[1]   They probably fled into the Isle of Axholme, for from Lincoln John
went by way of Barton[2] and Scotter to Stowe, where he
stayed three days, and whence he appears to have sent his   Sept.
mercenaries across the Trent to ravage the Isle with fire   26-28
and sword.   He returned to Lincoln on the 28th, to find
that Alexander had spent two or three days there in his
absence,[3] and had slipped past him into Yorkshire.   John,
however, was less eager for the capture of "the little sandy
fox" than for vengeance upon the English rebels.   From
Lincoln northward to Grimsby, and thence south again to
Spalding, the Lincolnshire fields—now, at the beginning of
October, all white to harvest[4]—were given to the flames,
and the houses and farm-buildings sacked and destroyed by
the terrible host with the king at its head.[5]   On October 9
he appeared before Lynn;[6] here the townsfolk, like most of
their class throughout England, were on his side, and they
gave him not only a joyous welcome, but a substantial contribution in money.[7]   He committed the custody of the
town and the duty of fortifying it to Savaric de Mauléon,[8]
whom on September 30 he had sent back to Crowland to
"seek out and capture the knights and men-at-arms, enemies
of the king, who were hiding in secret places" among the
fens around the monastery.   Savaric had "failed to find
those whom he sought"; but he had dragged some fugitives
out of sanctuary in the abbey, and brought back a valuable
spoil of flocks and herds to his master at Lynn.[9]

Louis had now been besieging Dover for more than two
months, and had made no progress at all.   The strength of

---

[1] R. Wendover, vol. iii. p. 382 ; for date see *Itin.* a. 18.
[2] *Rot. Claus.* vol. i. p. 289 ; probably one of several small places so called,
on the eastern side of the Trent.
[3] Cf. W. Coventry, vol. ii. p. 231, and *Itin.* a. 18.
[4] R. Wendover, vol. iii. p. 381.
[5] Cf. *ib.*, W. Coventry, vol. ii. p. 231, and *Itin.* a. 18.
[6] *Itin.* a. 18.
[7] R. Wendover, vol. iii. p. 384.
[8] R. Coggeshall, p. 183.
[9] W. Coventry, vol. ii. p. 232.

1216 the castle, the skill and valour of Hubert de Burgh and the hundred and forty knights who, with the usual complement of men-at-arms, constituted its garrison, were more than a match for all his forces. He swore that he would not quit the place till he had hanged every man within its walls;[1] but even the fall of one of its towers seemed to have brought him no nearer to effecting an entrance.[2] He could only turn the siege into a blockade, and wait till starvation should accomplish the work in which battery and assault had failed. In the country at large he was distinctly losing ground. Throughout the summer he had been set at nought in Sussex by a young Flemish adventurer called William of Casinghem, who, "scorning to do him homage, gathered together a thousand bowmen, lodged in the wilderness and woods with which that country abounded, and gave the French great trouble all through the time of war, slaying many thousands of them."[3] On September 2 John wrote a letter of encouragement to an association extending through Sussex, Kent, Surrey and Hampshire, composed of persons whom he describes as "sworn and confederate together for fealty and service to ourself," although they had been compelled against their will to swear allegiance to his rival. The "barons"—that is, the citizens—of Hastings, Sandwich, Dover, Hythe, Romney, Winchelsea, Rye, Pevensey, Shoreham and Portsmouth, who had also, under compulsion, taken the oath to Louis, had likewise assured John of their devotion to himself, and were in return assured of his favour; while the men of Seaford had resisted all the pressure put upon them by their lord, Gilbert de Laigle, to forsake their allegiance, and were on September 3 warmly thanked by John for their loyalty.[4] Soon after the beginning of the siege of Dover Louis was joined from over sea by the count of Perche, and in September or October by Peter of Britanny;

---

[1] R. Wendover, vol. iii. p. 380.

[2] *Hist. des Ducs*, p. 179.

[3] R. Wendover, vol. iii. p. 370. The leader's name comes from *Hist. des Ducs*, p. 181; M. Paris, *Chron. Maj.* vol. ii. p. 655, has corrupted it into "Collingham." See also *Ann. Dunst.* a. 1215. On William de Casinghem's relations with John see *Rot. Pat.* pp. 185, 186. He figures frequently in the Rolls of the next reign.

[4] *Rot. Pat.* p. 196.

the arrival of this last, however, brought no real gain, for   1216
as soon as Peter reached England, his brother, Robert of
Dreux, returned to France. Louis's English partizans, too,
were falling away. Earl William of Albemarle offered his
repentance and his services to John, who of course " forgave
him most kindly." [1] Of yet greater importance was the
return to allegiance of William of Salisbury ; it was he who,
in conjunction with Falkes de Bréauté, captured or put to
flight a body of Louis's adherents who were besieging Exeter.[2]
At last, however, a gleam of light fell across the gloomy
prospects of the French party. Towards the middle of
October Hubert de Burgh and his lieutenant, Gerard de
Sotinghem, felt that they could not hold out much longer,
and asked for a truce, that they might send to John either
for succour, or for leave to surrender the castle. The truce
was granted, and on the 14th the siege of Dover was
suspended.[3]

The crisis had come ; it had, however, really come not
on the cliffs of Kent, but on the shores of the Wash.
Sumptuously entertained by the burghers of Lynn, John,
who—unlike most of his race—was a notorious glutton,
feasted till his excesses brought on a violent attack of
dysentery [4] which he himself seems to have recognized as
the beginning of the end. One of the latest entries on the
Patent Rolls of his reign is probably significant of the
remorse awakened in him, for one at least of his many
crimes, by the terror of approaching death ; on October 10
he granted to Margaret, wife of Walter de Lacy, some land
in the royal forest of Acornbury, that she might build thereon
a religious house for the souls of her father, mother and
brother [5]—William, Maud and the younger William de
Braose. He could not rest ; ill as he was, he moved next   Oct. 11
day from Lynn to Wisbeach ; and early on the following
morning he set out again. "Like a swiftly advancing   Oct. 12

---

[1] *Hist. des Ducs*, p. 179.
[2] *Ann. Dunst.* a. 1215.
[3] R. Coggeshall, p. 182. Cf. *Hist. des Ducs*, p. 180, and W. Coventry,
vol. ii. p. 232.
[4] R. Coggeshall, p. 183. Cf. W. Coventry, vol. ii. p. 231.
[5] *Rot. Pat.* p. 199.

1216 storm," before which all men fled, he swept northward to
the mouth of the Welland, and thence in his impatience set
out to cross the Wash without waiting either for the ebb of
the tide or for any one who knew the way to guide him
across the treacherous soil, covered as it was with brackish
water. Suddenly the whole host, while struggling with the
waves, felt the ground opening beneath its feet. The king
himself and a part of his troops with difficulty reached the
further shore ; the rest of his followers and the whole of his
baggage train, with all his treasure and his lately gathered
spoils, men, horses, arms, tents, provisions, "everything in
the world that he held most dear, short of his own life,"
went down into the quicksand.[1] When at night he reached
Swineshead abbey, rage and grief threw him into a fever,
which he aggravated by supping greedily on peaches and
new cider.[2] With great difficulty he made his way on the
14th to Sleaford.[3] There he was found, probably on the
15th, by the messengers whom Hubert de Burgh had sent
from Dover to seek him. Their tidings brought on a fresh
access of fever, which bleeding failed to relieve.[4] Nothing
Oct. 15-16 could check his restlessness ; that night or next morning
he set out for Newark, and in spite of grievous bodily
suffering, he set out on horseback. He had, however, ridden
only three or four miles, "panting and groaning," when
increasing sickness compelled him to dismount, and he bade
his followers make him a litter in which he might travel more
easily. There was no workman to make it, and nothing to
make it of ; all that his men could do was to cut down with
their swords and knives the willows by the roadside, weave
them together as best they might, and throw a horse-cloth

[1] Cf. R. Wendover, vol. iii. p. 384 ; M. Paris, *Hist. Angl.* vol. ii. p. 190 ;
and R. Coggeshall, pp. 183, 184.
[2] R. Wendover, vol. iii. p. 385 ; M. Paris, *Hist. Angl.* vol. ii. p. 191.
The later legends about the cause of John's death are not worth notice.
[3] R. Wendover, *l.c.*, says John left Swineshead "summo diluculo." The
Itinerary shows him there on October 12 and 13, and at Sleaford on the
14th and 15th.
[4] R. Coggeshall, p. 183. Louis had raised the siege of Dover only on the
14th, but the truce must have been arranged and the messengers despatched
at least a day or two earlier, or the latter could not possibly have overtaken
John at Sleaford. They must in any case have travelled with marvellous
rapidity.

over them.   This litter, without cushions or even straw to   1216
relieve its hardness, had for want of carriage-horses to be
either slung between some of the high-mettled destriers
of the knights, or carried on the shoulders of the men.
Its shaking and jolting soon proved intolerable : " This
accursed litter has broken all my bones, and well-nigh
killed me," cried the king in an agony of pain and rage.
Matthew Paris quotes a French rime concerning the sons
of Henry II. which thus foretold their fate : " Henry, the
fairest, shall die at Martel ; Richard, the Poitevin, shall die
in the Limousin ; John shall die, a landless king, in a litter."
The prediction was all but fulfilled ; John, however, gathered
up strength and spirit enough to avoid a literal fulfilment
of its closing words, and to ride " on an ambling nag " into
Newark.[1]

   For three days, in the bishop of Lincoln's castle whose Oct. 16-18
ruins still look down upon the Trent, the king lay dying.
The abbot of Croxton, who was skilled in medicine, attended
him as his physician,[2] and also ministered to his soul, for he
persuaded him to confess his sins and receive the Holy
Communion.[3]   Then the one natural affection traceable in
John's character broke out in anxiety for his two little sons,
especially for the elder of them, to whom the crown must
devolve.   He solemnly declared Henry his heir, made those
around him take an oath of fealty to the boy, and sent letters
to the sheriffs and the constables of the royal castles, bidding
them look to him as their lord.[4]   He had already, on October
15, before leaving Sleaford, dictated a letter entreating for

   [1] M. Paris, *Hist. Angl.* vol. ii. pp. 191, 192.   He relates all this as having
occurred on the road from Swineshead to Sleaford, where he makes John die ; a
characteristic piece of confusion, illustrative of Matthew's careless way of reading
the author on whose work his own is based.   The itinerary given by Roger of
Wendover, vol. iii. p. 385, is perfectly accurate and perfectly clear.
   [2] M. Paris, *Chron. Maj.* vol. ii. p. 668.
   [3] R. Wendover, vol. iii. p. 385.   The long account inserted by Matthew
Paris in his *Hist. Angl.* (vol. ii. p. 193)—*not*, it is to be observed, in his *Chron.
Maj.*—of John's forgiveness of the barons and good advice to his heir is evidently
intended for the edification of Henry III. and of posterity, and if it has any
foundation at all, it is inserted in a wrong place ; for it is put after John's last
Communion, whereas the abbot obviously must have insisted upon John's declaring
himself to be in charity with all men (the barons, by implication at least, included)
before he gave him the Sacrament.
   [4] R. Wendover, *l.c.*

1216   Henry the special protection of the Pope.[1] He now appointed Peter de Mauley guardian of his younger son Richard, whom he had apparently left under Peter's charge in Corfe castle. There was but one man in England to whom he could confidently entrust the guardianship of the heir to the throne. "Before he died, he sent word to William the Marshal, the earl of Pembroke, that he placed his eldest son, Henry, in God's keeping and his, and besought him for God's sake that he would take thought for Henry's interest." [2]

The abbot of Croxton then asked the king where he wished to be buried. "I commend my body and my soul to God and to S. Wulfstan" was John's reply.[3] His last act seems to have been the dictation of the fragmentary document which has come down to us as his will. "Being overtaken," he says, "by grievous sickness, and thus incapable of making a detailed disposition of all my goods, I commit the ordering and disposing of my will to the fidelity and discretion of my faithful men whose names are written below, without whose counsel, were they at hand, I would not, even if in health, ordain anything; and I ratify and confirm whatsoever they shall faithfully ordain and determine concerning my goods, for the purposes of making satisfaction to God and Holy Church for the wrongs I have done them, sending help to the realm of Jerusalem, furnishing support to my sons for the recovery and defence of their heritage, rewarding those who have served us faithfully, and distributing alms to the poor and to religious houses for the salvation of my soul. And I pray that whosoever shall give them counsel and assistance herein may receive God's grace and favour; and may he who shall violate the settlement made by them incur the curse and wrath of God Almighty and the Blessed Mary and all the saints. First, then, I desire that my body be buried in the church of the Blessed Mary and S. Wulfstan of Worcester. Now I appoint as ordainers and disposers of my will the

[1] Baronius, *Annales* (ed. Mansi), vol. xx. p. 397.
[2] *Hist. des Ducs*, p. 180. Cf. *Hist. de G. le Mar.* vv. 15167-88.
[3] R. Wendover, vol. iii. p. 385.

following persons :—the lord Gualo, by God's grace cardinal   1216
priest of the title of S. Martin, legate of the Apostolic See ;
Peter, lord bishop of Winchester ; Richard, lord bishop of
Chichester ; Silvester, lord bishop of Worcester ; Brother
Aimeric of Ste. Maure ; William the Marshal, earl of
Pembroke ; Ranulf, earl of Chester ; William, earl of
Ferrars ; William Brewer ; Walter de Lacy ; John of Mon-
mouth ; Savaric de Mauléon ; Falkes de Bréauté." [1]   Here,
without date, signature or seal, the so-called will breaks off
abruptly ; evidently the testator had not time to complete
it. At midnight a whirlwind swept over Newark with such Oct. 18-19
violence that the townsfolk thought their houses would fall,
and in that hour of elemental disturbance and human
terror the king passed away.[2] A monk named John of
Savigny, entering the town at daybreak, met the servants Oct. 19
of the royal household hurrying out laden with everything
of their master's that they could carry. The corpse—for
which they had not left even a decent covering [3]—had
meanwhile been hastily embalmed by the abbot of Croxton ;
John having, it is said, made a grant of his heart, with ten
pounds' worth of land, to Croxton abbey.[4] The abbot, too,
fled as soon as his work was done and his strange relic
secured ; it was John of Savigny who, at the request of the
constable of Newark, kept the last watch beside the body
and offered his mass that morning for the soul of the dead
king.[5] The body was then dressed in such semblance of
royal attire as could be procured, and the remnant of John's
soldiers—nearly all foreign mercenaries—formed themselves
into a guard for its protection on the journey from Newark
to Worcester. The grim funeral train, every man in full
armour, passed unhindered across England, and John was
buried by Bishop Silvester in Worcester cathedral according
to his desire.[6]

---

[1] *Foedera*, vol. i. pt. i. p. 144.

[2] R. Coggeshall, p. 184. Cf. W. Coventry, vol. ii. p. 231, and R. Wendover, vol. iii. p. 385.

[3] R. Coggeshall, *l.c.*

[4] Cf. W. Coventry, vol. ii. p. 232 ; M. Paris, *Chron. Maj.* vol. ii. p. 668 ;
and *Hist. Angl.* vol. ii. p. 194.

[5] R. Coggeshall, *l.c.*

[6] R. Wendover, vol. iii. pp. 385, 386.

Within this tomb lies buried a monarch's outward form,
Whose inner man's departure hath stilled war's raging storm.

Thus may be roughly rendered the opening lines of an epitaph on King John preserved by Roger of Wendover.[1] The poet's words are true ; John's death virtually ended the war. From his burial the Marshal, the Legate, and the bishops passed to the crowning of his heir and the publication, in the boy-king's name, of the Great Charter in a revised form to which Gualo had no hesitation in giving the papal sanction, and which, thus safeguarded, left the revolutionary party no excuse for continuing the struggle. Thenceforth it was idle for Louis and his adherents to pretend that they were fighting for England's deliverance from bondage ; all men could see that they were fighting for her enslavement to a foreign conqueror. The majority of the barons had already become conscious of the blunder, or worse than blunder, which they had committed in calling the stranger to their aid, and were ready now to join in a national movement for his expulsion. His enterprise was doomed to fail when the kingdom ceased to be divided against itself ; and the one insuperable obstacle to the healing of its divisions was removed in the person of John. It was John whose very existence had made peace impossible. "Forasmuch as when he came to die he possessed none of his land in peace," says Matthew Paris, "he is called Lackland."[2] John had indeed earned for himself in a new sense the name which his father had given him at his birth ; and he had earned it not by blunders in statecraft or errors in strategy, not by weakness or cowardice or sloth, but by the almost superhuman wickedness of a life which, twenty years before its end, a historian of deeper insight than Matthew had characterized in one memorable phrase—" Nature's enemy, John."

1 " Hoc in sarcophago sepelitur regis imago,
    Qui moriens multum sedavit in orbe tumultum."
                                    R. Wendover, vol. iii. p. 386.
    2 M. Paris, *Hist. Angl.* vol. ii. p. 191.

NOTE I

JOHN AND THE DE BRAOSES

The fullest account of the quarrel of King John and William de Braose is contained in a document printed in *Foedera*, vol. i. pt. i. pp. 107, 108. This is a letter or manifesto addressed by John, after the fall of De Braose, "to all who may read it," witnessed by the justiciar (Geoffrey Fitz-Peter), the earls of Salisbury, Winchester, Clare, Hertford, and Ferrars, Robert Fitz-Walter, William Brewer, Hugh de Neville, William d'Aubigny, Adam de Port, Hugh de Gournay, William de Mowbray "and others," and evidently intended as a public defence of the king's conduct towards William. Coming from John, and under such circumstances, its truthfulness is necessarily open to suspicion ; but it is hardly conceivable that so many witnesses of such rank and character as those enumerated should have set their hands to it if it contained any gross misrepresentations of matters which must have been well known to most of them ; one of these witnesses, indeed, the earl of Ferrars, is stated in the letter itself to have been De Braose's own nephew, and another, Adam de Port, his brother-in-law. The only point on which the letter seems to be at variance with any other contemporary authority is the amount of the debt owed by De Braose to the king at the end of 1207 or beginning of 1208. John says (*l.c.* p. 107), that William then owed him the whole of the 5000 marks due for the honour of Limerick, and had only paid him one sum of 100 marks for the ferm of the city "which he had held for five years" (strictly speaking, it was, at the utmost, four years and a half). The Pipe Rolls of 1206, 1207, 1208, 1209, and 1210 (8-12 John), however, all state the sum still owed by William for the honour of Limerick as £2865 : 6 : 8 (= 4298 marks), thus implying that £468, or 702 marks, had been paid before Michaelmas 1206. In the Roll of that year the city of Limerick is not mentioned ; but in each of the later Rolls William is said to owe £80 for its tallage, and 100 marks for its ferm for one year (Sweetman, *Calendar*, vol. i. pp. 46, 55, 58, 68). This does not necessarily imply that the ferm for the other years had not been paid ; for the original grant of the custody of the city of Limerick to De Braose in July 1203 and the writ ordering its restoration to him in August 1205 both specify that he is to pay its ferm "to our exchequer *in Dublin*" (*Rot. Chart.* p. 107 b ; *Rot. Claus.* vol. i. p. 47). As there are no remaining records of the Dublin Exchequer of so early a date, we cannot certainly know what was or was not paid in there.

The strange thing is not that the English Exchequer should claim only one year's ferm for Limerick, but that it should have any claim at all in the matter.   The restoration of the city to De Braose in August 1205 was ordered to be conditional on his finding security, within forty days, for the payment of the arrears of the ferm.   That the restoration was actually made, and therefore that he gave the security, is plain; but there is nothing to show that he ever redeemed his pledge, or that he paid the ferm for the succeeding years.

The story of John's vengeance on the family of De Braose appears, in slightly varied forms, in almost every chronicle of the period.   Ralph of Coggeshall (p. 164), Roger of Wendover (vol. iii. p. 235) and the *Brut y Tywysogion* (a. 1209) say the victims were "slain in Windsor castle"; the Annals of Dunstable and of Oseney (a. 1210), that they "died in prison," without specifying where or how.   The Barnwell Annalist (W. Coventry, vol. ii. p. 202) and the Annals of Margan, Tewkesbury, Waverley, Winchester, and Worcester (a. 1210) say they were starved to death.   The *Hist. des Ducs de Normandie* (pp. 114-115) says they were imprisoned "el castiel del Corf," with no food save "une garbe d'avoine e i bacon cru," and describes with gruesome minuteness the attitudes in which, on the eleventh day, they were found dead.   Ralph of Coggeshall makes the victims William de Braose's wife and "sons" (*filii*); Roger of Wendover, his wife, eldest son, and that son's wife; the *Ann. Winton.*, wife and "younger" son; the *Ann. Tewkesb.*, wife and "children" (*liberi*); while the *Ann. Dunst.* say: " Cepit [rex] Willelmum de Lacy, et Willelmum de Brause juniorem, et sororem ejus, et Matildem matrem ejus; qui in carcere post modum perierunt."   All the other writers speak only of the wife and one son, whom the *Ann. Osen.* call "Willelmus primogenitus ejus," and the *Ann. Wigorn.* "haeres."   This latter version is undoubtedly the correct one as to the last point; of De Braose's three sons, the eldest, William, alone was in John's power; Giles, the second, was bishop of Hereford and safe beyond the sea, while the third, Reginald, had escaped capture, and lived to recover the greater part of the family heritage.   One of the daughters—the wife of Hugh Mortimer—had been taken prisoner with her mother and eldest brother (*Foedera*, vol. i. pt. i. p. 107); but she did not share their fate, for she was set free in 1214 (*Rot. Pat.* vol. i. p. 122); and Roger of Wendover is certainly wrong about the younger William's wife, who was still living in July 1220 (*Royal Letters*, ed. Shirley, vol. i. p. 136).   The elder William died, an exile in France, about a year after this tragedy (R. Wend. vol. iii. p. 237).

NOTE II

EUSTACE DE VESCI AND ROBERT FITZ-WALTER

Eustace de Vesci and Robert Fitz-Walter have long figured in history as typical examples of the way in which individual barons were goaded into hatred and vengeance against John by his invasions of their domestic peace, and also as foremost among the "patriots" to whom England is supposed to be indebted for her Great Charter. On both aspects of the lives of these two men— especially of the life of Fitz-Walter, whom Professor Tout has glorified as "the first champion of English liberty"—a few considerations may be offered here.

1. The earliest mention of John's unsuccessful attempt to entrap the wife of Eustace de Vesci is in an addition made by a chronicler at Furness Abbey, writing c. 1270-1298, to the Stanley chronicler's continuation of the history of William of Newburgh. This Furness writer (Howlett, *Chron. of Stephen*, etc., vol. ii. p. 521) merely states the bare fact, without any details, in the briefest and simplest way, and without any clue to the date. Walter of Hemingburgh, who was living in 1313, tells the story in an elaborate form which is certainly not impossible, perhaps not even very improbable, although it somewhat resembles a story in Procopius (see *Dic. Nat. Biogr.* "Vesci, Eustace de"). Walter gives it as an illustration of John's character, of which he inserts a picture—painted in the most frightful colours—between the coming of the Franciscans in 1212 and the rising of the barons in 1215; but he connects the incident directly with the latter event, representing Eustace as inducing those of his fellow-barons whom the king had injured in a similar way to join him in a common effort for vengeance, which widens into the struggle for the Charter (Hemingburgh, vol. i. pp. 247-9). The affair would thus seem to have occurred some years after Eustace's desertion from the king's host and flight from England in 1212; a desertion for which, therefore, it cannot serve as an excuse.

2. The legend of Robert Fitz-Walter's daughter which became famous in prose and verse in the sixteenth and seventeenth centuries is based upon a passage in the Chronicle of Dunmow, printed in *Monasticon*, vol. vi. pt. i. p. 147. This chronicle, written in a monastery of which the Fitz-Walters were patrons, begins with the year 1054, but the MS. (Cott. Cleopatra C. iii.) is of the end of the fifteenth century; it ends at the year 1501. The story is placed in 1216, and is briefly this: John demands Robert's

U

daughter, the fair maiden Matilda; her father refuses to give her up to him; the civil war breaks out, and the city of London joins the barons; afterwards they are worsted, whereupon the king destroys Robert's fortress in London—Castle Baynard—and causes Matilda to be poisoned at Robert's manor of Dunmow. Meanwhile Robert has fled to France. War continues on both sides of the Channel. Presently John goes to France, and has a conference with Philip Augustus; Robert Fitz-Walter displays his prowess in a single combat in presence of both the kings; John admires his valour, they are reconciled, and remain friends from that time forth.

On a tale so monstrous and so nonsensical as this, comment is needless. There is, however, a much earlier and more rational account of the quarrel between John and Fitz-Walter. According to the contemporary *Histoire des Ducs de Normandie*, Robert Fitz-Walter, "qui estoit uns des plus haus homes d'Engletierre et uns des plus poissans" (he was lord of Dunmow in Essex, of Baynard's Castle in London, and also, by his marriage with an heiress, of large estates in the north), had two daughters, of whom the elder was married to Geoffrey de Mandeville, eldest son of Geoffrey Fitz-Peter, chief justiciar of England. "Une fois" when the king was visiting Marlborough, a quarrel for lodgings arose between the servants of this young Geoffrey and those of William Brewer; they came to blows, and Brewer's chief "sergeant" was slain by the hand of Geoffrey himself. Geoffrey, fearing the wrath of the king, whom he knew to be jealous of his father's power and wealth, fled to his wife's father, who went to intercede for him with the king; John, however, "jura les dens Diu que non auroit (merchi), ains le feroit pendre, se il le pooit tenir." Robert in return swore " Par *Corpus Domini*, non ferés ! ains en verriés ii. m. hiaumes laciés en vostre tierre, que chil fust pendus qui ma fille a." At last John promised a "day" for agreement between himself and Geoffrey at Nottingham, intending to seize him at his coming; but Robert, "ki le roi connissoit à moult gaignart," came with his son-in-law, and with five hundred knights at his back. The king then proposed another "day," and the same thing happened a second time. Then John began to plot vengeance upon Robert; he sent secret orders to "ses bourgois de Londres, qui se faisoient apelier baron," to pull down Castle Baynard; and they, not daring to disobey him, did as they were bid. Robert, knowing very well that they had acted on an order from the king, fled over sea with his wife and children. On reaching the Continent "il fist à entendre par tout que li rois Jehans voloit sa fille aisnée, qui feme estoit Joffroi de Mandeville, avoir à force à amie, et por chou que il ne le vaut soufrir, l'avoit il chacié de sa tierre et tout le sien tolut." This

was the tale which he also told to King Philip of France, at whose
court he—after staying some time at Arras—presented himself just
as Philip was preparing to invade England. When the invasion
had been checked by John's submission to Pandulf and Pandulf's
prohibition to Philip, Robert went to "Pandoufle le clerc" and to
him told another tale: "li dist que il s'estoit partis d'Engletierre
por le roi qui escumeniiés estoit, car il ne voloit pas estre en la
compaignie des escumeniiés; et por chou li avoit li rois toute sa
terre tolue"; wherefore he begged Pandulf, now that the king was
excommunicate no longer, to make peace for him and get him
back his land, which Pandulf accordingly did (*Hist. des Ducs*, pp.
115-25).

Here, at any rate, it is clear that the date of the quarrel cannot
have been later than the spring of 1213; perhaps, as we are not
told how long Robert stayed in Flanders before going to France, it
might be some months earlier. This agrees with the date assigned
to Robert's flight from England by the Barnwell annalist, Ralph of
Coggeshall, and Roger of Wendover, all of whom place it in the
latter part of 1212 (see below, p. 292). The cause of the flight,
however, still remains doubtful. It will be observed that the writer
of the *Histoire des Ducs*, speaking in his own person, makes the
quarrel between John and Robert arise out of John's enmity to
Robert's son-in-law, Geoffrey de Mandeville, and also makes that
enmity originate in the king's jealousy of Geoffrey's father (the
Justiciar), without a word about Geoffrey's wife; but that he
represents Robert Fitz-Walter as having given to different
persons two different accounts of the matter, both of which are
quite distinct not only from the account given by the writer himself, but also from each other. To the third of these three accounts
—the assertion which Robert is said to have made to Pandulf, that
he left England because he would not keep company with an excommunicate sovereign—it is hardly possible for any one who has
read the story of the years of interdict to attach any weight.
Robert's appeal to Pandulf, moreover, is chronologically out of
place; it is represented as having been made after John's agreement with Pandulf, whereas in reality the restoration of Robert
Fitz-Walter, and also of Eustace de Vesci, was one of the conditions
of that agreement. The statement which Robert is said to have
made "everywhere," on the other hand, is only too likely to be true,
and may well contain the true explanation of John's designs against
the husband of Fitz-Walter's daughter; while none of the three
versions is incompatible with either of the others. Still the fact
remains that three different versions are thus given—two on the
alleged authority of Robert Fitz-Walter, one on his own authority—
by a writer who was strictly contemporary, and who ranks as one

of the best, and certainly the most impartial, of our informants on the closing years of John's reign; and this fact leaves a somewhat sinister impression as to the opinion which that writer, at least, entertained of the truthfulness of the "first champion of English liberty."

The main facts which can be gathered from other sources as to Robert Fitz-Walter's relations with the king are these. In 1203 he and Saher de Quincy were jointly charged by John with the defence of the castle of Vaudreuil. They surrendered the place to Philip Augustus under circumstances so exceptionally disgraceful that Philip himself felt constrained to make an example of them as cowards and traitors of too deep a dye to be left unpunished, and flung them into prison at Compiègne, whence they were only released on payment of a heavy ransom (R. Wend. iii. 172; R. Coggeshall, pp. 143, 144). "Ex qua re," adds Ralf of Coggeshall, "facti sunt in derisum et in opprobrium omni populo utriusque regni, canticum eorum tota die, ac generositatis suae maculaverunt gloriam" (cf. *Hist. des Ducs*, p. 97). Alone, the sovereign whom they had betrayed sought to shield their reputation at the risk of his own. Of course he acted from a motive of self-interest. As neither Robert nor Saher held any lands in Normandy, their money was to Philip more useful than their personal adhesion could have been. But for John the friendship of two barons of such importance in England was worth buying back, and he endeavoured to secure it by treating them with an exaggerated generosity which was evidently designed to impress them by its contrast with Philip's severity; he issued (July 5, 1203) letters patent declaring that they had surrendered Vaudreuil under a warrant from himself, and ordering that neither they nor its garrison should be made to suffer for their act (*Rot. Pat.* vol. i. p. 31). Fitz-Walter therefore came back in peace to his English possessions. Like Eustace de Vesci, he joined the host which John gathered for a Welsh war in 1212; like Eustace, too, he withdrew from it secretly on learning that John had received a warning of treason in its ranks (*Ann. Waverl.* a. 1212); and like Eustace, again, he did not come when summoned to make his "purgation" with the other barons, but, as has been already seen, fled the country instead (W. Coventry, ii. 207; R. Coggeshall, p. 165; R. Wendover, iii. 240). The Barnwell annalist (W. Coventry, *l.c.*) dates the demolition of Castle Baynard, and of Robert's other castles, after his flight; the Annals of Dunstable place the destruction of Castle Baynard a year earlier, viz. in 1211.

There remains the question: What was the reason for the special mention of Eustace de Vesci and Robert Fitz-Walter in the terms of reconciliation between the Pope and John? At first glance it seems natural to infer that there must have been some peculiar injustice in John's outlawry of these two men, to make their restoration a matter for intervention on the part of the Pope. But, as has been seen, all the ascertained facts of the case point the opposite way. If indeed Fitz-Walter's alleged assertion to Pandulf, that he had fled on account of the king's excommunication, were true, he would naturally be among the "laicis ad hoc negotium contingentibus" (R. Wendover, iii. 248), while the fact that the rest of these lay sufferers seem to have been all of lower rank might possibly account for his being specially mentioned by name. But it was not true ; and with regard to De Vesci no such assertion is mentioned. Nevertheless, it is extremely probable that both Fitz-Walter and De Vesci may have contrived to represent to the Pope or his commissioner the cause of their exile in the way in which Fitz-Walter is described as representing his own case to Pandulf; and neither Pandulf nor Innocent could have at his command the means of knowing what all the evidence now available goes to show—that these two men had fled their country and left their property to fall into the king's hand, not for conscience's sake, but because their consciences accused them of treason.

INDEX

THE END